Contents

Preface

Readership and Scope

We have designed this book to support courses in consumer behaviour at Master's level. It is also suited to more advanced teaching at first-degree level. Our intended audience is those who see consumer behaviour as a research-based discipline that addresses problems raised by marketing and consumer policy. The problems we explore are found in all advanced economies and, for this reason, we believe that the book will be useful throughout the world.

This book, with two additional authors, extends the coverage of the earlier *Consumer Behaviour: Advances and Applications in Marketing*. In particular, we have provided new chapters on market dynamics and word-of-mouth influence, while chapters on loyalty, brand equity, information processing and decision-making, satisfaction, the retail environment, price reactions and advertising response have been completely rewritten. Very considerable developments have occurred in many of these fields and we have tried to deal with these changes without lengthening the book. We think that this has made the treatment more focused. We see the book as a support to students who will be reading original papers; they need a text that assists, rather than replaces, this activity.

Consumer Behaviour: Applications in Marketing stresses aspects of consumer behaviour that are of widespread importance and draws on work in adjacent disciplines, particularly psychology. After an introduction, we describe the patterns of purchase that are usually observed in market economies and the way these patterns can be explained and applied. We then look at research that has illuminated our understanding of decision-making and show how this can be used. The last part of the book deals with the response to market intervention and covers price, promotion and advertising. In this part, we include a chapter on word of mouth as this topic has assumed increasing importance with the growth of the Internet.

Approach

Most textbooks in consumer behaviour are extensive and well illustrated, but may present the subject in a rather uncritical manner. Often, the treatment illustrates fashionable topics rather than providing evidence about long-standing marketing problems. Such books do not make sufficient call on the expanding research in our field and, when they do cite research, may give limited attention to the uncertainties or opposing views that persist in our discipline. In practice, there are competing findings and explanations, and we have tried to illustrate these where they arise.

This touches on a problem familiar to those who teach business students. Some of these students find arguments from evidence quite unfamiliar and may instead provide accounts of current business practice as though these were conclusive. Our approach opposes such uncritical thinking. We believe those who learn to use evidence as students acquire a technique that will serve them well as practitioners.

One hazard of research-based texts is the sheer weight of evidence. We have tried to emphasize the most recent work and key papers on topics but we have kept the work of early researchers. Those who first identified issues in consumer behaviour deserve mention. We therefore make no apology for some of the more ancient citations in this book, as these help to describe the origin of current thinking.

As subjects become more fragmented, textbooks acquire importance as integrators of different perspectives. In consumer behaviour, we can discern two rather different approaches to research and application. On the one hand, there is the tradition that dominates in the large conferences of the *Association for Consumer Research*. Put baldly, this endorses theorizing and hypothesis-testing, often within experimental designs, and tends to emphasize explanations in terms of the beliefs, preferences and the culture of consumers – a cognitive orientation. In contrast to this is the approach of those who belong to the *Marketing Science* grouping, who place emphasis on behaviour, measures rather than concepts, generalization from an accumulation of findings rather than testing hypotheses, and on the use of mathematical models rather than psychological theories for explanation. Textbooks have generally emphasized the cognitive tradition. We give more space than usual to the marketing science orientation; in particular, we emphasize behavioural explanations, the role of habit and the modelling of market patterns and market change. At the same time, we provide a full treatment to the techniques and theory that underlie the cognitive approach to consumer behaviour.

Consumer behaviour is a changing field. New techniques are giving answers to questions of major importance and, in due course, will give rise to a new breed of professional marketer. At the same time, the academic advance of consumer behaviour is raising issues in psychology and other disciplines and is contributing to the development of these subjects. All three authors report on their own research in this book; we hope that, in doing so, we manage to convey the excitement that new discoveries arouse.

Exercises

Good education gives students the confidence to use and criticize ideas. We try to enlarge this confidence through practical exercises that help the reader to apply and reflect on ideas about consumer behaviour. The exercises require self-appraisal, calculation, observation, measurement of attitudes and the use of computer programs. In many cases, they are quickly done and the reader will benefit by doing them as they occur.

Plan of the Book

The book is divided into four Parts. Part 1 (Chapter 1) introduces the reader to explanations for the different forms of purchase. Part 2 (Chapters 2, 3, 4 and 5) focuses on the patterns of purchase; we cover customer loyalty and brand equity and the recurrent features of stationary and changing markets. Part 3 (Chapters 6, 7 and 8) focus on decision-making; we deal with methods for predicting and explaining decisions, the way that decisions can be biased and the post-decision effects relating to satisfaction and quality. Part 4 (Chapters 9, 10, 11 and 12) deals with the responses of consumers to conditions that affect consumption. These are price, the retail environment, social influence and advertising.

Acknowledgements

A number of people have assisted us in the production of this book: Dag Bennett, Brian Birkhead, Walter Carl, Cullen Habel, Bruce Hardie, Paul Marsh, Jenni Romaniuk, Deborah Russell, John Scriven, Byron Sharp, Mark Uncles and Jim Wiley. Finally, we appreciate very much the influence of our students. With them in mind, we have tried to be relevant and clear.

Part 1
Introduction

1 Ideas and Explanations in Consumer Research

LEARNING OBJECTIVES

When you have completed this chapter, you should be able to:

1 Explain why it is important to study consumer behaviour.
2 Discuss the limitations of a common-sense approach to consumer behaviour.
3 Compare and contrast different approaches to decision-making by consumers.
4 Discuss the effects of the external environment on consumer choice.
5 Explain how markets are usually classified.

OVERVIEW

In this chapter, we show that findings in consumer behaviour can be quite unexpected and that research is needed if we are to answer the questions posed by marketers and regulators. Then we describe three ways in which consumer choice can occur. First, consumers may carefully assess alternatives before choosing; we argue that this cognitive approach to decision-making is rare. Second, consumers may be steered by the opportunities and reinforcements in their environment; this creates patterns of learned behaviour. Third, the learned behaviour may become habitual so that it occurs when related stimuli are present in the environment and no longer needs reinforcement. Following this, we introduce some classifications that are commonly used in marketing and consumer research.

SECTION 1: THE SCOPE OF CONSUMER BEHAVIOUR

How do people buy and use goods and services? How do they react to prices, advertising and store interiors? What underlying mechanisms operate to produce these responses? If marketers have answers to such questions, they can make better managerial decisions. If regulators have answers, they can form better policy. It is the role of consumer behaviour research to provide these answers.

In this book we provide an up-to-date survey of knowledge in consumer behaviour and show how this knowledge can be applied to marketing problems. Knowledge has grown rapidly in some areas, and we have reflected these advances by describing some work in more depth. In such cases, we explain why an issue is important, how it is investigated and what the findings are. This approach culminates in *empirical generalizations*. These are general findings that have stood the test of repeated investigation. Such general findings summarize the state of our knowledge and are useful to practitioners and researchers alike. All too often, textbooks contain little evidence of this sort and it is our purpose to reverse this pattern.

Where our knowledge is still sketchy, we have tried to indicate doubts about the evidence or its interpretation. Such uncertainty propels research and, as a result, creates new knowledge. Though not always welcome to students, doubt is part of good education. Students who see the uncertainties in consumer research should be more sceptical and may be better placed to adapt to new findings when these emerge. Each of the authors is an active researcher and has struggled to understand the complexities of consumer behaviour. We hope that this sharpens the account that we give. Inevitably, we have omitted some fields of knowledge; in particular, we have left out topics that are well covered in texts that are more elementary.

Chapter 1 launches the book by introducing some general ideas, which are explored in following sections. These ideas are grouped into:

- the sort of *questions* raised by marketing and the *answers* that are offered by consumer behaviour,
- models that provide descriptions of *consumer decision processes*,
- the *classifications* and *explanations* that we use.

Questions and Answers

There is a close affinity between marketing and consumer behaviour. In a sense, marketing is a customer of consumer research. Marketers want answers to a number of problems raised by their practices and consumer researchers can provide these answers. Examples of marketing practices are:

- the use of price incentives,
- the use of particular colours, music and aromas in stores,
- launching new products using existing brand names (brand extension).

Often, the direction of an effect fits common sense; for example, consumers buy more when the price is dropped. However, the benefit of a discount depends on the *amount* of extra sales generated by, say, a 10 per cent price cut and here common sense does not supply an answer. For informed action, we need to conduct systematic research, which allows us to measure the size of any effect. Evidence is gathered using the methods of market research, psychology and the social sciences. Using such methods, we seek answers to questions such as:

- How much do sales change when the price is cut by 10 per cent? What happens to sales after a discount has ended? Why do these effects occur?
- How much do colours, music and aromas affect behaviour in a store? What underlying mechanisms explain any effects?
- When a new product is launched under an old brand name, how much does the old name affect purchase of the new product?

Another set of questions comes from legislators and regulators, who have to set rules that affect marketing. Examples of their questions are:

- How do consumers react to product benefits such as energy efficiency and high nutritional value? What explains their behaviour?
- Do childproof packs save lives? How are such packs used?

Sometimes, practical marketers give little attention to the explanation for an effect. An example is the identification of specific groups who buy more of a category. If such people can be identified, they can be selectively targeted. This type of empirical approach can work well but explanation still helps. If we know *why* some groups buy a product more than others, we may be able to design communications that capitalize on this and also predict other products that these groups will want.

In any applied subject, practitioners need to use their judgement when evidence is lacking. Those who have to take decisions cannot delay action until problems have been fully researched. However, it is important that practitioners do accept new evidence when this becomes available. Some apparently sensible practices may need to be adjusted because of new findings. For example, it has been assumed that the childproof packs for medicines increase safety, but this may be illusory. Viscusi (1984) found evidence that child-resistant bottle caps were associated with an *increase* in child poisoning, possibly because parents left medicines accessible when they thought that a cap was childproof, or because the closure was so much trouble that the container was left open. Viscusi's work suggests that packs should carry more specific advice about use and possibly be redesigned so that they are less likely to be left open. More generally, this type of work reminds us that common sense does not replace empirical tests.

SECTION 2: CONSUMER DECISION MODELS

The traditional approach to problems in consumer behaviour employed a comprehensive model of the purchase decision process. Such models were often

the centrepiece of undergraduate consumer behaviour texts, and were expressed
with boxes and arrows representing all the components and connections of an elaborate rational decision. In these models, the consumer is supposed to attend to
product information and process it into memory. Such memories are recovered
when a need emerges and, after further search and evaluation of all relevant alternatives, a purchase is made. After this, post-purchase evaluation may create
satisfaction or dissatisfaction with the chosen product and this can result in a review
of needs for later decisions. Figure 1.1 shows the basic form of such a model.

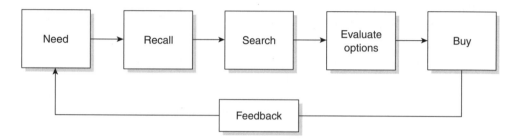

Figure 1.1   Is this how you choose?

   These days, there is less enthusiasm for such models. One problem has always
been that they are hard to test because it is difficult to find satisfactory measures
for all the components (Ehrenberg, 1988). Another problem with comprehensive
models is that they overstate the rationality of choice. If there is plenty of time and
the decision is important, then *sometimes* people will set out the alternatives, evaluate them and select the one that seems to be the best, but we know from our own
experience that we often simplify the process. Sometimes, we choose first and justify our behaviour afterwards, if we justify it at all. Thus, although rational decision
models might suggest what people *ought to do* (normative), they are a poor guide
to what people *actually do* (descriptive). In practice, managers want to know what
people actually do since it is this behaviour that they seek to influence.
   Textbooks now give more attention to 'partial decision models' where the
rationality of the process is incomplete; also, it is accepted that much repeat purchase occurs automatically as a habit. Often, this range of decision-making from
rational to automatic is related to the degree of *involvement*. People are likely to
be more involved and give more thought to the choice when it has high-value
outcomes and it is new to them. To explain decision-making in more detail, we
focus on three models of consumer decision, which have different implications
for managers (see Box 1.1). The models are:

1   **Cognitive,** treating purchase as the outcome of rational decision-making processes.
2   **Reinforcement,** treating purchase as behaviour which is learned and modified in response
    to the opportunities, rewards and costs present in the consumer's environment.
3   **Habit,** treating purchase as already learned behaviour, which is elicited by particular
    stimuli in the consumer's environment.

Box 1.1	**Models of consumer choice and managerial control**

The cognitive model. This assumes rationality. The decision rests on beliefs about alternatives, which are investigated and compared. The managerial control of cognitive decision-making is achieved by providing information that leads the consumer to prefer or reject alternatives.

The reinforcement model. Choice is controlled by factors in the environment that reward and facilitate some alternatives more than others. Managerial control is achieved by changing the consumer's situation. However, what is rewarding to some persons may not be so to others and this limits influence.

The habit model. Choice is controlled by managing stimuli (brand name, logo, pack features, etc.) that have become associated with a product as a result of past purchases. Sometimes this is called stimulus control.

The Cognitive Model

When consumers make an important purchase for the first time, they may reflect on alternatives and discuss pros and cons with others with the intention of securing benefits and avoiding costs. This model, sometimes called *extended problem-solving*, has always had its critics. Olshavsky and Granbois (1979: 98–99) noted:

> for many purchases a decision never occurs, not even on the first purchase ... even when purchase behavior is preceded by a choice process, it is likely to be very limited. It typically involves the evaluation of few alternatives, little external search, few evaluative criteria, and simple evaluation process models.

It is quite hard to find behaviour that fits the elaborate sequence of extended problem-solving. Beatty and Smith (1987) found that people did not search much before the purchase of durables and Beales et al. (1981) found that few people in the USA consulted *Consumer Reports*. Fully thought out decision-making is only likely for first purchases but these are quite rare, even in consumer durable markets, since most purchasers are either buying a replacement for an existing product or making an additional purchase. In a study of white goods purchases in the USA, Wilkie and Dickson (1985) found that two-thirds of the purchasers had bought the category before and Bayus (1991), quoting US industry sources, found that 88 per cent of refrigerators and 78 per cent of washing machines were replacements. In these circumstances, a carefully thought-out comparison of brands is likely to be the exception rather than the rule.

But is a carefully thought-out decision likely to result in the best choice? When people attempt to be rational about a first-time choice, they may make mistakes because they lack experience. However, they are likely to make a better choice than those who abandon any rational processing and plump for an alternative (see Box 1.2).

Box 1.2	**When pension is converted to an annuity**

People build up pension funds over their working lives and then convert the accumulated investment into an annuity when they retire. They may use their pension company for the annuity or search for better value from another company. According to Hargreaves Lansdown, a large financial services firm in the UK, the majority of people buy their annuity from their pension company. Since rates can vary by as much as 15 per cent, this careless choice can mean that many retirees lose income that they could have enjoyed for the rest of their lives. The most likely explanation for this behaviour is that the retirees had a very poor understanding of the issues and they plumped for the company with which they were familiar.

The tendency to simplify decision-making is also observed in industry. One study of investment decisions in British industry revealed that these were often made first and then justified later. Marsh et al. (1988) found that faulty financial analysis and lack of coherence with stated strategic objectives were common. More generally, industrial decisions often fit a 'satisficing' model (Simon, 1957). Simon describes how executives tend to accept the first option that is good enough to solve a problem; this means that there is assessment of one or more of the alternatives but little comparison between alternatives. Klein (1989) found that many decisions in operational settings follow a pattern that is consistent with Simon's ideas. Typically, people assess the situation and generate a prospective action based on this assessment. Then, they evaluate this action to see whether it will provide a solution. If it fails, they generate another prospective action and evaluate this, but they do not usually compare these prospective actions.

When the satisficing model applies, the order in which products are evaluated is important since the first satisfactory solution will be the one that is adopted. This means that more prominent alternatives have a better chance of selection (see Box 1.3). Managers may be able to use this fact to advantage.

Box 1.3	Diagnosis

Even in medicine, decisions may be simplified. Often, the symptoms are assessed and a preliminary diagnosis is made; then other symptoms are checked to see whether they confirm this diagnosis. Only if these other symptoms fail to support the first diagnosis is a second one considered. This procedure may lead to the over-diagnosis of common illnesses.

These examples of decision-making in industry and medicine suggest that the simplification of choice is the norm rather than the exception and we might expect consumers to follow much the same pattern. For example, if the freezer needs replacing and a preliminary inquiry establishes that there is an appropriate model in a convenient shop, consumers may complete the purchase there and then. If the shop does not offer a suitable freezer, they may then try other stores and look at other models.

Although satisficing may not result in the optimal solution, it may use time efficiently when this is scarce. However, when the outcome of the decision is important, consumers and managers would make better decisions if they considered a second alternative before deciding.

Influences on Decision-making

It is easy to fall into the trap of assuming that decisions are made by people acting on their own. Many choices are made in groups and, even when people decide on their own, they are often influenced by word of mouth from other people. At other times, people may base their decisions on information received through the mass media (e.g. advertising, newspaper and television comment). In later chapters on word of mouth and advertising, we consider how these influences may affect a choice. People are particularly likely to seek advice on matters that are obscure or difficult to test in other ways; this is common when the recipient of the advice is choosing for the first time or choosing in changed circumstances, such as when they move home and need to find a new dentist.

Since advice affects consumer decisions, managers need to take account of this process. For example, advertising can include information that is easily passed on in conversation and the design of the ad can reflect the process of giving advice. However, word of mouth is under direct consumer control, not managerial control so normally managers can only affect it indirectly.

EXERCISE 1.1   DECISION-MAKING

Identify an important purchase that you have made, for example a holiday, durable, financial investment or education course.

- Were you clear about what you wanted?

- How much investigation did you do before purchase?

- Did you consider one option and move on to others if it was unsuitable, or did you keep several alternatives in mind before choosing?

- Did you use the Internet?

- Did you consult others?

In retrospect, you may be able to see defects in your decision-making process. Often we lack enough prior experience, time or motivation to fully compare the options.

Purchase as Learned Behaviour

A person's environment controls behaviour in two ways. First, the environment makes some actions possible and other actions impossible to perform; for example, brands can only be bought if they are stocked by retailers. Second, when actions lead to positive outcomes they are more likely to be repeated and, conversely, negative outcomes make it less likely that the action will be repeated. These controls on behaviour have been examined in *learning theory*; this is a systematic description of the relationship between behaviour, its outcomes and subsequent behaviour, which is relevant to both the reinforcement and habit models.

Reinforcement

Early research in learning theory was done by Thorndike (1911), who confined a hungry cat to a cage and placed food outside. The erratic movements of the cat eventually released a simple catch and the cat escaped. The cat took less time on subsequent trials and eventually it released the catch immediately when it was placed in the cage. Thorndike called this *trial and error learning* and it has some relevance to consumption. People entering new markets are faced with a range of brands and may make near random trials of alternatives until they come upon a brand that they like.

In Thorndike's work, the cat's actions were driven by the outcomes: gaining food and freedom. Skinner (1938, 1953) called such outcomes *reinforcers*.

Skinner defined a reinforcer as an experience that raises the frequency of responses associated with it, while a punisher reduces the frequency of such responses. Reinforcers may be rewards or reductions in cost while punishers may be costs or reductions in reward. Reinforcement has most effect when it occurs at the same time as, or just after, the response. Skinner placed emphasis on the way in which reinforcement changes the frequency of the response, but reinforcement also strengthens the association between stimulus and response and this is important for the habit model. Figure 1.2 illustrates the effect of reinforcement.

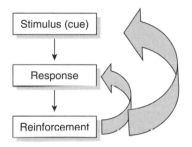

Figure 1.2   Reinforcement learning

The principles of reinforcement are applied in many sales promotions, such as discounts that offset the cost of a product. Skinner also introduced the idea of *shaping*, the process whereby behaviour is gradually shifted from one form to another by selectively reinforcing those performances that show change in the desired direction. Shaping is sometimes apparent in sales techniques where the salesperson moves the prospect towards the sales goal by reinforcing shifts in the preferred direction with nods, agreement and approval. Products also shape us. We become more expert at using computers and cars, partly because of the reinforcers that such products deliver; as a result of this, we may seek more sophisticated models.

Learning can be reinforced each time a response is produced, i.e. *continuously*, or *intermittently*. Learning is faster if the reinforcement schedule is continuous but the final effect of a given amount of reinforcement is greater when it is used intermittently. This helps to explain why people are prepared to lose money by gambling on fruit machines. The cost of playing a slot machine is a fairly continuous punishment but the machine rewards intermittently. Over time, the gains are less than the losses, but the effect on behaviour of the irregular reward is greater than the effect of the regular cost.

Both stimuli and reinforcers can lose their effect if they are used too frequently. Stimulus satiation, called *desensitization*, helps people to put up with recurring unpleasant experiences. An important effect of desensitization in consumer behaviour is the way in which people get used to conditions that are inadequate or unpleasant and, as a result, may not complain or demand compensation. Examples of this are the way people tolerate litter in streets, overcrowding on public transport and being kept waiting on the phone. Similarly, consumers may put up with defective goods because they have grown used to the defects. Examples are lumpy mattresses, broken refrigerator shelves and inadequate carving knives. The job of the marketer is to overcome the inertia in these situations so that the consumer sees the problem afresh and seeks a solution.

Stimulus Control: Classical Conditioning

One type of learning, called classical conditioning, was studied by Pavlov (1927). Pavlov noticed that dogs started to salivate at the sight of the person who fed them. The older dogs showed this most and Pavlov thought that, over time, the salivation reflex that normally occurred at the presentation of food had become associated with a new stimulus, the dogs' handler. Pavlov set up a series of experiments to demonstrate this process of classical conditioning using the sound of a buzzer as the conditioned stimulus instead of the dogs' handler. Figure 1.3 illustrates this process.

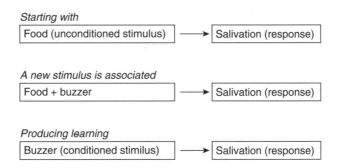

Figure 1.3   Classical conditioning: Pavlov's experiment

Classical conditioning has considerable relevance to consumer behaviour. Packaging, brand names, colours, smells, music and the contexts of purchase and consumption may become associated with the buying of particular products. Some advertising is clearly intended to forge associations between brands and particular stimuli that can be used in further advertising and at the point of sale, e.g. Marlboro and cowboys, McDonalds and the big 'M' sign and, more generally, a variety of logos and their respective brands and companies. The idea here is that the conditioned stimulus may help in identification and add to purchasing tendency. It is also noticeable that, to compete in some markets, manufacturers have to adopt the colours and pack shape that are conventional for that type of product. The power of such associations is revealed by a trip to an unfamiliar country. The absence of familiar features makes the high street confusing. A simple task, like posting a letter, requires investigation and effort in order to identify the colour, shape and location of the post box.

A stimulus that is associated with a rewarding product may induce a more generalized tendency to buy other products that appear similar. A direct application of such generalization in marketing is the use of an existing brand name for a new product. By this process of *brand extension*, some of the buying propensity for the old brand may attach to the new brand. For example, Mars used the positive propensity towards the brand when introducing Mars ice-cream and this was helped by the similarity in the appearance of the ice-cream and the confectionery bar.

Habits of Purchase

The cognitive and reinforcement models emphasize the *modification* of consumer behaviour and thus may explain the *changes* that occur in our purchasing. However, much consumption has a settled form; people buy the same brands and use the same stores over long periods. This habitual aspect of consumption is of great value to firms.

We say that people have a habit when they regularly produce much the same behaviour on encountering a particular stimulus. In the case of supermarket goods, important stimuli are the colour, size and shape of the pack. Williams (1966) found that colour affected impact most, followed by size then shape. Response to such stimuli is automatic, so that no conscious thought is required when we pick a laundry detergent brand in the supermarket. Habits sidestep cognitive decision-making and leave us free to concentrate on other problems where experience does not provide us with a ready response. However, even in novel situations people may trade on already acquired habits. Consider the person who is about to buy a car for the first time. Most first-time car purchasers are familiar with cars, have been to car showrooms before, may have bargained for goods before, may be knowledgeable about the ways of salespersons and may understand credit arrangements. Thus, even first-time car purchasing may reflect previous learning, some of which may have become habitual. Viewed in this way, even complex and novel behaviour may call upon behaviours in a habit repertoire.

The habit model of consumption excludes planning before action but does not imply that consumers never think about their habitual behaviour. People may reflect on their actions *after* purchase either because of discussion with others or because their purchase outcomes were exceptionally good or bad. But this is unusual; generally, habit restricts experimentation and, as a result, consumers may be unaware of improvements in products from which they could benefit. This suggests that, although habitual purchase is frequently satisfactory, it is not always the best solution. Exercise 1.2 may draw your attention to habits that you have which are sub-optimal.

EXERCISE 1.2   HABITS

It is hard to detect habits that work against your own interests but consider two areas:

1   Taking sugar in tea and coffee are habits that add to body weight and contribute to tooth decay. When people give up sugar they get used to it fairly soon and after a few weeks may prefer unsweetened tea or coffee. Is this not a habit worth changing?

2   If you make a regular journey to work, is the route optimal? People can discover journey improvements after years of using a less suitable route that has become habitual.

How should marketers present their brands when purchase is strongly habitual?

When purchase is habitual, a new brand must be marketed in a way that disrupts habit and provokes a review of past purchase. This is not easily achieved. Advertising may be ignored, while discounts and free samples may be used without thought. Most of the time, consumers carry on buying what they have bought before. But who said that marketing was easy?

How Free Are Consumers?

It is often claimed that the consumer is king but this may exaggerate the flexibility of action that consumers have. To be free you should be able to choose from more than one option without pressure, and be able to reject all options if they are unattractive. The account that we have given suggests that many consumer choices are controlled by the environment rather than by the reflective thought of the consumer, and this casts doubt on the freedom of action of consumers.

The constraints on consumers are considerable and are not just environmental. Consumers may *lack knowledge* of alternatives when these are not displayed. Sometimes, people *have to use* products; they must put petrol in a car and laundry detergent in a washing machine and the fact that they have a choice between near identical brands is often, to them, a matter of indifference. Freedom of action is also affected by *limited access* to goods and services, by *physiological dependence* on products like cigarettes and alcohol and by *psychological dependence* when the consumer is a compulsive purchaser or gambler.

People do many things that they would prefer to avoid, e.g. going to work on congested public transport and waiting for flights in airports. In many areas, such as education, medicine and legal advice, the opportunity to influence a service by withdrawing custom or complaining is effectively limited by the continuing need to use the service. There are other areas where a lack of money prevents people from doing the things they might wish to do; large houses and luxurious cars are possible for only a few. For these reasons, we are sceptical about claims that consumers exhibit much autonomy. However, the growth of the Internet has raised access to knowledge about goods and services and has assisted purchase; this may increase consumer choice.

Decision-making on the Internet

The increased use of the Internet and the facilities that websites offer may change the rationality of choice. In many fields, price levels seem to be lower on the Web and the increasing proportion of consumers who use the Web for purchasing will therefore tend to reduce average prices paid. The *New York Times* reported (December, 30 2005) that, according to Nielsen figures, online purchases in the USA accounted for 27 per cent of total spend in 2005, up from 22 per cent in 2004 and 16 per cent in 2002. It seems that Web purchasing is rapidly increasing as more people use computers to buy a wider range of categories. There is some variation by country. Nielsen data show the percentages of Internet users who buy via the Web as:

UK	70
Sweden	61
Australia	56
France	47
Hong Kong	42
Spain	35

The Internet makes it easier to compare prices and specifications, and can take some of the effort out of shopping. Search engines such as Google.com and Froogle.com assist in the identification of sources and alternatives, while chat rooms and blogs often provide user comment on different brands. Comparison sites such as Shopping.com show the prices charged by different suppliers. Other sites, such as Uswitch.co.uk, can compute the best value among service providers and may facilitate transfer to a new provider. Websites for those buying houses, shares, books and many other items aid choice by providing easy comparison between alternatives. For example, an Australasian buyer can use a site such as realestate.com.au to specify properties by location, price and type, and can then inspect pictures of interiors. This helps to focus attention only on those properties that meet the needs of the buyer. A subscriber buying shares through a Web-based stockbroker such as Hargreaves Lansdown, (h-l.co.uk), can see the past return on specific shares over different periods and can compare this performance with other shares and with standard indexes. On Amazon.com, customers can read reviews of a book before buying and be provided with information on new books that are related to their previous purchases. On airline sites such as ba.com, a traveller can pick travel times that are cheaper. Quite clearly, the Internet *can* be used by consumers to assess alternatives better but how much do consumers do this to improve their choices and lower their costs?

A study by Zettelmeyer, Morton and Silva-Risso (2006) suggests that Internet customers may bring down the price that they pay for cars by an average of 1.5 per cent; this may seem modest but it accounts for 22 per cent of the dealer's gross margin. However, consumers who use the Internet may be more price-sensitive and these people might also drive a hard bargain in an offline context. Also, it appears that even Internet customers rarely secure the lowest price. According to Shopping.com, 80 per cent of Internet customers pay more than they have to. It seems that use of the Internet to obtain better value is restrained by loyalty to particular websites. Once they are familiar with a site, consumers may return to it later because it is easy to use and saves time. A consumer might agree that a book might be cheaper elsewhere but still use Amazon because of convenience. Similarly, buyers normally use one online grocer because of the trouble of getting to know another site. In short, habits take over.

This evidence presents a somewhat confused picture. The Internet *can* assist people to make better decisions and buy more cheaply, but the technology may discourage experimentation when goods are regularly bought. In addition, there are some sectors, such as groceries, where choice limitations and delivery cost raise the price that is paid online. We will have a clearer picture when more evidence is available, covering a wider range of categories.

SECTION 3: CLASSIFICATIONS AND EXPLANATIONS

Disciplines must organize and classify information in order to explain it. Marketing is no exception and uses a number of classifications, some of which are shared with other subjects. We start with one distinction that is so ubiquitous that we scarcely notice it. This is the use of comparison in the assessment of evidence.

The Principle of Comparison

Any judgement rests on implicit or explicit comparison. When we say 'that's cheap', we are comparing the price that is presented with some standard. The standard might be given by another brand that is physically present, or it might be an internal standard that we have built up from experience. Such comparisons are fundamental in human judgements. We make sense of any raw data by comparing it with objective standards, or with personal or social norms. Comparison also occurs in the scientific assessment of findings.

Table 1.1   How owners rated their current car

Rating in comparison to the best alternative make that could have been purchased instead	Current car (%)
Much Worse	1
Worse	8
The same	27
Better	38
Much better	26

To illustrate this, consider Table 1.1. This table shows the ratings that owners gave to their car compared with the best alternative that they could have purchased instead. The data come from an Internet survey of 495 owners that we conducted in 2003. The numbers show that 64 per cent of respondents thought that their car was better than the best alternative and 9 per cent thought that it was worse. This seems to show great confidence among respondents in their choice of car. Our finding reflects a general phenomenon called the endowment effect: objects are rated more highly once they are owned (Kahneman, Knetsch and Thaler, 1991a). From a more objective standpoint, we can argue that the assessments shown in Table 1.1 are difficult to justify. When there are many alternatives, most of which are not evaluated, it is quite likely that another brand would have been better than the one chosen. Thus, there seems to be an optimism bias in the assessment of possessions which is revealed by making the question comparative. In Chapter 7, we study these judgemental effects in more detail.

Sometimes the standard of comparison that people use for judgements has an objective basis; for example, the average price of a basket of goods in the different supermarket chains or the fuel economy of different cars. But notice that consumers have to discover and accept such standards if these are to affect their judgements. Sometimes, standards are affected by marketing communications but, mostly, people appear to acquire price or quality norms from experience. Such internal norms will be based on observations, discussions with other consumers and information from the media and are likely to be quite stable. In these circumstances, what changes when marketers are successful in modifying consumer behaviour? Usually, marketing activity alters the immediate perception rather than the internal norm. When the price is cut, and more people buy, it is because the new price is seen as cheap, compared with the norm.

Categories, Brands, Variants and SKUs

Classifications are also made on the basis of the context in which decisions are taken. So products are divided into *categories* such as soup, wine, mobile phone airtime suppliers, cars and hotels. Within a category there will be a number of brands available for consumers to choose from. Brands are easily recognizable entities – such as Nokia, Ford and Marriott – and customers can become attached to one brand rather than another when making repeated choices. Sometimes there are sub-brands, e.g. Volkswagen has Polo, Golf, Passat, etc. The branding is signalled primarily by name, but also by logo, and the shape, colour and design of the pack or product when this has a physical form. Advertising may attach other associations to the brand, such as cartoon animals and musical themes. In many cases, a company name is synonymous with the brand, e.g. BP, but in other cases, the company owns a variety of brand names, e.g. General Motors, Procter & Gamble and Unilever each manage many brand names. Variants are subdivisions of the product type so the Volkswaken Passat is available as a saloon or estate, and Heinz soups are available in different flavours.

In business, the term SKU (stock keeping unit) is used widely. This is a unique combination of brand, variety, pack size and so on that is required for filling the shelves. The SKU is coded so that automated systems can specify it in production scheduling and stock control. Manufacturers and retailers often analyse consumer choice at the level of the SKU.

The consumer's brand preference controls the profit that is made by different suppliers; marketing activities are therefore coordinated to promote brand or sub-brand preference. This means that the branding must be distinctive enough for consumers to distinguish one brand from another but, at the same time, the brands in a category often have features in common which help the consumer to recognize what they are buying. As a result, brands often share characteristics such as pack size, colour and shape. In fact, one brand does not have to be physically different from other brands in a category. For example, at one time Volkswagen, Seat and Ford offered SUVs that were the same except for the name badge and the price. Similarly, there may be no detectable difference between the granulated sugar offered by two different manufacturers; consumers know this, but this does not stop them from regularly buying one brand rather than another.

Often, each brand will cover much the same range of variants. Sugar brands will offer granulated, castor and Demerara variants, soup brands will have much the same range of flavours, and car brands will be available in SUV, sports, saloon and estate forms. In fact, the differences between the variants of a single brand are often much greater than the differences between the corresponding variants of different brands.

The use of sub-brands can raise problems in the car industry when a new model comes out. Should the sub-brand be retained because consumers attach value to it (brand equity) or is a new sub-brand used to emphasize the novelty of the new model? Volkswagen retains sub-brand names, Citroën abandons them, while in other cases the sub-brand may not be used for a while and may then reappear (e.g. Ford Escort).

In many fields, the brands in a category compete only with each other for the customer's attention, e.g. Macleans versus Crest toothpaste. However, in the food and entertainment fields this is less true. A frozen meal brand competes with home cooking and restaurants, as well as with other brands of frozen meals. Similarly, beer competes with wine and ten-pin bowling competes with the cinema.

Other differentiators beside brands are used to distinguish one market offering from another. An interesting example is provided by wine. French wine has traditionally been branded by the producer, sub-region and region, e.g. Château Cheval Blanc is a St Emilion in the Bordeaux region. This produces a complex choice for the consumer. By contrast, Australasian wine is sold more on the basis of grape variety. Although there are many varieties of grape, a small number dominate the field (particularly Shiraz, Cabernet, Pinot Noir, Sauvignon, Chardonnay and Pinot Grigio) and several are grown in each region. This provides an easy 'handle' for the consumer and marks major differences between wines. When the grape variety has been chosen, regions like the Barossa, producers like Penfolds, and the year of the vintage may be used by the more discriminating buyer.

Goods and Services

A familiar grouping of categories is into goods and services. A good has physical form, e.g. a bed, whereas a service is intangible and is used by the recipient as it is created, e.g. nursing. Thus the essence of a service is that it exists in time and must be consumed at that time if loss of sale is to be avoided (e.g. places in a restaurant). By contrast, goods, such as frozen peas, can be stockpiled and supplied when there is demand. Most service products incorporate a goods component, e.g. the meal in a restaurant and the replacement hip inserted by a surgeon.

Goods can be subdivided into classes such as groceries, electronics and fashion. Similarly, services divide into classes such as transport, surgery and professional advice. The fact that there are textbooks devoted to the marketing of services suggests that this is substantially different from the marketing of goods. One difference is that, because they are delivered over time, services can suffer problems of uneven demand, leading to inefficient use of resources and delay and frustration among customers. We cover research on the consumer response to delay in Chapter 8. There are also differences that arise from the interaction between the service supplier and the customer; Keaveney (1995) found that a large part of all service switching occurred because of failures in the service encounter and this has no parallel with goods. It may be harder to evaluate services than goods before purchase. For example, most goods can be examined before purchase and this helps consumers to evaluate them. It may not be possible to examine services in this way and, as a result, those who are thinking of adopting a new service provider may seek advice from existing customers whose word of mouth provides a proxy for personal experience.

In other respects, goods and services are similar. Our three models of consumer decision-making apply to both, and so does the distinction between repertoire and subscription categories that we discuss below.

Vargo and Lusch (2004) have suggested that services rather than goods are the fundamental product form since goods are made by the service of workers. This new 'dominant logic' in marketing has echoes in the work of early economists, particularly in Marx's theory of value, expounded in *Capital* (1930), which relates value to the labour input. At the time, economists argued that the value of goods was defined by an exchange process; it is what others are prepared to give for the goods and no amount of labour input will raise the price of something that people do not want. The character of transactions may have changed and become more cooperative but, in our view, such exchanges remain the basis of value. Marketers must be concerned with profitable trading and, for this reason, we are sceptical about making service fundamental in marketing.

Repertoire and Subscription Categories

Categories can be divided into those that are repertoire, where consumers commonly purchase more than one brand (e.g. most groceries, restaurants and airlines) and subscription, where consumers mostly use only one brand at a time (e.g. current bank accounts, hairdressers and refrigerators). A paper by Sharp, Wright and Goodhardt (2002) shows that most categories fall clearly into either the repertoire or the subscription division. In repertoire categories, we can measure a type of brand loyalty called *share-of-category requirement* (SCR). This is the percentage of category purchases that a customer gives to a specific brand over a period. For example, if a person buys instant coffee on ten occasions in a year and five purchases are Maxwell House, the customer's SCR for Maxwell House is 50 per cent. By contrast, loyalty in subscription categories is shown at the time of repurchase when the customer either retains the brand or switches to another.

Market Concentration

In many categories, there are relatively few brands. Laundry detergents, toothpaste, supermarkets and mobile phone airtime supply are examples. In other fields, such as wine and cheese, there are a great many producers, none of which commands a large market share. In some other fields, such as fashion stores, chemists and investment advisers, a few large chains compete with many smaller suppliers in Western markets. When a few producers command a large part of the category, we describe the market as *high concentration*. Usually, large suppliers are more profitable because of economies of scale in manufacture, distribution and advertising. Retailers feel compelled to stock more familiar brands because of demand and this helps the manufacturer to maintain the price paid by the retailer.

Consumers are not necessarily disadvantaged by high market concentration. The large scale and efficiencies of big producers mean that product development can occur and the wide distribution of big brands ensures that consumers can easily find the larger brand. One concern is that high concentration may reduce competition but it is not difficult to find high levels of competition in concentrated markets. For instance, the worldwide cola market is highly concentrated, yet both Pepsi and Coke remain fiercely competitive suppliers.

Market Share

Ehrenberg (1988) has explained that many aspects of aggregate consumer behaviour can be seen as an outcome of market share. For example, the average SCR loyalty for a big brand tends to be higher than that for a small brand. In Table 1.2, we illustrate how another variable, the share of recommendation, relates to market share in the mobile phone category.

Table 1.2   Market share and share of recommendations of mobile phone brands (unpublished UK data gathered in 2005)

Brand	Market share (%)	Share of recommendations (%)
Nokia	40	40
Sony-Ericsson	25	21
Motorola	14	20
Samsung	10	11
Siemens	4	2
Others	7	4

Table 1.2 shows that the share of recommendations closely follows the market share of the brand to which the recommendation is related. There is no mystery about this. As we saw earlier with regard to cars, people are usually happy with the products that they own and East, Hammond and Wright (2007) found that about 80 per cent of recommendations related to the informant's main brand. So, the bigger the brand, and therefore the greater the number of users, the larger will be the share of recommendations. For this reason, managers need to take account of market share before they assess the word of mouth about their brand. In Table 1.2, Motorola is doing well because the rate of recommendation is ahead of market share. If the rate of recommendation was assessed without taking account of market share, Nokia would come top, but we can see that its performance is just average for its size.

EXERCISE 1.3   DO BIG BRANDS GET MORE, OR LESS, NEGATIVE WORD OF MOUTH?

Recommendation is positive word of mouth. What about negative word of mouth? Develop ideas about how negative word of mouth is produced. What will be the resulting relationship between market share and the share of negative word of mouth?

When you get to Chapter 11, you will see our evidence.

Segment Comparisons and Causal Relationships

We often compare population segments: those who retain a brand versus those who switch, heavy viewers versus light viewers of TV, high recommenders versus low recommenders, men versus women, etc. If we have evidence about the consumption habits of different segments, we can target those that appear to be most open to change. This is an approach that is very popular in marketing; it can work well even when we do not know why the behaviour of one segment differs from another. For example, a method used by those trying to harness word of mouth is to try to identify those consumers who give more advice than others (the *influentials*). Once they have been identified, the job of the marketer is to recruit them on behalf of a promoted brand.

However, in consumer behaviour, we want to explain behaviour, preferably by finding causes for it. Why is it that one segment is more active in advising others than another? We can investigate how segments differ with respect to possible causes. Once we understand the causes of an effect, we can influence it in a more sophisticated way than by targeting segments. As the picture of the different factors underlying recommendation builds up, a new strategy becomes available to marketers. Instead of identifying a segment, marketers can try to influence the factors that cause word of mouth and this can be done *without* identifying the influentials.

Behaviourism and Cognitivism

Does a change in thinking cause change in behaviour, or does a change in behaviour cause change in thinking? The answer is that we can find support for both processes. In psychology, the primacy of behaviour was called *behaviourism*. This approach was developed by Skinner (1953). The traditional behaviourist rejects the idea that thought and feeling are the initiators of action. Instead, action is explained by reference to the environmental circumstances that act on a person. This fits the reinforcement and habit models of consumer decision.

To a traditional behaviourist, thought and feeling are *effects but not causes*; like ripples on the surface of a pond they indicate the fish's movements but do not move the fish. If this account is correct, we can use people's thoughts and feelings as indicators of their potential behaviour but not as explanations for it. Such narrow behaviourism is usually rejected today. One reason is that it is difficult to describe action without taking account of the thought and feeling that lie behind it; words become insults or praise only through an understanding of the motives of the person uttering them. The behaviourist position is not subtle enough to deal with this complexity in the nature of human behaviour.

Opposed to behaviourism is the view that thought and feeling can produce change in action directly. This is *cognitivism* and it lies behind rational accounts of consumer decision-making. In its strongest form, experience is interpreted and used to change attitudes and knowledge, which then control behaviour. From a cognitivist perspective, behaviour may be modified by communications that change attitudes and knowledge. Some support for the cognitivist position can be found in the way public information campaigns change behaviour.

There are also examples where behaviour precedes attitude. Clare and Kiser (1951) asked parents of completed families about the number and sex of the children that they thought were desirable. There was a strong tendency for parents to prefer both the size and the sex mix of the family that they already had. At the time of the study, there were no ways of controlling the sex of offspring, so the preference for the same sex balance can only be explained as a product of experience.

In many other cases the priority between attitude and behaviour may be in doubt. The preferred number of children is a case in point. Parents might have had two children because they wanted two; or, having had two children, they might have come to prefer this number. Such alternative explanations can often be seen in the social sciences. For example, Marx argued that it was not ideology that determined social relations but social relations that determined ideology. This is the sociological equivalent of the primacy of behaviour over attitude and it is contrasted with Hegelian philosophy favouring the primacy of ideas. Sometimes Hegel's account fits; paradoxically, Marxism itself was a revolutionary ideology that created change.

Some studies in consumer research show the effect of prior behaviour. Bird and Ehrenberg (1966) found that two thirds of those who have used a brand at some time express an intention to buy it. A declining brand has a long tail of past users and, as a result, a larger number of consumers state that they are going to buy it again, compared with a brand with level consumption. There is also evidence that brand attitudes follow the purchase of groceries. Dall'Olmo Riley et al. (1997) found that brand attributions seemed to depend on recent purchase. Sandell (1981) examined the relationships between brand attitudes and purchase using panel data and found that attitudes were aligned with purchase immediately after buying, but then, over time, these attitudes reverted to the pre-purchase pattern.

SUMMARY

Key questions for consumer behaviour come from marketing and consumer policy. In order to answer these questions we need an understanding of how consumers make decisions. When people face difficult and involving choices, the cognitive model of choice may describe the process of decision-making, but the process is often simplified. When action is steered by the environment, the reinforcement model provides an explanation of how consumption patterns are learned: action is constrained by the opportunities available and directed by the rewards and costs that are present. Once actions are learned, they may be induced by specific stimuli, such as brand name, and the habit model can apply. To change the behaviour of consumers, the influencing agent must either alter the beliefs and values involved in a complex decision or, where the context controls behaviour, modify the consumer's environment. Learning principles help us to explain some marketing practices, such as brand extension.

The growth of the Internet suggests that people are able to make better choices (more suitable brands, lower prices) but it is not clear yet how much this occurs.

In this chapter, we also introduced some of the ways in which data are organized to create meaning: the use of comparison, types of category, brands and variants, goods and services and market share.

Additional Resources

For more detail on the challenge to comprehensive models of consumer behaviour, read Olshavsky and Granbois (1979). Also look at other textbooks; Solomon et al. (2006) *Consumer Behaviour: A European Perspective*, chapter 8 is quite close to our position.

Part 2
Consumption Patterns

2 Customer Loyalty

LEARNING OBJECTIVES

When you have completed this chapter, you should be able to:

1 Report the different terms and measures that have been used to describe customer loyalty.
2 Explain how different ideas about loyalty developed.
3 Explain how customer loyalty is divided between brands in repertoire categories.
4 Describe other habitual features of consumer purchase.
5 Discuss and criticize the main ideas in favour of promoting retention in consumer markets.
6 Report research on the associations between different forms of loyalty.
7 Report on the reasons for defection in services.

(Loyalty schemes, which are really forms of retail promotion, are covered in Chapter 10.)

OVERVIEW

There are three types of loyalty behaviour that consumers can show. First, when they buy several brands in a category, consumers can give a high share to one of them. Second, they can continue to buy a brand for a long time; this is retention. Third, they can recommend a brand to others and recruit new customers. These three forms of customer loyalty – share, retention and recommendation – ensure a continuing revenue stream and reduce the need for companies to promote brands. Marketers therefore want to find and keep customers who exhibit these forms of loyalty and, where possible, they want to encourage this behaviour. Marketers are also keen to understand why customers switch away from a brand.

(Continued)

A second aspect to loyalty is the feeling that customers have about brands. We talk of being satisfied by or liking a brand, being committed to the brand and, in the case of business and service suppliers, trusting and being dependent upon them.

This subject is quite complicated. We have a common term, loyalty, but it has many different forms and one form of loyalty may have a strong or weak relationship with another. Also, the form of loyalty that we use depends on the category. We use repeat purchase to show retention of consumer durables and duration as a customer to show retention of utilities and other services. We can use both share and retention to show the loyalty of customers to grocery brands, stores and airlines. To explore these issues, we approach the subject historically, show how the different forms of loyalty have originated, and we examine some of the evidence associated with each form of loyalty.

SECTION 1: BRAND LOYALTY IN REPERTOIRE CATEGORIES

Early Research

Research on brand loyalty, as a share of purchase, began with a paper by Copeland (1923) in the first issue of the *Harvard Business Review*. Copeland discussed a phenomenon, which he called brand insistence, that occurs when a consumer refuses to substitute one brand for another. Copeland was concerned with repertoire markets like groceries, where consumers often purchase more than one brand in a category. In these markets, brand insistence is an extreme form of share loyalty and is now called sole-brand loyalty.

Initially, research into this field was held back because there were no sound methods for measuring brand purchases. Retrospective surveys of purchase may be used but consumers can easily forget some of the purchases that they have made. To reduce this recall error, Churchill (1942) advocated the use of panels of consumers, who agreed to make regular reports about their household purchases. The methods for measuring purchases by panel members have evolved. Initially, members were asked to provide weekly reports of their household's purchases usually by keeping a diary of daily purchases. An alternative form of measurement was the 'dustbin' method where the consumer retained all wrappers and agency staff counted purchases from the wrappers. But wrappers may not be kept, so this method is also fallible. When bar codes became universal, panel members were given a bar-code reader and they used this to record their purchases when they brought their groceries home. This method is still used today by

Nielsen. An alternative method is used by Information Resources Inc. (IRI) in the USA. They own the checkout scanners in the stores of a number of communities where they conduct research. When panel members use a store they show an identification card and the store scanner sends data on their purchases directly to IRI for processing.

The first regular panel was run by a newspaper, the *Chigago Tribune*. Brown (1953) used data from this panel and found that brand loyalty in a household fitted one of four patterns:

- Sole-brand loyalty.
- Divided brand loyalty (polygamous).
- Unstable loyalty (switching, between brands).
- No brand loyalty (promiscuous).

Brown classified people on the basis of runs of purchase of the same brand. Thus AAAAAA shows sole brand loyalty; a mix such as AABABA indicates loyalty divided between A and B and AAABBB might indicate unstable loyalty with a switch from A to B, though it is clearly impossible to distinguish true switching from divided loyalty without an extended period of measurement. It is now clear that divided (or multi-brand) loyalty is the usual pattern of grocery purchase (see Box 2.1). This understanding was assisted by further research on the *Chicago Tribune* panel by Cunningham (1956), who examined the share of purchase devoted to each brand, rather than runs of sole-brand loyalty.

Box 2.1	Reasons for divided loyalty

Why do people buy more than one brand in a category? There seem to be two sorts of explanation for having a portfolio of brands which we call genuine and apparent.

Genuine portfolio

This may occur because:

1 There is little brand awareness and the consumer does not remember previously bought brands.
2 The category is one where consumers appreciate variety (biscuits, cereals, wine).
3 Customers buy discounted brands, which spreads their range of purchase.
4 The brand that customers wanted was not available.

(Continued)

Apparent portfolio

1 The panel collects data on *household* expenditure. Members of a household may prefer different brands. Individually, they could be 100 per cent loyal but, as a household, they could show divided loyalty.

2 A household may buy different brands in sub-categories such as biological and non-biological detergent. The household could be 100 per cent loyal in each sub-category. We need to remember that the categories used by market researchers may differ from the product groupings in the minds of consumers.

Share of Category Requirement

Cunningham's share of purchase approach is now standard and is illustrated with invented data in Table 2.1. In the table, the last three numbers of row 1 show that, over one year, Household 1 devotes 50 per cent of purchases to Brand A, 30 per cent to Brand B and 20 per cent to Brand C. These percentages are the share-of-category requirement (SCR) measures that were introduced in Chapter 1. Another measure that is often used is first-brand loyalty. This is the share given to the most heavily bought brand (e.g. Household 1 has a first-brand loyalty of 50 per cent). We see in Table 1.1 that purchase is irregular and that some households buy very little.

The last three columns give the loyalty to brands of each customer and the means at the base of these columns give the average SCR per brand; Brand A, with a score of 64 per cent, is more popular than Brands B and C.[1]

EXERCISE 2.1   MARKET SHARE AND AVERAGE SCR

How do average SCRs relate to market share? Are they the same or different? Think about this before looking below.

The average SCRs per brand are quite close to market share. The main reason for a difference is that light buyers tend to focus on market leaders (like consumers 6 and 10 in Table 2.1). This means that the average SCR of brand leaders tends to be a little above their market share. Fifty-one of the 89 purchases in Table 2.1 are for Brand A, which gives it a market share of 57 per cent, slightly below the mean SCR of 64 per cent.

Another measure is the average first-brand loyalty in a category. What is the average first-brand loyalty in Table 2.1? This is 50 + 60 + 67 + 50 + 64 + 100 + 56 + 50 + 80 + 100 divided by 10, which is nearly 68. Figures of 50–70 per cent are common for grocery brands.

Table 2.1 Hypothetical brand purchase data (assumes only three brands in the category)

House hold	Purchases of Brands A, B and C in each month												Total purchases (all brands)	% over year		
	Jan	Feb	Mar	Apr	May	June	July	Aug	Sept	Oct	Nov	Dec		A	B	C
1	A	B	B	A	C		A	C	B	A		A	10	50	30	20
2	B	C		C	A	AC		C	B		C	C	10	20	20	60
3	AA		AB	B	AA		AB	A	A		B	AB	15	67	33	0
4	C	A	A	B	C	CC	A	A	AC	B	A	A	14	50	14	36
5	AB		AB	A	B	C	A	A		A	A		11	64	27	9
6	A			A		A				A			4	100	0	0
7	A		C	C		A		AB		AC		A	9	56	11	33
8	C	C		A	A	A		A	C	A	C		8	50	0	50
9	A		A		A			B		A			5	80	20	0
10			A			A				A		A	3	100	0	0
Mean													**9**	**64**	**15**	**21**

Customers who buy a brand only once in a period must have an SCR of 100 per cent; when the brand is bought twice, the SCR cannot be less than 50 per cent; and when it is bought three times, the minimum is 33 per cent. These small-number effects mean that customers who rarely purchase in a period tend to have higher SCRs than average and, conversely, those who are sole-brand loyal are often light buyers.[2]

Loyalty Proneness and its Correlates

Cunningham (1956) also wanted to know whether the loyalty that a consumer showed in one category was related to loyalty in another; he called this, *loyalty proneness*. Cunningham found little evidence of loyalty proneness. Among 21 correlations between share loyalties in different categories, the highest was 0.3. However, Cunningham removed the consumers' discount purchases from the calculation of loyalty and, if he had not done this, he might have shown more loyalty proneness. It seems likely that it is the attraction of a deal that often draws people away from their usual brand and that this *deal proneness* should not be excluded. East et al. (1995) found correlations averaging 0.46 between share-loyalty measures across four grocery categories in a survey. This evidence of loyalty proneness means that it is realistic to average a consumer's loyalty scores across a range of categories in order to investigate the factors associated with share loyalty. Using this method, East et al. found that a customer's share loyalty to grocery brands was correlated with their store loyalty (measured as share), total supermarket spending, lack of interest in discounts and household income. The fact that heavier spenders are more loyal in supermarkets makes high-loyalty customers doubly valuable to the store owner because they buy a larger proportion of a larger amount. This seems to be a particular feature of supermarket customers. Work by Knox and Denison (2000) also showed this effect in supermarket spending but it did not occur in other retail fields.

The association between brand loyalty and store loyalty that East et al. found has been noted in other studies and a number of explanations have been offered. One possibility is that loyalty to retailer brands (own label, private label) explains the effect because the customer who buys more of a particular retailer brand has to shop with that retailer. However, Rao (1969) and East et al. (1995) both found that the correlation persisted after removing store-brand loyalty and Flavián, Martínez and Polo (2001) found that brand loyal customers bought fewer private label goods. Another explanation is that those who use a wider range of stores (low store loyalty) have a wider range of brands to choose from and this would tend to reduce their brand loyalty. A third possibility is that the correlation between brand loyalty and store loyalty may be explained if these forms of loyalty are habits, and that some people are more habit-prone.

This explanation is supported by the finding that those with high brand and store loyalty are more likely to show another habit by having a routine day for supermarket shopping (East et al., 2000). Habit proneness could relate to personality or lifestyle. Habits, by their nature, tend to exclude new experience but they may save time and effort (see Box 2.2).

Box 2.2	The habits of Gilbert and George (from The *Observer Magazine*, 28 January 2007)

They wear the same tailored suits day in, day out, and follow the same routines 365 days a year. They get up at 6.30am and go round the corner to a café for breakfast (they do not have a kitchen at home). They then work till 11, when it's back to the café for lunch, after which they put in a full afternoon until Paul O'Grady's show comes on ITV at 5pm. ... Dinner is taken in the same Turkish restaurant in Hackney every night. ... They are often asked about these routines and complain that no one ever seems to grasp that they stick to them, not for show, but to save time.

Other Habits

Purchase habits also apply to brands that we routinely *do not buy*. Most of us will admit to avoiding certain brands and service providers. Research by Hunt, Hunt and Hunt (1988) has thrown light on the way consumers hold grudges against such brands or providers. Hunt et al. find that grudges persist for a long time and usually begin with an emotionally upsetting experience as a customer. Grudge-holders often give negative word of mouth about the offending product when talking to others. Brand avoidance would seem to have dire consequences for a manufacturer but, despite this, it has received little systematic study.

Beside brands, there are other product differentiators and consumers can be loyal to pack size, price level, country of origin, flavour and formulation characteristics. For example, Romaniuk and Dawes (2005) found that, although people bought a variety of different wines, they tended to have a consistent pattern of preference for price tiers. Singh, Ehrenberg and Goodhardt (2004) have illustrated regular patterns of purchase with regard to other category divisions. The point that we emphasize here is that no emotional commitment is needed for such effects. We argue that most patterns of purchase, including loyalty, reflect habit rather than deeply felt commitment.

SECTION 2: THE RISE OF RELATIONSHIP MARKETING: CUSTOMER LOYALTY AS RETENTION

Relationship marketing (RM) has been described as 'attracting, maintaining and enhancing customer relationships' (Berry, 1983: 25). RM is an industrial philosophy that replaces the competitive transaction between buyer and seller with a more cooperative relationship.[3] This is described by Grönroos (1994). One basis for this approach is the fact that cooperation between long-term partners has the potential to use resources more efficiently. In a cooperative relationship, partners learn to trust each other and to reveal more detail about their needs to the other, which improves the quality of mutual support. Relationship marketing seems to work well between industrial partners (business to business, or B2B).

Relationship Marketing in B2B

One outcome of relationship marketing has been the improvement in manufacturer–retailer relations due to the work conducted for Procter & Gamble by Buzzell, Quelch and Salmon (1991). Buzzell et al. found that the proliferation of new lines and sales promotions took much of the time of executives and cost money to implement. One of the reasons why manufacturers introduce new lines is to gain more space in supermarkets because this leads to more sales. If the retailer is willing to guarantee store space, the manufacturer can eliminate small-selling lines and save money. Similarly, if the retailer is willing to accept everyday low prices (EDLP) and not seek discounted product from the manufacturer for price promotions, more money can be saved. Thus, a movement based on these ideas called *Efficient Consumer Response* (ECR), developed in supply chain management. As a result of Buzzell et al.'s work, more cooperative arrangements were established between Procter & Gamble and Wal-Mart. Line ranges were reduced, prices were kept low and there were fewer promotions. Also, the restocking of the retailer could be simplified because the customer (Wal-Mart) and supplier (P&G) shared data. Without promotions, executives saved time and the demand for goods was more regular, which eased supply to stores. It is claimed that consumers also saved money as a result of these arrangements. These changes were reported in a book by Barbara Kahn and Leigh McAlister (1997) called *Grocery Revolution: The New Focus on the Consumer*.

Relationship Marketing in B2C

Relationship marketing has also been applied in the business-to-consumer (B2C) field, particularly by those concerned with services. As in B2B, some service relationships (e.g. dentist and patient) can be characterized by trust and cooperation but this does not apply so well when the business is larger. There is still interdependence between a large firm and its customers but any initiatives are likely to come from the firm and to be automated with the help of the customer database. Firms call this customer relationship management (CRM). Much of the CRM conducted by large firms is designed to increase sales by exploiting customer purchase habits and this has little to do with cooperation. Most firms follow good-practice rules so that their customers can trust them, but it does not go much further than that. For their part, customers can be quite calculating. For example, they may participate in loyalty schemes because they get a discount on purchases, or gain other benefits, rather than because they like the firm.

In relationship marketing there is more emphasis placed on retaining existing customers than attracting new ones. CRM can help here; for example, when a lack of spending indicates that a customer has switched supermarkets, vouchers can be issued that may bring the customer back. Most firms are keen to see increases in satisfaction among customers because this is thought to retain customers. This emphasis on retaining customers is based on the idea that it is more expensive to acquire customers than to retain them. So, instead of losing a customer and gaining another, it is cheaper not to lose the customer in the first place. A review by Rosenberg and Czepiel (1984) suggested that the average company spends six times as much acquiring a customer as keeping a customer. The 'six times as much' rule has now become an item of marketing folklore; the reality is that the relative cost varies with the category. Supermarket customers are acquired at little cost whereas credit card customers are expensive to acquire because they must be checked with credit agencies and offered financial inducements to switch.

The idea that customer retention increases long-term profit was given added impetus by Reichheld and his associates in a series of papers (Reichheld and Kenny, 1990; Reichheld and Sasser, 1990; Reichheld, 1993; Jones and Sasser, 1995; Reichheld, 1996a). These ideas were brought together in a book by Reichheld (1996b). Reichheld suggests that the value of a customer grows with the length of time that they remain a customer (called customer tenure). The reasons for this are illustrated in Figure 2.1. Reichheld argues that, for each added year of tenure, the profit from a customer rises as the acquisition cost is amortised, and as the customer spends more (revenue growth), becomes easier to deal with (cost savings), introduces more new customers (referrals) and is more tolerant of higher prices (price premium). Also, and not shown in Figure 2.1, the longer customers stay, the more likely they are to remain in the following year. This means that long-term customers are likely to give more profit in the future than short-term customers. An admirable feature of Reichheld's work is that he is very precise about the potential effects of customer retention so that others can test these claims. Reichheld's own evidence tends to be based on case studies. Case studies serve well for teaching about management practice but, as evidence, they are not as valuable as systematic studies that are set up to test a hypothesis.

Case study evidence is already available when marketers begin to hypothesize and they may unintentionally focus on the evidence that fits their theory. Now, we review Reichheld's claims.

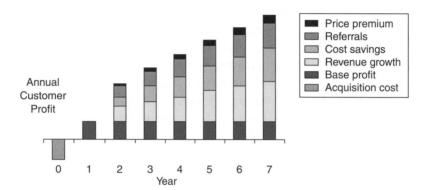

Figure 2.1   Factors in customer lifetime value (adapted from Reichheld, 1996b)

Customer Tenure and Profitability

First, do long-term customers spend more? East, Hammond and Gendall (2006) reported on 17 services where customers were asked how much they spent and how long they had used the supplier. Examples of services were supermarkets, credit cards, dry cleaners, fashion stores, mobile phone airtime and car servicing. Of the 17 studies, only three showed a statistically significant positive association between tenure and spending: credit cards (UK), outdoor clothing (USA) and mobile phone airtime (UK). The average correlation between tenure and spend for the 17 studies was 0.09. This shows that, usually, there is no substantial association between tenure and spending that would justify management attention. In a few categories, long-term customers may spend significantly more than new customers, but such cases need to be established by research and not assumed by managers.

Second, are long-term customers cheaper to serve? Long-term customers become familiar with company procedures and need less 'hand holding' but they may also exploit company services more. Dowling and Uncles (1997) first expressed doubt that long-term customers were cheaper to serve. Later, Reinartz and Kumar (2000, 2002) found that long-term customers in one firm made more use of the free services available, thus raising their cost to serve. It seems that costs do not routinely decline with tenure.

Third, do long-term customers refer more new customers than recently acquired customers? Long-term customers may value their providers more for two reasons. First they may *learn* more about the merits of the supplier's offering over time and second, as those who dislike the supplier switch, the more appreciative customers remain.

Despite these effects, Smith and Higgins (2000) and Fournier, Dobscha and Mick (1998) have illustrated how relationships can sometimes sour over time. Also, a brand may be salient when first acquired but may then become so familiar that consumers give it no thought and therefore do not talk about it. This loss of salience is more likely when the category does not change much (e.g. house insurance) and/or is frequently used (e.g. credit cards). When there is change, for example in the merchandise of a fashion store, the brands can be recommended again whereas a relatively unchanging product, for example motor insurance, does not merit a second recommendation.

In their review of previous evidence, East et al. (2005a) found either no association between recommendation rates and tenure (e.g. Kumar, Scheer and Steenkamp 1995; Verhoef, Franses and Hoekstra 2002) or a negative association (e.g. East, Lomax and Narain, 2001; Wangenheim and Bayón, 2004). In their paper (2005a), East et al. reported evidence from 23 studies (shown in Table 2.2). They found that the overall association between tenure and recommendation was neutral (−0.01) but that individual associations ranged from significantly negative to significantly positive.

Table 2.2 Correlations between variables in 23 service studies (from East, Gendall et al., 2005)

Service (country)	Customer tenure and recommendation
Cheque book service (UK)	−.44*
Credit card (UK)	−.39*
Car insurance (UK)	−.36*
Credit card (UK)	−.28*
Main supermarket (UK)	−.09
Mobile airtime (UK)	−.04
Motor insurance (UK)	−.03
Dentist (UK)	−.03
Dry cleaning (UK)	−.02
Internet provider (UK)	0.02
Leisure centre (UK)	0.04
House contents insurance (UK)	0.04
Main supermarket (Mexico)	0.06
Main fashion store (UK)	0.07
Car insurance (Mauritius)	0.07
Favourite restaurant (UK)	0.08
Email (UK)	0.10
Hairdresser (Mexico)	0.12
Search engine (UK)	0.13
Main fashion store (Mexico)	0.18*
Car servicing (UK)	0.20*
Car servicing (Mauritius)	0.20*
Car servicing (UK)	0.25*
Mean	−.01

*significant at $p < 0.05$

The significant negative associations were cheque accounts, credit cards and car insurance. The significant positive associations were for car servicing and main fashion stores in Mexico. Car servicing is infrequent so it takes time for a new customer to be reassured about the quality of work. Car servicing was one of the service categories mentioned by Reichheld so, in this specific case, the evidence shows that long-tenure customers recommend more. More generally, East et al. (2005a) do not support Reichheld's claim and indicate that, in a minority of fields, significantly more recommendations will come from recent recruits than from long-tenure customers. Notice that East et al. studied credit cards and car servicing twice in the UK; the pairs of studies gave similar results and this makes the work more convincing.

Fourth, are long-term customers more price-tolerant? Price tolerance is particularly exploited by providers of financial services. Firms allow the interest on accounts to drop without telling the account holders and mortgage, insurance and credit card offers to new customers are often better than those to existing customers. These inertia tactics may produce short-term profit if a large proportion of existing customers do not notice them but, when they do take note, they may be irritated and become regular switchers in order to get introductory discounts. This could be very damaging to long-term profits. Reichheld makes it clear that this sort of exploitation of customers is likely to be damaging in the longer run. However, in other fields there may be no long-term price premium. In three B2C companies that they studied, Reinartz and Kumar (2002) found that long-tenure customers did not pay more than short-term customers for the same goods. They also found that long-tenure customers were *more* price-sensitive and that these customers expected better value when compared with recent customers.

Fifth, do defection rates decline with tenure? In general, this is true. Reichheld finds that a company typically loses about 15 per cent of its current customers in the first year and 50 per cent over five years. Recent recruits, who have usually defected from another supplier, are particularly likely to defect. If we follow a cohort of customers and examine them over a period, we find that fewer and fewer customers defect each year and that the decay curve levels out, as shown in Figure 2.2. A study by East and Hammond (1997) estimated defection rates for a range of groceries and found an average of 15 per cent defection in the first year. In the second year, defection halved. This means that the customer's prospective lifetime value increases with tenure. However, there must come a time when changes in life stage (and even death) mean that customers do not need the category and defection may then rise. In addition, there are some products and services which are only used for a limited period, for example disposable nappies and crèche facilities, and here we would see a different pattern from that shown in Figure 2.2.

The Strategy of Customer Retention

This evidence indicates that the benefit of customer retention in consumer markets has been exaggerated and that the benefits from retention differ substantially

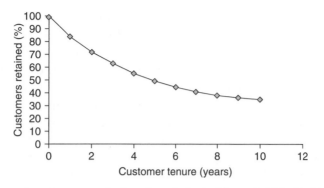

Figure 2.2   Normal customer survival pattern (adapted from Reichheld, 1996b)

between categories. One implication of this evidence is that customer acquisition may bring more advantage than is conventionally recognized, relative to retention. We need more evidence of the relative cost of gains through customer acquisition and retention and we need more evidence on how increases in share come about – are changes due primarily to acquisition or retention of customers? Two relevant studies are by East and Hogg (1997) and Riebe, Sharp and Stern (2002). East and Hogg found that, when Tesco overtook Sainsbury in 1995, the Tesco gains came equally from increased customer acquisitions and reduced defection. Sainsbury lost customers because of reduced recruitment, not increased defection. Riebe et al. found that changes in drug prescription among doctors came mainly from changes in acquisition.

There are a number of other points that are relevant to the retention versus acquisition argument. First, it is quite difficult to reduce defection. Reichheld's calculations suggest large gains in profit if customer defection is reduced from 15 per cent to 10 per cent but a one-third drop in defection is a substantial amount. Reichheld did have some examples where defection averaged only a few per cent a year but, in services where there is a specific location for service delivery, a large part of the defection occurs because of the relative inaccessibility of the service. For example, East, Lomax and Narain (2001) found that 43 per cent of the defections from a main supermarket were because the customer had moved home or because a more convenient store had been built nearby. This sort of customer loss is very difficult to counter.

A second point is mentioned by Reichheld but is sometimes forgotten by those who espouse his arguments. This is that the customers who are retained by a successful marketing intervention or service improvement are not necessarily typical of the other customers of the service provider. Customers who defect are obviously more mobile; when these customers are retained by a marketing intervention, they may be more likely to defect later.

A third point is that it is in the nature of loyal customers that they stay put. They may not need incentives to stay; if so, rewards and product improvements may give little return. Similarly, it may be very difficult to prise away the loyal customers of competitors. This leads to a paradox of loyalty. The most loyal customers may have the highest value but they may not be the best segment for marketing intervention because of their inertia. So which customers should be targeted when we have evidence of their loyalty? Should Tesco target high-share customers, who cannot increase their share much and may not be willing to change?[4] Or medium-share customers, who can increase their share and may be more changeable? Or low-share customers, who can increase their share substantially, may change more easily but may be prone to change again later? This is a complicated problem which requires experimental comparisons; we understand that Tesco focuses on the medium-share customers.

Although customer retention is emphasized in relationship marketing, this evidence shows that customer acquisition may be more important. Reichheld (1996b) does not ignore customer acquisition. He gave the example of the MBNA credit card organization. This company managed to acquire high-spending and high-retention customers by the careful design of the service and by well-chosen targeting. It is also well accepted that not all customers are profitable. Company costs can exceed returns on small-spending customers and sometimes retail facilities are so overstretched that more profit is made when some customers defect.

EXERCISE 2.2   BRAND SWITCHING

Consumers switch for many reasons which may vary across categories. Your own experience may be a guide. If you have switched banks, mobile phone companies, doctors, hairdressers, supermarkets or alcoholic beverages, why did you do this? Choose two categories which you have switched:

1   List the key reasons for your switch.

2   Identify four things the supplier could have done to try to retain you.

3   Evaluate how effective each of these initiatives would have been in your particular case.

SECTION 3: COMBINATION DEFINITIONS OF LOYALTY

So far we have described loyalty in terms of share, retention, satisfaction or trust. We have not combined these different forms of loyalty into a more complex definition. Most marketing scientists use a single behavioural definition, usually share or retention (see East et al. 2005a). By contrast, most of those who have theorized about loyalty suggest that loyalty is not behaviour alone, and many feel strongly that attitude should appear in the definition. For example, Jacoby and Olson (1970) defined loyalty as:

1   the biased (i.e. non-random)
2   behavioral response (i.e. purchase)
3   expressed over time
4   by some decision-making unit (e.g. household, person)
5   with respect to one or more alternative brands
6   which is a function of psychological processes (decision-making, evaluation)

Customers who stay with suppliers because of unthinking habit or simple convenience are not regarded as loyal according to this definition, because of point 6 which implies that feeling about the brand is required in addition to behaviour. Oliver (1999: 34) emphasized the role of feeling as well as behaviour when he described loyalty as 'a deeply held commitment to re-buy or re-patronize a preferred product/ service consistently in the future, thereby causing repetitive same-brand or same brand-set purchasing, despite situational influences and marketing efforts having the potential to cause switching behavior'. Also, Day (1969) suggested that 'true' or intentional loyalty occurred when there was a positive attitude to the brand and he distinguished this from 'spurious' loyalty where purchase of the brand was not supported by any commitment. Another widely quoted paper by Dick and Basu (1994) used Day's distinction and divided customers into four segments in the typology shown in Figure 2.3. True loyalty occurs in the top left-hand quadrant of Figure 2.3. Latent loyalty covers those who would like to buy the brand but who have not been able to do so in the past because it was not available, too expensive or because they had no need for it. Spurious loyalty occurs when consumers buy the brand but regard it as little better than others. In this typology, 'relative attitude' means that the attitude measure includes a term such as *compared with available alternatives*. Then, if a brand gets a high score, it is because it is rated much higher than the nearest alternative.

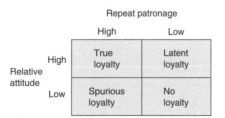
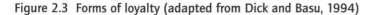

Figure 2.3 Forms of loyalty (adapted from Dick and Basu, 1994)

So should we see loyalty simply as behaviour or as behaviour with attitude? Ryanair and Wal-Mart can make profits from customers who use them regularly but may not like them. Indeed, for brands in some utilitarian categories like bleach and sugar it is difficult to have much feeling. But when loyal behaviour is supported by a liking for the brand, retention may be greater and more profit may be made. There are brands like Harley-Davidson which are clearly liked by their owners.

Definitions relate to the type of explanation that the researcher seeks to make. In Chapter 1, we introduced *segment comparisons* and *causal relationships*.

Dick and Basu's typology allows researchers to make comparisons between the four segments with respect to retention, share, recommendation and overall profitability, though we have been unable to find research that does this. Pritchard, Havitz and Howard (1999) used the Dick and Basu typology to show a number of differences between travellers who were classified according to the four segments but the authors did not investigate behaviour such as recommendation and retention. Macintosh and Lockshin (1997) also found significant differences between customers divided according to the Dick and Basu typology, but they investigated *intention* to repurchase rather than actual retention, and intention to repurchase may not relate closely to actual retention. Combination definitions of loyalty may be useful if retention and recommendation differs across segments, but we need to see evidence on this matter.

East et al. (2005a) investigated whether relative attitude and past patronage both predicted later retention and recommendation. For supermarkets and cars, they found that greater relative attitude was associated with more recommendation but had little relationship with retention. They also found that customers who bought mostly from one supermarket or who had bought the same make of car on the last two occasions (high past patronage) were somewhat more likely to retain the supermarket or the last make of car, but that the level of past patronage had no effect on word of mouth. Figure 2.4 summarizes these relationships with the dotted line indicating a weak relationship. We conclude that retention and word of mouth have largely different causes. One simple way of explaining the relationships in Figure 2.4 is that 'like correlates with like'. Past patronage and later retention are alike because they are the same measure at different points in time. Relative attitude and recommendation are alike because the reasons that people have for liking a brand are likely to be much the same as the reasons they give when they recommend it.

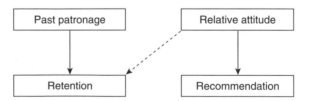

Figure 2.4   Consequences of different forms of loyalty

Other research has shown a weak positive association between satisfaction and retention. Crosby and Stephens (1987) found that life assurance renewal was slightly greater when customers were satisfied with the provider. Kordupleski, Rust and Zahoric (1993) found limited evidence that satisfaction increased retention in company research by AT&T. Reichheld (1993) reported that between 65 per cent and 85 per cent of customers who defected were satisfied with their former supplier.

Ennew and Binks (1996) did not find clear evidence of a positive association between retention and service quality (usually closely related to satisfaction) and Hennig-Thurau and Klee (1997) generally found moderate associations between satisfaction and retention in a review of studies. Against this weak evidence we can find a few stronger findings but these are where *dissatisfaction* has caused customers to switch. Andreasen (1985) studied ten patients who reported serious problems with their medical care and found that six of them switched physicians; Bolton (1998) found that dissatisfaction with a mobile phone airtime provider led to switching if the users had recently adopted the service and lacked knowledge of the supplier's longer-term performance. A forthcoming paper by Winchester, Romaniuk and Bogomolova (2008) shows that defection is indicated by prior negative beliefs about the product. Overall, this work indicates that satisfaction with a brand or supplier provides a limited prospect of increased retention but dissatisfaction may be a spur to switching.

Some readers may find it puzzling that feelings like satisfaction have such a weak relationship with retention but there are some good reasons why this should be so. One reason is that, usually, the measure of satisfaction employed is not *relative*. People retain a supplier because of the *superiority* of that supplier over others and a relative satisfaction measure would be more sensitive to this relative difference between alternatives. A second reason for the weak association between satisfaction and retention can be found in the reasons for defection. In services, defection often occurs as a consequence of specific failures, price changes or the emergence of superior competition, which we discuss later (Keaveney, 1995); such reasons are unlikely to be anticipated by an earlier measure of satisfaction. The same could be true of some goods. A third reason why satisfaction fails to predict defection well is that the defection may be involuntary, as was found by East, Lomax and Narain (2001). People who move house will change their main supermarket if their old one is now inaccessible; this does not mean that it was unsatisfactory.

What does all this mean? Those who propose combination measures of loyalty need to show that this approach is useful and that the segments in Dick and Basu's typology behave in different ways. In particular, they need to show that the top-left loyalty segment shows more retention, share loyalty and recommendation than other segments, at least in some categories. If they cannot do this, the case for combination measures fails. Meanwhile, those who are interested in the prediction of retention and recommendation need to present separate theories and evidence on these behaviours, so that we understand what will change them.

SECTION 4: REASONS FOR DEFECTION

Retention is often inertial. Behaviourally, consumers remain loyal by continuing to do what they have done before. In some cases, the inertia can be quite thoughtless as people continue with savings accounts and utility suppliers, even when better value is available. In the case of consumer durables, where an act of repurchase is required for retention, there may be more thought but, even here, the process may be fairly automatic. A study by Lapersonne, Laurent and Le Goff (1995) on car choice showed that 17 per cent of the respondents considered only the brand of their current car. But when people do defect and change the pattern of their past behaviour, they often have reasons. These reasons for defecting from service providers were studied by Susan Keaveney (1995).

Keaveney used her postgraduate students as investigators. They gathered evidence from people outside the university, asking them to focus on their most recent service defection, report what the service was and describe what happened. The narratives of what happened were reviewed by judges, who produced a typology of eight reasons for defection plus an 'other' category. Then the frequency of the different reasons was assessed from the narratives. Some people had more than one reason for defection and, in Table 2.3, we show the percentages for all the reasons cited and the percentages when one reason was given. There is not much difference between these two sets of percentages and we treat the average as typical of what Keaveney found (column 4).

Table 2.3   Reasons for switching from a service (adapted from Keaveney, 1995)

	All reasons (%)	When only one reason given (%)	Mean (%)
Core service failures	25	25	25
Failed service encounters	19	20	20
Response to failed service	10	0	5
Pricing	17	20	18
Competition	6	7	6
Ethical problems	4	4	4
Inconvenience	12	10	11
Involuntary switching	4	7	5
Other	5	7	6

The method used by Keaveney, called Critical Incident Technique (CIT), is suitable for establishing the typology but rather less appropriate for measuring the frequency of the different reasons since some memories are more easily recalled because of *retrieval bias*. This was described by Taylor (1982: 192), who states 'colorful, dynamic, or other distinctive stimuli disproportionately engage attention and, accordingly, disproportionately affect judgments'. Events are more changing and distinctive than conditions and are thus more easily retrieved. In Keaveney's list of reasons, the first three (core service failures, failed service encounters and responses to failed service) are clearly events, whereas inconvenience and involuntary switching are likely to relate to persisting conditions. Thus there is a danger that Keaveney's method raises the proportion of events at the expense of conditions. Keaveney, herself, was careful to describe her method as exploratory but others, when citing her findings, have been less cautious.

East, Grandcolas and Dall'Olmo Riley (2007) used a different method of measurement. They put Keaveney's reasons into one item of a questionnaire and asked the respondents to state which of these reasons was the most important in their decision to defect. This method should have reduced retrieval bias because all the possible reasons were prompted. Keaveney aggregated the data on all services mentioned by respondents but East et al. specified the services. They chose some services that were delivered in a particular location (e.g. a favourite restaurant) and some services where delivery was independent of location (e.g. mobile phone airtime). They reasoned that conditions would be much more important as a reason for defection when service delivery was located because the inaccessibility of some locations could cause inconvenience and involuntary switching. East et al. combined data on the three types of service failure event and the two conditions and presented their aggregate results in Table 2.4, which also shows Keaveney's frequencies.

Table 2.4   Condensed table of reasons for defection compared with Keaveney's results (Precentages by row) (from East et al. 2007a)

	N	Service failure events	Pricing	Competition	Ethical problems	Conditions	Other
Located services	523	12	12	23	1	47	6
Non-located service	369	27	35	20	0	8	9
All services	892	18	22	22	1	31	7
Keaveney	211	50	18	6	4	16	6

Table 2.4 shows a much lower proportion of service failure events (18 per cent instead of 50 per cent) and a higher proportion of conditions (31 per cent versus 16 per cent). The conditions came mainly from the located services, as expected. There were two other interesting findings. One was that the reason for defecting from non-located services was often pricing. This suggests that locations give some defence from price competition. Although location may force defection on some customers because of inconvenience, it may encourage continued use among others because alternatives would be inconvenient.

The second point was the role of competition which, at 22 per cent, was much higher than Keaveney's 6 per cent. Customers who give competition as the reason for their defection imply that they discovered a better supplier, and then they abandoned their current supplier. Other reasons suggest that the current supplier was abandoned first, and then a new supplier was found. We need more evidence on the sequence of events governing defection because we will then be better able to influence the process. It is probable that the reasons that people give for keeping a brand are rather different from those given for switching a brand. An unpublished study at Kingston by Maria Francolini on car replacement compared the reasons given for car purchase when the car brand was repurchased and when it was switched. Table 2.5 shows that consumers use rather different criteria once they have decided to switch.

Table 2.5 Reasons given for retaining or switching the make of car (Maria Francolini, unpublished)

Reasons for repurchase of same brand	N=138 (%)	Reasons for switching to new brand	N=162 (%)
Reliability	43	More money to spend	17
No choice	15	Needed bigger car	15
Safety	13	No choice	12
Economy	11	Good deal on old car	11
Performance	7	Old car unreliable	7
Holds value	5	Recommendation	7
Goods size	2	Bad servicing	6
Comfort	2	Other reasons	19

One of the inferences that Keaveney draws from her data is that managers can prevent defection in many cases. Let us assume that managers cannot control defection when it is based on conditions and competition. Then, according to Keaveney's evidence, 78 per cent of the reasons for defection are controllable. According to East, Grandcolas and Dall'Olmo Riley, 72 per cent of reasons are controllable in non-located services but only 30 per cent in located services. It appears that defection is difficult to stop in located services. This suggests that more emphasis should be placed on customer acquisition in such services.

SUMMARY

Several behaviours indicate customer loyalty. These are share-of-category requirement (SCR) in repertoire markets, and retention and recommendation in all markets. Feelings also indicate loyalty. The main feelings are attitude, satisfaction, commitment and trust.

Early work investigated SCR in grocery purchase and showed that consumers frequently divided their purchasing across several brands in a category. Divided loyalty patterns persist over long periods and may reflect consumer habits.

With the rise in relationship marketing, attention turned to the retention of customers, particularly with regard to services. Reichheld (1996b) argued that there was substantial profit to be gained if customers could be retained for longer periods but many of his arguments have been undermined by subsequent research.

Marketing scientists have generally used behaviour measures such as share and retention but others have argued that loyalty should be seen as a composite of attitude and behaviour and be tested by segment comparisons. The best-known model is by Dick and Basu (1994) but, although differences in behaviour have been demonstrated between the population segments defined by this model, there is little evidence that these differences relate to loyalty behaviours such as retention and recommendation.

Defection from services has been studied by Keaveney (1995), who developed a typology of eight reasons for defection. Recent work has suggested that the reasons for defection depend on the type of service. Customers often leave services that are delivered in a specific location because of problems of accessibility.

Additional Resources

The papers by Reichheld and his colleagues are clearly written and are more concise than his book. Keaveney's (1995) paper is worth reading. Reinartz and Kumar (2002) provide a critical review in this area.

Notes

1 We do not describe the average SCR per brand as *brand loyalty* because there is no consistent usage here and the term 'brand loyalty' is mainly used to cover the loyalty of a customer to a brand.
2 When more cases are obtained by gathering data over a long period, the small-number effect disappears and then light buyers are found to be somewhat less loyal (Stern and Hammond, 2004).
3 Sometimes, relationship marketing is contrasted with transactional marketing but this is unhelpful since transactions still take place in relationship marketing even if they are approached more cooperatively.
4 Tesco estimate the share of each customer's purchases that they get (they call it *share of stomach*).

3 Brand Knowledge, Brand Equity and Brand Extension

LEARNING OBJECTIVES

When you have completed this chapter, you should be able to:

1 Understand ideas about the mental representation of concepts.
2 Understand what is meant by brand image, brand awareness, brand strength and brand equity.
4 Explain the potential gains and losses from brand extensions.
5 Understand how brand shares alter when new brands enter a market.

OVERVIEW

Managers search for ways of exploiting their brands better by introducing line extensions (new variants in the established category) and category extensions (products in different categories). These brand extensions are not without risk. If the extension fails to capture new sales, then marketing effort will have been wasted. In addition, if the introduction of new products confuses customers and lessens their allegiance to the brand, all the sales associated with the brand could suffer. We start by considering how consumers store brand knowledge through a network of related concepts. Then we consider the idea of brand equity. Finally, we examine research on brand extension and the way in which new entrants to a market take sales from existing players.

SECTION 1: THE MENTAL REPRESENTATION OF BRANDS

In this chapter, we are concerned at first with the way in which concepts such as companies, brands, services and categories are represented in memory. Such mental representations should define how a brand is linked to other concepts and what developments of the brand would be consistent with the way in which it is perceived. The fundamental idea is that memory is an *associative network* of interlinked nodes in which each node is a concept. The meaning of a concept is therefore given partly by the interrelationships it has with other concepts. These interrelationships may be established through experience and from information received from other persons and from the mass media. Once established, such links may be strengthened by further experience and information. Smith and Queller (2001) provide a useful review of this field.

In mental representations theory:

- Perception activates nodes that correspond to the perceived object.
- Thinking occurs when these activated nodes spread activation to other linked nodes.
- Links between nodes are strengthened slowly over time by such activation.
- The concepts relating to more frequently activated nodes are retrieved from memory.
- Nodes are valenced (positive or negative), which is the basis for attitude.
- Long-term memory is the single, large associative structure covering all concepts whereas short-term memory is a currently activated subset.
- Simultaneous activations may occur (parallel processing), but much of this processing is unconscious.

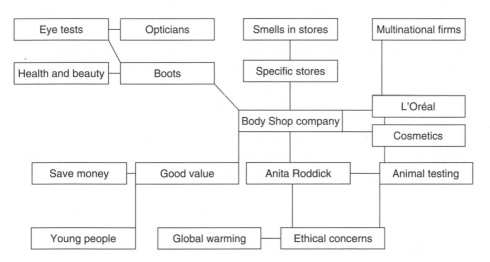

Figure 3.1 Concepts that might be associated with Body Shop

To illustrate this thinking we have set out a mental representation of Body Shop and related concepts in Figure 3.1. A mental node for Body Shop might be linked to concepts such as environmental concern, good value, young people, specific shops, pungent smells in the store and to the different products it sells. Some people would know that Body Shop is now owned by L'Oréal but may continue to link it to the ethical ideals of Anita Roddick, its founder. More peripherally, the concepts associated with Body Shop include its competitors, such as Boots, which will have further associations. In the process of thinking, a person might pass from cosmetics to eye tests and from multinational firms to global warming or young people. Conversely, thoughts about distant concepts may eventually lead to Body Shop.

Figure 3.1 helps us to think about two aspects of brand knowledge, *brand image* and *brand awareness*. The set of nodes and linkages in Figure 3.1 represents the brand image of Body Shop. This is created from customer experience of the firm and its stores, and by word of mouth and mass communications. To the extent that consumers have similar customer experiences and similar exposure to word of mouth and mass communication, we expect them to have similar brand images for Body Shop.

Brand awareness concerns the way in which ideas are brought to mind. There are two mechanisms, *recall* and *recognition*. When people recall something, they use the links between concepts in their mental representation to get to the idea that is recalled. For example, they might need a cosmetic and then think of Body Shop. Recognition involves a direct match between an external stimulus and a mental representation; this occurs when a person sees a branch of Body Shop and knows what it is. When the stimulus is partial or the mental representation poorly defined, the matching will be harder to complete.

This distinction between recall and recognition is well exemplified by the children's memory game in which 30 objects are placed on a tray, shown for a minute, and then concealed. The children then have to recall as many objects as they can. Usually, the objects that they cannot recall are retrieved when they are asked questions such as 'Was there a comb, a paper clip, a balloon?' The second type of retrieval is a form of recognition because partial object cues are provided. Human beings have very great powers of recognition, e.g. the ability to recognize people from their face, voice and other cues.

Box 3.1	Schemas

Mental representations also include schemas (or schemata), which cover classifications and relationships. Schemas are abstract and generalized rather than concrete. The classifications that we use in marketing are schemas (goods and services, brands and categories, etc.). Schemas help us to think by directing attention, classifying and relating external phenomena and by guiding the retrieval of information from memory. Schemas tend to be seen as parallel to associative networks though they are presumably based on similar structures. There is more on schemas in Chapter 7.

Brand Image in More Detail

Gardner and Levy (1955) introduced the idea of brand image; they believed that brands have a social and psychological meaning as well as a physical nature and that these feelings and ideas about brands direct consumer choice. The idea of brand image is also expressed by other terms, such as 'the symbols by which we buy', 'brand personality' and 'brand meaning'. These more experiential or symbolic aspects of brand image may prompt brand recall as easily as more precise descriptions. For example, people wanting a subtle white wine, a romantic weekend or a book that lifts the spirit may think of particular products that they associate with these concepts, just as they would in response to more straightforward stimuli such as white wine, hotel or an author.

Using the terminology of mental representations, brand image is the set of concepts associated with the brand. These associations differ in respect of valence, number, uniqueness and linkage strength, and these factors determine brand attitude and brand strength, as shown in Figure 3.2. Brand strength is important because it is thought to be related to ease of retrieval, range of association and resistance to change (not shown in Figure 3.2), which are also aspects of brand equity, which is discussed later.

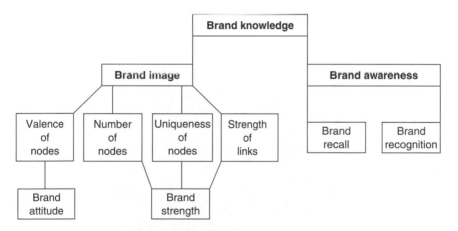

Figure 3.2   Main forms of brand knowledge

Retrieval is thought to be easier if there are many strong links to the central concept. If the number of links affects strength, we might expect brands with more links to be found more often in the choice set. Supporting this, Romaniuk (2003) has shown that brands with more image attributes are more likely to be considered for choice, and Romaniuk and Gaillard (2007) noted that the biggest brands had more attributes. Romaniuk and Sharp (2003) also found that respondents stated that they were less likely to defect from brands with a greater number of positive attributes. More associations will anchor the brand image so that consumers find it harder to change.

If brand strength is affected by the uniqueness of nodes, retrieval should also be greater when nodes are uncommon and differentiated from others in the brand image. The evidence does not support this effect of uniqueness. Romaniuk and Gaillard (2007) did not find that consumers thought that the brand that they bought had more unique attributes than brands that they did not buy, and they found that larger brands had much the same proportion of unique characteristics as smaller brands. Although we have included uniqueness in Figure 3.2, it is likely that this feature is overemphasized. Customers need to be able to differentiate brands but this can be accomplished through quite trivial differences (see Box 3.2).

Box 3.2	**Consumer confusion and look-alike brands**

The term 'consumer confusion' is used in a variety of ways. In courts of law, it relates to *passing off*, when one manufacturer makes a product that is very similar to that of another manufacturer. In these circumstances, consumers may make mistakes and buy the wrong brand. This has been a concern in marketing but there is often no confusion in this sense. For example, a person buying Perigan's gin will normally know that they are not buying Gordon's gin, despite some similarities of bottle shape, colour and label design. But Gordon's gin has built up a buying propensity that is associated with the

The illustration shows Gordon's and Perigan's gin. Both spirits are in squared bottles, use yellow and orange on the labels and have similarities of label design.

uniqueness of its pack, and some element of this buying propensity may attach to look-alike competitors even when consumers are well aware of the differences between brands. This means that Perigan's is using brand strength that they did not create. However, it is not clear that their product damages Gordon's gin – it could even strengthen this brand because it draws attention to the Gordon's design. Also, if a brand is sold at a distinctly different price from another in the same category, there will be limited direct competition.

As noted, the strength of a mental representation will depend partly on the strength of the links between concepts. Fazio and Zanna (1981) have shown that knowledge that is established through experience is more readily retrieved and has a stronger effect on behaviour than knowledge established from communication. This means that one concept can have the same valence as another but have more effect on behaviour because of the way in which the concept was established.

Brand attitude is the positive or negative feeling about the brand. This is likely to vary from context to context since different situations will tap different parts of the mental representations map. Notions like animal testing are often negative, in which case concepts that are linked to this will acquire some negativity. The overall attitude will depend on the balance of linkages to positive and negative nodes.

A number of techniques are used for measuring brand image. Driesener and Romaniuk (2006) review three commonly used methods. Brands can be rated or ranked on a criterion, or all those with a characteristic can be named – the 'pick-any' method. These techniques can be used for evaluative criteria such as good value, or for more descriptive criteria such as French-made. A third method – the expected-value formulation developed by Fishbein (1963) – may also be used to measure brand attitude (discussed in Chapter 6).

One concern about the theory of mental representations is the extent to which it can cover the full range of connected concepts. Obvious features seem to be covered but there may be a substantial amount of unconscious processing behind our conscious thinking. We should be wary of drawing too close a parallel between mental representations and the evidence from brain research, but there is clearly some correspondence between the neurons in the brain which are connected to other neurons by synapses and the nodes connected by links in mental representation theory. Brain research shows that cerebral activity occurs on a vastly greater scale than that used to illustrate mental representations. Consciousness is associated with a massive activation of portions of the brain, involving hundreds of thousands of neurons; each neuron has as many as two thousand synapses connecting it to other neurons (Greenfield, 1997). This suggests that mental representations theory indicates only a small part of the processing that goes on when people think.

Box 3.3	Brand Images

Weak brand image

In the UK, one of the DIY store groups called Do-It-All found, some years ago, that the extra sales raised by its advertising were much the same as the extra sales they received when their competitor B&Q advertised. It seemed that the public made little differentiation between DIY stores; advertising reminded them of work that they had intended to do and they got any necessary supplies from the most convenient store. Thus, the advertising of any one store group had the effect of promoting the DIY retail category as a whole, rather than the named store group. In situations like this, where brand awareness is weak, store groups may set up sales promotions and advertise these. In this way, consumers only gain advantage when they patronize the advertised store group.

Strong brand image

In Britain, the case of Hellman's mayonnaise (Channon, 1985) illustrates the way in which a strong brand awareness can pay off. In 1981, Hellman's was priced well above other brands of mayonnaise and was open to fierce competition from these other brands, particularly retailer brands. The advertising used the term 'Hellman's' rather than 'mayonnaise' to reinforce the brand name. The campaign was successful in making Hellman's the effective name of the category and the brand still has a large share of the market. Becoming synonymous with the category has always been an attractive possibility for a leading brand. In the UK, 'Hoovering' means vacuum cleaning and is perhaps the best known example of this effect.

Brand Awareness in More Detail

Brand awareness is about the retrieval of a brand from memory and the retrieval can take two forms, recall and recognition (Bettman, 1979). We introduced these concepts above and now we look at them in more detail. Recall is often a general to specific process; for example, the thought of an aperitif might bring the idea of a Ricard to mind. Often, the cue is the category or a need for the category. Clearly, a number of alternative brands can be recalled. Also, people may think of other matters, such as the previous time they were thirsty, rather than a drink. Recall is also involved in spontaneous thinking where one concept cues another. Recognition occurs when the brand is presented to a consumer in whole or in part. Recognition is a specific to general process in the sense that it involves identifying the class of the stimulus; for example, the bottle of Ricard is recognized as a type of French aperitif that goes cloudy when mixed with water.

The strength of brand recall may be measured as top of mind. This is the first brand retrieved in response to a category stimulus; for example, Federal Express might be recalled when a courier service is needed. Ease of recognition may be measured as speed of response when a brand stimulus is presented and accuracy of recognition might be estimated by asking people to report whether a particular brand is present when a picture of several brands is exposed briefly.

Brands are thought about and chosen in a variety of contexts and these contexts affect whether recall or recognition is used to retrieve a brand from memory. For example, a person might want to repair a broken jug and recall that Loctite will do the job. Alternatively, the person might be in a DIY store and see Loctite on the shelf, recognize it, and remember that this product is needed to repair the jug. Brands with a physical form are generally suitable for recognition because the brand 'makes itself known' to the consumer in the store. Services are often harder to represent in the environment and here the need for the category often occurs first, and then the brand is recalled in response. Rossiter and Bellman (2005) use the distinction between recall and recognition as a cornerstone of their approach to designing effective advertising and choosing suitable media. Visual media such as television are good for representing physical brands because they aid recognition, whereas radio is good for strengthening the link from category to brand and this medium therefore aids recall.

The distinction between recall and recognition would have little relevance if advertising and brand experience facilitated recall and recognition equally. However, the linkages in the mental representation have direction and a person who has a *brand* → *category* recognition may not have the same degree of *category* → *brand* recall, even though the same nodes are linked. The measurement of brand awareness should test these links separately.

SECTION 2: BRAND EQUITY AND BRAND EXTENSION

Brand Equity

Biel (1991) describes brand equity as the value of a brand beyond the physical assets associated with its manufacture or provision and says that it can be thought of as the additional cash flow obtained by associating the brand with the underlying product. Because brand knowledge changes slowly, a brand that is currently profitable is likely to continue to be so. We should therefore conserve and exploit brands in the same way that other assets are used. Some marketers have taken a *financial* approach and have tried to value the additional profit potential offered by a brand.[1] A second *customer-based* approach has focused on consumer responses to the brand as measured by image, awareness, quality, loyalty and specific market advantages (e.g. Aaker, 1991); without these consumer responses to the brand, there would be no extra revenue stream or scope for brand extension. In consumer behaviour, we are primarily interested in this second approach and Figure 3.3 shows brand equity as the outcome of brand attitude, brand strength and context effects. Context effects cover such matters as market size, prominence of the category in everyday life, opportunity to purchase and the accumulated effect of marketing support.

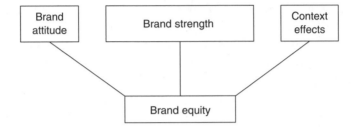

Figure 3.3   Determinants of brand equity

Because of the difficulty of measuring these different components of brand equity, and uncertainties about how they should be aggregated, customer judgements of quality are often used as a proxy for brand equity. Using brands of high and low quality, Krishnan (1996) compared the number of associations, valence, uniqueness and how the associations were formed (by experience or indirectly through communication). Krishnan's results were generally in the direction expected but there is a problem about using quality as a measure of brand equity; few people doubt the quality of Porsche but most lack the means to buy such cars, which reduces Porsche's brand equity. The results were generally in the direction expected. Kamakura and Russell (1991), and Keller (1993), have proposed an alternative measurement of brand equity. Instead of trying to measure aspects of brand knowledge, these researchers suggest that it can be measured through the consumer evaluation of marketing elements. Specifically, they propose blind tests that compare the consumer responses to changes in the product specification, price, promotion and distribution of a named brand with the corresponding responses for an unnamed or unfamiliar product.

EXERCISE 3.1   THE SCOPE FOR BRAND EXTENSION

1   Put in order of brand quality the following brand names: Samsung, Toshiba, Sony, Bush.

2   What does this suggest about the profit potential of the four brands?

3   What, in particular, do you associate with Sony?

4   Does the quality order stay the same for a new category, e.g. electric toothbrush or food processor?

In western countries, Sony usually tops the list and Samsung does less well (but not in South Korea where it is a premium brand). Sony's ascendancy probably reflects product quality, innovation and advertising sustained over many years. However, Sony is particularly focused on electronic goods and the assurance offered by the brand name is usually less clear when it is related to electric toothbrushes or kitchen equipment. This suggests that extensions to these categories may not carry much brand equity.

New Brand or Brand Extension?

Strong brand equity will affect the success of line, category and geographical extensions. A line extension is a variant within the category of a parent brand (e.g. fun-size Mars bars). A category extension occurs when a brand name used in one category is applied in another category (e.g. Mars Mini rolls). A geographical extension occurs when a brand name that is famous, but marketed only in some countries, is introduced to other countries (e.g. the introduction of US car brands such as Chrysler to Europe). In addition to extensions, companies with a strong brand may gain by taking over other companies and extending their name to the acquired company's products. For example, a well-established hotel brand, like Marriott, may be able to make more profit out of another hotel company's assets because of the strength of the Marriott name. Similarly, brand combinations can work well; the name Sony-Ericsson on mobile phones combines pre-eminence in consumer electronics (Sony) with a very strong engineering reputation (Ericsson).

The picture shows the parent product, the Mars bar (top left) and the line extension, the fun-size Mars bar (right). At the bottom is the Mini roll category extension.

Line extensions are very common. In the USA, Aaker (1991) estimated that about 90 per cent of new products in the packaged goods industry were line extensions. Generally, the description of a product as a line extension is appropriate when the variant competes with its parent. For example, those who buy fun-size Mars will usually do so instead of buying the normal size Mars bar. Sometimes, a line extension will raise additional sales but often the line extension is defensive and is designed to counter competition and prevent sales erosion to new variants produced by competitors. Normally, category extensions do not compete with sales of the parent. For example, Porsche sunglasses do not compete with the sale of Porshe cars and Caterpillar boots will not compete with the sale of the company's earth-moving equipment. Exceptions to this rule occur in food categories; it is likely that sales of Mars ice-cream and Mars Mini rolls affect sales of Mars bars because of the common flavouring.

Although there may be substantial value attaching to a brand name, it is not easy to decide whether to introduce a product with a new brand name or to extend an existing brand name. A brand may be inappropriate for some extensions. Sometimes, there will be an incompatibility between categories that makes it unrealistic to extend a name. Procter & Gamble would have problems in extending the Pampers brand (disposable diapers) to food though they might be able to use the name on baby clothing. Toyota, a very strong mass-market, brand was deemed unsuitable for the launch of a new luxury brand. As a result, Toyota developed Lexus. By contrast, high-quality brands such as BMW and Mercedes have chosen to offer smaller cars and utility vehicles under their brand name. This underscores a general observation that high-quality brands are more extendable than low-quality ones. In fact, it is rare to find an extension from a low-quality brand.

Box 3.4	**The model name dilemma**

The launch of a new car raises naming problems. Should the old model name be abandoned or kept? Some equity attaches to a model name which is lost when the name is dropped. On the other hand, it is important to show the novelty of the new model and a break with the past helps this. Some companies, such as Volkswagen, have a policy of retaining model names such as Golf and Passat, whereas other manufacturers, such as Citroën, always drop the model name. Peugeot normally dropped model names but when faced with the continuing popularity of the 205, retained this name when updates were introduced.

Nesting a new model name with the old one is not normally used in the car industry but it had to be used in Australia when Daihatsu found that their rather bizarre model name, Charade, was better known than Daihatsu. When the time came to end the Daihatsu Charade, they introduced the new model as the Daihatsu Charade Centro (*Sydney Morning Herald*, 7 July 1995).

Managers must decide whether to launch new products as extensions or as new brands. If a new name is used, it must be (1) different from other brand names, (2) easy to remember, (3) translate well (the Vauxhall Nova was unsuitable in Spain because it implied that the car would not go), (4) be available (many brand names are registered but unused by major manufacturers) and, most importantly, (5) cover potential extensions since these may make money and justify using a new brand name. One reason for the loss of interest in descriptive names such as 'I Can't Believe It's Not Butter' is that such names offer limited scope for extension.

Box 3.5	Extensions may affect core business

In 1993, the British security firm Group 4 extended its operations from moving money to moving prisoners. In the first week three prisoners escaped, other disasters followed and the press castigated the firm for its incompetence. Group 4 became the butt of jokes: 'What was Group 4 originally called? Group 5 but one got away'. According to Stephen Moss in *The Guardian* (24 May 1993), the company considered pulling out of its private prison contracts because of the ridicule and possible damage to the rest of its £500 million a year security business.

New brand names are expensive. McWilliam (1993) found that cost saving was the most frequent reason cited by marketing practitioners for using an extension. Smith and Park (1992) studied the effect of extensions on market share and advertising efficiency and concluded that extensions capture greater market share and can be advertised more efficiently than new brands. Doyle (1989) also found that extensions needed less advertising and noted that they are more readily accepted by distributors as well as by customers. Tauber (1988) noted that the use of an existing name helps a brand to gain shelf space in stores.

Failure with a brand extension may damage the parent brand. This may occur because the extension so enlarges the associations of the brand name that it loses impact and all products under that name suffer in consequence (Tauber, 1981). One case cited by Trout and Ries (1972) was the rapid diversification of Protein 21 by Mennen into a confusing set of alternatives. This was associated with a loss in share rather than the expected gain. However, new extensions need not cause confusion. Smith and Park (1992) did not find that the efficiency of a new extension was reduced by the number of extensions already made. Dacin and Smith (1993) found that consumer confidence in a new extension was unaffected by the number of existing extensions, provided that the new entrant was compatible with its predecessors. Dawar and Anderson (1993) found that new lines were more acceptable if they were introduced in an order that made them coherent with the products that had already been introduced. Aaker and Keller (1990) found that potentially negative associations could be neutralized by focusing on the attributes of the new brand rather than the strengths of the parent brand. In a subsequent study, Keller and Aaker (1992) examined how consumers saw the extensions to a brand when there were, and were not, prior extensions. They found that, if the prior extensions were regarded as successes, they improved the evaluation of a new extension; if the prior extensions were unsuccessful, they degraded the evaluation of a new extension. This suggests that brand owners should be wary of extensions after a failure.

Consumer Acceptance of a Category Extension

Although we can explain the management issues affecting the launch of new products, the theory is not well enough defined for us to predict whether a specific extension will be a success or not. However, we have a good idea of the factors that determine success as a result of work by Aaker and Keller (1990). They took six well-known brand names and examined how consumers reacted to 20 possible category extensions. For example, they considered the ideas of Crest extending to chewing gum and Vidal Sassoon offering perfume. They found that three factors predicted the attitude of consumers to the potential extension. One of these was the *fit* between the categories of the parent and offspring. A second was the quality of the parent brand. The third factor was whether the extension required some effort to imagine. These relationships are shown in Figure 3.4.

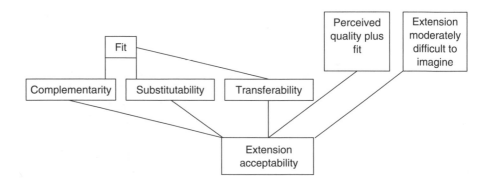

Figure 3.4   Factors contributing to extension success (adapted from Aaker and Keller, 1990)

Fit was measured as complementarity, substitutability and transferability. Complementarity concerns the matching of the new product with the parent, thus skiing goggles would be a complementary product for a maker of skis. Substitutability applies when the new product could be used instead of the parent product; for example, snow boards would substitute for skis. Transferability relates to manufacture rather than usage; whether or not the producer of the parent product is believed to have the capacity to produce the offspring product. For example, a firm that made skis would not necessarily be seen as the best organization to manufacture snow-making equipment but would be accepted for ice skates. This account of fit is neat but it may be inadequate when faced with brands like Chanel which embrace a wide variety of product types. Although these products share a quality image, in other respects they are diverse.

The second factor, the perceived quality of the parent brand, was positively associated with the acceptability of the extension, but only when there was a good fit.

The third factor was whether the extension required some effort to imagine. This means that extensions that are very easy or very difficult to imagine are less successful. Aaker and Keller suggest that consumers might think that an easily imagined extension was overpriced. An alternative explanation relates to the cognitive effort involved. A very simple extension requires little effort to comprehend and may therefore not disturb a person's mental representations. When people have to do cognitive work on an idea they may connect it with existing concepts, thus raising awareness of the extension. However, if the cognitive work required is too complicated, the extension may be rejected. Related to this explanation, Hartman, Price and Duncan (1990) suggest that people will try to make sense of an extension but, if it differs too much from the parent product, they will dismiss the idea of the new product or just fail to recognize it. Hartman et al. suggest that consumers may make sense of large discrepancies between parent and extension when the products are high involvement but warn that people could also react negatively if they have to make a lot of effort to comprehend an association. Supporting Hartman et al., Meyers-Levy and Tybout (1989) showed that one unusual characteristic increased cognitive processing but too many unusual characteristics reduced it. In sum, the very obvious may be ignored and the inexplicable may be rejected.

Sunde and Brodie (1993) failed to replicate Aaker and Keller's (1990) findings. Following this, Bottomley and Holden (2001) reviewed the evidence on the acceptability of brand extension. They used data from the original Aaker and Keller (1990) study and from seven replications. They found that the original contentions of Aaker and Keller were broadly supported: fit makes an extension more acceptable and the quality of the parent brands increases acceptability provided that there is some fit. We might also note that Aaker (1991) presents some very persuasive examples of successful and unsuccessful extensions that indicate that one key to success is the fit between parent and the extension. However, we should note that Aaker and Keller's method is quite weak; it rests on the judgement of respondents about how they will behave in hypothetical circumstances and, in practice, they may not know this, or other factors may intervene and induce them to behave differently.

Effective Marketing

Some poorly fitting extensions have worked because the appropriate marketing structures were available. Marks and Spencer, originally known for clothing, successfully diversified to food because they had an effective system of sourcing and distribution; Bic, known for disposable ballpoints and lighters, succeeded with a sailboard extension. McWilliam (1993) points out that marketers are very reluctant to see a failure as the result of poor marketing, but this is often the reason, rather than fit. Similarly, Barwise (1993) suggests that effective marketing is often ignored. The potential of a category extension is affected by market size, product quality, market growth, economies of scale, distribution structures and profit margin, all of which should be considered by the marketer. From this standpoint, some incongruous extensions may succeed because they are well marketed.

EXERCISE 3.2   POTENTIAL EXTENSIONS

Dell, Nokia, Pampers, Shell and the BBC are brands that have few extensions. Suggest extensions which might be appropriate and successful. Give reasons for your suggestions. Why have these brands not been extended?

Review

It is clearly important that we understand how brands are accepted or rejected and what scope there is for extracting more profit from a brand. However, the subtlety of human thought makes this a difficult enterprise. First, it seems likely that the unconscious cognitive activity involved in brand choice is large and, because it is unconscious, it is difficult to measure this activity. One reason why we suspect that there is a substantial amount of unconscious activity is because the brain structure that makes this possible is vastly more elaborate than any of the descriptions that we may make of our conscious processing. A related problem is that brand choice is contextual. It occurs under a variety of circumstances and these different circumstances will relate to different parts of a consumer's mental representation map.[2] This problem is aggravated when we take account of the way mental representations differ between people. The theory of mental representations may serve as a description of why certain effects are found, but it has limited value as a predictive model.

We are also rather sceptical about the value of findings from the studies that have been conducted to determine the acceptability of potential extensions. It is not that we dispute the findings of this work, now checked by Bottomley and Holden (2001). What we dispute is the generalizability of these findings to every-day life. In the laboratory, people will report on perceived quality and fit but, in the field, marketing activity and consumer adaptability may overcome the apparent unacceptability of an extension.

Despite these problems, there are some areas of promise. It is clear that brands do have value in the sense that people will associate more benefits with well-known brands and may pay more for a branded product than a functionally equivalent anonymous product. Tests based on such comparisons are likely to indicate brand strength and extension potential.

SECTION 3: SALES LOSSES BY THE PARENT OF A LINE EXTENSION

Sometimes a new entrant enlarges a market so that all the brands gain. One example was when Pampers entered the disposable diapers market in South Africa (Broadbent, 2000). Their campaign helped the category to become estab-lished as an alternative to cloth diapers and this helped Pampers' competitors to sell more volume. But this is unusual. Normally, markets are fairly stationary so that one player's gain is another player's loss. When this applies, it is important to know how a new entrant takes sales from the existing players since this helps to decide a manager's strategy. This sales loss is often large for the variants of a brand when a line extension is launched because existing lines can easily be sub-stituted by the new line: the new line *cannibalizes* the existing lines. Sometimes, cannibalization is enforced by retailers who refuse to give manufacturers addi-tional shelf space for a new line and stipulate that some other line must be abandoned in order to provide space. 'Line in, line out' is the terse name for this retailer practice. When extra space is given and the new line can compete with the previously established brands, there are two sales patterns that can occur:

- Existing brands may lose sales to the new entrant in proportion to their market share. This is the basic effect that may be expected when there are no special affinities between brands.
- An extra loss of sales occurs among brands that are perceived to be similar to the new entrant. With a line extension the main similarity is likely to be the common brand name, with the result that the parent loses more sales than would be expected from market share alone. Extra losses may also be incurred when there are similarities of for-mulation, packaging, pricing, positioning, targeting, distribution and physical proximity to other brands in the store.[3]

Table 3.1　Brand market shares and percentage of Wisk gain 20 weeks after Wisk launch

Brand	Midland market share before Wisk launch	Contribution to Wisk sales after launch
Persil	28	27
Ariel	17	22
Surf	16	8
Bold	14	12
Daz	9	11
Other brands	16	15
No previous purchase	–	5

Source: AGB data, 1987

Some data on the British detergent market illustrate the way in which consumers shift support from existing brands to a new brand. Table 3.1 shows how, 20 weeks after launch, the first liquid detergent on the British market, Wisk, was taking customers from other brands (right-hand column). Wisk was a new brand and took share from other brands roughly in relation to their market share, though Surf, with its value-for-money positioning, seemed to resist loss better. Because the sales loss is proportional to existing share, big brands lose more volume than small brands.

This effect was further investigated in a study by Lomax et al. (1996). Using new data, this work confirmed that Wisk took share in relation to the market share of the other brands. A second study showed the cannibalization effect of the same brand name when a concentrated version of a German detergent took disproportionately more sales from its parent than from other brands. In a third study, Lomax et al. examined the gains of the Ariel Liquid detergent that followed Wisk onto the British market. Here there was a parent powder brand and it was anticipated that this would be cannibalized by the new liquid formulation, but this did not occur. Instead, Ariel Liquid gained sales at the expense of the whole powder section. Though unexpected, this finding is consistent with a notion of *cannibalization barriers* introduced by Buday (1989). Consumers apparently saw the new product in relation to its formulation rather than its branding. In the language of mental representations, there may be limited linkage between versions of the brand in different formulations. This seems to be an advantage but there is a danger that, when this occurs, the new entrant will gain less benefit from the common brand name. A fourth study examined the sales of Persil Liquid, which was launched after Ariel Liquid; again the parent powder was not disproportionately affected and the total liquid detergent share increased.

This work shows that cannibalization may be prevented but more research is required before we can claim to fully understand these processes. Firms must give careful attention to cannibalization when they launch a line extension; small gains in overall sales may not be justified if each variant sells less. Cannibalization may be reduced by differential pricing, targeting and positioning of the brand so that it is more similar to competitor brands and less similar to the manufacturer's existing brands. In addition, advertising at launch can support the parent as well as the extension.

SUMMARY

Knowledge can be represented as a network of interlinked nodes. Thinking involves the activation of parts of this network. The whole network represents long-term memory. Short-term memory is the currently activated section of the network. Within this system, brand knowledge has two aspects: brand image – the range of brand associations – and brand awareness, which is the retrieval of the brand by recall and recognition.

Brand equity is the value added by a brand to the basic product. Brands with high brand equity can be used to extract more profit from assets. It is thought that brand equity is greater when the attitude to the brand is more positive, when the range of associations is large, unique and strongly linked, when awareness is high and where the brand is prominent, well marketed and has large market share. In practice, there is no coherent way of measuring and aggregating all these factors so either perceived quality is used as a proxy for brand equity or it is measured by showing the difference in the value attaching to the marketing of branded and unbranded products.

Marketers want to know whether a category extension will succeed. This has been approached by examining consumer judgements about different extension propositions. Acceptance is greater when the off-spring product *fits* the parent because it complements or substitutes for the parent product and when the parent producer is seen as suited to producing the offspring product. Acceptance of a fitting product is increased when the parent is seen to be high quality. However, this laboratory approach has been criticized for ignoring marketing expertise in the launch of an extension. Some fitting extensions have failed and some non-fitting ones succeeded and it is likely that success or failure owes a great deal to marketing.

When line extensions are launched, they often take a large proportion of their sales from the parent. Sometimes, this is accepted as part of the evolution of the product, but it is attractive to get extra sales from a line extension. There has therefore been interest in how a new entrant to a market draws sales from existing players. Sometimes, the sales losses of the parent are modest because consumers use formulation, price or an other factor to distinguish the new line from the parent.

Additional Resources

Read Keller (2002) to get a more detailed picture of his ideas about brand equity. You can get an overview of the research in brand extendibility by reading the analysis by Bottomley and Holden (2001).

Notes

1 The best known method of valuing brands in this way is by the Interbrand Group. Seven factors are considered: leadership, stability, market stability, internationalization, trend, support and protection. Simon and Sullivan (1993) describe a method that compares branded and unbranded cash flows. Others have used the stock market to indicate the value of brands by subtracting the value of fixed assets from the market valuation.
2 An interesting study by Cowley and Mitchell (2003) illustrates how brand knowledge may be structured in different ways. They found that some consumers stored knowledge about categories in a simple way without sub-categorization whereas other consumers organized brands by sub-category when they encoded information. The effect of the first pattern was to limit retrieval to the same brand set, regardless of the needs of the situation. Those who encoded using sub-categories could retrieve different sets of brands that related better to need.
3 These affinity effects are also seen when consumers buy more than one brand in a category. When they do this, their selection of brands may be linked by a common characteristic such as brand name or product formulation. This is discussed in Chapter 4.

4 Stationary Markets

LEARNING OBJECTIVES

When you have completed this chapter, you should be able to:

1 Describe the typical patterns of purchase found in mature, stationary markets.
2 Explain the role of stationary market models in evaluating brand performance.
3 Discuss the importance of both light and heavy buyers to sales.
4 Explain how market regularities set limits to marketing objectives.

OVERVIEW

Research on market patterns is done by analysis of the data provided by market research companies. In particular, academic researchers use the findings of the consumer panel studies, described in Chapter 2, which are conducted by companies such as IRI, Taylor Nelson Sofres, GfK and Nielsen. Consumer panels record the purchases of households for several years. From such records we can see that most mature markets are approximately stationary (i.e. brand sales change little from year to year).

In order to judge how a brand is performing in a stationary market, we need to know the patterns of purchase that are commonly found in such markets. Then we can see whether a brand is behaving in a normal manner, or whether there are exceptional aspects to its sales. Marketing scientists have established elegant mathematical models that are very effective at mimicking the patterns found in stationary markets that are revealed by panel data. These models have been so successful that they now provide us with sales norms that can be used to assess the performance of a brand. When brand performance differs from the stationary market prediction, we can investigate why this is so. This work applies primarily to frequently purchased repertoire markets.

SECTION 1: MODELLING MATURE MARKETS

The Stability of Mature Markets

In this chapter, we are mainly concerned with established markets rather than new markets. Established, or mature, markets cover the majority of our purchases. An important feature of these markets is that they usually do not change much and are therefore described as *near-stationary*. Changes do sometimes occur in mature markets: whole sub-markets may decline, e.g. the 1980s saw a decline in the consumption of bitter beer and a corresponding rise in lager drinking in the UK. Normally, such changes occur quite slowly over a period of years. Only exceptionally do we see rapid changes that become permanent for specific brands or for the whole category. Such changes may occur when adverse publicity about a product damages its reputation, or when an advertising campaign is particularly successful (e.g. Stella Artois gained substantial share in the British lager market in the mid-1980s following a very successful advertising campaign). Markets may also change over short periods because of sales promotions but, usually, these gains are not maintained when the promotion finishes (Ehrenberg and England, 1990; Ehrenberg, Hammond and Goodhardt, 1994). Because promotions run for short periods, the gains they produce have little effect when averaged over several months and, often, promotional gains are counter-balanced by losses when competitors run promotions. As a result, the market looks quite stable over a period of several months or a year.

One reason for the relative stability of markets has been explained in Chapters 1 and 2. Individuals form habits of purchase that limit change. In Chapter 2, we noted that a typical brand loses about 15 per cent of its customers over a year, and that these customer losses are usually offset by customer gains.

The Value of Mathematical Models

If a market does not change, brand performance measures, such as repeat purchase, the distribution of heavy and light buyers and the pattern of purchase across the brands in a category will be much the same each time they are measured for the same period. An effective mathematical model will let us predict these brand performance measures from other simple brand statistics. If a model is routinely effective, it acquires diagnostic value. When the observed brand performance does not fit predictions from the model, we need to find out why this is so and we may have to adjust our marketing support for the brand. The model used to predict the purchase patterns for a single brand is the negative binomial distribution (known as the NBD), while the more complex model used for predicting purchase in a brand field (i.e. several brands at once) is the Dirichlet (pronounced: *Dir-eesh-lay*).

Early research on brand modelling was conducted by Ehrenberg (e.g. papers in 1959, 1969); this early work was brought together in *Repeat Buying: Theory and Applications* (Ehrenberg, 1988, first published 1972). This book attacked conventional beliefs in marketing and caused a reappraisal of some of the traditional ideas about brand loyalty, brand positioning, the effects of advertising and the way in which sales grow. Work in the USA focused more on the mathematical properties of stationary market models and Morrison and Schmittlein (1981, 1988) gave detailed attention to the precision of models and to the modifications that might improve this precision.

Mathematical models can also be applied to other forms of stable repetitive behaviour. For example, Goodhardt, Ehrenberg and Collins (1975, updated 1987) used such models to study television audiences. Another application has been to store choice, with store groups being treated as brands (Kau and Ehrenberg, 1984). It is also possible to subdivide the brand and model part of the purchasing, such as Persil in a particular pack-size or Heinz tomato soup. Also, models can be used to predict the performance of brand aggregations (e.g. all private label brands in a category).

Stationary market research does not explain *why* some people buy more than others and one brand rather than another. Some critics argue that the lack of attention to such motivational issues limits the application of this work, particularly when the marketer is trying to induce change. What do you put in advertisements if consumer motivations are unknown? Do those who buy more have different reasons from those who buy less? Why do people avoid some brands? When markets do expand or contract, these changes may reflect changes in motivation, income or other household circumstances. But theorists such as Ehrenberg do not claim to cover all the problems that arise in marketing and specifically exclude motivation. What they do describe is the quantitative form of stable markets; if a market is stationary, the numerical predictions from the model are usually very close to the observations derived from panel data. If the market is not stationary, the difference between the observed facts and the model prediction is often instructive and may help us to understand how brands are performing.

Definitions

Before we examine the patterns found in mature markets, the reader should be clear about the meaning of a number of terms. First, we usually work with *purchase occasions* rather than sales. On a purchase occasion, a buyer buys one or more units of a brand. In most markets, consumers buy one unit at a time so that purchase occasions are approximately equal to sales. Other important definitions are:

- The *penetration, b*, which is the proportion of all potential buyers in a population who buy a brand at least once in a period. (Think: *b* for b̲uyers.)
- The *purchase frequency, w*, which is the average number of purchases made by those who purchase *at least once* in a period. (Think *w* for purchase w̲eight.)
- The *mean population purchase rate, m*, the number of purchase occasions in the period made by an average member of the population. (Think *m* for m̲ean.) When *b* is expressed as a percentage, *m* will be the sales per hundred buyers.

These variables are linked by the *sales equation*:

$m = bw$

Thus when the penetration of Tide over three months is 0.25 and the purchase frequency is 4, $m = 0.25 \times 4$ or 1. (In words: *when a quarter of the population buy Tide, on average four times, then the average purchase occasion rate in the whole population is one.*)

When people buy more than one unit per purchase occasion we multiply by a correcting factor to get the sales rate. For example, if people buy, on average, 1.2 units of Tide per purchase occasion then the mean population *sales rate m_s*, will be given by

$m_s = 0.25 \times 4 \times 1.2$ which is 1.2.

EXERCISE 4.1   APPLYING THE SALES EQUATION

1   In a stationary market, the penetration of Senso toothpaste is 0.07 over 24 weeks. Over 24 weeks, 21 per cent of the population buy Senso. What is the purchase frequency?

2   How many purchase occasions per 100 consumers will there be in 48 weeks?

3   If the purchase frequency for the 48-week period is 4.6, what are the mean sales and penetration?

Answers:

1   0.21/0.07 = 3.

2   In a stationary market, you double the purchase occasions if you double the period: 42 per 100.

3   $b = mw$. Therefore 0.42 = b × 4.6. So b = 0.42/4.6 = 0.09, or 9 per cent.

SECTION 2: SINGLE BRAND PURCHASE PATTERNS

The Impact of Recent Purchase

How does recent purchase experience affect the next purchase? In particular, is there a bias towards purchasing the same brand as last time? Consider two people who have both bought Persil and Tide an equal number of times over the last six months, as below:

Philip: Tide, Tide, Persil, Persil
Elizabeth: Persil, Tide, Persil, Tide

Who is most likely to buy Persil at their next purchase? If people learn more from their recent experience, Philip is more likely to buy Persil next time. This is a *first-order* explanation because it relates to the last purchase. A *zero-order* explanation takes no account of the order of prior purchases and here there would be no difference between Philip and Elizabeth in terms of their likelihood of purchasing Persil. When the explanation is zero-order we can predict the likelihood of a future brand purchase only from the ratio of past brand purchases.

Since people do occasionally switch, their most recent purchase should be a slightly better guide to their next purchase than earlier purchases, and Kuehn (1962) did find some evidence to support a first-order effect. But a study by Bass et al. (1984) showed that the majority of purchases in most markets are zero-order. All studies have their weaknesses and Kahn, Morrison and Wright (1986) argued that, because *household* panel data were used by Bass et al., the first-order behaviour of *individuals* might have been obscured. However, on balance, it seems likely that a zero-order pattern of purchase is more common in stable markets and habit, rather than learning, provides the best way of thinking about repetitive purchase.

Do Consumers Buy at Regular Intervals?

We have habits about *what* we buy, but are we also habitual about *when* we buy? Purchase time habits would show up in panel data as an individual tendency to buy a brand each week or month. Habits of this sort would mean that a purchaser's probability of buying rises sharply at intervals. This pattern is found for some frequent purchases, such as newspapers or cigarettes. It also applies to shopping trips (Dunn, Reader and Wrigley, 1983) and Kahn and Schmittlein (1989) report that households tend to be loyal to a particular day for grocery shopping, and East et al. (1994) found that the majority of supermarket users were also loyal to particular times of the day.

Despite the routine timing of many shopping trips, brands are usually bought at irregular intervals. There are several reasons for this. First, we should note that most brands are bought quite infrequently, for example a typical US household buys a specific coffee brand about three times a year and the category about nine times a year. This gives an average inter-purchase interval between purchases of any brand of instant coffee of five to six weeks. Actual intervals are quite varied because household consumption may fluctuate and shoppers may stockpile or run out. The prediction of when a specific brand will be re-bought is even more irregular because other brands may be bought instead. So brand purchase, although it has a long-term average frequency, occurs at irregular times. Mathematicians describe this random pattern as a *Poisson* distribution.

However, people rarely buy a brand again immediately after purchasing it. Because of this 'dead time' after purchase, the Poisson distribution does not fit well for short periods. Over the longer periods covered in panel research, the fit of the Poisson assumption is close and provides a basis for the mathematical models described later.

How Does Purchase Frequency Vary?

People differ widely in how much they buy. The range of purchase frequencies in a sample of buyers has a form that is described by a statistical model called a *Gamma* distribution, illustrated in Figure 4.1. This is a histogram in which the largest number of buyers usually occurs for the lowest purchase frequency.

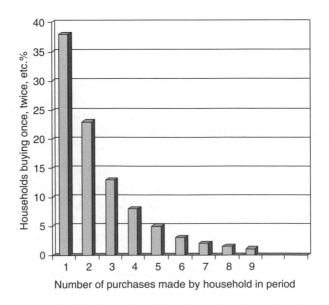

Figure 4.1   Gamma distribution of purchase for a brand showing that there are many light buyers and few heavy buyers

Few people buy heavily but those who do so are responsible for a large proportion of a brand's sales. Table 4.1 illustrates this with the purchases of Kellogg's Corn Flakes in the USA. In Table 4.1, you see that a sample of 100 purchasers have produced 210 purchases, 2.1 per person, in three months. This average is based on the 55 per cent who bought once, 22 per cent who bought twice, 8 per cent who bought three times and so forth (a Gamma distribution). When we work out the sales from these sub-groups we get the NBD distribution. This is the bottom row of Table 4.1 and it shows how important the few heavy buyers are for sales. Those who bought six or more times – 5 per cent of all purchasers – were responsible for 20 per cent of sales.

Table 4.1   Three-month sales of Kellogg's Corn Flakes in the USA (adapted from Ehrenberg and Goodhardt, 1979)

Penetration (%)	Purchase frequency	Out of 100 purchasers, the number buying:						
20	2.1	Once	Twice	3 times	4 times	5 times	6+ times	Total
		55	22	8	5	5	5	100
		Number of purchases:						
		55	44	24	20	25	42	210

In general, a substantial proportion of purchases are made by relatively few heavy buyers; one rule of thumb, the *heavy-half* principle, is that the lighter buying 50 per cent are responsible for about 20 per cent of all purchases while the heavier buying 50 per cent are responsible for the other 80 per cent. When this rule applies, the heaviest 20 per cent are responsible for about 50 per cent of sales. If you inspect Table 4.1 you will see that the 55 per cent buying once are responsible for 26 per cent of purchases and the heaviest 23 per cent (buying three or more times) are responsible for 53 per cent of purchases, so the data in Table 4.1 fit the heavy-half rule quite well. Other ratio rules are more extreme; the best known is the 80:20 rule. This is that 80 per cent of purchases are made by the heaviest buying 20 per cent of customers. The precise ratio depends partly on the category. For example, if we investigated savers, we might find that very few heavy savers were responsible for a large part of the total savings in a savings institution. The ratio is less extreme when there is a natural ceiling on purchase, e.g. people rarely buy more than one newspaper.

The ratio also depends on the period of time used to collect data. Because they buy frequently, most heavy buyers will be found in a short purchase period. Light buyers may not get round to buying in a short period but, as the period lengthens, more of them are captured. Therefore, if purchase data for instant coffee are collected over a period of years instead of months, a greater proportion of light buyers are recorded and the ratio moves from approximately heavy-half to approximately 80:20. Ratio rules were first highlighted by Pareto, an Italian economist and they are reviewed by Schmittlein, Cooper and Morrison (1993).

The heavy-half principle shows that heavy buyers are an attractive segment in many markets and marketers may therefore try to focus their efforts upon them. For example, promotions may give progressively more attractive benefits to those who buy more and the frequent-flyer schemes that airlines run are designed to benefit the heavier users. Sometimes, it is possible to target the heavy buyers by using a particular distribution system. For example, a wine warehouse, which sells wine by the case, may secure a larger proportion of heavy wine buyers. Also, it may be useful to focus research on heavy buyers since they are responsible for so much of the profit (e.g. Hammond and Ehrenberg, 1995). In B2B marketing, *key account management* has become a recognized speciality (the key accounts are the few big ones).

Ratio rules can apply to any phenomenon and Box 4.1 provides an interesting example. Another application has been to the imprisonment of offenders. If most crimes are committed by a relatively small group of offenders, crime will go down if these offenders are imprisoned for longer.

Box 4.1	**Weight of consumption among feline consumers (Churcher and Lawton, 1987)**
An interesting demonstration of how consumption varies was provided by a study of what the cat brought home to households in a Bedfordshire village. Over 70 domestic cats were studied and their tendency to kill and bring home sparrows, frogs, rabbits, mice and so on was studied. One cat was responsible for 10 per cent of the total kill while, at the other end of the distribution, several cats brought back nothing in a whole year.	

The ratio of light to heavy buyers depends on the break point chosen but we can compare the top 20 per cent of customers that is typically responsible for 50 per cent of sales with the bottom 80 per cent of customers that is responsible for the other 50 per cent. On this basis, light buyers are four times as numerous as heavy buyers. Because of their numbers, light buyers *in aggregate* may offer more scope for sales gain than the heavy buyers. However, when purchasers of a brand are considered *individually*, it is clear that more attention should be given to the few heavy buyers. This is partly because they could buy more and partly because their loss could be very damaging. Mass communications such as advertising are effective at reaching the large number of light buyers but, when the approach to customers needs substantial resources, it is better to concentrate on the heavy buyers.

It is easy to be confused by stationary market evidence. Although relatively few heavy buyers are responsible for a substantial proportion of sales, this does not mean that heavy buyers are responsible for most of the gain or loss when sales change. First, as noted, this depends on the proportion of buyers that are treated as 'heavy'. If this is only the heaviest 20 per cent, the light buyers have a numerical advantage. Second, we find that light buyers tend to change their purchasing *proportionately* more than heavy buyers. As a result, light (and new) buyers are responsible for a large part of any gain in sales when a brand improves its market share. But when the new pattern of sales has stabilized, we find that the heavy-half rule still applies since sales gains have occurred across the distribution. This analysis means that marketers must not ignore the light buyers since their purchasing is more changeable and, from their ranks, some new heavy buyers may emerge.[1]

How Does the Type of Product Affect Purchase?

One category is likely to differ from another but, if two brands in quite different categories have the same purchase frequency and penetration, do they also have much the same sole brand loyalty and repeat purchase rates? Panel research shows that they do. Effectively, the purchase characteristics of a brand are captured by purchase frequency and penetration, and a variety of other brand performance statistics can be predicted from these measures. This means that the specific brand or category need not be known for the prediction of brand performance, provided that we know the purchase frequency and penetration.

Repeat Purchase

If we compare any two adjacent sales periods, e.g. two quarters, we find that many of the buyers of a brand in quarter 1 (Q1) return in Q2, particularly the heavier buyers. But some do not return and these 'lapsed' buyers are replaced by an approximately equal number of 'new' buyers. The 'new' buyers are mostly light buyers of the brand, like those that they replace, and although they did not buy in Q1, they have usually bought the brand before and are not really new. At Q3 about the same proportion of Q2 buyers drop out and are replaced by others, including some of those who lapsed after Q1. This intermittent pattern of purchase does not show loss of loyalty but instead reflects the fact that many people buy a brand so infrequently that they often miss quarters. The change of buyers at each quarter is explained mainly as a probability effect, though a small part of the effect is due to defection.

This analysis helps us to understand that repeat purchase rates depend mainly on purchase frequency. A household that buys four times in one quarter is more likely to re-buy in the next quarter than one that bought only once, since the latter household may not need to buy again so soon. Because heavier buyers are more likely to repeat, we find that the purchase frequency of repeat purchasers is higher than the rate for the whole sample (by about 20 per cent). New purchasers tend to be light buyers and their purchase rate usually does not rise much above 1.5 for any period.

Although repeat-purchase rates depend mainly on purchase frequency, penetration does have a small effect, illustrated in Table 4.2. Compare columns 1 and 2 and you see that a tenfold increase in purchase frequency has a substantial effect on repeat purchase, raising it from 57 per cent to 85 per cent; compare columns 1 and 3 and you see that repeat purchase moves only three points when the penetration increases tenfold. Note that it is the repeat purchase *rate* that is slightly affected by penetration. The *number* of repeat purchasers is directly affected by penetration.

Table 4.2   Repeat purchase for given purchase frequencies and penetrations

	Baseline case	Tenfold increase in penetration	Tenfold increase in purchase frequency
Penetration as %	2	2	20
Purchase frequency	2	20	2
Repeat purchase as %	57	85	60

Repeat purchase is an important diagnostic measure. If the purchase frequency for a period indicates a repeat purchase rate of 50 per cent under stationary market conditions, then consistent deviations from this figure indicate that the market does not have the normal stationary characteristics. One application of this thinking was reported by Ehrenberg (1988: 97–98). A brand launched 18 months before was being heavily advertised but, despite this, sales were constant. Two explanations were possible:

- The advertising was ineffective and the brand was creating normal repeat purchase.
- The advertising was effective, consumers were trying the brand, but not repeat purchasing so the brand was not gaining sales.

To distinguish these two we derive the normal repeat-purchase rate for a stationary market and see whether this is what is found in the panel data. Evidence that repeat purchase is normal favours the first explanation and means that the advertising should be changed or stopped. Evidence that the repeat purchase is below the normal level supports the second explanation. This suggests that the brand is weak, and that sales will collapse when the pool of potential trialists is exhausted. In this case the brand should be dropped before more money is wasted. This case is presented in Exercise 4.4 below.

NBD (Negative Binomial Distribution) Theory

Negative binomial distribution (NBD) theory is a mathematical model that permits the prediction of repeat purchase and other measures from data on the penetration, purchase frequency and period. NBD theory is based on the assumptions that the purchasing of a brand is stationary, that individual purchases follow a Poisson distribution, and that the long-run average purchase rates of individuals follow a Gamma distribution. These assumptions are set out by Ehrenberg (1988: ch. 4).[2]

Box 4.2	Does the NBD give the best prediction?

Marketing scientists have tried to improve on the predictions derived from the NBD by adjustment of the mathematics. One suggestion is that NBD theory might be modified to allow for the temporary loss of buying interest following a purchase. But any gain would be marginal since the theory is already very close to panel evidence. Usually, the random variation in panel data is rather larger than any difference between the predictions of competing mathematical models. In a comparison of theories, Schmittlein, Bemmaor and Morrison (1985) concluded that the NBD model was hard to beat. A further paper by Morrison and Schmittlein (1988) identified three ways in which real behaviour tended to depart from NBD assumptions but noted that these effects tended to cancel each other out so that the NBD remained a good predictive model.

Program NBD

When purchase frequency and penetration are known, program NBD estimates a range of brand performance statistics. This computer program accepts data on the penetration, purchase frequency and period and computes repeat purchase and new purchase rates for different periods. The Gamma distribution of persons buying once, twice, etc. is worked out for each period and the proportion of sales attributable to different rates of purchase is calculated (the negative binomial distribution). These figures are tabled on the screen and the user then has options to change the rounding and to express data as proportions, percentages or actual numbers. A copy of the screened figures can be recorded as a file for printing.

Table 4.3 shows the output for Kellogg's Corn Flakes using the figures shown in Table 4.1 (a three month penetration of 20 per cent and a purchase frequency of 2.1). Because the program does not have a three-month column, the figures were assigned to the 12 weeks period (highlighted). If you look down this column you see the input penetration and purchase frequency, then the predicted repeat purchase rate of about 62 per cent. Below this is the purchase frequency of repeat buyers, which is about 20 per cent higher than the purchase frequency of the whole group, and the purchase frequency of new buyers. The program estimates the number of buyers buying once, twice, etc. and then calculates the sale proportions contributed by these segments.

Table 4.3   Output from program NBD (figures rounded to 2 decimal places)

	1 day	1 wk	4 wks	12 wks	24 wks	48 wks	1 yr
Penetration (b)	0.00	0.03	0.10	0.20	0.28	0.36	0.36
Purchase frequency (w)	1.02	1.11	1.40	2.10	3.04	4.73	5.01
Repeat purchase (%)	2.97	16.82	40.99	61.65	71.61	78.88	79.60
Purchase frequency of repeat buyers	1.03	1.18	1.63	2.55	3.67	5.60	5.91
Purchase frequency of new buyers	1.01	1.09	1.24	1.38	1.45	1.49	1.49
Proportion –							
not buying	1.00	0.97	0.90	0.80	0.72	0.64	0.64
buying once	0.00	0.03	0.07	0.11	0.11	0.11	0.11
twice	0.00	0.00	0.02	0.04	0.06	0.06	0.06
3 times	0.00	0.00	0.01	0.02	0.03	0.04	0.04
4 times	0.00	0.00	0.00	0.01	0.02	0.03	0.03
5 times	0.00	0.00	0.00	0.01	0.01	0.02	0.02
6 +	0.00	0.00	0.00	0.01	0.04	0.10	0.10
Proportion of sales due to those buying –							
once	0.97	0.82	0.52	0.25	0.14	0.07	0.06
twice	0.03	0.15	0.26	0.21	0.13	0.07	0.07
3 times	0.00	0.03	0.12	0.15	0.12	0.07	0.07
4 times	0.00	0.00	0.05	0.11	0.10	0.07	0.06
5 times	0.00	0.00	0.02	0.08	0.09	0.06	0.06
6 +	0.00	0.00	0.02	0.19	0.43	0.66	0.69

In Table 4.4, the empirical data from Table 4.1 are compared with the theoretical predictions (using three places of decimals). If you inspect Table 4.4 you will see that the agreement is close.

Table 4.4   Quarterly sales of Corn Flakes in the USA (Observed (O) and Theoretical (T) values)

Out of 100 purchase, the number buying:

Once		Twice		3 times		4 times		5 times		6+ times	
O	T	O	T	O	T	O	T	O	T	O	T
55	53	22	22	8	11	5	6	5	4	5	6
Giving sales of:											
55	53	44	44	24	33	20	24	25	20	42	36

The output of program NBD also allows us to see how penetration and purchase frequency change when periods of different duration are used. Table 4.5 shows how the penetration and purchase frequency rise as the period of time is successively doubled (Table 4.5 is obtained by assigning figures to incorrect time periods in program NBD, e.g. the 12-week figures are assigned to 48 weeks so that the nominal 12 and 24-week figures are then actually 3 and 6 week). Mean sales are given by the product of penetration and purchase frequency; in a stationary market, these must keep step with the time period, as recorded in the bottom row. Table 4.5 shows that each doubling in the period produces about the same absolute penetration increase. When the penetration is low, changes in sales are mainly related to changes in penetration. When penetration is high and approaching a ceiling, the sales changes appear as changes in purchase frequency.

Table 4.5 Change in purchase data over time (theoretical)

	3wks	6wks	12wks	24 wks	48 wks	96 wks	192 wks
Penetration (b)	0.08	0.13	0.20	0.28	0.36	0.44	0.51
Purchase frequency (w)	1.3	1.6	2.1	3.0	4.7	7.8	13.5
Mean sales (bw)	0.1	0.2	0.4	0.9	1.7	3.4	6.9

Program NBD is easy to use and is needed to answer questions in Exercises 4.2 to 4.4. It has one technical limitation: when the penetration is high and the purchase frequency is very low the mathematical procedure for estimating the parameter k breaks down and the user must then extrapolate from results obtained with lower penetration figures.

EXERCISE 4.2   USING PROGRAM NBD: HOW THE PERIOD AFFECTS THE DATA

1 Assume that 0.05 of the population buys an average of 1.5 Snickers in each 4-week period. Use program NBD to establish the penetration, b, and the purchase frequency, w, and mean sales, m $(= bw)$ for the given periods and fill in the table below. (If you enter the 4-week data as 1-week data all results will be for four times the tabled period.)

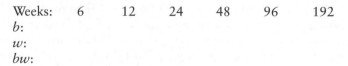

Weeks: 6   12   24   48   96   192
b:
w:
bw:

2 Can you compute the proportion of the population who buy *no* Snickers in four years?

3 Notice that the purchase rate for new buyers is relatively constant for longer periods. See whether it remains so for different b and w input data.

EXERCISE 4.3   COLLECTING PANEL DATA FOR COMPARISON WITH NBD PREDICTIONS

NBD predictions can be tested against panel data gathered by the class. You – and others – must keep a diary and record when you engage in a consumer activity such as phoning your friends or drinking beer. Table 4.6 records the data from 224 students for one day together with the distribution that is predicted from the NBD model. You can see that the fit is close.

Table 4.6   Number of students making 1, 2, 3, etc. telephone calls in a day

Number calling:	Once	Twice	3 times	4 times	5 times	6 + times
Observed	75	30	8	0	0	1
Predicted:	75	28	8	2	0	0
$b = 0.51; w = 1.46$						

EXERCISE 4.4   MARKETING ANALYSES

1   Brand R was launched 18 months ago. With continuing advertising support it has maintained a penetration of 4 per cent and a purchase frequency of 1.4 per quarter, but is scarcely viable. Panel research shows a repeat purchase rate of 21 per cent. Should you stop the advertising? Withdraw the brand? Maintain both? To answer this you need to calculate, using program NBD, the theoretical repeat purchase and see whether it agrees with the observed figure. If the actual repeat purchase is below the stationary market norm, the brand is failing. Also, see the earlier section on repeat purchase.

2   The consumption of soup rises in the winter and falls in the summer. Find out whether all those who buy soup reduce consumption in the summer or whether there are two groups: those who buy it all the year with much the same frequency, and those who buy it only in the winter. Panel data show that those who buy soup in the summer show a penetration of 32 per cent and a purchase frequency of 5 over 12 weeks. When these people are followed into the higher consumption winter period, panel data show that their quarterly repeat purchase is 79 per cent. What do you conclude? You need to calculate, using program NBD, whether this repeat purchase is the norm for a stationary market. If it is, then you have two separate groups: the all-year stationary buyers and seasonal buyers who only enter the market in the winter. For more information, see Wellan and Ehrenberg (1990).

SECTION 3: PATTERNS OF PURCHASE IN THE WHOLE CATEGORY

We now address the following questions:

- How do penetrations and purchase frequencies vary in a product category?
- What changes do we see in penetration and purchase frequency when market share changes?
- Can we predict the buying frequency and penetration of a new entrant to the market when it achieves a given market share?
- When people buy more than one brand, how is purchase distributed between the different brands?
- Does the evidence of cross purchase support the idea of niche positioning?
- Is television watching like brand purchasing?
- How is multi-brand purchase modelled mathematically?

Purchase Frequencies and Penetrations in a Product Field

Double jeopardy

Table 4.7 presents data on the US instant coffee market in 1981, ordered by average sales. You can see that bigger brands (shown in the right-hand column) have greater penetrations and slightly greater purchase frequencies. This is typical of what is found in most packaged goods markets. It means that changes in brand sales will be seen mainly as changes in penetration. The low variation in purchase frequency is not so surprising. Why should one brand of instant coffee be drunk more often than another? And often the people who drink Folgers are also the people who drink Maxim.

Table 4.7   Penetrations, purchase frequencies and mean sales in the US instant coffee market

	Penetration (b) (%)	Purchase frequency (w)	Mean sales (bw)
Maxwell House	24	3.6	86
Sanka	21	3.2	69
Taster's Choice	22	2.8	62
High Point	22	2.6	57
Folgers	18	2.7	49
Nescafé	13	2.9	38
Brim	9	2.0	18
Maxim	6	2.6	16
Mean	**17**	**2.8**	**48**

Source: (MRCA panel data for 48 weeks, 1981)

The relationship between penetration and purchase frequency in a product field fits the pattern known as *double jeopardy* (Ehrenberg, Goodhardt and Barwise, 1990). Double jeopardy (DJ) was described by the sociologist McPhee (1963: 133–140), who credits the original idea to the broadcaster Jack Landis. McPhee noted how less popular radio presenters suffer in two ways: fewer people have heard of them and, among those who have heard of them, they are less appreciated. Applied to brands, DJ implies the pattern seen in Table 4.7, that less popular brands are not only bought by fewer people (lower penetration) but are also bought less often (lower frequency) by those who do buy them. Ehrenberg, Goodhardt and Barwise show that DJ is a ubiquitous phenomenon, occurring in such fields as the viewing of TV programmes and the purchase of consumer durables, industrial goods and newspapers.

Although DJ is easily seen, the explanation for the effect is less clear. McPhee's explanation took account of differential awareness. People who are aware of less popular presenters are usually also aware of more popular presenters and thus are more likely to 'split their vote' compared with those who have only heard of the more popular broadcasters. But the DJ effect is seen even in categories where consumers are fully aware of all the major brands in a market, for example in the case of supermarkets.

We see DJ as a statistical effect. Consider a board with 100 slots that can receive counters. If you throw counters on to the board, the early ones will each tend to get a slot on their own and each time that you do this, they raise the percentage of slots with a counter (the 'penetration'). As more counters are thrown on to the board, they will increasingly land on slots where there are already counters and this will raise the average number of counters in occupied slots (the 'frequency'). Figure 4.2 shows the theoretical relationship that applies; further analysis of the theoretical double jeopardy line can be found in Habel and Rungie (2005). Notice that the relationship is approximately linear for much of the penetration range. The statistical relationship between penetration and frequency will be disrupted in a number of ways in real markets. In particular, there may be feedback effects so that, once consumers have bought a brand, they may be more, or less, willing to buy the brand again. A second empirical effect is that some consumers will never buy in some categories. For example, those who do not own a cat, rarely buy cat food. This effect will vary across categories and buying segments and it means that calculated penetrations will underestimate penetrations that are based only on those who are willing to buy.

What Changes When Sales Change?

Table 4.7 is useful in showing the way in which penetration and purchase frequency may be expected to change. Major changes over short periods of time are rare, but if Brim were to treble its sales, it is unlikely, looking at Table 4.7, that it could do so by getting its existing buyers to use three times as much instant coffee. The closeness of brand purchase frequencies means that sales have to grow

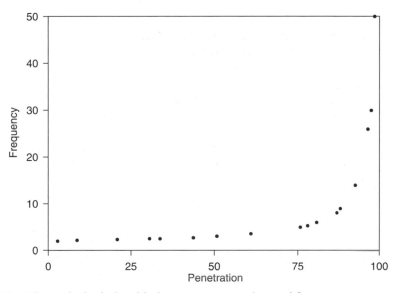

Figure 4.2 Theoretical relationship between penetration and frequency

mainly by increase in penetration. Sometimes a gain in frequency may be possible by persuading consumers to find new uses for a product, e.g. by pouring bleach down drains to disinfect them, or by eating cereals at tea-time, but this is a new use of the *category* which is likely to raise the purchase frequencies of all brands.

Some evidence on what changes when a brand gains sales comes from advertising cases. In 1982, advertising substantially increased the purchasing of Curly Wurly, a chocolate coated toffee liked by children. Sales then remained approximately constant for the rest of the year (Channon, 1985: 168). From the published data, it appears that among 7–11-year-old children the two monthly penetration increased by 60 per cent while the purchase frequency increased by a mere 6 per cent. Among adult purchasers the main gain was also in penetration. Thus, sales gains came mainly from penetration gains, in line with the DJ pattern. Other evidence comes from the sales of Hellman's mayonnaise (Box 4.3).

Box 4.3	Attempts to raise purchase frequency

There are some situations where increased consumption of a brand might be expected to come from more frequent use by existing buyers rather than by increased penetration. One such situation arose in the case of Hellman's mayonnaise when it was new to the British market. The manufacturers found that the British used Hellman's mayonnaise on little else but salads, a habit they had

(Continued)

probably learned from earlier experience with salad cream, which looks rather like mayonnaise. The advertising for Hellman's was therefore designed to expand the number of uses of the product and this could have led to more frequent purchase.

The case report (Channon, 1985) shows that, following the advertising, 40 per cent of users were trying the product in the new ways suggested in the campaign. This suggests that there could have been some gain in purchase frequency relative to other brands but figures were not reported. However, there was clearly a substantial gain in penetration which accounted for much of the increase in sales.

The relative constancy of purchase frequency is also important to those who are hoping to break into a market with a new brand. With enough advertising money and a sound product, marketers may occasionally achieve a high market share. If they succeed with the new brand, the DJ pattern will define how that success will depend upon penetration and purchase frequency. Supporting this, Wellan and Ehrenberg (1988) found that, after rapidly established leadership in the UK market, a new soap called Shield registered a purchase frequency appropriate to its new position, i.e. slightly more than its competitors.

For the periods used in market research, most changes affect penetration but Treasure (1975) pointed out that when sales figures are aggregated over longer periods, changes in purchase level appear to be based more on changes in purchase frequency and less on penetration. This difference arises because of the way in which light buyers are counted over short and long periods. Over short periods, an infrequent buyer tends to be a non-buyer in the reference period and is therefore registered as a penetration gain when he or she buys in a later period. Over longer periods, the infrequent buyer is more likely to purchase in the reference period and therefore any gain in purchase in later periods will be recorded as a purchase frequency gain. Treasure's observation is thus an effect of data presentation and points to the importance of light buyers when sales change, which was discussed in the previous section.

Patterns of Multi-brand Purchase

As we saw in Chapter 2, most buyers buy more than one brand in the category. In many grocery markets, the average share-of-category requirement (SCR) is around 30 per cent; this means that for every three purchases of a given brand, the average buyer makes seven purchases of other brands. Ehrenberg (1988) remarks that 'your buyers are the buyers of other brands who occasionally buy you'. In the cereal market, where people seek variety, the SCR can be even lower. Table 4.8 shows SCRs for two cereal brands in the USA and the UK.

Table 4.8   Share-of-category requirements in cereal purchase (adapted from Ehrenberg and Goodhardt, 1979)

Brand	SCR (%)
Nabisco Shredded Wheat (USA)	10
Nabisco Shredded Wheat (UK)	18
Kellogg's Corn Flakes (USA)	15
Kellogg's Corn Flakes (UK)	30

Is there a pattern to this multi-brand buying? There are two possibilities. One is that certain brands are mutually substitutable. If most buyers see brands X and Y as almost the same, we would expect a higher than average purchase rate for Y among purchasers of X and vice versa. Such cross-purchasing of brands would create purchase subsets or *market partitioning*. Ehrenberg and Goodhardt (1979) demonstrate that this effect does occur, e.g. in children's cereals where those who buy one sweetened cereal are more likely to buy another sweetened cereal rather than an unsweetened brand. An alternative pattern is that the purchase of one brand is unrelated to the purchase of other brands and purchase rates simply reflect the penetrations of the other brands. We find both effects in grocery markets. The basic pattern is that other-brand purchasing is directly proportional to the penetrations of the other brands. Ehrenberg (1988) calls this the *duplication of purchase law*. Superimposed on this pattern are some cases of market partitioning.

Some people expect more market partitioning because they see some brands as close alternatives. But, although many of us will have our own personally preferred groupings of brands, there may be little agreement between individuals. One person may buy Colgate and Crest, another Crest and Macleans, a third Macleans and a retailer's private label. When these diverse combinations are put together, the different individual cross-preferences will average out so that, usually, there is not much evidence of market partitioning at an aggregate level. When partitioning does occur, it can usually be connected with distinct product features such as price, product form (e.g. flavour, pack) or a common brand name, rather than with the less tangible claims of the brand that may be identified in advertising. Collins (1971) has reviewed this issue.

Table 4.9 shows how buyers of one brand of toothpaste also bought other brands. The brands are arranged in market share order by column and row. The second row from the bottom shows the average cross-purchase, i.e. the mean percentage of people buying a 'column' brand in addition to their 'row' brand. In this example, the cross-purchases are about 50 per cent greater than the corresponding penetrations (compare with the bottom row, which shows the

Table 4.9   Cross-purchase in the British toothpaste market

% buyers of:	Market share	Colgate GRF	Aquafresh	Crest	Macleans Fresh	Mentadent	Colgate gel
			Who also bought:				
Colgate GRF	18	–	19	18	20	12	32
Aquafresh	9	30	–	26	28	14	23
Crest	8	32	28	–	23	17	24
Macleans Fresh	8	31	27	20	–	12	21
Mentadent	7	28	21	22	18	–	20
Colgate gel	7	53	24	23	23	15	–
Av duplication (all brands)		35	24	22	23	14	24
1.5 x penetration		36	22	21	24	15	21

Source: AGB data, 1985

penetrations multiplied by 1.5). The multiplier (known as the duplication con-stant, D) varies across categories.

Table 4.9 shows some partitioning. There is a higher level of cross-purchase between Colgate GRF and Colgate gel than is implied by penetration. Compare the 32 per cent for Colgate gel bought by GRF buyers with 24 per cent and com-pare the 53 per cent for GRF bought by gel buyers with 35 per cent. This effect is common where two products with the same brand name compete in the same field and provides a basis for line extension since some of the tendency to buy a brand seems to pass to the new line (see Chapter 3).

Cross-purchase and Positioning

In marketing, much importance has been given to positioning. This is the set of beliefs about the brand that the manufacturer and advertising agency seek to establish in the minds of potential purchasers: it is an *intended brand image*. One implication of the cross-purchase evidence is that new brands do not need to have some unique formulation to succeed, a finding which has worried those who attach strong importance to brand positioning. If cross-purchase between brands depends largely upon penetrations with exceptions relating only to price, formulation or brand name, we must conclude that positioning, with its implication that each brand occupies a distinct niche in the minds of consumers, is poorly supported. When advertising does succeed, it may be because it has produced high brand awareness and not because a brand is seen as subtly dif-ferent from other brands in its category. Indeed, many successful brands may do well because they are perceived as typical of other brands in the category rather than as different from those brands. Thus, Ehrenberg (1988) recommends that manufacturers focus on the strategy which is often called 'me-too', i.e. copying the formulation and appearance of existing successful brands and thereby trading on established purchase habits. This is a strategy that is much used by retailers when they offer private label brands.

The Tesco pack has much the same shape and design as the more established Head & Shoulders brand of Procter & Gamble.

Positioning assumptions are well established in marketing. It is hard to abandon the idea that a brand has a unique selling proposition (USP), which is appreciated by consumers. The niche approach rests on the idea of positioning. A niche brand is appreciated by a consumer segment but not by others, even though they could buy it. This sometimes happens in fashion (see Box 4.4).

Box 4.4	Niche brands

Niche brands are those that are bought by one part of the population but not by other parts that could afford to buy them (in this sense, expensive brands, like Porsche, are not niche brands). To show such niche brands it is necessary to compare the consumers who buy different brands to see whether they differ in terms of demography or beliefs. One study compared the demographic profiles of brand buyers in different grocery categories (Hammond, Ehrenberg

(Continued)

and Goodhardt, 1996). This work showed very little difference between the buyers of different brands except in the case of cereals where certain brands were bought only when there were children in the household. Given this evidence, the realistic assumption is that there is normally little difference between the buyers of any two brands in a packaged goods category. This is not so surprising when we remember that the buyers of one brand are often the buyers of another brand.

But niches can occur. One interesting case arose when the fashion designer Burberry was taken up by chavs. In the UK, chavs are 'uneducated and uncultured people' (Wikipedia) who wear tracksuits and gold jewellery (called 'bling'). Their endorsement of Burberry was unwelcome for the fashion house because other potential buyers then avoided the brand.

The close association between other-brand purchase rates and penetration will fail when brands lack a common distribution structure since the availability of brands obviously affects choice. Thus, local variation in distribution will produce local variation in other-brand purchases. This can occur with beer brands since many are regional and are not easily available in parts of the country. Uncles and Ehrenberg (1990) have shown this effect with stores; in the USA, the cross-purchase between Safeway and Lucky is higher than predicted because these chains tend to have stores in the same areas.

Watching Television

Television viewing has been shown to have similarities to brand purchase in studies by Goodhardt, Ehrenberg and Collins (1987). When the programme is a serial, viewing the next episode is like repeat purchase and we can ask how much programme loyalty exists, as measured by repeat viewing. The evidence shows that there is loyalty, particularly for the serial with a very high rating. In the UK, about 55 per cent of those watching a serial will repeat view in the following week but this figure is derived from several different loyalties. Some people watch more than others (i.e. they are loyal to the medium) and this raises their chance of being a viewer of the next episode; some people are channel loyal so that serials on favourite channels have a better repeat-viewing chance; and some people watch more at particular times of the day so that time loyalty may enhance repeat viewing. These three loyalties ensure that people who have been watching a serial are quite likely to be tuned to the same channel at the same time of the week *after the serial has ended*. The difference between this end-of-serial viewing and the repeat viewing when the serial is running indicates the true loyalty to the programme. This analysis has similarities to other ways of partitioning loyalty, e.g. to the way in which loyalty to a car is divided between brand, model and specification and may be affected by loyalty to a distributer.

Goodhardt, Ehrenberg and Collins (1987) also found some programme partitioning, e.g. those who watch one sports programme are more likely to watch other sports programmes, but they also note that people watch a wide variety of programmes so that cross-viewing has limited partitioning. Terrestrial TV is a *broadcast*, not a *narrowcast*, medium and this makes it difficult to target specific social groups accurately using the main television channels. However, television transmission by cable and satellite are likely to increase the degree of partitioned viewing because these modes offer channels that are dedicated to sport or music, thus coupling together channel and content loyalty.

The Dirichlet Model

The Dirichlet is a mathematical model that can predict brand performance statistics for *all* the brands in a product field. It was described in work by Chatfield and Goodhardt (1975) and developed by Bass, Jeuland and Wright (1976). It was presented in a comprehensive form by Goodhardt, Ehrenberg and Chatfield (1984). The assumptions are similar to those for the single-brand NBD model but, in addition, it is assumed that the market has no partitioning; the model does not apply if there is appreciable evidence of brand clustering on any other basis than penetration.

Table 4.10   Observed and predicted purchase frequencies and sole brand buyers in the US instant coffee market (MRCA panel data over 48 weeks, 1981)

	Purchase frequency (w)		% buyers who are 100% loyal	
	Observed	Dirichlet	Observed	Dirichlet
Maxwell House	3.6	3.2	20	18
Sanka	3.3	3.0	20	17
Taster's Choice	2.8	2.9	24	16
High Point	2.6	2.9	18	16
Folgers	2.7	2.9	13	15
Nescafé	2.9	2.8	15	14
Brim	2.0	2.6	17	13
Maxim	2.6	2.6	11	13
Mean	**2.8**	**2.9**	**17**	**15**

Programs running Dirichlet analyses can give predictions of penetration, purchase frequency, sole buyers, sole-buyer purchase frequency, proportions of buyers at different frequencies and the repeat-purchase rates of those buying with different frequencies. Table 4.10 shows the real data for US instant coffee together with the Dirichlet norms. The fit is fairly close. Often, brand leaders exceed the Dirichlet norms for purchase frequency and sole-brand buying and this is so for Maxwell House in Table 4.10. The purchase frequency of Brim is below the norm; this could have occurred as a result of a larger than usual number of sales promotions, which raised the proportion of one-off purchasers and therefore reduced the purchase frequency.

The Value of Models in Marketing

Ehrenberg, Uncles and Goodhardt (2004) point out that mathematical models provide norms against which real markets can be assessed. One management application of such norms is to set out the realistic options that are open to those who want to improve the share of their brand or who want to launch a new brand on the market. Models also provide norms for cross-purchase in an unpartitioned market and illustrate the long-run propensity to buy a repertoire of brands. When markets are partitioned, e.g. powdered and liquid detergent, we can see the extent to which this partitioning affects cross-purchase. In some cases the market analysis, coupled with Dirichlet norms, may help to show how much of a market is accessible to competition. For example, if a new environmentally friendly detergent is being contemplated, is the competition all detergents, or all detergents that make environmental claims?

However, a major value of this work lies in management education. An understanding of stationary markets helps managers to read their own brand statistics and to understand the ways in which change may, or may not, be brought about. When change does occur and the market stabilizes again, the new brand performance statistics will fit the Dirichlet norms.

One criticism of stationary market research is that it has generally been confirmatory in approach, showing the fit between data and models, rather than testing for exceptions. Exceptions need to be zealously pursued because it is information on such exceptions that may help us to see how to 'buck the market'.

SUMMARY

Over periods of three months to a year the sales of most established brands are approximately stationary: short-term fluctuations are averaged out and longer-term trends are too slow-acting to have much effect. The steady state of such markets arises because most buyers in a category maintain their propensities to buy the same group of brands for long periods of time.

The penetration, purchase frequency and market share of a brand are key statistics. These measures encode most of the buying propensities of consumers so that there is no need to know anything more about the brand in order to predict other brand performance statistics. This makes mathematical modelling possible.

Brands have few heavy buyers but these are responsible for a large part of the sales; the heaviest 20 per cent of buyers typically makes 50 per cent of the purchases. However, because there are many light buyers and some new buyers, a change in their purchasing can have a substantial effect on sales. Over shorter periods (3–12 months), sales changes are mostly seen as a change in penetration, with only a small change in purchase frequency in line with the rule of double jeopardy.

The NBD and Dirichlet models rest on assumptions that purchase incidence is Poisson, purchase rates in a population of buyers are Gamma, and that (in the case of the Dirichlet) there is no market partitioning. The predictions from such models usually fit the data derived from panel research. When the fit is poor, the model provides benchmark norms for interpreting any exceptional brand performance.

Analysis of cross-purchase suggests that there is limited market partitioning. The absence of substitution patterns between specific brands indicates that the different brands in a category are seen by consumers in much the same way. In these circumstances, a positioning strategy based on brand differences may have little relevance.

Additional Resources

A clearly written but technical account of the NBD can be found in Morrison and Schmittlein (1988), while the phenomenon of double jeopardy is well explained by Ehrenberg, Goodhardt and Barwise (1990). For a useful review of the Dirichlet and its applications see Ehrenberg, Uncles and Goodhardt (2004). Finally, an exercise designed to bring home the features of stationary markets is available in Ehrenberg, Uncles and Carrie (1994).

Notes

1 Firms sometimes conduct Pareto analyses and delete the worst performing brands or discourage the customers who buy the least. It is important to consider whether such brands and customers could change. For example, a customer at a DIY store could buy little for several years but become a heavy buyer after moving house.
2 Within these assumptions it is possible to derive an expression for the probability of making r purchases in a period, p_r. For those interested in the technicalities: $p_r = (1-m/(m+k))^{-k}$ where k is a parameter that is estimated from the purchase frequency and penetration. Expressions of the form $(1+x)^n$ are called binomial; the equation for p_r is a negative binomial because the exponent is negative. The calculation of the NBD requires the solution of the equation $1-b = (1+m/k)^{-k}$ to obtain the parameter k; this is done by program NBD.

5 Market Dynamics

LEARNING OBJECTIVES

When you have completed this chapter, you should be able to:

1 Sketch a 52-week sales curve showing seasonality and sales promotions.
2 Explain what will happen if there is an imbalance between customer defection and customer acquisition.
3 Explain why the effects of marketing actions may take some time to become obvious.
4 Explain the social basis of diffusion theory.
5 Describe and sketch the technology substitution model, the Bass model, and the typical trial growth curves for frequently bought products.

OVERVIEW

Chapter 4 described the regular patterns of purchase found in mature, stationary markets. But what if a market is not stable? Sales and market share do sometimes change and new products sometimes gather sales and become established. In this chapter, we explore aspects of this change.

In the first section, we discuss sales fluctuations in mature markets due to seasonality and sales promotions. These can be large, making it harder to spot long-term trends. The second section describes the dynamic patterns in loyalty that underlie stable markets. We document these, show how they lead to dynamic equilibrium and discuss the effects of disturbing this equilibrium. In doing so, we extend some of the material from Chapter 4. In the third section, we consider the launch of major innovative new products. These may create new markets or lead to the complete substitution of an old way of doing things. We draw on the theory of innovation diffusion, as summarized by Everett Rogers, introduce the technology substitution model and give an overview of Frank Bass' model of new product adoption. Finally, we consider frequently bought categories, such as grocery products. These categories exhibit recurrent minor product innovation, but with a different social dynamic from that found in the work of Everett Rogers and Frank Bass. We document the growth of first purchases for these minor innovations, and discuss theories of the development of loyalty to such new products.

SECTION 1: CHANGES IN AGGREGATE SALES

Variations in Demand – Seasonality and Sales Promotions

To understand sales changes in markets, it is important to first understand the fluctuations present in markets that are stationary. It would be easy to assume that, if sales are fairly stable from year to year, they are also fairly stable from month to month or week to week. Nothing could be further from the truth. Most businesses experience large swings in demand that relate to the time of the year, holidays, sales promotions and other events. More butter and soup are sold in winter. There is little demand for Easter Eggs at Christmas. Americans buy barbecue sauce in summer, with demand skyrocketing for the 4th of July, assisted by heavy sales promotion. Similar patterns can occur in durables and business-to-business markets. The weather, holidays and tax refunds all nudge consumers towards buying certain products. Even sales targets and discounting policies can lead to seasonality in demand (see Box 5.1).

Box 5.1	**Discounts create irregular sales**

Early in his career, one of the authors worked for a large American computer company where the need to meet sales quota led to a crescendo of effort at the end of the year. If sales were slow, management would authorize company-wide promotions in the final quarter, in the hope that they could still achieve their targets. Some IT managers responded to this by adjusting their capital purchase cycle. When pressed about low sales mid-way through the year, sales staff would tell management that their customers 'liked to buy at the end of the year, when the discounts are offered'.

These patterns are founded on individual consumer choices, but they are usually observed in aggregate sales figures. So it is important to be familiar with the variations in demand seen in such sales figures. Figure 5.1 provides an example.

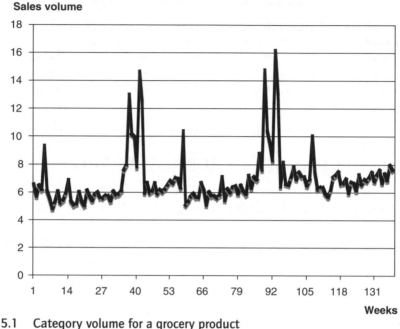

Figure 5.1   Category volume for a grocery product

Source: Simulated data based on known patterns

The graph covers two and a half years of weekly data, and is representative of one of the yellow fats (butter, margarine, olive oil spreads) in a major western economy. The x-axis shows intervals of 13 weeks, or a quarter, which is a common management reporting period. The base of the y-axis is zero, so differences in the height of the graph are directly proportional to percentage differences in demand.

This figure shows spikes that increase sales by as much as 150 per cent above the baseline level. They tend to be about four quarters apart. In other words, the spikes occur at the same time (or season) every year. Why are these sales spikes so large? Because sales promotions are often timed to match holidays or seasonal upswings in demand, giving a large combined effect. As mentioned in Chapter 4, despite the magnitude of these changes there is usually little long-term effect. This is because most of the extra sales come from a brand's existing users (Ehrenberg, Hammond and Goodhardt, 1994; Gupta, Van Heerde and Wittink, 2003).

Many managers are surprised when they first see such period-to-period sales variations, so it is important to be aware of them. The size of these variations can cause supply problems and managers should take steps to avoid stock-outs during periods of heavy demand.

Measuring Long-term Sales Performance

It can be difficult to identify underlying trends in the face of all this period-to-period change. Figure 5.1, for example, shows a steady upward trend over time, although this is hard to pick out at first glance. The need to smooth out these variations is one reason why market share is a popular measure of performance. Seasonality and holidays should affect all competitors equally, so market share is a more stable measure of performance than raw sales data. Even so, many companies find it necessary to measure market share using statistical techniques to reduce the period-to-period variation in the data.

Large companies may apply seasonal decomposition to remove seasonality effects, or exponential smoothing to reduce the impact of random variations. Some advanced econometric techniques, such as ARIMA (Autoregressive Integrated Moving Average), may combine both methods, include estimates of trend lines and use dummy variables for holiday effects. By using statistical models to identify the seasonal, promotional and holiday effects, the underlying trend is more clearly revealed.

SECTION 2: DYNAMIC EFFECTS AND BRAND LOYALTY

The Changes Underlying a Stable Market

Section 1 examined short-term fluctuations in sales that occur in markets that are stationary in the longer term. In this section we examine fluctuations in purchase rate and loyalty and whether these may or may not be a source of sales change. We know from Chapter 4 that the NBD model describes normal patterns of light buying and repeat purchase. We can expand on this, using a technique called conditional trend analysis (CTA) developed by Goodhardt and Ehrenberg (1967). Conditional trend analysis extends the NBD to different classes of buyers, so that repeat purchase can be predicted for light versus heavy buyers, for example. Managers should be particularly interested in this, due to the sales importance of heavy buyers. They are often concerned that a loss of loyalty from heavy buyers presages a decline in brand sales and share.

Consider a brand that is bought by 15 per cent of category purchasers, on average 1.6 times in a 13-week period (many occasionally bought grocery categories follow a similar pattern). The NBD analysis in Chapter 4 tells us the expected repeat purchase rate in the next 13-week period is about 50 per cent (i.e. half of the people who bought the brand in the first period will buy again in the second). But the NBD does not tell us how repeat purchase is distributed between light and heavy buyers. To compare actual repeat purchase with the norms for heavy buyers, we need to undertake CTA. Table 5.1 reports some results from both normal NBD analysis and CTA, broken down by the number of purchases made in the first period.

First, look at the set of buyers who made a single purchase in period 1. They are important, as they make up 65 per cent of all buyers. Given that they bought once (on average) in period 1, a manager may expect them to continue buying at the same rate. It may be a surprise to find that this set of buyers

Table 5.1   Purchase and repeat purchase over consecutive 13-week periods

| Number of purchases | Initial purchases – Period 1 | | Repeat purchases – Period 2 | |
	% of buyers	% of sales	Average purchases per Period 1 buyer	% repeat buying
1	65	41	0.6	40
2	21	26	1.2	61
3	8	15	1.7	74
4+ (av. 4.8)	6	18	2.7	87

makes just 0.6 purchases (on average) in the second period. Likewise, the set of buyers who bought twice in the first period drops to 1.2 purchases in the second period and the heaviest buyers have gone from an average 4.8 purchases down to 2.7.

It would be easy to interpret this as an erosion of loyalty, and to conclude that you need to find the source of the problem and recruit replacement customers. That would be a mistake, though not an uncommon one. It is what Andrew Ehrenberg calls the 'Leaky Bucket Theory' (most recently, in Ehrenberg, Uncles and Goodhardt, 2004), the idea that customers are steadily leaking away, requiring replacement by freshly recruited buyers.

In fact, the values in Table 5.1 are theoretical norms. They are exactly what we would expect in a normal, mature stationary market. Period 1 shows familiar NBD patterns; most buyers make only one purchase, and 35 per cent of buyers account for 59 per cent of sales. In period 2, we simply see how the NBD plays out over time. We see how the 50 per cent repeat-purchase rate is distributed across heavier and lighter buyers, and that the average number of purchases for each period 1 group declines in period 2. Instead of thinking of this as undesirable, we should recognize it as the typical pattern of purchasing over time. Heavier buyers show higher repeat rates simply because they are heavier, more regular buyers to start with.

Total sales remain stable because those who do not repeat purchase in period 2 are balanced by an influx of other regular buyers. These are households who did not purchase in period 1, but are nonetheless established buyers of the brand. Similarly, a reduction in purchase frequency by some buyers will be matched by an increase in purchase frequency by others. Rather than a 'leaky bucket' in need of constant replenishment, this is the normal pattern of buying in repertoire markets.

Some large companies do monitor erosion of loyalty by examining repeat-purchase rates for heavy buyers. This is sometimes called buyer flow analysis. If you want to do this, be sure to use the NBD and CTA for a benchmark. You will find that much apparent erosion is simply the normal pattern of occasional purchasing.

Erosion of Loyalty in Repertoire Markets

That is not to say that there is no true erosion of repeat purchase loyalty. There is, but it is smaller than implied by a simple analysis of repeat purchase rates. For example, East and Hammond (1996) examined repeat-purchase rates for super-market products and found that they declined from around 55 per cent to 47 per cent over a year. Erosion is the difference between the repeat purchase rates at the start of the study and a year later. This is 8 percentage points, and 8/55 is 15 per cent of buyers. Similar observations can be found in Zufryden (1996). In a study of four brands in two segments, he observed year-to-year retention of first-brand loyalty ranging from 79 per cent to 86 per cent. Thus, erosion ranged from 14 per cent to 21 per cent. These values are a little higher than those of East and Hammond (1996). This may be because a loss of first-brand loyalty, as measured by Zufryden (1996), does not necessarily represent a complete switch. It may simply be a downgrade to a lower position in a customer's repertoire, such as moving from favourite to second-favourite brand. So, there is erosion, but it occurs slowly. The leaky bucket theory is not wrong but the holes are quite small.

Defection and Churn in Subscription Markets

Leakage is often more obvious in subscription markets, such as insurance, banking, utilities and mobile phones airtime. These markets may be based on an annually renewable contract, as in the case of insurance, or they may be a 'tenure' contract in which the subscription continues until terminated, as with banking or utilities. Customers often have relationships with more than one financial institution, so banks are generally interested in whether they are a customer's main bank and have the largest share of wallet. Such main bank relationships tend to be long-lasting, as shown by relatively low annual defection rates and valuable to the bank. Some markets, such as hairdressing or the family doctor, are thought to show the same kind of persistent subscription-like behaviour, even when choice is not constrained by a contract (Sharp, Wright and Goodhardt, 2002).

In subscription markets, a loss of loyalty often represents a complete loss of revenue from the customer concerned. Thus, the rate of defection (or retention) is a key performance metric and a leading indicator of a brand's fortunes. Defection rates in subscription markets typically range from 4 per cent to 20 per cent of a brand's customer base. Lees, Garland and Wright (2007) report a figure of 3.6 per cent for a main bank. Gupta, Lehmann and Stuart (2004) found figures of 5 per cent for online stock trading and 15 per cent for a credit card company. Wright and Riebe (2007) calculated, but did not report, category switching rates. However, we can reveal figures of 4.1 per cent for the main bank and 20 per cent for annual industrial pipe contracts. Reichheld (1996b) claimed that defection varied quite widely but averaged about 15 per cent across a range of services.

Turnover in the customer base, often called churn, is not always due to defection. First-time market entry and market exit both play a role. People may enter these markets as they reach independence or form households, and leave them as they cease to support households. There may also be churn due to upgrades or downgrades in the product used and because of competitive pricing.[1] In some fields, change may be linked strongly to life-stage.

Consider the use of banking services. Over a lifetime an individual may move from a child's savings account, to an overdraft, to a mortgage, to an on-call cash management account. People may move house or be affected by a major life event such as their first job, marriage, birth of a child and so forth. This can affect the types of product and service they require and thus their loyalty to previously purchased brands. Some car models are suitable for young people, others for executives and others for families. Similarly, there are regional banks in many countries that cannot offer a full range of services in large cities. A young family that moves from a regional centre to a large city may be forced to change their bank.

Some evidence on the reasons for switching banks comes from Lees, Garland and Wright (2007). They found that, in New Zealand, change of main bank was due to better offers 32 per cent of the time, product or service failures 31 per cent of the time, reasons beyond the bank's control (such as moving house) 22 per cent of the time and a combination of these reasons 15 per cent of the time. Chapter 2 reported results for other categories.

Change from Market Imbalances

If erosion, or switching, from a brand is exactly matched by customer acquisition, a dynamic equilibrium will exist in which market share remains constant. An imbalance between the two will lead to a change. For example, reducing a brand's defection rate while maintaining customer acquisition will lead to an increase in market share. Defection reduction has been recognized as a possible source of growth for some time (Reichheld and Sasser, 1990). More recently, Reichheld (2003) pursued the idea of growth coming from dynamic forces through his 'net promoter' score, which takes account of the balance between positive and negative word of mouth (see Chapter 11). Recent work has also integrated defection rates into an understanding of customer lifetime value (Gupta, Lehmann and Stuart, 2004) and compared the relative returns of customer acquisition and defection reduction efforts (Reinartz, Thomas and Kumar, 2005) to support an optimal allocation of the marketing budget.

However, some work in this area tends to overlook the fact that defection reduction is *bounded*. That is, if a brand has 6 per cent defection, it can only reduce it by this amount. Furthermore, no matter how superior the product or service, some loss of customers will occur due to market exit or changes in customer requirements.

EXERCISE 5.1   DEFECTION REDUCTION AND SHARE GROWTH

Question: Imagine you have a brand with a 3 per cent market share and an annual defection rate of 10 per cent. How long will it take to increase your market share from 3 per cent to 10 per cent, simply by halving your defection rate?

Answer: Assuming your market share has been in a dynamic balance and that all customers buy at the same rate, your 10 per cent annual defection rate will have been matched by a 10 per cent annual customer acquisition rate. If your defection rate halves to 5 per cent while your customer acquisition rate remains constant, you will grow by 5 per cent of your customer base per annum. That is, your market share after T years can be found by a simple compounding formula, as follows.

$$3\% \times (1 + .05) \wedge T$$

We suggest you conduct a simple spreadsheet analysis to find the answer. We did this and found that market share will rise above the 10 per cent threshold in the *24th year*. However, defection reduction can be an expensive exercise so there is a risk that market share growth will not be matched by profit growth.

Comment: This example is somewhat similar to that of MNBA, outlined in Reichheld and Sasser (1990). Reichheld and Sasser were more concerned with customer lifetime value than with growth. However, we hope our example makes it clear that brand growth requires a broader explanation than just defection analysis, especially when brands have a relatively low market share.

Ask yourself the question: what else could lead to brand growth?

Observing Market Change

One consequence of occasional buying and the relatively low levels of erosion is that marketing actions can take a long time to bear fruit. Exposure to advertising, for example, cannot affect brand choice until the next purchase occasion. Similarly, defection reduction programmes seek to plug a leak that may be fairly small to start with. So it may take some time to see an effect.

Similarly, market problems, such as a drop in perceived quality, may not be immediately noticeable. It may be some time before affected customers are ready to purchase the category again, or to renew a contract and have the opportunity to make a different choice. By that time, quite a weight of dissatisfaction may have accumulated so that many switch. This makes it important to monitor brand performance metrics such as penetration, average purchase frequency and, repeat purchase as well as satisfaction or perceived quality, because these may indicate potential problems and allow a manager to respond before the problems gather too much momentum.

SECTION 3: THE DYNAMICS OF NEW PRODUCT ADOPTION

So far we have examined change in mature markets. What about the more fundamental changes that result from the launch of new products? Whether they satisfy a previously unmet demand, or replace a previous technology, new products can result in faster and more enduring change than is otherwise seen in mature markets.

How, then, are such innovations adopted by a population of consumers? While there is a large literature on this topic, we will restrict ourselves to examining three approaches of particular importance to marketers. These are Rogers' innovation diffusion curve, Fisher and Pry's technology substitution model, and the Bass model.

Rogers' Approach to Innovation Diffusion

Most marketers have some awareness of work on the diffusion of innovations. The most well-known author in this area is Everett Rogers (1962, 2003), whose book on the subject is a widely cited classic. Rogers brought together studies from many disciplines, but gave emphasis to sociology. He followed influential work by Gabriel Tarde (1903), who noted that cumulative adoption followed an S-shaped curve and saw adoption or rejection as a critical decision, George Simmel (1908), who introduced the idea of a social network and Ryan and Gross (1943), who undertook a landmark study into adoption of hybrid corn. Later work incorporated Granovetter's finding (1973) that the spread of an innovation through a social system was helped if people were loosely bonded to many different groups.

In Rogers' work, these ideas are more fully developed, with diffusion defined as 'the process in which an innovation is communicated through certain channels over time among the members of a social system' (Rogers, 2003: 5). He believes that the adoption follows a normal distribution curve, with time as the x-axis and number of adopters as the y-axis. Figure 5.2 shows this normal curve. There are two versions: the standard normal curve of (non-cumulative) adoptions in each

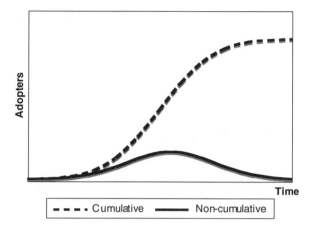

Figure 5.2   A normal adoption curve

period and the S-shaped curve of total (cumulative) adoption. Historical examples include black and white televisions, 286 computer chips, air conditioning units, facsimile machines and first-generation mobile telephones. Modern examples might include high-definition colour televisions, DVD recorders and third-generation mobile telephones.

Characteristics of an innovation

Innovations do not always follow this curve. They may fail. Or they may diffuse so slowly that the left tail, or lead-time, of the adoption curve extends for many years. Rogers cites as examples the British navy's resistance to citrus juice as an anti-scurvy agent, resistance to the use of boiled water in Peru and the failure to displace the QWERTY keyboard on which this book has been rather inefficiently typed. He became interested in the characteristics affecting the innovation adoption rate and posited that it depended on:

- The *relative advantage* that an innovation has over previous methods of meeting the same need. Some innovations, such as facsimile machines and the Internet, also have strong network effects, so that relative advantage increases with the number of adopters.
- *Compatibility*, or the consistency of an innovation with the existing experiences, needs and values of the adopting population. Cultural and religious incompatibilities may be particular risks for the adoption of innovations.
- *Complexity*, or how easy an innovation is to use and describe to others and whether it requires specialized expertise or substantial learning.
- *Trialability*, enabling experience to be gained with the innovation before purchase or full adoption.
- *Observability*, increasing both awareness and social influence, as we are influenced by seeing others use new products and tend to follow the consumption habits of the communities we live in.

There is also the perceived risk, or cost, of an innovation. The higher the price, the less the confidence in after-sales service, or the harsher the returns policy, the more reluctant people will be to adopt. Rogers' adoption characteristics have an indirect impact on perceived risk; it will be reduced by trialability or observability and increased by problems with compatibility or complexity.

Adopter categories and innovativeness

Perhaps the most famous part of Rogers' work is the division of the normal curve into adopter categories. The first 2.5 per cent of the normal curve in Figure 5.2 are labelled the innovators and the next 13.5 per cent the early adopters. Then we have the early majority (34 per cent), late majority (34 per cent) and laggards (16 per cent). These adopter categories are reproduced in most consumer behaviour textbooks, together with comments about their typical characteristics.

This approach has come in for some serious criticism. Bass (1969) famously described Rogers' approach as 'largely literary'. Wright and Charlett (1995) pointed out that Rogers' adopter categories were a *post hoc* tautological classification system, of no value for forecasting. This is because Rogers' categorization depends on the standard deviation from the mean time to adopt. Innovators are all those up to two standard deviations before the mean time to adopt; early adopters are between 2 and 1 standard deviations from the mean time to adopt and so on. Yet neither the mean nor the standard deviation can be calculated until the diffusion of the innovation is complete, at which point the adopter categories have little managerial value.

A counter-argument is that innovativeness is a normally distributed trait, associated with other consumer characteristics in a predictable manner, allowing innovators and early adopters to be identified and targeted. Rogers claims that there were 26 characteristics that varied between adopter categories, including socio-economic variables, personality values and communication behaviour. However, empirical findings do not always support this claim. Taylor (1977) found that a striking characteristic of 'innovators' in grocery products was that they were heavy buyers of the category, a finding that was recently confirmed for pharmaceuticals (Stern and Wright, 2007). This hardly suggests an enduring personality trait. A more popular modern view is that innovativeness varies by product category (e.g. Crawford and Di Benedetto, 2006: 372).

The long lead-time that can occur before an innovation takes off is sometimes explained by the characteristics of the most innovative people. Rogers notes that innovators are often 'deviants', somewhat apart from the rest of the social system: they might be hermits in the wood or perhaps the archetypical computer geek. While such people may be innovative, they may have little social influence, so their behaviour has little effect on the broader community. Diffusion will only take off when more influential people, well connected within the social system, adopt the innovation. In a primitive village, this might be the chief or the chief's wife. In western social networks, it may be opinion leaders or celebrities, or people who offer marketplace advice to many others, such as Feick and Price's (1987) 'market mavens' (if they can be found, see Chapter 11). Rogers places such people in the early adopter category.

While these ideas offer insights into ways of speeding up adoption within particular social systems, they are not necessary to explain the S-shaped curve that we see in practice. A long lead-time can be explained through the cumulative effects of social forces, as we shall see later. Nonetheless, Rogers' work is very useful. The concept of an idea spreading through a social system via specific communication channels underlies much subsequent work on innovation diffusion. The insight that adoption follows a normal curve has been borne out in many product categories.

Fisher and Pry's Technology Substitution Model

Rogers' adopter categorization exploits the properties of the S-shaped normal distribution curve, but is not helpful for forecasting. Marketers need to make forecasts to assist launch decisions on new products, set targets against which performance can be assessed and allocate marketing expenditure.

Fisher and Pry (1971) showed how to use an S-shaped curve to forecast the replacement of an inferior technology with a better one that meets the same need. This process is called technology substitution. They dealt with the problem of an indeterminate lead-time by assuming the substitute technology must achieve several per cent market share before complete substitution could be guaranteed to occur. They then treated substitution as a logistic function of time.[2] This has the practical effect of transforming the S-shaped cumulative adoption curve into a straight line. Extrapolation through regression then yields a forecast. They validated this model over 17 diverse data sets and found surprisingly accurate results.

Figure 5.3 is an example of the raw pattern of technology substitution, using some previously published data on diesel and steam locomotives in the USA. These data are expressed in relative percentages of the total number of locomotives. You will see that the growth curve for diesel locomotives is similar to the cumulative normal adoption curve shown in Figure 5.2.

Although quite old, Fisher and Pry's (1971) model is likely to be of great importance in the next decade, as we undergo accelerating technological substitution in areas such as telecommunications, computing and home electronics. This model has the useful feature of forecasting the dynamic decline of the old technology as well as the growth of the new one. This is potentially very helpful to companies in fields such as telecommunications, where there are substantial but declining revenue streams from products such as fixed line connections and dial-up Internet access.

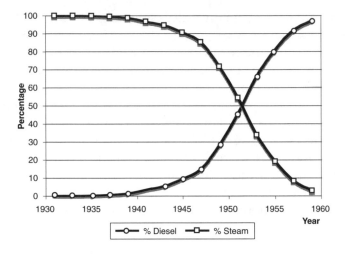

Figure 5.3 Cumulative substitution of locomotives

Source: Interstate Commerce Commission, Statistics of Railroads 1925–1960, as cited in Moore and Pessemier (1993: 79)

By way of example, consider the following forecast (Box 5.2). This applies the Fisher and Pry model to publicly available information on dial-up and broadband Internet connections in Australia. We describe the workings so you can see how easily the model is applied. Note that the date had to be adjusted to an equal interval scale to allow the statistical analysis to take place. Figure 5.4 graphs the example in Box 5.2, in this case in fractions rather than percentages.

Box 5.2	The growth of broadband

We applied the Fisher and Pry model to forecasting the decline of Australian dial-up Internet access and, conversely, the growth of Broadband in that country. Using Nielsen net ratings figures published at http://www.dcita.gov.au, we converted the proportions of Internet users that had dial-up and broadband access to a log odds ratio (LOR) and ran an OLS regression. The OLS regression predicted that LOR = 3.214– .068 × adjusted date. (We had to use an adjusted date to ensure an equal interval scale, as the time between reports varied.) We put future dates into this equation to predict changes in LOR and then converted these changed LORs back to predicted proportions of dial-up and broadband connections. Figure 5.4 shows our forecasts. Forecasts like this give useful long-range expectations about the size of the customer base and the support infrastructure needed from capital equipment to call-centre staff. They are also useful to help forecast market potential for Internet services relying on a broadband connection, such as Internet TV.

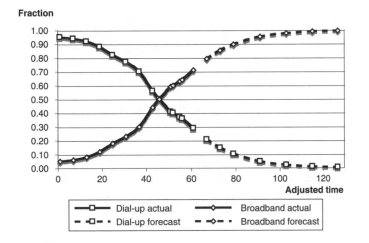

Figure 5.4   Cumulative substitution of Internet access

The technology substitution model gives impressive forecasting ability, but it does not offer much explanation. It is also constrained by the simplicity of the assumptions. In their original article, Fisher and Pry (1971) applied their model to the substitution of margarine for butter, water-based for oil-based paints and artificial for natural fibres. We now know that those substitutions are partial – there is a limit on their potential that is less than the total usage of yellow fats, paint and clothes fibre respectively. Furthermore, both Rogers and Fisher and Pry assume a strict S-shaped diffusion and do not allow a different process.

It would be ideal to have a model of innovation diffusion that offered the forecasting ability of Fisher and Pry, the explanation of Rogers, a variable ceiling on the number of adopters and allowed the adoption curves to take shapes other than a strict normal distribution. As it happens, there is such a model in marketing – the Bass model.

The Bass Model

Frank Bass's approach to diffusion of innovation (1969) is one of the most well-known models in marketing. Bass drew on epidemiological theory – the theory of the spread of diseases – to examine the spread of an innovation throughout a connected social system. Bass modelled the effect of both innovative and imitative forces in promoting adoption up to a saturation point. He saw innovative forces as those external to the social system, such as advertising and personal selling. Innovation therefore acts right throughout the diffusion process rather than being limited to the first 2.5 per cent of adopters. Conversely, imitative forces reflect social influence, which is internal to the social system. This is exerted by previous adopters as they model and recommend the innovation to others. For example, you might buy an iPOD simply because you see an advertisement (innovation), but your purchase becomes more likely the more you see people listening to one, the more your friends and family own them, and the more they tell you about it (word of mouth). Unlike earlier researchers, Bass found a way to quantify these social influence variables within a mathematical model. An early success of the Bass model is illustrated in Box 5.3.

Box 5.3	A Strong Test of the Bass Model

The Bass model is lauded for having passed the key scientific test – prediction. Bass used his model to predict the peak of the colour television adoption curve in the USA. He was roundly criticized at the time by industry figures for his 'pessimistic' forecasts. However, when actual sales figures became available, he was proved right. Ignoring his forecasts led the consumer electronics industry to build too much production capacity, at considerable cost.

Parameters, Shape and Equations

Bass's model is elegant. It requires only three parameters: innovation (p), imitation (q) and the eventual number of adopters, known as market potential (m). The dependent variable is either cumulative or non-cumulative adoption by time period – $Y(T)$ or $y(t)$ respectively. Importantly, sales data can be equated with adoption data if the purchase is a high-value durable or service that is bought once and does not need replacement for some time.

In the first period (usually a year), the probability of adoption, given that no adoption has yet taken place, is simply p and the predicted number of adopters is $p \times m$. However, as more of the population adopt, social influence (q) increases and the probability of adoption becomes $p + q \times (Y(T)/m)$. This basic equation can be expressed in a variety of forms, both algebraic and probabilistic and for either cumulative or non-cumulative adoption.

The mix between internal and external influence can be seen in the Bass curve in Figure 5.5, estimated on data for first-time use of a telephone enrolment system at Massey University in New Zealand. The parameters of this curve are $p = 0.10$, $q = 0.47$ and $m = 5,788$. This p value is quite high for Bass modelling, so the adoption curve starts at a point well above zero, peaks early and is over quickly. This shows the extra flexibility of the Bass model compared to a simple normal distribution curve.

Validation, Replication and the Extension of the Bass Model

Box 5.3 notes a famous case of forecasting success for the Bass model but Bass may have been lucky on this occasion. More cases are needed to assess the model. In a review of early replications, Wright, Upritchard and Lewis (1997)

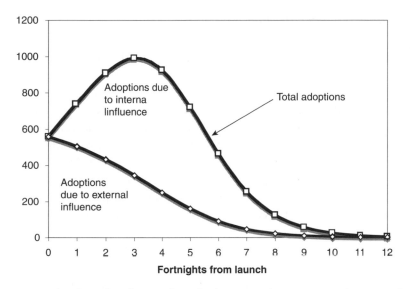

Figure 5.5   Adoption of an interactive telephone enrolment system (non-cumulative)

Source: Model parameters from Wright, Upritchard and Lewis (1997)

noted that a poor fit was sometimes found for the model outside North American and European settings. They also found that the predictive ability of the model was limited by variations in the early data. As early sales (or adoptions) are quite few, fluctuations have a large effect on long-term forecasts. Putsis and Srinivasan (2000) subsequently found that Bass model forecasts generally do not stabilize until the peak of the adoption process had passed. Also, the assumption of constant social influence may be an over-simplification. As we shall see in Chapter 11, word-of-mouth production may vary with the period a person has owned a product.

Notwithstanding this, there has been a wealth of successful research on the Bass model, including applications to other historical data sets, methodological improvements and many useful extensions, such as allowing population size to vary or modelling the successive generations of new technologies. Bass models have accurately described innovations in areas as diverse as consumer durables, consumer electronics, education, agriculture services, telecommunications and even United Nations membership. In these areas, only one purchase is normally made; thus sales (or membership) data gives a direct measure of diffusion, up to the point where replacement purchases commence. If you are interested in this area, you should start by reading the summary, review and meta-analysis articles that draw this literature together (Bass, 1995; Mahajan, Muller and Bass, 1990; Sultan, Farley and Lehmann, 1990) and also Bass, Krishnan and Jain (1994), who found a way to include marketing variables in the generalized Bass model.

Using the Bass Model to Predict

To predict the sales of an innovation using the Bass model, we need to know the values of p, q and m. The usual way to estimate these is through non-linear regression against sales data for the first few periods. However, this requires several years of such data and some degree of statistical skill. Furthermore, as noted earlier, the results tend to be unstable until the data includes the peak of the adoption process.

It would be much more helpful to apply the model before the launch of a new product. Then it could be used for initial sales forecasting, launch decisions, capacity planning and marketing budgeting. Two traditional approaches to doing this are to forecast by analogy or to use management judgement.

To forecast by analogy, known values of p and q from other innovations are used. Sultan, Farley and Lehmann (1990) report the results of a meta-analysis of these parameters, and tables of them have been published elsewhere (e.g. Lilien and Rangaswamy, 2002). However, Rogers' theory tells us that the characteristics of the innovation and the characteristics of the social system are the key drivers of adoption, so it is questionable whether p and q values are generalizable unless they are from a similar innovation in a very similar social system. For the m parameter, the value cannot be derived by analogy, but may be estimated through market research.

The techniques for applying managerial judgement are not made very clear in the literature and should generally been seen as a last resort. Managers are unlikely to understand the social basis or typical values of the Bass model parameters p and q. Managers will therefore have little basis to apply their judgement. Also, Armstrong (1985) has evaluated evidence on the performance of subjective estimates – managerial judgement – in forecasting. He found that they do not perform well compared to forecasts from objective methods and that integrating objective information with managerial judgement typically provided substantial improvements over managerial judgement alone (Armstrong, 1985: 387–420). So it is doubtful whether management judgement will show much accuracy unless the judge already has substantial experience with the Bass model and takes steps to combine this judgement with other, objective, information.

Lessons for Market Dynamics from the Bass Model

What lessons does the Bass model offer us in understanding market dynamics? First, consider the domain of the model. It concerns new products, not brands. It is typically applied to high-value products or services that have long inter-purchase times. These may be completely new or substantial technological improvements (although it can be applied to other behaviours if true adoption data is available, as in Figure 5.5). Bass modelling has shown that sales curves following the introduction of such products and services will be roughly normal or S-shaped.

Second, the exact shape of the curve will depend on social factors relating to the social system involved. Understanding the relative importance of these external and internal influences will give richer insights for marketing planning and more accurate forecasts of product sales growth.

Third, a long lead-in time can be explained simply by the values of the parameters. It will occur if the innovation parameter, p, is relatively low. Rapid acceleration of adoption will then occur if the innovation parameter, q, is relatively high.

Therefore, knowledge of the Bass model gives a good understanding of market dynamics following the introduction of a new product, at least for durables or high-involvement services. However, the Bass model has little to say about frequently bought products or new brands in established markets. We address this in the next section.

EXERCISE 5.3   THE FLEXIBILITY OF THE BASS CURVE

The following graphs show how changes to the parameters affect the shape of Bass curve. Examine each one of the four examples and then consider the questions that follow.

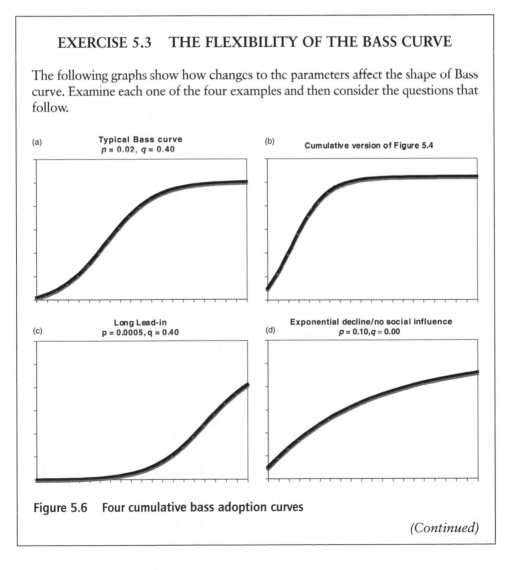

Figure 5.6   Four cumulative bass adoption curves

(Continued)

1   For each curve, identify a social system and innovation it could be describing. (*Hint: think about the level of innovation and the extent of word-of-mouth recommendation.*)

2   Consider Rogers' innovation characteristics. How might they affect the shape of the cumulative adoption curve?

3   Which do you think are the most and least common shapes? Justify your answer.

SECTION 4: THE SALES DYNAMICS OF FREQUENTLY BOUGHT CATEGORIES

Are Frequently Bought Items Different?

Section 3 described what we know about sales changes that occur when new categories are introduced, or when technological substitution causes a wave of change in an existing durable category. However, we cannot expect the same processes in low-value items that may be bought several times in a year, such as groceries or doctors' drug prescriptions. New products in these categories are most often 'me-too' or incremental innovations. These rely on familiarity and existing memory structures, as discussed in Chapter 3, and most sales come from repeat purchases rather than from the initial adoption decision. Occasionally, there may be a major innovation, such as the first olive oil spread or low-fat calcium enriched milk. However, even these are typically presented as new brands launched into a familiar category (yellow fats and milk, respectively).

Nonetheless, diffusion theory offers some useful insights. In general, we can expect trial and adoption will be affected by influences external to the social system (advertising, promotion and personal selling) and influences internal to the social system (observation of others and word-of-mouth recommendation). We expect high-value durables will be more visible, and will tend to be a topic of conversation, because of their novelty or because the high price level leads people to seek pre-purchase recommendations. The result is that social influence increases with the number of previous adopters, leading to the S-shaped cumulative adoption curve.

Consider a low-value, frequently bought item. The low value means lower risk. Also, it may be one of many dozens of regularly purchased product categories. The category is less likely to be a topic of conversation – who talks much about toilet paper, bleach, milk, baking powder, flour, light bulbs, butter and the like? Of course there will be exceptions – a cooking club may talk a great deal about a new type of flour. However, such exceptions represent a small fraction of the buyers and indeed the authors are not aware of any corresponding light bulb-changing or milk-drinking clubs.

Thinking of Rogers' adoption characteristics, we suggest that low-value incremental innovations in frequently bought categories are familiar (compatible), simple (not complex), cheap (trialable) and widely present on the shelf (observable). This means there are few barriers to adoption of a new product, provided it has a relative advantage. Conversely, such products are less likely to be topics of conversation, so there will be relatively little social influence. Consequently, the probability of adoption remains constant over time, while the number of adopters falls each period as the pool of those who have not yet adopted shrinks. The result is a curve whose shape is known as exponential or an exponential decline. Figure 5.6(d) in Exercise 5.3 shows the pattern of cumulative adoption for such an exponentially declining adoption curve.

EXERCISE 5.4   SKETCH AN EXPONENTIAL DECLINE CURVE

It's easy to see for yourself how an exponential decline curve works. Imagine that a population of 100 people has an adoption rate of 10 per cent. In the first period, 10 will adopt, in the second period, 9 (10 per cent of the remaining 90 who had not yet adopted), in the third period 8.1 are expected to adopt (10 per cent of the remaining 81) and so on.

1   In Excel, calculate the number of adopters for each of the first 20 periods. Assume a population of 100 and an adoption rate of 10 per cent. (*Hint: you might find it helpful to have columns for those yet to adopt, adopters in the period, and total adopters to date.*)

2   Graph both the cumulative and non-cumulative adoption curves.

3   Repeat the exercises for adoption rates of 30 per cent and 5 per cent.

Empirical Patterns in First Purchases

A complicating factor for new products in frequently bought categories is that, unlike durable products, the first purchase is not necessarily an adoption. It may simply be a trial of the new product. However, before discussing this point, we must ask: what is the empirical pattern found for these first or trial purchases? Do they accumulate in an S-shape, suggestive of internal influences, or an exponential shape suggestive of little internal influence? Wright and Stern (2006) examined 12 national product launches and 19 controlled test market product launches for a variety of frequently bought categories. They normalized cumulative first purchases to year-end values so the results could be averaged across data sets. Figure 5.7 sketches some of their findings. It is noteworthy that the individual product launches showed similar patterns, despite varying degrees of innovativeness in the product or brand being launched.

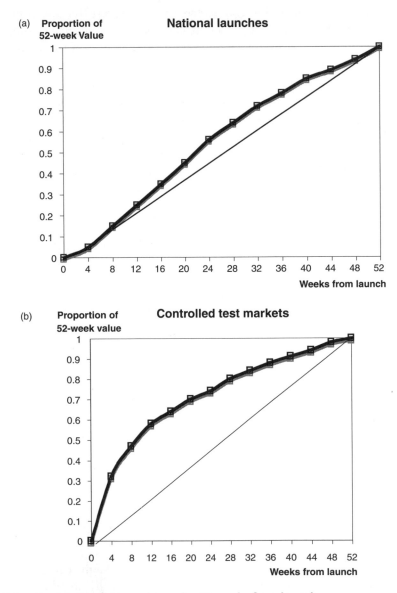

Figure 5.7 Cumulative first purchases for 52 weeks from launch

Source: Values reported in Wright and Stern (2006), partly derived from data downloaded from www.brucehardie.com

These curves are not obviously S-shaped and so show little evidence of an increasing word-of-mouth effect. Rather, they show an exponentially declining pattern of growth in first purchases. There is a slight bend in the curve for national launches, although this may be due to distribution growth. Yet even with this, the curve still generally follows the declining exponential pattern.

If the q parameter of the Bass model is set to zero, the result is such an exponentially shaped curve, with maximum adoption in the first period tailing off over time. However, a Bass model does not quite make the best assumption in this case. It assumes members of the population all have a chance of purchase in the first period. Light buyers may not buy the category for months at a time. Also, achieving distribution coverage can take several months for a national launch (although it is immediate in a controlled test market). More importantly, if the model has an unnecessary parameter (q), it will over-fit, resulting in poor forecasting performance. So even if it is theoretically correct, the Bass model may be practically inadequate. Thus, it should be no surprise to find that the Bass model does not do a good job of forecasting first purchases for frequently bought categories (Hardie, Fader and Wisniewski, 1998). Instead, Wright and Stern (2006) and Hardie, Fader and Wisniewski (1998) found that exponential models fit these curves well. So, we have theoretical and empirical reasons to believe that word-of-mouth recommendation is either very low or crowded out by launch advertising in frequently bought categories.

There is a complication. As with the Bass model, the early data show considerable fluctuations, partly due to the effects of marketing actions such as distribution growth, advertising and promotions. This variation obscures the underlying process and can make it difficult to forecast the number of first/trial purchases achieved by the end of the year. One solution is to use controlled test markets, such as the BehaviorScan service, in which distribution is guaranteed, the populations are homogeneous and marketing influences are tightly controlled. However, even within these markets it takes 12 weeks of data *and* the inclusion of marketing-mix elements in the model to get accurate forecasts. Without marketing mix elements being included, a period of 20 weeks or more is needed for accurate forecasts (Fader, Hardie and Ziethammer, 2003).

After the First Purchase

For durable products, adoption and sales are measured by the simple act of a purchase. As noted earlier, the picture is not so clear for frequently bought items. The exponential models of cumulative first purchase do not confirm that trialists will adopt the new product, or tell us what the long-term purchase frequency will be.

We might expect buyers of these new products to make one or two trial purchases before choosing either to drop the new product or to include it in their repertoire. This is the traditional view in most consumer behaviour texts and is consistent with Rogers' theories on innovation diffusion, with exposure being followed by evaluation and then an adoption or rejection decision.

However, light buyers may only buy the category two or three times a year, so trial will continue for some time. It is hard to say when a light buyer will have completed evaluation their, or even whether such a question is meaningful. If somebody makes a low-involvement purchase of a brand once or twice a year, it is not clear that this involves much cognition or post-purchase evaluation. Conversely, early buyers are more likely to be heavy buyers; Taylor (1977) demonstrated this, Fourt and Woodlock (1960) made a similar assertion and Stern and Wright (2007) have confirmed it. These heavy buyers may complete trial purchases and evaluations quickly.

A further complication is that sales data include a mix of first and repeat purchases and so do not reveal whether a new product is establishing a base of loyal customers. Repeat purchases rates can be calculated with individual panel data. Yet these may still be misleading, as they combine heavy buyers, whose repeat purchase rate has settled down, with lighter buyers who may still be making evaluative purchases. So the overall repeat purchase figure will keep changing until light buyers have finished making evaluative purchases.

A popular solution to this problem was introduced by Eskin (1973). He recategorized purchase data for new products into depth-of-repeat classes. The depth of repeat indicated how many purchases of the new product had been made by each household. These could be trial purchases, first repeat purchase, second repeat purchase and so forth. For each purchase he recorded not just the depth-of-repeat class, but how long it had been since the previous purchase by that household. By modelling the transitions from one depth-of-repeat class to the next he could predict better the growth of sales over time. To avoid biased estimates, he removed the initial, evaluative purchase before estimating transitions. He was able to predict the final long-run level of repeat purchase – and thus sales – to be expected once the trial process was complete. There have been some major recent advances building on Eskin's (1973) approach that we will discuss shortly. First, however, we consider an alternative approach to understanding demand for these types of new product.

Near Instant Loyalty or Adoption-Rejection?

A competing approach can be found in the near-instant loyalty hypothesis of Ehrenberg and Goodhardt (2001). They found that, surprisingly, the long-term average purchase rates for a new brand are achieved almost instantaneously. In a study of 22 grocery product launches, they compared average purchase frequencies for new brands with those of the existing brands. In the first quarter, the new brands had an average purchase frequency of 1.4 – a little lower than established brands, which averaged 1.9. In subsequent quarters, the new brands showed purchase frequency of 1.8, 1.9 and 2.0, virtually identical with the established brands. Wright and Sharp (2001) found similar results for an Australian grocery product launch. This is inconsistent with the traditional idea that a trial purchase is followed by an adoption or rejection decision. How could such near-instant loyalty come about? One explanation is that new brands in low-involvement categories are immediately included in the consumer's repertoire. The trial curve may then just reflect distribution growth, the occasional nature of category purchases and the shuffling of category purchases around the consumer's repertoire.

The Alternative View

Yet contradictory evidence is emerging. An unpublished student project at Victoria University of Wellington, New Zealand, tracked monthly penetration for new products over three data sets (Seidler, 2006). Note that this is not the same as cumulative first purchase, as one purchaser can buy more than once in the year. There was a slight peak for monthly penetration at about six months, followed by a slight decline. This suggests at least some degree of genuine trial, rather than just near-instant loyalty, otherwise we would not expect the peak and decline in month-to-month penetration. Rather, once they started buying, consumers would keep it up at the same rate.

A further criticism of the near-instant loyalty hypothesis is that it is supported by evidence on *average* purchase frequency (the average volume of purchase in a single period) rather than *repeat* purchase frequency (the proportion purchasing in consecutive periods). Repeat purchase is a more direct measure of loyalty. There is little evidence on patterns in repeat purchase frequency for new products. However, when Ehrenberg and Goodhardt (1968) did analyse repeat purchase rates for a new brand, they found them well below the levels expected from the NBD model.

A final – and very important – piece of evidence against the near-instant loyalty hypothesis comes from Fader, Hardie and Huang (2004). They took a standard trial-repeat model and allowed a consumer's mean buying rate to be revised after experiencing the new product. This is a weak form of the adoption-rejection approach; it allows experience to affect future purchases without requiring a complete adoption or rejection. The result was extremely accurate forecasting performance for the data set that they examined. This suggests that their assumptions – that purchase rates are revised following experience – are reasonable ones to make, although replication across other data sets would give more confidence in their findings. Fader, Hardie and Huang (2004) did not use the traditional criterion of adoption or rejection. Their model simply allowed the mean purchase rate to get a little higher or lower with experience.

So is there near-instant loyalty? The evidence is mixed. There seems to be post-purchase evaluation involving revision of the consumer's purchase rate, rather than a complete adoption or rejection. For the most accurate forecasts, particularly when a substantial launch budget is involved, it is worth using Fader, Hardie and Huang's (2004) model to predict take-up in low-value frequently bought categories.

SUMMARY

Markets undergo sales change for many reasons. At a basic level, the time of year, holidays, sales promotions and other events have a temporary effect. At a more sophisticated level, a dynamic equilibrium

(Continued)

underlies stable markets and change will result from disturbances to this equilibrium. However, the effects may be small, with growth likely to occur in small increments over several years. Changes often occur slowly due to the low rate of erosion or switching and the long inter-purchase times of occasional buyers.

The launch of new products is a major source of more rapid and enduring change. Sociology helps us to understand the underlying forces, while models such as the technology substitution model and the Bass model provide tools for analysing and forecasting new product adoption. Social forces may be different for low-value, frequently bought items. We can capture the first purchase process in these markets with exponential models (which assume little social influence). For repeat purchase, the analysis is a little more complicated, due to early trial by heavy buyers, the large number of light buyers and the unclear role of evaluative purchases. One approach is to undertake depth-of-repeat modelling. Another is to assume near-instant loyalty. The most sophisticated is to use statistical models that allow purchase rates to be revised after experience with the new product.

In studying or managing markets, you need to know what to expect. From this chapter, we hope you have developed a good understanding of how the sales of brands change and thus of how changes in market volume, adjustments to market share and the introduction of new brands or products will play out over time.

Additional Resources

The classic text on the diffusion of innovations is Rogers (2003); it gives a good review of the diffusion literature and offers many interesting examples, although it has little on alternative models. For an appreciation of the technological substitution model, go straight to Fisher and Pry (1971), which remains readable and interesting and has a number of case studies. The Bass modelling literature is not so accessible, but Mahajan, Muller and Bass (1990) provide a comprehensive overview that is accessible to a wider audience. Finally, if you wish to know more about new product development, there are many excellent textbooks in the area, such as Crawford and Di Benedetto (2006).

Notes

1   The term *churn* is widely used in industry but, if the defection and recruitment rates are different for a brand, what is the churn? We prefer to use 'churn' to describe the average replacement rate in a category. Average defection and acquisition will be the same across the category if it is stationary.

2   A logistic function is a function of logits, or log-odds ratios. Odds ratios are simply the ratio of possible outcomes. If a football team is expected to win 80 per cent of the time, the odds of victory are 8:2 (or 4:1), and the natural logarithm of this is ln (4), which is 1.39. The logit is widely used in some other types of market modelling, such as the multinomial logit choice model.

Part 3
Explaining Decision-making

6 Predicting And Explaining Behaviour

LEARNING OBJECTIVES

When you have completed this chapter, you should be able to:

1 Define attitude, belief and intention, and explain how these concepts are measured.
2 Understand the expected-value theory of attitude applied to products.
3 Report on the research linking attitude and intention to behaviour.
4 Describe the theory of planned behaviour, its applications, strengths and weaknesses.
5 Understand the problems of predicting behaviour from attitude.

OVERVIEW

The cognitive approach to consumer behaviour has relied on understanding consumers' attitudes, beliefs and intentions in order to explain their behaviour. Here, researchers have applied models developed in social psychology to consumer decision-making. Among these models, the theory of planned behaviour has been most successful, although a number of problems with this theory have yet to be resolved. We first examine the nature and measurement of attitudes, beliefs and intentions and their relationship with behaviour, and then we explain how the theory of planned behaviour can be used to predict and explain behaviour. This has a clear relevance to marketing: we need to predict purchase and to understand why people prefer one brand to another if we are to create products in the right quantity and of the right quality.

SECTION 1: DEFINITIONS AND MEASUREMENTS

Attitudes are what we feel about a *concept*, which may be a brand, category, person, theory or any other entity about which we can think and to which we can attach feeling. An important class of concepts are *actions*, particularly commercially relevant behaviour such as buying, renting, using, betting and steal-ing. We focus on attitudes to such actions because these attitudes help us to predict such behaviour. Thus, it is the attitude to *playing* the National Lottery or *buying* a mobile phone that most concerns us. The attitude to the object (the National Lottery or the mobile phone as a product) is less directly related to the action.

A person's attitude may be inferred from his or her actions or measured using a systematic questioning procedure. According to the mental representations model, introduced in Chapter 3, a concept is a node linked to other nodes. The linkages to other nodes can be seen as beliefs about the central concept. When the concept is an action, the beliefs often concern the outcomes of the action. If I play the National Lottery, there are outcomes such as dreaming of untold wealth, being excited by the draw and, usually, being disappointed by the result. Such beliefs have an outcome likelihood (or belief strength) and an evaluation which can be measured by the scales below:

If I play the National Lottery I will be excited by the draw

unlikely −3 | −2 | −1 | 0 | 1 | 2 |3 likely

extremely   quite   slightly neither slightly quite   extremely

Being excited by the draw is:

bad   −3 | −2 | −1 | 0 | 1 | 2 |3 good

extremely   quite   slightly neither slightly quite   extremely

These seven-point measures are often called semantic differential scales and were developed in early work on the measurement of meaning by Osgood, Suci and Tannenbaum (1957). We may use more than one scale to cover those situations where people have mixed feelings towards an action. Often people are ambiva-lent when an action carries quite different short-term and long-term implications. For example, many smokers would say that giving up cigarettes is both good *and* unpleasant and for this reason we would use both bad–good and unpleasant–pleasant scales to measure this attitude.

We usually denote the likelihood measure as b (for belief) and the evaluation measure as e. The full outcome measure is the product of b and e, which we call the *expected value* of the outcome. An expected value can be negative as well as positive because the evaluation can be negative.

The Expected-value Theory of Attitude

Most of the alternatives from which we choose are *multi-attribute*. To assess the value of going to Wales for a holiday I have to take account of weather, cost, travelling effort, food, opportunities for recreation, etc. Using the method above, we can measure an expected value for each outcome and my overall (or global) attitude to going to Wales for a holiday should be given by the sum of the expected values. So, if A is the global attitude:

$$A = b_1e_1 + b_2e_2 + b_3e_3 + \dots$$

or $\quad A = \Sigma b_ie_i$

Rosenberg (1956) pioneered this approach in attitude theory and Fishbein (1963) tested the relationship by separately measuring the global attitude, A, and the sum value, Σb_ie_i, using a sample of 50 people. If A is related to Σb_ie_i, then subjects with high scores on one measure will have high scores on the other; similarly, low scores on one measure should be matched by low scores on the other. Thus, by correlating respondents' scores on the two measures, we can find out how much A is related to Σb_ie_i. Fishbein found that the correlation between the sum score and the global measure was 0.80, which gave strong support to the idea that global attitudes are based on the sum of the expected values of the attributes. Fishbein's expected-value treatment of attitude has been supported in a large number of published studies though the correlations are generally lower than 0.8 (typically, in the range 0.4 to 0.6).

Fishbein's treatment of attitude assumes a process of compensation: for example, that the unspoilt beaches of Wales can offset the frequently wet weather. At best, compensation is likely to be partial. Just taking account of the main outcome of one alternative requires some thought and when several outcomes are involved the assessment is obviously more complicated. As noted in Chapter 1, extended thought before choice is a rarity but we probably consider more attributes when important decisions are taken. When a person has a choice of several options we expect him or her to take the one with the largest expected value. Edwards (1954) described this as the subjective expected utility (SEU) model of decision. This way of thinking about decisions treats any product as a bundle of expected gains and losses.

Box 6.1	Conjoint analysis and choice modelling

There is another type of utility measurement that is famous in marketing: conjoint analysis and choice modelling. These methods present respondents with a carefully designed range of alternatives and obtain ratings, rankings or choices from respondents for these alternatives. Statistical procedures are then used to infer the utility of each feature in the choices being tested. This can provide good predictions of the attractiveness of different options. Conjoint analysis is widely used in product and service design, and is supported by a large literature. For an introduction to the field that does not assume much prior knowledge, see the textbook by Hensher, Rose and Green (2005).

Modal Salient Beliefs

Fishbein's theory of attitude is about what *individuals* think and feel, but it has to be tested on *groups* of people and each member of the group may have a somewhat different basis for their attitude. To take account of this, some studies have asked each person separately about the attributes that he or she thought were important, e.g. Budd (1986) on cigarette use and Elliott and Jobber (1990) on company use of market research. This raises the association between global and sum measures but the procedure is laborious. Fortunately, on many issues there is substantial agreement between people on the factors that are important and the same questionnaire can be used on all respondents with only a modest loss of precision.

   To establish the commonly held beliefs about a concept it is necessary to perform an *elicitation,* which is described in Exercise 6.1. This is a series of questions about the positive and negative associations of the concept which are put to members of the target group. The beliefs that come easily to mind are recorded and those that occur frequently in a group, called *modal salient beliefs,* are used for the questionnaire. In an elicitation, the questioning should be low pressure. Fishbein and Ajzen (1975) ('Ajzen' is pronounced 'Eye-zen') argue that beliefs which have to be dredged up from the recesses of the mind are unlikely to have much effect on behaviour. Exercise 6.1 anticipates developments later in the chapter so that the elicitation covers not only the gains and losses of a prospective action, but also the influence of other people and the personal and environmental factors that make the action easier or more difficult to perform.

EXERCISE 6.1   ELICITING SALIENT BELIEFS

1 **Define the action clearly.** For example, 'buying Snickers', 'getting a new computer', 'giving blood when the blood transfusion service comes to the campus'.

2 **Define clearly the target group.** For example, you might be particularly interested in children buying Snickers, or women wine buyers.

3 **Elicit salient beliefs.** In a sample of people from the target group, ask each person questions about the advantages and disadvantages of the defined action. After each response prompt with: 'anything else?' but do not press hard for ideas. Record the responses for each person. A typical encounter might be:

Q.   Can you tell me what you think are the advantages of getting a new computer?
A.   You get a lot for your money now.
Q.   Anything else?
A.   Probably more reliable.

Q.   Anything else?

A.   Not really.

Q.   Can you tell me what are the disadvantages of getting a new computer?

A.   It will have to be set up with the right programs.

Q.   Anything else?

A.   I'll have to get used to a different operating system.

Q.   Is there anything else that you think of about getting a new computer?

A.   No.

4   **The negative action.** Certain actions may have different salient beliefs associated with *not* doing the action. For example, 'not having children' and 'not taking drugs' may be seen as actions with their own rationale and are not just the opposites to having children and taking drugs. When this is likely it is wise to elicit salient beliefs about the negative action.

5   **Salient referents.** Ask each respondent in the sample whether there are people or groups who think that the respondent should do the defined action. Repeat with 'should not'. Ask if there are other people or organizations that come to mind when they think of the action. Use the prompt 'anyone else?' but do not press for responses.

6   **Control factors.** Ask each respondent about conditions that make the action easier or harder to perform. Again, prompt with 'anything else?' In the case of a new computer there may be problems of transferring files or the unsuitability of software on new systems.

7   **Refine the list of beliefs.** Combine similar beliefs. Compile a list of modal salient beliefs using the ones most frequently mentioned. The decision to include a belief depends on the frequency with which it is mentioned and the time and money available to support the research. When the questionnaire is intended to be used *both before and after* exposure to advertising or the product, it is important to include beliefs that may *become* salient as a result of this exposure.

8   You can use the computer program NEWACT to make up a questionnaire according to the methods of planned behaviour theory which is explained later.

After similar responses have been grouped together, the list of modal salient beliefs is usually quite short. Complex issues, such as getting married or using oral contraceptives, may have ten or more salient beliefs relating to attitude; simpler issues, such as buying chocolate, may have rather fewer.

Do Attitudes Predict Action?

Our interest in attitudes is partly based on the belief that they predict behaviour. Following Allport (1935), an attitude is usually seen as 'a preparation or readiness for response' and thus should be a predictor of behaviour, except when freedom of action is restricted. Correctly measured, attitudes do predict behaviour though the connection is sometimes weaker than expected. However, when Wicker (1969: 65) reviewed 47 studies on this matter, he concluded that: 'It is considerably more likely that attitudes will be unrelated or only slightly related to overt behaviors than that attitudes will be closely related to actions'.

Schuman and Johnson (1976) suggested that other unreported variables affected behaviour in addition to attitude. This was supported in work by Fishbein and Ajzen (1975), Ajzen and Fishbein (1980) and Ajzen (1985, 1991). As we explain later, these researchers showed that, in addition to attitude, behaviour is controlled by beliefs about the wishes of important persons and groups and by beliefs about the way personal ability and the environment can affect behaviour.

In addition to the 'other variables' explanation for poor prediction of behaviour, Ajzen and Fishbein (1977) pointed out that researchers frequently measured the wrong attitude. As we have explained, the correct attitude for predicting behaviour is the attitude to that behaviour. Fishbein and Ajzen (1975: 360) concluded that 'many of the studies that have been viewed as testing the relation between attitude and behavior are actually of little relevance to that question'. Thus, if you want to predict quitting smoking, it is the attitude to quitting smoking not the attitude to cigarettes, or even smoking, that should be measured. This lack of compatibility between the attitude and behaviour measures is neatly demonstrated by an unpublished study conducted on 270 women by Jaccard, King and Pomazal (reported by Ajzen and Fishbein, 1977). In this work, three attitudes relating to birth control were measured and correlated with the use of birth control. As the attitude comes closer to the specification of the behaviour, the correlation rises (see Table 6.1).

Table 6.1   Correlations are greater when measures of attitude and behaviour are more compatible (Ajzen and Fishbein, 1977)

Attitude to ...	Correlation with use of the birth control pill
birth control	0.16
the birth control pill	0.34
using the birth control pill	0.65

This effect is readily explicable if we think of the motivations of different women. For example, a woman who wanted to become pregnant would neither use the pill nor be positive in her attitude to using it (giving a high correlation), but she might still be positive about the pill and birth control in general (giving a low correlation with her non-usage of the pill). Similar results were obtained in another study of the correlations between attitudes to 'religion', 'church', 'attending church this Sunday' and actual church attendance.

Another example of using the wrong attitude takes the form of trying to predict what people *will* do from measures of *past* satisfaction. As we saw in Chapter 2, satisfaction is an indifferent predictor of future behaviour and this is partly because people can be positive about their past experience with a product without necessarily wanting to use it in the future. Needs change and sometimes products change so that what was satisfactory in the past may not be satisfactory in the future. A somewhat better prediction of retention would be obtained by using the attitude to buying the product again.

Specifying Measures

The more compatible the measures of attitude and behaviour, the more they will correlate. Compatibility is specified by Target, Action, Context and Time (think TACT). In the case of oral contraceptive use, the target is the oral contraceptive, the action is using it and the context/time is implicit in its use. In other cases, the context or time could be more important. For example, shopping in my local supermarket on a Saturday morning might be avoided because the local store is so busy at that time. In addition to the TACT variables, it is important to ensure that respondents are talking about their own attitudes and behaviour rather than some general idea. Ajzen and Fishbein (1977) applied these compatibility criteria in a meta-analysis of 142 attitude–behaviour associations. They sorted the studies into those with low, partial and high compatibility between the measures and sub-divided the last group because some measures were not clearly specified. Table 6.2 shows their findings. It is clear that compatibility criteria explain why many previous studies showed a weak connection between attitude and behaviour.

Table 6.2   Analysis of attitude–behaviour studies (adapted from Ajzen and Fishbein, 1977)

Compatibility	Significance of attitude–behaviour relationship		
	Nil	Low	High
Low	26	1	0
Partial	20	47	4
High–questionable measures	0	9	9
High–appropriate measures	0	0	26

One problem occurs when attitudes embrace a *set* of behaviours rather than one specific behaviour (Ajzen and Fishbein, 1977). For example, a measure of a person's attitude to the environment might give a rather low prediction of their bottle recycling behaviour because specific factors may affect the decision to recycle bottles. If a multiple-act measure of environmental behaviour is constructed that also includes use of recycled paper, use of low-energy bulbs, installing insulation, recycling of metals and newsprint, donations to environmental groups, refusal to buy tropical hardwoods, boycotting the products of environmentally suspect firms, chiding women in fur coats, etc., we would expect this measure to have a stronger correlation with the attitude to the environment. This is because the specific factors affecting each action tend to cancel each other out in the combined measure leaving the common theme of helping the environment. Consistent with this, Weigel and Newman (1976) found that the attitude to environmental preservation correlated better with a multiple-act measure of environmentally concerned behaviour than with single measures.

In consumer research, the compatibility principle means that attitudes to the *purchase*, *hiring*, and so on of the product must be measured if it is these actions that we want to predict. This simple lesson about using compatible measures has not been well learned. Usually attitudes to the brand are studied rather than attitudes to purchasing the brand. Often there is substantial overlap between these measures but, as Ajzen and Fishbein show (1980: ch. 13), this is not always so. Many of the studies reviewed by Wicker (1969) used incompatible measures, thus explaining the low association that he found between attitude and behaviour. The notion of compatibility has given us a major methodological advance in attitude research.

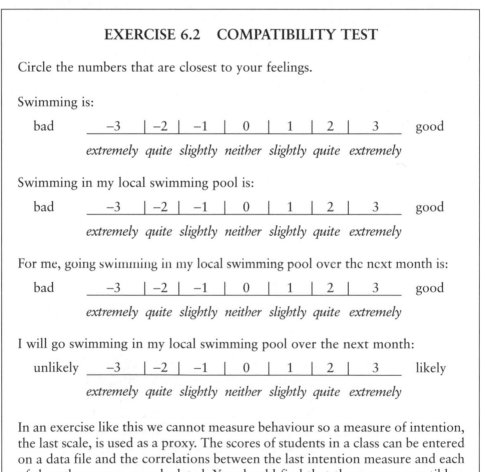

EXERCISE 6.2   COMPATIBILITY TEST

Circle the numbers that are closest to your feelings.

Swimming is:

    bad   −3 | −2 | −1 | 0 | 1 | 2 | 3   good

                 extremely quite slightly neither slightly quite extremely

Swimming in my local swimming pool is:

    bad   −3 | −2 | −1 | 0 | 1 | 2 | 3   good

                 extremely quite slightly neither slightly quite extremely

For me, going swimming in my local swimming pool over the next month is:

    bad   −3 | −2 | −1 | 0 | 1 | 2 | 3   good

                 extremely quite slightly neither slightly quite extremely

I will go swimming in my local swimming pool over the next month:

    unlikely   −3 | −2 | −1 | 0 | 1 | 2 | 3   likely

                 extremely quite slightly neither slightly quite extremely

In an exercise like this we cannot measure behaviour so a measure of intention, the last scale, is used as a proxy. The scores of students in a class can be entered on a data file and the correlations between the last intention measure and each of the other measures calculated. You should find that the more compatible a concept is with the intention measure, the higher the correlation between the measures.

Purchase Intentions

Intentions may predict behaviour but do not tell us why the behaviour is undertaken. In marketing, prediction may sometimes be all that is needed. Purchase behaviour may be predicted either from stated intention or from a person's estimate of their purchase probability. Work on purchase prediction goes back to research by Katona (1947) and Ferber (1954), who investigated consumers' 'purchase plans'.

Measures of intention have been well tested in the field of consumer durable purchase. Pickering and Isherwood (1974) found that 61 per cent of those who said they were 100 per cent likely to purchase actually did so; this compares with the 5 per cent of respondents who made a purchase even though they had expressed no intention to purchase the durable in the next 12 months. These findings were close to those obtained by Gabor and Granger (1972) in a similar study.

Since intention-to-buy measurements can discriminate quite well between prospective buyers and nonbuyers it is possible to compare prospective purchasers and non-purchasers in the same way that users and non-users are compared. This suggests that market research may be used to predict those consumers who will buy before they have actually done so and, also, by using additional questions, to find out why they are going to buy. Such research could be used for refining the product specification.

There are two reasons for discrepancies between predicted and actual purchase: first, the true probability of purchase may be inaccurately measured by the scale point checked and, second, people may change their intention or be unable to fulfil it (Bemmaor, 1995). The second inaccuracy is difficult to avoid but the first type of discrepancy is reduced by improved scaling. Juster (1966) used an 11-point, verbally referenced scale to measure the likelihood of purchase (see Box 6.2). In a review of intention measurement Day et al. (1991) argue that the best results are obtained using a Juster Scale and Wright and MacRae (2007) show that predicted purchase proportions obtained using the Juster scale were unbiased estimates of the actual purchase proportions found from panel data or purchase recall.

Box 6.2	The Juster scale

This is an 11-point scale with verbal descriptions and probabilities associated with each number:

10	Certain, practically certain	(99 in 100)
9	Almost sure	(9 in 10)
8	Very probable	(8 in 10)
7	Probable	(7 in 10)

(Continued)

6	Good possibility	(6 in 10)
5	Fairly good possibility	(5 in 10)
4	Fair possibility	(4 in 10)
3	Some possibility	(3 in 10)
2	Slight possibility	(2 in 10)
1	Very slight possibility	(1 in 10)
0	No chance, almost no chance	(1 in 100)

Intention measures are used in the planned behaviour research reported next. In this field, the seven-point semantic differential scale has usually been used, either as a direct measure of intention or as a self-prediction by the respondent that he or she will perform some behaviour. Often, there is little difference between the two measures but self-prediction seems likely to be more accurate because it may take more account of conditions that may prevent action. For example, people may intend to give up cigarettes but be more realistic if asked to estimate the likelihood that they actually will give up. However, Sheppard, Hartwick and Warshaw (1988) reviewed a large number of attitude–behaviour studies and found only marginal superiority for self-prediction over true intention measures.

Normally, with durable goods like cars, a large majority of people express no intention of buying in the next year so that even a small percentage of this group who do buy provides a large fraction of the total number of buyers. Pickering and Isherwood (1974) found that 55 per cent of all buyers came from the group expressing no intention to buy. Theil and Kosobud (1968) in the USA, and Gabor and Granger (1972) in Britain, found that 70 and 65 per cent of purchasers respectively were in the group stating a zero purchase probability.

The extent to which people fulfil their intentions has been reviewed by McQuarrie (1988), who assembled data from 13 studies. McQuarrie found that those who intended to purchase did so, on average, 42 per cent of the time whereas those not intending to purchase did not purchase 88 per cent of the time; this asymmetry is probably related to the fact that it is easier not to do something than to do it (see Box 6.3).

Box 6.3	**Reasons for inaction**

Why don't people do what they intend? One study found only two-thirds of those intending to apply for shares in British Government privatizations actually did so. When the other third were asked why they hadn't followed through on their intention, they were equally divided between changing their mind, for example because the investment looked less advantageous and inertia, such as simply forgetting or finding that, when the time came, they could not be bothered (East, 1993).

Another study investigated failure to follow through an intention to buy a consumer durable. In this case respondents had usually changed their mind due to unforeseen circumstances, such as lack of money, or because their current durable was lasting better than expected (Pickering, 1975).

Discrepancies between attitude and behaviour may also increase with the period that elapses between attitude measurement and behaviour measurement. The longer the period, the more opportunity people have to change their minds in response to new information or changed circumstances. For example, the attitude to voting for a political party may be affected by political events and a measure of voting attitude taken close to an election should have more predictive value than one taken years before. However, although this effect of time lapse seems common sense, a study by Randall and Wolff (1994) found no evidence that the length of the interval was related to the correlation between intention and behaviour.

One study has raised some concern about the prediction of behaviour from intention. Chandon, Morwitz and Reinartz (2005) found that correlations in surveys between intention and subsequent behaviour are artificially increased by the process of asking about the respondent's intentions. The research process affects the respondents so that they increase the consistency between what they say and what they do.

SECTION 2: THE THEORY OF PLANNED BEHAVIOUR

Attitudes, intentions and behaviour have been combined in a comprehensive model of consumer choice called the theory of planned behaviour. Figure 6.1 illustrates this theory and Figure 6.2 shows it applied to playing the National Lottery.

The theory of planned behaviour (TPB) was developed over a long period, starting with Fishbein's (1963) expected-value theory of attitude. This theory was extended in a number of studies to predict intention and behaviour (e.g. Ajzen and Fishbein, 1969; Ajzen, 1971; Ajzen and Fishbein, 1972). In addition to attitude (A_B), the authors included subjective norm (SN) as a determinant of intention. SN measures an agent's beliefs about what other important persons think the agent should do. The most complete account of this work appeared in *Belief, Attitude, Intention and Behavior* (Fishbein and Ajzen, 1975). This extended model was renamed the theory of reasoned action by Ajzen and

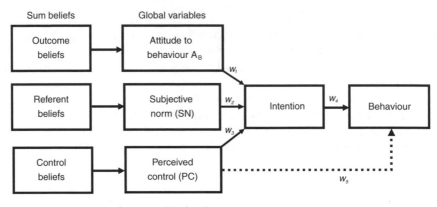

Figure 6.1   The theory of planned behaviour

Fishbein (1980) in a book in which they applied the theory to practical concerns such as health, consumer behaviour and voting. In 1985, Ajzen perceived control (PC) introduced the theory of planned behaviour (TPB) by adding as a determinant of intention, and slightly modified this theory in 1991. PC measures an agent's beliefs about the opportunities for an action which are based on the environment and the agent's abilities. The relative strengths of A_B, SN and PC in determining an action are given by the weights w_1, w_2, and w_3. Since these weights vary from category to category, they are established empirically, using regression or structural equation modelling.

From one point of view the inclusion of PC in the TPB lacks logical support. If, for example, someone was only 50 per cent sure that they could do something, then all likelihoods and hence payoffs should be halved, thus covering this uncertainty in the measurement of outcomes. This reasoning probably delayed the development of the TPB. However, the ultimate test is empirical and, often, there is little relationship between PC and either A_B or SN. On this basis, PC has earned its place in the theory.

As can be seen from Figure 6.1, the three global variables determine intention, which then determines behaviour. The weight w_4 reflects the fact the circumstances may stop people from realizing their intentions, or that their intentions could change. Finally, the model includes a second direct effect of perceived control on behaviour, with weight w_5. This covers behaviours such as giving up smoking and eating less where lack of personal control can undermine intention.

This theory covers altruistic behaviour, which can be driven by the subjective norm, and it takes account of the way people are more or less likely to do things, depending on their self-assessed abilities and opportunities. As such, it is an advance on simple subjective expected utility (SEU) models that do not allow for such influences. The subjective norm is an internalized influence, exerting its effect through the agent's memories. Therefore, the people and groups that are recalled need not be present, or even exist, for them to have an effect. Among other behaviour, the TPB has been applied to: taking exercise, attaining grades, condom use, health self-examinations, escaping addiction, blood donation,

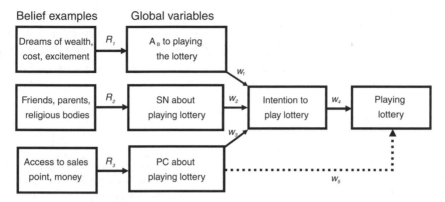

Figure 6.2   The theory of planned behaviour applied to playing the National Lottery

mother's diet management of their babies, food choice, recycling, buying environmentally friendly products, Internet use, reducing risky driving, accident avoidance, seeking funding, buying gifts, applying for shares in initial public offerings and complaining. It is suitable for any behaviour where there are reasons for action but it is more appropriate for explaining category use than brand use if there is little difference between brands. Armitage and Connor (2001) review the behaviours to which the TPB has been applied.

Many studies predict intention and do not measure behaviour, so it is important to know how strong is the link (w_4) between intention and behaviour. One study illustrates this. Conner et al. (2007) measured intention and actual behaviour with regard to breaking speed limits using an extended model of planned behaviour. The model predicted 82 per cent of intention but only 17 per cent of actual behaviour was predicted. A review of 185 studies by Armitage and Conner (2001) found that 39 per cent of intention was predicted and 21 per cent of objectively measured behaviour. However, these figures may have been inflated by the effect of prior questioning, as indicated by Chandon, Morwitz and Reinartz (2005). In marketing, we are concerned with behaviour since this is where money is made and the relatively modest link between intention and behaviour is a matter of concern.

Using the Theory of Planned Behaviour

Different sorts of explanation can be drawn from the TPB, depending on the measures considered.

Level 1: Behaviour

The immediate precursors of behaviour in the TPB are intention and perceived control, so one form of explanation concerns the relative impact of these two factors. This has been examined by Madden, Ellen and Ajzen (1992). Usually, perceived behavioural control is the weaker factor and may have no direct impact on behaviour. As noted above, PC directly affects behaviour when people try to achieve a goal over which they have limited control, such as giving up cigarettes or controlling diet, but this has limited relevance to consumer behaviour.

Level 2: Intention

The next level of explanation is the relative importance of A_B, SN and PC in predicting intention. This varies from application to application. For example, Jaccard and Davidson (1972) found that, among college women, the use of the contraceptive pill was associated more with A_B than with SN; this probably reflected the importance of avoiding pregnancy for this group. Davidson and Jaccard (1975) found that married women with children placed somewhat more emphasis on the normative component.

Box 6.4	**An application to giving up cigarettes**

In 1978, the UK Joint Committee on Research into Smoking recommended that a new study should be undertaken on attitudes towards smoking. One stimulus to this work was a 1977 report on attitudes and smoking behaviour prepared by Fishbein for the US Federal Trade Commission. This recommended a shift of focus from 'attitudes to smoking' to 'attitudes to giving up cigarettes'. The new study was conducted by the Office of Population Censuses and Surveys by Marsh and Matheson. This was published by the government in 1983 but the main features appear in work by Sutton, Marsh, Matheson (1990). The research measured A_B and confidence in being able to stop smoking, which was a form of PC measurement, but it did not measure SN. This work provided one of the most substantial tests ever given to a theory in social psychology.

The researchers predicted behaviour on the basis of the difference between the expected values of stopping and continuing to smoke. It is this difference that shows the personal gain or loss of taking one option rather than the other. The research showed that the majority of smokers accepted that smoking caused lung cancer (73 per cent) and heart disease (59 per cent), but the study showed that most of these people believed either that they did not smoke enough to do any damage or that any damage was already done and was irreversible. For such people, cessation held little promise of reduced risk. The only smokers who saw a benefit from stopping were the minority who believed both that they had an enhanced risk and that cessation would diminish this risk. The researchers predicted that these people would make more attempts to stop and this was confirmed when smokers were followed up six months later. This evidence therefore supports a causal process from attitude to action.

This research showed where to place emphasis in health education in order to get people to try to quit; for example, by explaining that the risk from cigarettes is related to the number smoked, that there is no threshold at which health hazards begin and that there are health benefits for nearly all people who stop smoking. The study also showed that eventual success in quitting was strongly dependent on confidence and that health education should therefore emphasize 'how to stop' methods which would build this confidence.

One interesting finding from a study conducted at Kingston University (East, Whittaker and Smith, 1984) was that the dominant reason given for taking exercise among students was the social contacts that it brought, not health and fitness, as might be supposed by health educators. This clearly has relevance to how the exercise facilities might be publicized. A number of applications of planned behaviour theory have related to consumer matters. East (1993) studied the applications for shares in privatizations. It might be predicted that the application for shares would be determined largely by the expected financial outcomes and therefore by A_B. However, in East's study, access to finance, a PC factor, was a major determinant of intention. This suggests that business people should not become too focused on the good value of an offering. Interest will often be constrained by finance or other control factors.

Level 3: Specific Factor Explanations

The third level of explanation relates specific outcome, referent and control beliefs to intention or behaviour. In the theory, specific beliefs relate to intention through the appropriate global variable but it is not always clear which global variable a factor belongs to when an investigation is being conducted. For example, embarrassment about complaining might be seen as an outcome or as a control factor. East (2000) found that embarrassment acted primarily as a control factor, obstructing complaining, rather than as a cost if complaint was made. This problem can be avoided by correlating beliefs directly with intention. Level 3 explanations help us to choose intervention strategies. For example, if a firm wants to encourage customers to express their grievances, the key factors affecting complaining must be addressed. If many people lack confidence about complaining, it is best to provide a clear procedure and to draw attention to this procedure in company literature and on receipts.

EXERCISE 6.3   RESEARCH USING PLANNED BEHAVIOUR THEORY

1   Choose an action that is individually performed and voluntary, e.g. watching a popular TV programme, using second-class post, carrying an organ donor card, installing solar water heating, going to the dentist regularly or playing the National Lottery. Make sure that the action is appropriately specified in terms of target, action, context and time.

2   Choose the target group.

3   From a sample of the target group elicit the salient outcome, referent and control beliefs about the action, using Exercise 6.1. Ideally, about 20 people should be used. Reduce the salient beliefs by merging similar ones and dropping those that appear rare.

4   Use the NEWACT program to create a planned behaviour questionnaire. The program asks for:

   - the title of the questionnaire,
   - the intention,
   - the outcome beliefs,
   - the referent beliefs,
   - the control beliefs.

The program sets up the different scales for each item and works out the form of some of the items by parsing your input. Mistakes and poor grammar in the questionnaire need to be eliminated by word processing. Often the phraseology for control items is clumsy and needs adjustment. Some items are added automatically but these may be deleted if not required. The questionnaire will usually cover two sides of paper when printed in two-column landscape format. The questionnaire looks better if scale referents such as 'extremely', 'quite' and 'slightly' are italicized. The scaling is designed for a proportional font such as Times Roman.

5   Gather data from 50+ respondents.

6   Analyse the data.

Use the COMPUTE function in SPSS to:

a)   Create products between outcome probability and outcome evaluation (and the corresponding products for the referent and control beliefs) (see later comment, Multiplying Ordinal Measures).
b)   Produce sum measures by aggregating products for the outcome, referent and control items.
c)   Aggregate measures for the global variables and intention when more than one scale is used. (A reliability test may be appropriate here to check that each scale is measuring the same variable.)

Then:

d) Test the correlations between sum and global measures (Spearman is appropriate).

e) Perform a structural equation analysis or regression analysis to test the theory and establish the relative weights of A_B, SN and PC in the prediction of intention. (If you use regression, ordinal regression is appropriate.)

7 Examine your analysis and answer the following questions:

- Is intention most related to A_B, SN or PC?
- Do the sum measures correlate with the corresponding global measure better than with the other two global measures?
- Which belief factors correlate most with intention?
- Which belief factors might be used to improve the product's design or positioning, if any?
- What are the shortcomings of this study and analysis?

Applying Evidence from Planned Behaviour Research

When the findings from planned behaviour research are used to influence others, the influence attempt may not succeed for a number of reasons. First, correlations do not mean that there is a causal relationship. Second, beliefs may be strongly anchored and resist change, or may not change because of the ceiling effect (no room for change). Third, the influence attempt may be interpreted in an unexpected way that does not bring about the intended change. Fishbein and Ajzen (1981) have stated that studies of the existing basis for action give only an indication of where to place emphasis in an influence attempt and argue that it is impossible to tell in advance how much a given item of information will influence a person's intention and behaviour. Even so, planned behaviour research suggests what may be important in decisions on product development, positioning and advertising themes. Usually ads can say little in the time available and evidence on what principally drives purchasers to buy a category is very useful for positioning a brand.

SECTION 3: ISSUES ASSOCIATED WITH THE THEORY OF PLANNED BEHAVIOUR

Multiplying Ordinal Measures

When measures were introduced at the beginning of this chapter, a bipolar scales (-3 to $+3$) rather than unipolar scales (1 to 7) were shown for the measurement of both likelihood evaluation. Although bipolar scales are normally used for evaluation, there is less agreement on the appropriate scaling for outcome likeli-hood and for the measures relating to referent and control beliefs. When products are derived from two measures such as outcome likelihood and evaluation and correlated with the global variable, the correlation varies, depending on which scale is used. As Bagozzi (1984) and others have explained, for the product terms we are using ordinal measurement instead of ratio-scale measurement and we do not know what conversion of the ordinal measure should be used to approximate to the ratio-scale measure. Ajzen (1991) recommends *optimal scaling*, i.e. adding a constant to each scale to produce the highest correlation between the sum and global variables. This procedure gives some benefit to random effects and there is no specific justification for taking the scaling that gives the best correlation. An alternative method is to use the four combinations or 1–7 and −3 to +3 and to see whether the results vary much. If similar results are obtained, whatever the scaling, there is more assurance about the results. The NEWACT program numbers all the scales 1 to 7 but the scales can be recoded in SPSS.

How are Salient Beliefs Best Established?

The methods for eliciting and selecting modal salient beliefs, shown in Exercise 6.1, are *ad hoc* and there is some interest in finding alternative methods. (However, any vagueness in the measurement counts against the theory in empirical test; if the theory works using these methods, the problems cannot be too great.)

Differences in salience have been illustrated by Kristiansen (1987), who showed that smokers and non-smokers have different beliefs. Similarly, Petkova, Ajzen and Driver (1995) found that the salient beliefs of those who were pro-choice on abortion differed from those who described themselves as pro-life. Generally, users have more salient beliefs than non-users and this complicates any comparison between them.

One approach has been to link salience with accessibility. Ajzen, Nichols and Driver (1995) measured accessibility by delay in response and found that beliefs that were more quickly elicited gave higher correlations with global variables.

From a practical standpoint it is necessary to set a criterion of exclusion when choosing salient beliefs in planned behaviour research. Non-salient items waste time and take space in the questionnaire, and they weaken correlations with global variables. Excluding these beliefs from the questionnaire is usually done on the basis of their frequency of elicitation but this may not be a full test of salience. Non-salient beliefs may also be excluded at the analysis stage; this pro-cedure is open to the charge of capitalizing on chance but any such effect seems slight. An unpublished study of playing the National Lottery included outcomes on becoming dependent on gambling, having social problems as a result of major winnings and being disappointed at losing. These items were generated in the elicitation but none of them was significantly related to either A_B or intention and, when they were excluded, the correlation between $\Sigma b_i e_i$ and A_B increased.

The Principle of Sufficiency

The TPB rests on beliefs. Therefore, any change in global variables, intention or behaviour must come about through the acquisition of new beliefs or the modification of existing beliefs. In other words, belief changes are a *sufficient* explanation for 'downstream' changes. Ajzen and Fishbein (1980) accept that variables *external* to the theory, such as past experience, personality, age, sex, and other social classifications will be associated with behaviour but they argue that this occurs only because these variables are related to relevant beliefs and hence to A_B, SN or PC. They state:

> Although we do not deny that 'external' variables of this kind may sometimes be related to behavior, from our point of view they can affect behavior only indirectly. That is, external variables will be related to behavior only if they are related to one or more of the variables specified by our theory. (Ajzen and Fishbein, 1980: 82).

Thus, beliefs and the other components of the TPB should mediate the effect of external variables as shown in Figure 6.3. This argument has been tested in a number of studies by including external variables in the regression analysis to see whether these significantly improve the prediction of intention compared with the global variables alone. Often, demographic variables have little effect; for example, Marsh and Matheson (1983) found no direct effects of age or sex on intention in their study on smoking cessation and Loken (1983) found no direct effect of external variables on television watching.

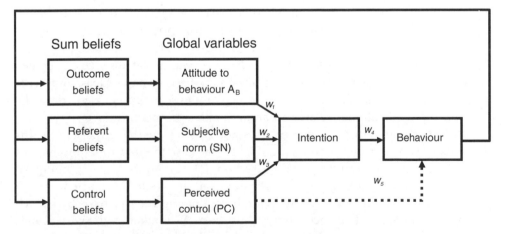

Figure 6.3   Feedback from experience should affect beliefs

However, it is usually found that past experience has a direct effect on intention and behaviour (Bagozzi and Kimmel, 1995). In the Marsh and Matheson (1983) study, the previous experience of attempting to stop smoking had a direct effect on intention and a small direct effect on attempts to stop smoking. Similar direct effects of past behaviour on both intention and subsequent behaviour have been found by Bentler and Speckart (1979, 1981), Fredricks and Dossett (1983) and Bagozzi (1981). One possible explanation is that people are partly controlled by their environment via stimulus control and habit and that is not fully captured by PC or other global measures even though people realize that they are more likely to do the action again and thus give higher scores for intention. Bentler and Speckart (1979), Fredricks and Dossett (1983) and Triandis (1977) take this view, i.e. that past behaviour establishes a habit which may affect intention and later behaviour without altering the beliefs measured in the TPB.

The Development of A_B, SN and PC

As experience increases, people become more informed and the belief basis for future action is changed. This is a situation that is particularly pertinent to consumer behaviour. Consumers are naïve when they enter markets that are new to them and, as they repeat purchase, they become more experienced. When the experience is positive, intention will be enhanced in a positive feedback loop; if the experience is negative, intentions will be reduced and further trial curtailed. Thus, under the voluntary conditions that attach to most consumer behaviour, we would expect to find that those who are highly experienced have stronger intentions. Applying the TPB, there should be changes in A_B, SN and PC as intention develops, as illustrated in Figure 6.3. This can occur because the beliefs underlying the global variables become more numerous and more strongly linked to the behaviour. If experience elaborates the belief basis of planned behaviour constructs, we may ask whether it has the same effect on A_B, SN and PC. East (1992) suggested that the progression from novice to expert consumer involves a movement from actions based mainly on SN to actions based more on A_B and PC. This proposal is founded on the idea that, in the absence of detailed knowledge, people have to make decisions on the basis of naïve ideas, and 'what others think I should do' is better known, or more easily guessed, than the benefits and opportunities related to an unfamiliar prospect.

East (1992) found three studies that supported the view that experience shifts the basis of choice from SN to A_B and PC. In one case the *first-time* purchase of a computer was found to be heavily based on SN; this study lacked a comparison with experienced computer purchasers but it would be surprising if a product with so many outcomes was purchased on a normative basis by knowledgeable consumers. The second study by East, Whittaker and Swift (1984) examined the prospective viewing of Breakfast TV (before it started in Britain) by two groups of people. In one group (novice) there was no explanation of the service to come. Here, SN was the stronger determinant of intention. In the second group (experienced), details and examples of Breakfast TV from the USA and Australia were provided. Here, A_B was the better predictor of intention.

Later, after the service had started, a sample of viewers gave responses that were similar to those of the experienced group. A third study by Knox and de Chernatony (1994) found that non-users of mineral water were much more influenced by SN than users.

East (1992) tested his hypothesis and reported conflicting results. Then, in a further ten studies, nine supported the prediction that, as experience increases, the determination of intention shifts from SN to A_B and PC. However, a further ten studies were accumulated and, in these, the effect was not supported. With these uneven results, the work was never published. The second group of ten studies were mainly financial decisions, such as the purchase of endowments and pensions, and these may not have permitted much development of knowledge from experience.

Despite the lack of support for the theory, the issue of how experience affects the different beliefs underlying intention and action is important and deserves further study. In many studies, SN is a relatively weak determinant of behaviour and there has been some tendency to downgrade this determinant (e.g. Sheppard, Hartwick and Warshaw, 1988). Armitage and Connor (2001) found that part of the weakness could be attributed to poor measurement. Our view remains that the relative contribution of A_B, SN and PC is likely to be related in part to experience, though clearly the association depends on the type of action.

Deliberate and Spontaneous Action

In an interesting review, Fazio (1990) divides the prediction of behaviour into two fields, one largely explained by the work of Fishbein and Ajzen, where decision-making is deliberate and the second, where action is undeliberated and spontaneous, and is explained by Fazio (1986) and his associates. Fazio's model is shown in Figure 6.4.

In Fazio's account, attitudes are automatically activated by observation of the attitude object. The attitude then guides perception and the individual becomes aware of parts of the environment related to the attitude. The definition of the event then occurs as these perceptions are associated with a normative under-standing of the situation and, out of this definition of the event, behaviour may follow. The main point here is that the environment is driving cognitive processes in an automatic way and attitude rather than belief is the foundation of this process.

Fazio argues that attitude activation occurs only when the object and its eval-uation have been well established in memory, usually through direct behavioural experience. Thus spontaneous production of behaviour is restricted to familiar contexts, leaving planned behaviour to explain the more unusual situations. However, this rather cosy division of the field has been disrupted by evidence from Bargh et al. (1992) that a wide range of objects can elicit attitudes. This

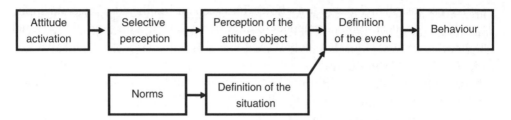

Figure 6.4   Fazio's (1986) theory of the attitude–behaviour process

casts doubt on the separation between automatic and deliberate control of behaviour. It seems possible that these two types of explanation may often both apply to the same phenomenon and work together. Fazio (1990) has shown that responses are affected in measurements of deliberate behaviour if people are asked to focus on objects before measurement. Baldwin and Holmes (1987) found systematically different measures were obtained when different social referents were visualized before response. These studies show the effect of automatic processes even when people are making considered responses.

Other Alternatives to the Theory of Planned Behaviour

A number of researchers have suggested modifications of the theory. Bagozzi and Kimmel (1995) and Bagozzi (1992) suggested distinctions between intention, desire and self-prediction for which Armitage and Conner (2001) found some support. There have been proposals to include a moral norm to cover the agent's personal normative control, but this seems to have an additional predictive function only for some actions.

Ajzen and Driver (1992) have distinguished between the short-term and expressive consequences of action and the longer-term and more cognitive consequences of action. Often, a short-term pain has to be balanced against a long-term gain. On this basis, A_B should be seen as having two components.

In its present form, the theory includes only one type of subjective norm – what agents think that others think that they *should* do. What others actually do (descriptive norm) exerts a separate influence on behaviour (Deutsch and Gerard, 1955). When descriptive norms are included, predictions are usually increased (Rivis and Sheeran, 2003). Armitage and Conner (2001) have examined alternative measures for the control element in the theory; clearly, there is the control that a person has by virtue of his or her abilities and the control that is made possible by the environment.

In the consumer behaviour context, the technology acceptance model (TAM) has been offered as an alternative method of predicting the intention to use new systems (Davis, 1989). This theory bases behavioural intention on two factors: perceived usefulness (usually related to enhancing job performance) and perceived ease of use (usually related to low effort). This account has the advantage of simplicity and avoids elicitation but it applies to a restricted field and may not give so much explanation as a belief-based model. Usefulness has some correspondence with A_B, and ease of use with PC, so the theory does not represent SN, which can be quite powerful when employers introduce new systems. Venkatesh and Davis (2000) have modified the model to incorporate SN. Generally, TPB performs better than TAM.

Reviewing Planned Behaviour Theory

The development of the theory of planned behaviour has been a success story. Social psychologists have emerged from the dark days of 1969 when Wicker claimed that there was little or no connection between attitude and behaviour. We now have a predictive and explanative model which works effectively though there remains a nagging doubt about the scale of behaviour prediction.

However, one problem about the validation of the theory has been the methods that have been used. If the theory is causal, it should be possible to instigate change by supplying information and then to follow how the effects of that change 'cascade' through the components of the theory. This requires research designs in which comparisons are made between experimental conditions that induce changes of belief. The fact that there is little evidence of this sort may indicate that little has been done or that the results of such research have not been coherent.

Finally, there is a need to use the theory more effectively in marketing. It may be used to study the activities of marketers – why they opt for or against particular practices (e.g. Elliott, Jobber and Sharp, 1995) and it applies to a host of consumer practices. The theory is of limited use in explaining the preference for one brand over another, unless the brands are markedly different (e.g. one restaurant versus another, or one holiday destination rather than another). Planned behaviour research can explain why categories are liked and therefore it can assist managers to position brands, target the more responsive segments and select themes for advertising.

SUMMARY

Attitudes are an evaluative response to a concept. The concept is a cluster of attribute beliefs, each with attaching value. Thus the attitude to the concept should relate to the aggregate value of the attribute beliefs. Generally, this view of attitude has been upheld by research and it fits the idea that the purchase of a product can be seen as the acquisition of a bundle of expected costs and rewards.

(Continued)

In many studies the correlation between attitude and behaviour measures has been weak. There are two reasons for such weak relationships. The first is that 'other variables' may swamp the association between attitude and behaviour. The second reason is that the measures of attitude and behaviour may not be compatible, i.e. these measures may not refer to the same action, target, context and time. A mismatch here means that the wrong attitude is being used to predict behaviour.

The closest prediction of behaviour is provided by measures of intention. In a number of studies, those who stated that they would buy a product were found to be much more likely to buy it than those who stated that they would not buy it.

The theory of planned behaviour (Ajzen, 1985, 1991) is built on this evidence. In this theory, there are three global variables – attitude to a behaviour, subjective norm and perceived control. These have a combined effect on intention. Behaviour is predicted by intention and perceived control. The global variables rest on beliefs about the outcomes of behaviour, the referents who think that a person should engage or not in the behaviour, and the ability and opportunity to engage in the behaviour. The theory of planned behaviour provides different levels of explanation which can be used in positioning, product development and advertising.

Additional Resources

Issues on the nature of attitudes and their relationship with behaviour are well discussed in chapter 4 of Eagly and Chaiken (1993). A review of the theory of planned behaviour is provided by Ajzen (2002) and by Armitage and Conner (2001). Ajzen's website is www.people.umass.edu/aizen/faq.html.

Information Processing And Decision-making

LEARNING OBJECTIVES

When you have completed this chapter, you should be able to:

1   Understand the way thinking is based on schemas and is affected by response competition.
2   Explain what is meant by a heuristic mechanism and describe how these mechanisms may bias decision-making.
3   Describe how human beings respond to objective probability and value.
4   Understand the ideas of framing, mental accounting and editing.
5   Describe how this work can be used to influence others and improve choice.

OVERVIEW

Many of the theories that we use work quite well to predict human behaviour but are inadequate as descriptions of information processing. Mental representation models are simplistic. NBD and Dirichlet theories model actions as if they were random and do not have causes. Similarly, the theory of planned behaviour does not really describe how people think. People do not assign likelihoods and evaluations, multiply them and sum the products to form their attitudes. Planned behaviour theory works as if people figure out their interests in this way, but no claim is made that they actually do so.

An alternative approach focuses on automatic mechanisms that guide information-seeking and choice. This approach seems to get closer to the thought processes (often unconscious) that govern behaviour. We deal first with the way schemas can guide thought and recognition. The repeated exposure of stimuli often leads to them being liked more and this effect of 'mere exposure' may be based on the resolution of response competition. However, the majority of the chapter is devoted to findings relating to prospect theory. This work by Kahneman, Tversky and many of their colleagues has transformed thinking about the way human beings process information and choose

(Continued)

in an intuitive rather than rational manner. Their methods have mainly used simple choices, presented to participants, with a count of the preferences expressed. Using such methods, they have documented many instances where judgement is biased and decision-making departs from economic assumptions.

SECTION 1: SCHEMAS AND ATTENTION

Schemas

In Chapter 3, we introduced the idea of the schema. According to Crocker, Fiske and Taylor (1984: 197), a schema is:

> an abstract or generic knowledge structure, stored in memory, that specifies the defining features and relevant attributes of some stimulus domain, and the inter-relationships among those attributes. ... Schemas help us to structure, organize and interpret new information; they facilitate encoding, storage and retrieval of relevant information; they can affect the time it takes to process information. ... Schemas also serve interpretive or inferential functions. For example, they may fill in data that are missing or unavailable in a stimulus configuration.

The notion of the schema was implicit in Bartlett's (1932) work on remembering. Bartlett wrote of the 'effort after meaning' and showed how unusual structures that fell short of representing any object were interpreted by reference to more familiar ideas. One of Bartlett's stimuli was a diagram of an ambiguous object that was variously recognized as a battleaxe, turf cutter, anchor or key, although it was not quite like any of them. People used schemas for more familiar objects as a way of making sense of the ambiguous object. When more than one schema fits, people experience *response competition* as they struggle to make sense of the stimulus (see Box 7.1).

Box 7.1	Response competition

This is demonstrated in the Stroop test. You are asked to call out the colour that is written on the overhead the moment that it is displayed. In one condition, the word is RED written using a red colour; in the other condition, RED is written using a blue colour and this gives a longer response delay than the first condition. In the second case, two competing responses are aroused: to say 'red' and to say 'blue' and the competition delays the production of the correct response.

More frequently encountered stimuli are more easily retrieved. In addition, stimuli with particular characteristics are recognized or recalled more easily. 'Colorful, dynamic, or other distinctive stimuli disproportionately engage attention and, accordingly, disproportionately affect judgments' (Taylor, 1982: 192). This leads to an idea that thinking is based on cognitive accessibility. The more rapidly an idea can be brought to mind, the more likely it is to figure in cognition and subsequent processing. This *retrieval bias effect* has parallels with accessibility in the physical environment. For example, people buy more from those supermarkets that are nearby. Search machines use a related process when they take account of the frequency of past interest in the search outcomes. Retrieval bias is quite efficient because it ensures that the more likely candidates are considered first. However, concepts that occur infrequently or are hard to visualize for other reasons will tend to be left out of cognitive processing. In general, experience-based concepts are more easily retrieved than communication-based concepts, events are favoured over states, recent occurrences over long-past occurrences and the clearly defined concept over those that are fuzzy.

Bartlett's problem involves the simplest of schemas, those used to classify objects. Somewhat more elaborate schemas include classifications of persons or groups, grammatical forms and social roles. In their most abstract form, schemas may cover relationships like logical validity, causality and symmetry. People might explain an occurrence in terms of causal relationship rather than simple association if causes are more easily retrieved than other associations.

Managing Schemas

Since thought is guided by schemas, it follows that negotiation and other forms of influence may succeed by manipulating the selection of schemas that people use to interpret their experience. One standard ploy in negotiation is to try to anchor the discussion around a particular range of outcomes. Early in the discussion, a negotiator might say 'The normal rate for this type of work is £1,000 a day'. This can constrain offers to those fairly close to the rate mentioned. Turning to advertising, schemas may be used to develop the product concept. An iPod is not just a device for delivering music to the ears of a user; it also indicates something about the user's style and ad copy may imply this. Similarly, since newspapers indicate the reader's knowledge, this may be implied in ads. For example, 'No FT, no comment' implies that those who read the *Financial Times* are likely to be better informed. Often public relations exercises can be seen as attempts to manipulate the schemas used for judgement. For example, firms may play up their green credentials by drawing attention to their energy-saving actions. Some interesting examples of schema management are shown in Box 7.2.

Box 7.2	New schemas for old

An activist group took on the tobacco companies in Australia in the 1980s. The group was called the Billboard Utilising Graffitists Against Unhealthy Promotions (BUGA UP) and they specialized in 'refacing' tobacco posters. When a cigarette company offered a car as a prize, their poster was given the caption 'From the people who put the 'car' in carcinogen'. The adjustments to the posters and the speeches in court when members of the group were prosecuted, gave entertainment to the people of New South Wales, who much appreciated the sight of multinational companies being humbled.

Many of BUGA UP's activities were legitimate. One took place when a tobacco company sponsored work at the Sydney Opera House; well-dressed members of the group distributed leaflets expressing regret at this unsavoury association between tobacco and the arts. Another BUGA UP enterprise sabotaged a Marlboro 'Man of the Year' competition in Australia. BUGA UP proposed their own candidate; their choice was a man disabled by smoking, confined to a wheelchair and smoking through the hole in his throat provided by a tracheotomy operation. The man himself was a willing accomplice and starred in a poster which was printed and sold in large numbers. The idea of the strong heroic figure that Marlboro had tried to cultivate was ridiculed. In its place were put the schemas of disease and disability which are more accurately related to smoking cigarettes. A further 'anti-promotion' counteracted the distribution of free cigarettes in shopping malls. To most people a gift is a kindness and the giver is regarded as well meaning. To oppose such promotions, BUGA UP arranged for children to parade around the mall with banners saying 'DANGER – DRUG PUSHERS AT WORK'. This changed the perception of the tobacco companies' motives from kindness to self-interest. Tobacco companies have a squalid history of refusing to admit to the hazards of their products; they *are* licensed drug sellers and an important part of their public relations has been to counter such facts by sponsoring orchestras, sport and research. BUGA UP's achievement was to reassert the drug seller schema as the one by which the tobacco company's actions should be judged.

Do People Like Response Competition?

Jokes are often based on response competition. People may anticipate one outcome and have their expectations confounded at the punch line. But other forms of response competition may be disliked. Even jokes may be disliked when a person is under stress. The explanation for this variable reaction is that it depends upon the degree of arousal of the person involved. Arousal is high when people are either under-stimulated or over-stimulated. People prefer low levels of arousal and are therefore guided to seek an intermediate degree of stimulation. Conceptual conflicts may be welcome when people are inactive or bored (e.g. when watching television) because, under these conditions, more stimulation will reduce arousal; at other times, unusual stimuli may raise arousal (Berlyne, 1965; Berlyne and McDonnell, 1965) and, when this occurs, the stimuli may be disliked. This explains why Harrison (1968) and Saegert and Jellison (1970) found that the objects that people investigated (because they were stimulating) were often liked less.

Mere Exposure

Response competition has been used to explain an interesting phenomenon first reported by Zajonc (pronounced Zi-onse, 1968). Zajonc observed that repeated exposure to a new stimulus often made people like it more. This effect of *mere exposure* was so called because a change in the observer's evaluation occurs without the use of reinforcement (discussed in Chapter 1). Zajonc observed this effect in both laboratory and field experiments, using nonsense words, obscure characters and photographs of unknown faces as the unfamiliar stimuli. For example, in Zajonc and Rajecki's (1969) field experiment, nonsense words such as NANSOMA were printed like advertisements in campus newspapers. Later, the researchers got large numbers of students to rate the words on evaluative scales and there was clear evidence that the frequency of exposure correlated positively with the evaluative rating. Zajonc's explanation for this was that the nonsense words created response competition in the minds of readers which was reduced when people developed a familiarity with the nonsense word after repeated exposure. If the response competition created by nonsense words is generally disagreeable, a reduction in competition should produce a more positive evaluation. Harrison (1968) measured response competition as the time delay before any response to the stimulus and found that the delay was reduced as the number of exposures increased. Lee (1994) offered another ingenious explanation which is based on the availability heuristic discussed later in this chapter. Repeated exposure speeds up recognition; the stimuli that we recognize more easily tend to be those that we like; this affects judgement and leads us to give the stimuli higher evaluations.

Not all stimuli become more liked on repeated exposure. This suggests that prospective brand names, which are frequently exposed, should be screened to see whether the are liked.

The Response to Thought and Feeling Stimuli

We tend to think that recognition is a necessary precursor to any evaluation of a stimulus. If you do not know what the concept is, how can you have any affective response to it? Strangely, it seems that we can have an evaluative response without recognition. Zajonc (1980) showed that thought and feeling are initially processed independently and Kunst-Wilson and Zajonc (1980) found that evaluative responses occurred slightly ahead of recognition. Zajonc points to the survival value attaching to a fast response to dangerous stimuli: it is better to jump without thought than to recognize that it is a car that is hitting you!

In a further experiment, Marcel (1976) used an instrument called a tachistoscope to present words or blank space with equal likelihood. Words were either short or long and either pleasant or unpleasant. If the subjects thought they saw a word, they were asked to judge its length against comparison words and to say whether the word was 'good' or 'bad'. A good word might be 'food' while a bad word might be 'evil'. The duration of exposure was reduced until the subjects were guessing the presence of words at chance level and could not therefore have been recognizing anything. At this duration, Marcel found that word-length judgements (also cognitive) were at chance level too. However, at this point the subjects were still scoring at above chance on their evaluative judgements of words, when these were present, indicating that the evaluative response was generated faster than the recognition response.

Zajonc's ideas have not gone unchallenged. Anand, Holbrook and Stephens (1988) and Anand and Sternthal (1991) have argued that affective judgements can rest on cognitive processes without recognition occurring. They propose that recognition is only one part of cognitive processing and that other cognitive responses may underpin the evaluative response. Vanhuele (1994) gives a review of this work.

Fast recognition judgements of the sort studied by Zajonc are quite different from the choices typically faced by consumers, but these studies show how unconscious mechanisms can underlie consciously experienced thought and feeling.

Attention and Value

In decision-making, the observable action is often restricted to the overt choice. However, when the alternatives are physically present, it is possible to observe the direction of gaze and to infer from this which alternative a person is thinking about. Gerard (1967) used this method of investigation; he employed two projectors to show two alternatives (pictures), while light reflected off a mirror attached to the back of the participant's head showed which alternative was receiving attention. A multi-channel recorder logged the data. Gerard reported that the participants looked most at the alternative that they did *not* choose and suggested that they were trying to come to terms with not having this alternative.

To test Gerard's result, East (1973) conducted two experiments using a battery of slide viewers connected to a hidden time recorder. The slide viewer equipment is illustrated. As in the earlier study by Gerard (1967), the choice was made between French Impressionist paintings. The participants were led to believe that they would get a poster of the picture that they chose. Control of

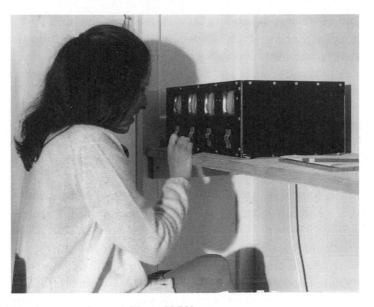

Using the slide viewer equipment (East, 1973).

the viewers was left entirely in the hands of the participant so that the time spent on the different alternatives was unconstrained.

East's first experiment presented subjects with two alternatives, while the second presented three alternatives. Both experiments had two levels of choice difficulty: high, between alternatives that had previously been rated equally by the subject and low, between alternatives that had been rated unequally.

The results showed that the subjects spent more time looking at the alternatives that they liked more, so that the ratio of attention times was an approximate function of the ratio of the evaluations (see Table 7.1). Thus there is a simple mechanism that directs attention to the more valued alternative. This mechanism is unconscious; when asked about their choice behaviour in such an experiment, people do not know which alternative they would look at most. This evidence suggests that the more valued features of a person's environment generally get more attention.

Table 7.1   Mean durations of attention to alternatives in choice experiments (East, 1973)

	Order of evaluation	Two alternatives Time spent (seconds)	Three alternatives Time spent (seconds)
High choice	1	46	25
difficulty	2	37	23
	3	...	21
Total time		83	69
Low choice	1	24	24
difficulty	2	18	16
	3	...	9
Total time		42	49

East's result was the opposite of Gerard's reported findings and it is possible that, with Gerard's rather complicated method for recording attention, the records were inadvertently linked to the wrong alternative. A study by Russo and Leclerc (1994) supports East's finding. These researchers used video equipment in a simulation supermarket situation and measured the number of eye fixations on alternatives (rather than duration of time spent) at different phases in the decision sequence. They found that in the main phase of the decision the number of fixations clearly favoured the alternative later chosen. In another study, Pieters and Warlop (1999) also found more attention to the alternative that was eventually chosen. This evidence does not tell us what people would attend to when the alternatives were unpleasant; people need to avoid loss so they are likely to attend most to the more unpleasant alternative, but evidence is needed here.

If evaluation guides attention, it means that second and third preferences will get proportionately less attention and their worthwhile attributes are less likely to be discovered. This mechanism therefore carries a bias in favour of existing preferences but it is an efficient way of allocating the scarce resource of time since it ensures that little time is wasted on low-rated prospects. But if investigation of the first preference leads to negative findings, and this alternative is down-rated, more time will be allocated to lesser alternatives. Given this evidence, people may be encouraged to buy a lesser brand by attaching information about this brand to a message on the preferred alternative. In this way it is more likely to receive attention. This may be done by using comparative advertising and there is evidence that small brands benefit from this (Grewal et al., 1997).

East found that total attention time was longer when the alternatives had similar evaluations, leading to greater conflict. This is a common effect but is not usually explained. One approach here is to see the decision as the outcome of obstructed motivation (or frustration). The tendency to choose one alternative obstructs the opportunity to have other alternatives. Table 7.2 shows how this might work if motivation is shown by evaluation and obstruction by the probability of not choosing. When the alternatives have equal evaluations, there is a higher score for obstructed motivation.

Table 7.2 Hypothetical data explaining the longer time to make high-conflict choices

Choice difficulty	Evaluation	Probability of not choosing	Obstructed motivation (evaluation x probability of not choosing (frustation)
High	5	0.5	2.5
	5	0.5	2.5
Total frustration:			5
Low	7	0.1	0.7
	3	0.9	2.7
Total frustration:			3.4

SECTION 2: HEURISTICS

EXERCISE 7.1   AVAILABILITY EFFECTS

In Britain, approximately 600,000 people die each year from all causes. How many people die prematurely each year from the following two causes? Enter the figures that you think apply:

Smoking:
Road accidents:

Schemas and response competition provide helpful ways of thinking about the processes involved in attention and choice. However, there is also extensive research on the biases found in people's evaluations and choices. We now consider such biases.

If you want to find the river, go downhill! This is a heuristic rule which often helps but may mislead when there is no river in the valley. The term 'heuristic' was used by Kahneman, Slovic and Tversky (1982) to cover inexact or rule-of-thumb processes which may be used unconsciously to assess likelihood when an event is uncertain. Kahneman et al. argue that people do not appear to follow the statistical theory of prediction when making such judgements. Instead, they rely on a limited number of heuristic processes which often yield reasonable judgements but sometimes lead to error. In particular, people seem to attach higher probability to ideas that are easily retrieved; this is called the *availability heuristic*. It arises because frequently experienced concepts are often more common and are easier to retrieve so that the likelihood and ease of retrieval become associated.

Markus and Zajonc (1985) provide an example of the way in which availability may quite unjustifiably support the prestige of the medical profession. People may get better without treatment but, when treatment has been given, there is a tendency to assume that it has helped recovery. The therapy is more cognitively available as a cause of recovery than ideas about the natural processes counteracting disease that occur unseen within the body. As a result, people may judge that therapy is more effective than it is.

The judgement of risk is notoriously erratic. Some of the reasons for this may lie in the poor information about actual risks in the media but judgement may also be distorted by the action of heuristics. Lichtenstein et al. (1978) have suggested that some risks are exaggerated by people because they hear about them more often in the media and therefore retrieve them faster, which invokes the availability heuristic. Those who completed Exercise 7.1 are likely to have overestimated the risk of death from road accidents because these events are more salient in media reports. Smoking deaths are less well reported and are likely to be underestimated. The approximate answers are given below.

Approximate annual numbers of deaths in Britain by cause:

All causes	600,000
Smoking	100,000
Road accidents	3,500

Risk misjudgement has also affected the use of oral contraceptives. Exaggerated fears have caused women to abandon the pill, even when the identified risk was very small in absolute terms. In 1996, a 10 per cent increase in legal abortion in Britain was attributed to earlier announcements that a number of contraceptive pills should be phased out because of small associated risks.

People seem to have difficulty in taking account of background risk and may focus instead on large percentage increases. For example, women may be shocked to hear that those over age 35 who smoke and take the contraceptive pill have 18 times the risk of pulmonary embolism compared with those who do neither of these actions. The '18 times' fact seems to be more available and to dominate in judgement, but embolisms are very rare in the 35–45-year-old range and other hazards present far more risk. A more responsible way of handling the data would be to report the personal increment in risk for smokers of using the pill. For example, that a smoker who takes the pill has an extra risk of dying of one in a million. The effect of the information on embolism was to encourage women to abandon the pill. They would have done better to quit smoking since one in six smokers die from smoking-related illnesses.

EXERCISE 7.2   WHO WAS TO BLAME?
(ABRIDGED FROM TVERSKY AND KAHNEMAN, 1980: 62)

Solve the following problem:
A cab was involved in a hit-and-run accident at night. Two cab companies, the Green and the Blue, operate in the city. You are given the following data:

- 85 per cent of the cabs in the city are Green and 15 per cent are Blue.

- A witness identified the cab as a Blue cab. The court tested his ability to identify cabs under appropriate visibility conditions. When presented with a sample of cabs (half of which were Blue and half of which were Green) the witness made correct identifications in 80 per cent of the cases.

Question: What is the probability that the cab involved in the accident was Blue rather than Green?
Decide on your answer before reading on.

The tendency to ignore base rates such as market share is the basis of the *representativeness heuristic*. This is the tendency to judge likelihood by reference to visible similarities rather than background probabilities. For example, a person may be seen as a barrister because of features of dress and delivery of speech. In this case, the judgement draws on the stereotype of a barrister, but such a judgement takes no account of the low number of barristers in society which makes it unlikely that a person belongs to this group.

EXERCISE 7.2 (continued)

Tversky and Kahneman (1980) put this problem to several hundred participants; the median response was 80 per cent. Thus participants tended to take note of the witness's skill in recognizing cabs and ignored the market shares of the two cab companies. Clearly, if there had been no Blue cabs, the witness could not have been right so the proportion of Blue cabs is relevant. The probability that the witness was right is the ratio of correct identification as blue to total identification as blue (both correct and incorrect). The chance that the cab was Blue (0.15) and was recognized correctly (0.8) is 0.15 × 0.8 and the chance that the cab was Green (0.85) and was recognized wrongly as Blue (0.2) is 0.85 × 0.2. The required ratio of correct identification to total identifications is therefore:

$$\frac{(0.15 \times 0.8)}{(0.15 \times 0.8) + (0.85 \times 0.2)}$$

$$= 0.41$$

In Exercise 7.2, the bias towards the witness test and away from the market shares of the two cab companies probably relates to the fact that the witness test is an event. As previously reported, events are more available than continuing states such as market share. We seem to be tuned to change and direct our thinking to the more active aspects of a problem. In contrast, data dealing with an unchanging background do not attract as much attention. This mechanism serves a useful purpose by drawing attention to aspects of the environment that require response but it can cause mistakes in particular cases. In particular, it means that individual economic decisions may be related to more active features of the environment rather than their impact on wealth. Wealth is a state rather than an event and does not usually figure in individual judgements even though, normatively, it should.

People are also prone to give more weight to causal data, which is related to change. To illustrate this we use a problem devised by Tversky and Kahneman (1980). Which of the following events is more probable?

(a)   A girl has blue eyes if her mother has blue eyes.
(b)   The mother has blue eyes if her daughter has blue eyes.
(c)   The two conditions are equally probable.

The correct answer is (c) but, among those who did not choose this answer, three times as many people preferred (a) to (b). The mother to daughter inheritance is causal, unlike the daughter to mother relationship.

The focus on events rather than states and the different heuristic rules are now described by Kahneman as intuitive thinking, for example, in his presentation following the award of the Nobel Prize for economics (2002). Kahneman likens such thinking to the way perception seems to be governed by mechanisms over which we have little conscious control. What you perceive is a function of the context from which reference points are drawn. Small changes in problems can affect the reference points and change the judgement. There are criticisms of this work; see, for example, Gigerenzer (1991), who has raised questions about the interpretation of effects. Kahneman and Tversky (1996) respond to this criticism.

Relevance to Marketing

The greater cognitive availability of events and causal data has a relevance to marketing. For example, we may exaggerate the impact of market interventions. As we saw in Chapter 4, conditions like market share control the likely outcome of interventions such as advertising, but these conditions may get less attention than they deserve because of their constancy.

In addition, retrieval bias will move decisions towards the option that is easier to bring to mind. This may lead us from the prevention of undesirable occurrences (by adjusting conditions) towards the active remedying of undesirable occurrences after they have happened. Good management is often proactive and stops problems from happening. However, the proactive approach is not always best. It depends on costs; sometimes it is best to let things happen and then to focus resources on the problem – management by exception – but in other cases, for example avoiding accidents, prevention is usually best.[1] Our point is that there is a bias against proactive intervention because successful prevention produces no visible outcome and is therefore less cognitively available. In addition to supporting reactive solutions, retrieval bias will operate in favour of the visible, well-defined event and against intangibles. This suggests that people may:

- give too much support to the status quo: what is happening is available, but what could happen is harder to bring to mind,
- make poor assessments of the opportunity cost, which is the alternative use of resources when a course of action is selected,
- find it easier to sell products that have a form that is easy to grasp.

SECTION 3: PROCESSING VALUE AND PROBABILITY

Objective value, expressed in money or other units and objective probability, measured or given, are processed by human beings to produce subjective evaluations of utility and subjective estimates of probability. The subjective representations do not bear an exact correspondence with the objective forms and this affects decision-making.

Value

The relationship between objective value and utility has a long history going back to Benoulli (1738), who described how the curve of utility against wealth flattens as wealth increases, and marginal utility therefore diminishes with each increment in wealth. Benoulli gave the example of a pauper who, finding a lottery ticket offering an equal chance of winning 20,000 ducats or getting nothing, might quite reasonably ensure a gain by exchanging his ticket for a guaranteed 9,000 ducats. The value function is curved, so that half the *utility* of 20,000 ducats is less than the utility of 9,000 ducats.

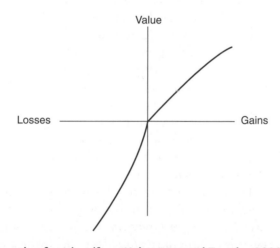

Figure 7.1   The value function (from Kahneman and Tversky, 2000)

This curvature assists exchanges. To a person who has enough of a good, the marginal utility of additional supplies is low and this will encourage exchanges with others who possess different goods that the person needs. Both parties in such an exchange can gain in utility. However, Benoulli was wrong to think that changes were reckoned against total wealth. Normally, people assess gains or losses against a more salient criterion – and this is often the zero point. This relationship between gains and losses relative to zero, and utility, is shown by the curve in Figure 7.1. You can see that the curve is concave to the x-axis for both gains and losses and that the response to losses is more extreme than the response to gains. This relationship has been established by observing the preferences expressed by individuals about different choices. Comparisons between positive and negative choices have been particularly interesting (see Exercise 7.3).

EXERCISE 7.3   POSITIVE AND NEGATIVE CHOICES

1 Which do you prefer?
   A: £9,000 for certain, or
   B: £10,000 with a probability of 0.9, otherwise nothing.

2 Which do you prefer?
   C: Losing £9,000 for certain, or
   D: Losing £10,000 with a probability of 0.9; otherwise nothing.

In Exercise 7.3 people generally prefer A to B. The shape of the value–utility relationship for gains explains why people prefer £9,000 for certain rather than have $0.9 \times £10,000$. What about the avoidance of losses? In Exercise 7.3 most respondents prefer D to C. The shape of the value function in the negative region means that losing £10,000 with a probability of 0.9 is less painful than losing £9,000 for certain and people prefer the smaller disutility. These outcomes mean that people are generally *risk averse on gains but risk prone on losses*. This pattern of preference reversal is regularly found and is called the *reflection effect*. However, in 1992, Tversky and Kahneman suggested that the data were more consistent with the idea that people are risk averse on gains and risk prone on losses when outcomes had medium or high probability and the reverse for low probability. This modification arises because of the way people weight low probabilities, as we explain later.

Figure 7.1 shows another interesting effect. This is the steepness of the negative part of the value function in comparison to the positive part. This effect is captured by the aphorism *losses loom larger than gains* and, more formally, as *loss aversion*. Loss aversion is behind the *endowment effect* which is the fact that people often demand much more to give up an object than they would be willing to pay to acquire it. The endowment effect has been demonstrated in a number of studies reviewed by Kahneman, Knetsch and Thaler (1991a). One simple example of the effect is the reluctance of people to engage in a 50:50 win/lose bet. On average, people will only wager a dollar on a coin toss if they can win more than two dollars. Generally, people will be reluctant to trade what they own, except at a high price. Not surprisingly, the endowment effect has been tested by critics, see for example Shogren et al. (1994).

As we stated, gains and losses relate to some reference point. Although this is often zero, in some cases it will relate to a prior associated cost. For example, a person may see the $20,000 cost of building work on a newly acquired house as an addition to the $1million price paid for the house. Viewed like this, the $20,000 seems a modest increment to the purchase price but, 10 years later, when the purchase of the house had faded into the past, such costs stand alone and will be psychologically more painful. Thaler (1999) points out that the extent to which a cost is psychologically linked to a benefit can vary. When people pay a fixed cost for a service, irrespective of their amount of use, usage is decoupled from the payment since any extra use is free. Another decoupling occurs when a credit card is used. This postpones payment and also aggregates costs into one bill where individual items are less apparent. The aggregation reduces the psychological cost compared with several smaller separate costs.

Probability

Faced with the choices in Exercise 7.4, 80 per cent of subjects preferred option B to A but 65 per cent preferred option C to D. This seems paradoxical because the ratio of the sums and the ratio of the probabilities is the same in each choice pair, yet the preference order reverses for most subjects. One explanation for this pattern is that probability is weighted as it is converted to subjective probability. Figure 7.2 shows how the weighting of objective probability reduces the subjective impact of high probabilities and increases the impact of low probabilities. The x-axis is objective probability and the y-axis is the weighted outcome. Applied to the data in Exercise 7.4, the weighting reduces the appeal of A and increases the appeal of C.

EXERCISE 7.4   THE ALLAIS PARADOX (ALLAIS, 1953)

Allais asked one group of subjects to choose between the two options:

A: $4,000 with a probability of 0.8; otherwise nothing.
B: $3,000 for certain.

Which do you prefer?

Another group were asked to choose between:

C: $4,000 with a probability of 0.2; otherwise nothing.
D: $3,000 with a probability of 0.25; otherwise nothing.

Which do you prefer?

No mathematical expression has been given for the probability weighting function; it is determined empirically. One partial explanation for the effect is that a rule of diminishing sensitivity with distance from a reference point applies.

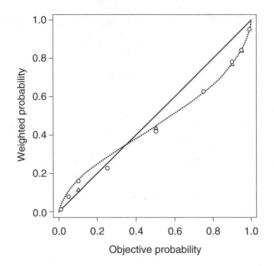

Figure 7.2   The probability function (From Kahneman and Tversky, 2000)

The probability function has two natural reference points, 0 and 1; the weights, or relative differences between subjective and objective probability, initially increase with distance from these anchors. However, as these relative differences are in opposite directions, they must come together again somewhere in the central area.

The weighting of small objective probabilities fits the evidence that people are positive about insurance and like to place long-odds bets.[2] Above an objective probability of 0.40, the weighting depresses subjective probability so that risks are subjectively discounted; for example, a 50 per cent probability is nearer to 40 per cent subjectively. At the extremes, the weighting is unstable; a one in a thousand chance may be dismissed as no chance or taken seriously. In 1992, Tversky and Kahneman suggested that gains and losses might have different weighting functions but research has shown that these are quite similar.

The sensitivity near the reference points (0, 1) is illustrated by Exercise 7.5. Most people will pay more in the 0 per cent and 99 per cent conditions but the long-run benefit of a one per cent increment in probability is the same at any point on the probability range.

EXERCISE 7.5   RISK PREFERENCES

Suppose that you have a 99 per cent chance of getting $1,000. How much would you pay to move that probability to certainty?

Suppose that you have a 50 per cent chance of getting $1,000. How much would you pay to move that probability to 51 per cent.

Suppose that you have 0 per cent chance of getting $1,000. How much would you pay to move that probability to 1 per cent.

Prospect Theory

Kahneman and Tversky (1979) and Tversky and Kahneman (1992) incorporate the subjective conversion of value and probability into a theory of choice called prospect theory and propose that the choice of an alternative (prospect) is established in two stages. In the first stage, the choices that are *framed* in a communication are restructured or *edited* by the receiver. Then, in the second stage, the receiver chooses the best option based on the values assessed in the first stage.

Framing refers to the manner in which the choice is presented to the decision-maker and editing refers to the processes used by the decision-maker to rethink the choice. In framing, a prospect may be presented either as a loss or as a gain, as in Exercise 7.6.

EXERCISE 7.6   LIFE AND DEATH (TVERSKY AND KAHNEMAN, 1981: 453)

An unusual disease is expected to kill 600 people. Two interventions are proposed. Which do you prefer on the basis of the following information:

If programme A is adopted, 200 people will be saved.

If programme B is adopted, there is 1/3 probability that 600 people will be saved and 2/3 probability that no people will be saved.

When you have decided, consider how you would react to these alternatives:

If programme C is adopted, 400 people will die.

If programme D is adopted, there is 1/3 probability that no one will die and 2/3 probability that 600 people will die.

The second pair of alternatives in Exercise 7.6 is the same as the first (A = C, B = D). Yet 72 per cent preferred programme A to B and 78 per cent preferred programme D to C. By framing the problem in terms of the gains (lives saved), it is possible to steer preference to the risk-averse option, A, rather than B. In the second choice pair, the framing in terms of lives lost makes people risk prone, and steers them to option D. Using the appropriate frame is clearly a lesson for anyone in the field of persuasive communication.

Thaler (1985) suggests some interesting implications of framing for those presenting gains and losses to others. Losses are best presented in aggregate, to minimize their impact, and gains are best presented singly to maximize their effect. It may also be better to offset some losses against gains because, separately, losses have more impact than gains. Framing effects seem to apply to the presentation of discounts. A saving of $10 on a $50 item may be presented as such or as a 20 per cent discount. When the percentage discount is small it may be best to present it as an absolute cost reduction.

In editing, complex choices may be simplified. Thus a person may see the price of a car, not as $20,000 but as $2,000 less than he or she expected to pay; another edit is to aggregate the cost of extra features with the basic price so that the purchase has a single price. Some information, such as the base rate, may be ignored in the editing process (as we saw with regard to cab recognition, Exercise 7.2).

Box 7.3	**Overpaid?**

The way bond traders are paid may help them to get very high remuneration. Bond dealers typically work on commissions that are very low percentages. A commission of 0.1 per cent does not seem much. However, if it is based on a principal of $100 million, it is $100,000. In general, people assess costs in proportional terms and will take more trouble to save $5 off a $20 item than $5 off a $100 item.

In negotiation, our editing processes may lead us into a poor deal and we should beware of the way the other side frames choices. It is wise to focus on the total cost of a deal. Give way on small items but resist concessions on the larger ones. It could even be worthwhile to include small items in a deal proposal that you can then concede.

Thaler (1999) introduced the term *mental accounting*, which covers some of the editing functions. This uses the metaphor of accounting to explain the way in which people organize, evaluate and keep track of financial activities. As in accounting proper, people maintain separate accounts for different activities, for example they may accept the idea of travelling business class to Australia at an extra cost of $5,000 but find it difficult to justify spending $5,000 to save two day's discomfort in another sphere. Also people may close an account after a defined period; gamblers on the race track tend to think of gains or losses over a day and investors in the stock market may operate with a one-year horizon.

SECTION 4: FINANCIAL APPLICATIONS OF PROSPECT THEORY

Prospect theory provides explanations for some puzzling behaviour. We now provide several examples of its explanatory power, drawing on a review by Camerer (2000).

Investment

One of the effects of loss aversion is that people tend to hang on to losers and sell winners in share markets. Investors may have some equilibrium concept in mind, believing that the swing of the pendulum will take a losing stock back towards its purchase price and that a rising stock could similarly fall. They may also be reluctant to sell a loser because this turns a potential loss into an actual loss, so that it is more painful. From a rational standpoint, the buying price should not figure in the decision to sell shares, except for calculating capital gains tax. The selection of an alternative to sell should be based on prospective return, based on the current valuation of the share.

A bias in favour of selling winners and keeping losers has been demonstrated experimentally by Weber and Camerer (1998) and in real data by Odean (1998). Such behaviour appears to be a mistake since Odean estimated that investors lost an average of 3.4 per cent in the subsequent year compared with selling losers and keeping winners. However, this behaviour by investors may contribute to the effective operation of share markets. These markets are potentially unstable since a loss of confidence could precipitate selling, which could further aggravate the loss of confidence and lead to a collapse of the market. In practice, panic selling on a large scale is rare and markets show corrections but do not usually collapse. If the market has fallen, many investors will bide their time and refuse to sell. There seems to be evidence that market professionals are much more willing to realize a loss (see Box 7.4). They may operate with a momentum rather than an equilibrium concept of the market. Computerized share trading may lead to more market instability if it circumvents the effects of loss aversion.

Box 7.4	**'Mutual-fund pros panicked in peso crisis while small investors stood their ground'. (Headline in *Wall Street Journal*, 13 January 1995.)**

Among share-trading professionals the folklore is to stay in a rising market and sell when it turns. Loss aversion suggests that small investors might find this difficult. In particular, once they see that the market has fallen, and that they have made a loss by reference to recent prices, they may resist selling because now they are risk prone. Also, by selling, they close the account so that the potential loss becomes a real loss. The headline suggests that ordinary investors follow loss aversion but that the professionals have learned to reverse it.

The Equity Premium

Equities have traditionally provided a greater return on investments than fixed interest investments (bonds). Sometimes bonds give a return that is little better than inflation, while equities have given an average return in the USA of about 10 per cent over the period 1926–2003 and 9.6 per cent in the UK over the period 1900–2003 (Dimson, Marsh and Staunton, 2004). Traditionally, the equity premium has been explained as a compensation for risk but the difference in returns is far too large to be explained in this way.

An ingenious explanation has been offered by Benartzi and Thaler (1995). A feature of equity markets is that they rise and fall in market value much more than bond markets. Investors who look at their equity investment a month after purchase are as likely to see a gain as a loss compared with the purchase price but, after ten years, there is nearly always a gain. Since losses loom larger than gains (the ratio is about 2.25), an investor with a short-term horizon will suffer more pain from the losses and may be put off from investing in equities. Benartzi and Thaler show that, over a one-year horizon, bonds and equities have equal *prospect* returns (i.e. the larger number of gains are counterbalanced by the smaller number of more painful losses). Thus, they explain the equity premium as the additional return required to compensate for the loss aversion effect. This explanation would be still more convincing if there were evidence that those investors with longer-term horizons held a greater proportion of their portfolios in equities rather than bonds.

Long-shot Bias and the Value Premium

As noted, when the probabilities are low, the psychological weighting of probability makes long odds more attractive. This seems to operate in betting. In racetrack betting there is a tendency to back outsiders or long shots – horses with high odds that are unlikely to win. This may reflect the overweighting of small probabilities. When the betting is via the Tote, disproportionate betting on outsiders will tend to reduce the odds on these horses and raise the odds on favourites. The result is that, in the long run, long shots do worse than favourites. This effect becomes more pronounced over the course of the day as betters lose money. Their mental accounting period is a day and, in order to end up 'in the money', they increasingly need to win on a long shot, so still more money goes on such horses. Under these circumstances, an each way bet on the favourite for the last race will make money, on average, even allowing for a 15 per cent tax on winnings (Ali, 1977).

Long-shot bias, or something rather similar, may lie behind the persistent value premium effect in share investment. Value or income stocks typically give fairly high dividends and sell at prices that are rather lower than is justified by their fundamentals. Value stocks are contrasted with growth stocks that pay low dividends. With growth stocks, investors forego current income and hope for more rapid growth. By analogy, the growth stock is rather like a long shot and some companies like Google emerge to give spectacular results. However, the fundamentals are just that and Dimson, Marsh and Staunton (2004) find that, in the long run, value stocks give a distinctly better performance and show a premium of about 3 per cent over growth stocks. This effect is transnational. In a comparison of 14 countries, only one country (Italy) showed superiority for growth stocks.

Impact on Economics

Economics is founded on rational assumptions. These include an assumption that the accumulation of wealth drives individual behaviour. Thus alternatives should be assessed against this wealth criterion. However, it is apparent that individuals do not think about their wealth but instead about gains and losses relative to norms defined by the context. Furthermore, they operate with a number of accounts so that a gain in one is not necessarily offset (in their minds) by a loss in another. This pattern of behaviour violates the principle of fungibility, that money in one account is as good as money in another account. Also, it is possible to construct choices where preferences violate the principle of dominance because people choose the alternative that is the lesser of two.

Thus, people do not think according to the canons of economic logic and economics has been severely challenged by prospect theory. Previously, economists have argued that wealth will increase most rapidly if people act rationally and money is fungible. This is a normative theory. Those who do not apply normative economic principles will lose out, so that self-interest or reinforcement will direct behaviour towards a rational pattern. Thus, actual economic behaviour will be driven towards the rational pattern. This argument has been turned on its head. If people do not act rationally, normative economics needs to take this into account. The most rational policy is to anticipate the irrationality of others and adapt to it. Therefore, a study of everyday decision-making is needed so that the rational person can exploit the systematic biases in the choices of others.

A matter of current interest among finance specialists is whether psychological biases affect asset pricing. We have been accustomed to thinking that fundamentals are objectively assessed but it seems likely that some biases operate here.

Problems with Prospect Theory

The possibility of using prospect theory to explain behaviour, choose profitably and negotiate successfully has seized the imagination of researchers but the potential may be reduced when the theory is more widely evaluated. Van der Plight and van Schie (1990) gathered evidence on risk aversion and proneness among European populations. Their work confirmed Kahneman and Tversky's findings, but the effects were less strong. Leclerc, Schmitt and Dubé (1995) find that people making decisions under risk were often risk averse about time loss when, according to prospect theory, they should be risk prone.

Many of the studies in prospect theory have used hypothetical and rather artificial examples. In these studies, the majority vote has been used to decide response and it would be interesting to know more about those people who do not fit the model. However, there is plenty of field evidence which supports the theory though, often, only after *ad hoc* assumptions have been made about the mental accounting period and the separation of accounts.

The most fundamental problem with prospect theory is the lack of an underlying rationale that could relate the different phenomena that are reported. Why do losses loom larger than gains? Why do costs affect consumers less than losses? Why is time different from money in terms of loss aversion? What we have in prospect theory is an accumulation of important findings but no fundamental explanation. One possibility is that effects are related to the relative frequency of different types of occurrence. We have seen that frequency affects availability but it may have a wider relevance. If there are more positives than negatives, reference points will tend to be based on the positives. As a result, negative outcomes are more at variance with assumptions and are therefore more disturbing. This is essentially the explanation offered by Fiske (1980) for the greater impact of negative information (considered in Chapter 11). However, in betting contexts, punters more often lose so that, in this case, the norm would be established on the basis of loss, and winning should be more disturbing (in a positive sense). Clearly, this idea is just that – an idea – and more work is required before it provides any sort of explanation.

SUMMARY

This chapter is about the automatic mechanisms involved in recognizing, evaluating, judging, investigating and deciding. One process that seems to underlie thought processes is the use of schemas – structures that are fitted to information to make sense of it. When the fit is poor, people may give more attention to the stimulus until a fit is achieved. Repeated exposure of a stimulus often leads to increases in evaluation.

The evaluative response to stimuli is often faster than the cognitive response and these responses, in the initial stages, seem to involve relatively independent processing. In choices, attention is proportional to the evaluation of alternatives.

When making judgements, people use simplifying processes called heuristics. They make more use of information if it is more available because it is more discrete, eventful, recent or established through personal experience and they tend to neglect information dealing with states. More available information is also given higher probability.

We convert gains and losses into utility and objective probability is weighted when it is used in decisions. The effect of this is that people are risk averse on gains and risk prone on losses at medium and high probabilities. At low probabilities, they are risk prone on gains and risk averse on losses. The value function is steeper in the negative region. This gives rise to loss aversion and makes people more reluctant to part with things that they own.

In prospect theory, the presentation of choices, or framing and the information processing of prospects by receivers, or editing, affect the way in which choices are evaluated. By manipulating the framing, people can be pushed towards particular alternatives. People tend to think in terms of different accounts which may be closed after different periods. Thus, mental accounting, loss aversion and risk tolerance will affect the evaluation of prospects.

These processes produce effects that are contrary to axioms in economics but they help to explain a number of puzzles. These include the preference for selling winning rather than losing shares, reluctance to fully invest in shares as opposed to bonds and preference for growth shares over income shares.

Additional Resources

In 2002, Kahneman was awarded the Nobel Prize for economics – no mean achievement for a psychologist. The lecture that he gave at the time is available at: http://nobelprize.org/nobel_prizes/economics/laureates/2002/kahneman-lecture.html.

Much of this work has been accumulated in two volumes edited by Kahneman, Slovic and Tversky (1982) and Kahneman and Tversky (2000). In particular, read Thaler (1999) 'Mental accounting matters' (reprinted in Kahneman and Tversky, 2000: 241–260).

Notes

1 'If you think that accident prevention is expensive, try having accidents' – interview with Stelios Haji-Ioannou, founder of EasyJet, talking about a shipping accident.

2 An alternative explanation is that the response to many long-odds options is dominated by ideas of what could happen. People have a tiny chance of winning the lottery but the dreams of untold wealth can preoccupy them so that they ignore the odds.

8 Consumer Satisfaction and Quality

LEARNING OBJECTIVES

When you have completed this chapter, you should be able to:

1 Describe how consumer satisfaction/dissatisfaction (CSD), and consumer complaining behaviour (CCB) have been studied.
2 Know the evidence on the relationship between satisfaction and company profit.
3 Explain the confirmation and disconfirmation models of consumer satisfaction.
4 Give an account of the development and criticism of the SERVQUAL model.
5 Report on research on CCB and on the response to service delay.
6 Report on the lessons for management from this work.

OVERVIEW

Until the 1990s there was a steady development of research on the post-purchase phase of consumption but the past decade has shown limited progress in our understanding of these issues. This field has two related aspects, the nature and measurement of consumer satisfaction and dissatisfaction (CSD) and the consequences of CSD in the form of consumer complimenting and complaining behaviour (CCB), retention/defection and word of mouth. We have covered the issue of retention/defection in Chapter 2 and word of mouth will be addressed in Chapter 11, so here we are more concerned with CCB.

In the USA, Hunt and Day set up the first conference on consumer satisfaction in 1976 and work in this field grew rapidly. In 1993, Perkins noted over 3,000 references relating to this area. In Europe, CSD and CCB have received rather less emphasis than in the USA and, starting with the work of Grönroos (1978), the focus has fallen on the perception of quality, particularly with regard to services. Satisfaction often depends on the quality of goods and services and, therefore, CSD research is closely associated with the measurement of quality. There is evidence that high-quality products are more profitable: they yield better margins, are more easily sold and extended and command higher loyalty. The measurement of quality has been developed in the USA by Parasuraman and his colleagues but this work has been widely criticized.

SECTION 1: INTRODUCTION

In the past, studies have indicated that products were quite frequently regarded as unsatisfactory by consumers. Andreason (1988) quoted a figure of 15–25 per cent dissatisfaction in the USA; Stø and Glefjell (1990) found similar figures for a range of goods and services in Norway. Peterson and Wilson (1992), in one part of their review, found that 17 per cent were neutral or dissatisfied. However, improvements in design and computer-controlled manufacturing have raised quality and it is likely that satisfaction ratings have risen for goods. It is more difficult to ensure high service quality. Consumers normally like goods to be of uniform design but attempts to do the same with services can be counterproductive. Service providers need to adapt to the needs of the customer and what suits one person may not suit another; for this reason, service standardization can produce a rather formulaic interchange with customers, which may not meet their requirements.

Maintaining the quality of a service is made more difficult because of the nature of services. A service is consumed as it is produced and any mistake by the provider becomes part of the service delivered. In contrast, mistakes in the production of goods can often be corrected before sale. Getting services right is important because these constitute an increasingly large fraction of modern economies. Koepp (1987) stated that 85 per cent of all new jobs created since 1982 in the USA were in the service sector. Shugan (1994) estimated that, in 1995, 77 per cent of all jobs in the USA were in service industries. Other commentators have suggested that over 80 per cent of the US economy is service-related (see, for example, http://www.ita.doc.gov/td/sif/PDF/ ROLSERV199. PDF).

Most services have goods components; medical treatment has drugs and restaurants deliver food. However, the greater fallibility of the service component means that it is this, rather than the physical product, that usually generates most complaint. In a study conducted by Technical Assistance Research Programs (TARP), unsatisfactory product quality occasioned less than a quarter of the complaints (see Table 8.1).

There are several reasons for an interest in satisfaction and quality. People like to deliver something that is appreciated but it is also be prudent to deliver

Table 8.1   Reasons for complaint (TARP, 1979)

Problem	Households reporting a problem (%)
Unsatisfactory repair or service	36
Store did not have advertised product for sale	25
Unsatisfactory product quality	22
Long wait for delivery	10
Failure to receive delivery	10

quality. Buzzell and Gale (1987) showed that quality was profitable; margins were larger and firms could grow more easily. Reichheld (1996b) and others have argued that it costs less to retain existing customers than to gain new ones and that retention was promoted by satisfying customers (though we qualified this argument in Chapter 2). Brand extensions are likely to be more successful when the brand has higher perceived quality. Those who deliver a lower quality than their competitors are likely to lose market share (see Box 8.1).

Box 8.1	**Quality in all things (abridged from the *Guardian*, 11 August, 1993)**

Heidi Fleiss, accused of running an expensive call-girl circuit for the elite of Hollywood, rebutted criticism from Madam Alex, the previous leader of the circuit, who claimed that she had stolen her clients. 'In this business', Heidi Fleiss is reputed to have said, 'no one steals clients. There is just better service.'

Consequences of Success and Failure in Delivering Quality

Hirschman (1970) suggested that perceived failure in the delivery of goods and services led to two types of consumer response, which he described succinctly as *exit* and *voice*. Exit is switching to other products or suppliers, or simply boycotting the product. Voice has a number of forms: complaining to suppliers and seeking redress, negative word of mouth to other consumers and, occasionally, formal complaints through legal or trade authorities. Blodgett, Granbois and Walters (1993) have suggested that when a complaint is made, the character of complaint handling will determine further loyalty and word-of-mouth behaviour. An interesting extension of Hirschman's outcomes by Huefner and Hunt (1994) details vandalism, theft, disruption and other activities that aggrieved customers use to retaliate against unsatisfactory suppliers.

Oliver (1980), Oliver and Swan (1989), Feinberg et al. (1990) and Fornell (1992) find that, although repurchase intentions are much reduced by dissatisfaction, many consumers are reluctant to change. For example, Feinberg et al. (1990) found that, after an unsatisfactory warranty repair, repurchase intentions for different goods were still 47–84 per cent compared with more than 90 per cent repurchase intention when the repair was satisfactory. There is, of course, some doubt about whether repurchase intentions are an adequate guide to actual behaviour in this context; we saw in Chapter 6 that inertia operates against change and it seems likely that many of those who say that they will defect do not do so. We must also recognize that it is often not feasible to change patronage; sometimes the product is satisfactory in many other respects and there may be substantial switching costs.

At the company level, increases in satisfaction may, literally, deliver dividends. If managers can increase product quality and satisfaction, a number of beneficial effects may follow, as detailed in Figure 8.1. These are more customers (either by retention or acquisition), more purchases per customer or more margin, either through an increase in price or a reduction in costs. Thus there is interest in whether companies that raise satisfaction do become more profitable and, if so, how this comes about. To investigate this, routine measures of satisfaction are used such as the American Customer Satisfaction Index (www.theacsi.org/) and the Swedish Customer Satisfaction Barometer (Fornell, 1992). These measure satisfaction with the firm rather than the firm's brands. When the company name and brand are the same, this is appropriate but in many cases the brands are different from the company name (e.g. Procter & Gamble and their range of grocery brands). Even so, there have been some impressive findings.

In a review of studies using such measures, Zeithaml (2000) found a wide range of support for a positive association between quality and profit and suggested that this was mediated by improved customer retention. Using the Swedish Customer Satisfaction Barometer, Anderson, Fornell and Lehmann (1994) were able to demonstrate small increments in return on investment (ROI) over five years as a result of increases in satisfaction. The authors suggest that the connection between satisfaction and profit could be mediated by a range of effects. They cite greater retention, reduced price elasticity, lack of interest in competitor offerings, reduced costs for future transactions, reduced costs from failure, lower costs of customer acquisition, advertising and new product advantage through increased reputation of the firm, more customer recommendation, greater willingness to trial products and stronger relationships with suppliers. These more specific explanations are largely covered by the more aggregate alternatives shown in Figure 8.1.

Anderson and Mittal (2000) examined the connection between satisfaction and company profit and emphasized the role of retention in the satisfaction–profit

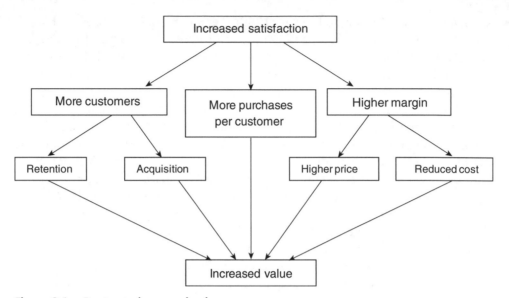

Figure 8.1   Routes to increased value

chain but they cite only one study showing clear evidence of *actual* repurchase as a function of satisfaction (Bolton, 1998). They can point to rather more examples where satisfaction is related to repurchase *intention* but this is an inadequate measure of actual retention.

Anderson, Fornell and Mazvancheryl (2004) have shown that increases in customer satisfaction are associated with increases in shareholder value, as measured by Tobin's q.[1] Anderson et al. argue that higher customer satisfaction may raise the bargaining power of a firm. Increased bargaining power may assist margin and sales and may thus contribute to shareholder value. Gruca and Rego (2005) found satisfaction influenced shareholder value by both increasing cash flows and reducing their variability; this provides a financial explanation of the relationship, but tells us little about the underlying changes in consumer behaviour. Fornell et al. (2006) examined the growth obtained from portfolios of high satisfaction companies. They found impressively high returns when compared against standard indices and they argued that this extra gain was achieved without incurring greater risk. A study by Netemeyer and Maxham (2007) suggests that supervisor ratings of company performance predicted customer outcomes, so this may be an alternative way of predicting company performance.

Although there is little *evidence* favouring any specific pathway from quality/ satisfaction to increased value, there has been some tendency to emphasize the retention route (Anderson and Mittal, 2000; Zeithaml, 2000). This emphasis on retention may be misplaced, since a review of the connection between satisfaction and retention generally found weak associations (Hennig-Thurau and Klee, 1997). We suspect that increased satisfaction may have more effect on profits via increased word of mouth, which leads to more customers. Word of mouth is considered further in Chapter 11.

SECTION 2: THEORIES OF CONSUMER SATISFACTION

The Confirmation Model

Early thinking about satisfaction treated it as meeting consumer expectations. This is the *confirmation model* of consumer satisfaction which is illustrated in Figure 8.2. Oliver (1989) described the outcome as *contentment*; for example, we are contented when a refrigerator continues to keep food cold. This low arousal state is matched by *discontent* when negative expectations are met. This applies to the routine use of inadequate services, such as congested roads, late buses and slow security at airports, and to unsatisfactory goods such as dripping taps, lumpy mattresses and toasters that eject the toast prematurely. In these situations, the discontent may be subdued because of habituation. People get used to a problem and their inertia becomes a habit. As a result, it does not occur to them to do anything about the problem and any feedback on consumption is weak (shown as a dotted line in Figure 8.2). Consumer contentment and discontent may not be expressed but are revealed when people are questioned, or when other factors raise the salience of a product's performance, for example others may comment on the dripping tap or an ad for beds may make people think of their own bedtime discomfort.

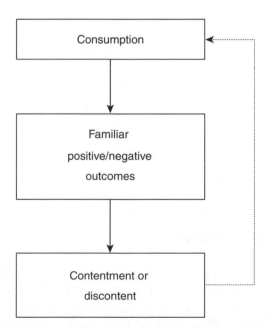

Figure 8.2   The confirmation model of consumer satisfaction: meeting expectations

The toleration of product deficiencies is explained by adaptation theory (Helson, 1964). This theory makes perception relative to some standard which may change over time in response to experience. As long as positive and negative deviations from expectation are small, they will be accommodated and will have little effect on the reference standard.

EXERCISE 8.1   LURKING DISSATISFACTIONS

Think of everyday products that you use, for example, refrigerators or car mirrors. Are these satisfactory? If you look at these products with a more critical eye, are there weaknesses that could be corrected? Does your refrigerator ice up or fail to drain condensation? Does your car use three mirrors and still leave blind spots?

   Now there are solutions to these problems but these might have been invented earlier; what is often missing is the application of an idea, rather than new technology. And people may not have had the ideas because habituation stopped them from recognizing a problem. See if you can think of products that we take for granted but which could be better.

If consumers have little awareness of the shortcomings of everyday products, they will feel little pressure to change their behaviour and this can be a matter of concern. Our tendency to adjust to our environment may be to our disadvantage. When poor products are frequently experienced, any improvement would be frequently experienced too; it is a pity if habituation leads to an absence of complaint or a lack of effort to find a better product. Although people may not notice deficiencies in currently used goods and services, they may well notice and appreciate the change when the product is improved because this change may surprise them. However, many of the discontents that we experience relate to public services (e.g. transport and parking constraints), and here, because of limited choice and influence, it may be difficult to achieve change. Research has moved away from the confirmation model but we can see that this explanation relates to much consumer behaviour, particularly the toleration of delay, which is considered later.

The Disconfirmation Model

Large deviations from expectation will affect perception and change the adaptation level (Helson, 1964). Most research has focused on this high arousal condition where the goods or services disconfirm expectation, either by exceeding it and giving satisfaction, or by falling short of expectation and causing dissatisfaction (see Figure 8.3).

   In the disconfirmation model the consumer is surprised by product features that are better or worse than expected. This model is often described as though the expectations are held in mind prior to the experience and then compared

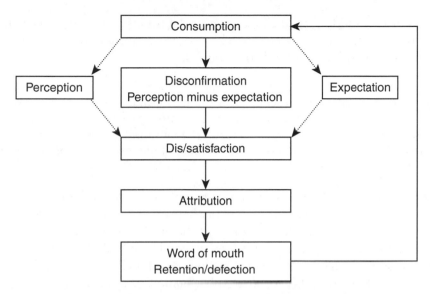

Figure 8.3   The disconfirmation model: exceeding or falling short of expectations

with the delivered product, but the experience, pleasant or unpleasant, usually causes us to bring to mind what would be appropriate in the circumstances, which we then call our expectation. In the disconfirmation model, the magnitude of surprise is related to the size of the discrepancy between expectation and experience. Two additional determinants are shown in Figure 8.3 – we show these with dotted lines because they are not part of the core disconfirmation model. The perception of the performance of the goods or services affects dis/satisfaction directly; the better it is, the more we like it. Expectation also has a direct effect, probably because it relates to the value of a product.

There is variation in the emphasis placed on the different determinants. Researchers have generally been most interested in the disconfirmation variable. Some researchers (e.g. Oliver, 1980, 1981; Swan and Trawick, 1981) have emphasized expectations, while others (e.g. Churchill and Surprenant, 1982; LaTour and Peat, 1979; Tse and Wilton, 1988) have given attention to perceptions. Several studies (e.g. Oliver, 1980; Swan and Trawick, 1980) found that satisfaction is influenced mainly by disconfirmation. At odds with these results, Churchill and Surprenant (1982) found that satisfaction with a video disc player was determined solely by perceived product performance and any disconfirmations had no additional impact on satisfaction.

The disconfirmation explanation of satisfaction has gradually evolved. Cardozo's (1965) laboratory work is often cited as the first empirical treatment of disconfirmed expectation and Howard and Sheth (1969: 145) were among the first to suggest that people use standards of assessment in judging products when they wrote that satisfaction was 'the buyer's cognitive state of being adequately or inadequately rewarded for the sacrifice he has undergone'. This cognitive account has now been modified to include emotional response. In more recent treatments the dis/satisfaction is described as a jag of arousal that modifies the attitude to the good or service. Satisfaction is:

> ... the summary psychological state resulting when the emotion surrounding disconfirmed expectations is coupled with the consumer's prior feelings about the consumption experience. Moreover, the surprise or excitement of this evaluation is thought to be of finite duration, so that satisfaction soon decays into (but nevertheless greatly affects) one's overall attitude toward purchasing products. (Oliver, 1981: 34)

However, Oliver's statement is an explanation of the formation or change of attitude, rather than a definition of satisfaction. In practice, satisfaction is determined by assessing the attitude to the past usage of the product. We can measure this by using rating scales or we can use the more elaborate method of attitude measurement discussed in Chapter 6, treating attitude as a bundle of costs and benefits. Westbrook (1980) tested this approach. He examined the way in which shop customers combined the bundle of dis/satisfactions relating to the store and found that a global measure of retail satisfaction correlated well with a simple addition of the satisfactions and dissatisfactions customers felt about different aspects of store service. Westbrook and Oliver (1991) showed that consumers subdivide consumer satisfaction and dissatisfaction (CSD) into three components: negative feeling, positive feeling related to surprise and positive feeling based on interest.

Attribution

Disconfirmations may be interpreted in different ways by consumers. The model in Figure 8.3 therefore has an *attribution* stage for the meaning assigned to product experience. This attribution of meaning will affect later behaviour by the consumer. When consumers explain a positive experience as a chance effect, they are unlikely to recommend the product. If a negative experience is attributed to neglect by the service provider, negative word of mouth and complaint to the provider are likely to ensue. Burns and Perkins (1996) cover a wide range of possible responses in such situations. The attribution that consumers make may be affected by other conditions and, in particular, the *availability of explanations* and *causal inferences* have been studied. Exercise 8.2 relates to attribution.

EXERCISE 8.2   YOUR EXPERIENCE

The apparently fresh Brie is acrid, the new vacuum cleaner blocks or the waiter in an expensive restaurant is unhelpful; here the dissatisfactions arise because we expected a better experience. Conversely, we may be pleasantly surprised and satisfied when expectations are surpassed, e.g. when the roads are unusually clear, the fruit in supermarkets is ripe or the plane arrives early.

Think back to the last time you were surprised by your experience as a consumer. Did the surprise make you satisfied, dissatisfied or neither? How would you explain what happened? Who was responsible? If you have the opportunity, will you try to repeat the experience?

Availability

According to the availability heuristic, more vivid events are more easily brought to mind than routine occurrences and are judged more probable (see Chapter 6). Folkes (1988) gives an interesting example of how this can work. She asked people who were approaching the escalators to their apartment in a six-storey building how often the escalators broke down. The escalators only went to the fourth floor so that those who lived on the fifth and sixth floors always had to climb the stairs for the last part of their ascent. Those who always had to use the stairs for part of their journey estimated that the escalators broke down *less* often than the people who used the first four floors, for whom an escalator failure was more vivid. The distinctiveness of a product failure raises its availability and the availability heuristic raises the perceived likelihood that it will occur again. This, in turn, raises dissatisfaction. The supplier should, therefore, try to make failures less distinctive. For example, if customers are occupied in some way when service quality is reduced, they may form a less distinct memory of the poor performance.

Worse-than-expected outcomes have more impact than better-than-expected outcomes (DeSarbo et al., 1994). This difference could be explained as an availability effect if failures are unusual and draw attention, or it may be a loss aversion effect (Chapter 7).

Causal Inferences

Weiner (1980, 1990) has examined the explanations given for success and failure and has suggested three causal dimensions that are relevant to consumer response: *stability*, *locus of causality* and *controllability*. Stability is shown when the cause can be consistently attributed to a particular person or feature of the environment; locus of causality relates to whether the purchaser, the supplier or some other party is seen to be at fault; and controllability reflects the ability of an agent to intervene and change outcomes. From the consumer's standpoint, an unstable negative event is less threat. For example, an out-of-stock item may be seen as exceptional (unstable) and unlikely to be repeated. It is, therefore, better for a seller if the cause of their failure is seen as unstable by the customer. By contrast, it is best to have stability in product success since this encourages continued usage. Folkes (1984) suggests that, when failure is perceived to be stable, a consumer will prefer to have a refund for a product failure since a replacement carries the same risk as the original; if the failure is seen as unstable, consumers will be more willing to accept a replacement. Stability may vary across customer segments. Bolton (1998) examined defection as a consequence of the failure of a mobile phone network. If the customer was long term, the failure was offset against past good performance and seen as unstable, so the customer was disinclined to defect. Recent customers who lacked this experience were more likely to see the failure as stable, blame the supplier and defect.

Weiner's other dimensions also affect consumer response after product failure. For example, with respect to locus of causality, persons may blame themselves when they purchase a poor product, and therefore expect no redress; but if they see the failure as the responsibility of the manufacturer or retailer, they may then expect replacement or refund. If people feel that they have no control over their outcomes, they may feel anger towards those whom they think do have control, for example when public transport services are inadequate.

SECTION 3: SERVICE QUALITY

SERVQUAL

SERVQUAL is a measuring instrument designed to assess any service using one standard set of questions. It was developed by Parasuraman, Zeithaml and Berry (1985, 1988). SERVQUAL measures customers' expectations of what firms should provide in the industry being studied and their perceptions of how a given service provider performs against these criteria. The 1988 version of the instrument contained 22 expectation questions covering such specific service facilities as up-to-date equipment, visually appealing premises and polite employees. In 1991, Parasuraman, Berry and Zeithaml modified the instrument slightly. They changed two items and altered the wordings of some others, the negative scoring on some items was removed and the wording of the expectation measures was changed so that respondents were asked what an 'excellent service would provide', rather than what 'firms in the industry should provide'. With the original phraseology most responses clustered at the top of the scale so that it was difficult to show much variation in the expectations about different attributes. Box 8.2 shows the expectation items in the 1991 scale, applied to telephone companies. A second set of questions (not shown), deals with the perceptions about a specific telephone company.

Box 8.2	SERVQUAL expectation components and classification (from Parasuraman, Berry and Zeithaml, 1991: 446–447)

Tangibles

1 Excellent telephone companies will have modern-looking equipment.
2 The physical facilities at excellent telephone companies will be visually appealing.
3 Employees of excellent telephone companies will be neat-appearing.
4 Materials associated with the service (such as pamphlets or statements) will be visually appealing in an excellent telephone company.

Reliability

5 When excellent telephone companies promise to do something by a certain time, they will do so.
6 When customers have a problem, excellent telephone companies will show a sincere interest in solving it.
7 Excellent telephone companies will perform the service right first time.
8 Excellent telephone companies will provide their services at the time they promise to do so.
9 Excellent telephone companies will keep error-free records.

Responsiveness

10 Employees of excellent telephone companies will tell customers exactly when services will be performed.
11 Employees of excellent telephone companies give prompt service to customers.
12 Employees of excellent telephone companies will always be willing to help customers.
13 Employees of excellent telephone companies will never be too busy to respond to customer requests.

Assurance

14 The behavior of employees of excellent telephone companies will instil confidence in customers.
15 Customers of excellent telephone companies will feel safe in their transactions.
16 Employees of excellent telephone companies will be consistently courteous with customers.
17 Employees of excellent telephone companies will have the knowledge to answer customer questions.

(Continued)

Empathy

18 Excellent telephone companies will give customers individual attention.

19 Excellent telephone companies will have operating hours convenient to all their customers.

20 Excellent telephone companies will have employees who give customers personal attention.

21 Excellent telephone companies will have the customers' best interests at heart.

22 The employees of excellent telephone companies will understand the specific needs of their customers.

Parasuraman, Zeithaml and Berry (1988) showed that these 22 items could be allocated to five dimensions as shown: tangibles, reliability, responsiveness, assurance (knowledge and courtesy of employees and their ability to inspire trust and confidence) and empathy (caring and individual attention to customers). However, the five-factor structure has not been well supported; Cronin and Taylor (1992) found only one general factor.

The idea that SERVQUAL will apply to a variety of services without much modification has also been contested. Carman (1990) found that some functions require additional measures for adequate explanation. Koelemeijer (1992) and Finn and Lamb (1991) found that the SERVQUAL instrument performed poorly in retail contexts. Dabholkar, Thorpe and Rentz (1996) developed a scale for retail quality measurement which customized the measure to the retail context. It is easy to argue that some of the items are inappropriate for certain services, e.g. religious services having modern-looking equipment, neat appearance in academic settings, or the providers of sexual services keeping error-free records. Thus, customization of SERVQUAL seems to be required for application to different services and, although Parasuraman, Zeithaml and Berry (1994) accepted this, the changes may need to be substantial.

The computation of quality judgement from the questionnaire responses has also raised problems. SERVQUAL uses the difference scores between expectation and perception so that a positive score occurs only when perceptions exceed expectations. Expectations tend to be uniformly high and show little variance. Although the difference measures correlate reasonably well with an overall measure of quality (Babacus and Boller, 1992; Cronin and Taylor, 1992; Parasuraman, Berry and Zeithaml, 1991), the low variance in the expectation measures makes these irrelevant to the score so that perception-only scores are equally predictive. For this reason, Cronin and Taylor (1992) recommended that the measure is restricted to performance perceptions (which they call SERVPERF), resulting in a questionnaire of half the length. An alternative to this is to measure the gap between expectation and perceived performance with a single question that combines the two elements. Babacus and Boller (1992) suggested a way of phrasing this and Box 8.3 shows the binary form and the combined measure. In a review of SERVQUAL's history, Smith (1995) concludes that few of the original claims remain undisputed. Another useful review is by Buttle (1996). The aim of generic measurement of service quality is attractive, but this goal may be unobtainable because of variation in the nature of services and because of a lack of agreement about concepts and measures.

Box 8.3	**Alternative scales**

1 SERVQUAL expectation and perception scales:

Firms in XYZ's field should have modern-looking equipment

Strongly disagree   1 | 2 | 3 | 4 | 5 | 6 | 7   Strongly agree

Firm XYZ has modern-looking equipment

Strongly disagree   1 | 2 | 3 | 4 | 5 | 6 | 7   Strongly agree

2 Combined item:

XYZ's modern-looking equipment

Greatly falls short off my expectations   1 | 2 | 3 | 4 | 5 | 6 | 7   Greatly exceeds my expectations

---

Managing Satisfaction

Work on CSD should help us to make goods and services better. A paper by Halstead (2002) summarizes the mistakes made in consumer satisfaction programmes. The disconfirmation model, by specifying how people become satisfied and dissatisfied, defines the targets for management action. Specific management decisions are required under three headings.

1 Refining Services

Customer preference

Provide the service that customers want, rather than the one that it is convenient to give. This requires regular assessment of customer satisfaction, monitoring of complaints, etc. Some satisfaction measures are too long. It may be better to focus on the best and worst aspects of a service rather than covering all the possibilities.

Communication

Make sure that senior management gets the information on customer perceptions of product quality. Many perceptions of service quality arise in the exchange between customers and, usually, junior staff such as receptionists. As a result, senior management may be unaware of dissatisfactions. Senior managers are responsible for policy on complaint handling, returned goods, compensation and the general quality of exchanges with customers. They must define this policy and communicate it to staff and customers. Since relatively junior staff often receive complaints first, it may be wise to empower these staff so that they can immediately resolve the problem.

Competitors

Customer expectations are set by the market so managements should monitor competitor practices.

Research

Managements should search for ways of adding value to the product and should monitor the customer response to any changes. Use customer complaints to improve the product.

2 Belief Management

Prime relevant expectations

People can have several expectations about a product. People may have views about what is fair, ideal, desirable, common, just adequate – and these can all be different. When we go to a post office, the ideal may be no queue, the minimum acceptable may be a short queue and the prediction may be a long queue. When a number of expectations are in play, the supplier should try to increase the salience of those expectations that the service can normally meet. The management of expectation also includes forewarning customers about problems with products, e.g. that ionizers produce dirty deposits on nearby walls. Marketing communications to trade users sometimes identify the limitations of a product. It is possible that suppliers would benefit if they were more open to consumers about product weaknesses, particularly when these deficiencies are quickly discovered by users.

Reveal hidden benefits

Another aspect of belief management occurs when marketing communications draw attention to benefits that would otherwise go unnoticed, even though they fulfil a need. An example might be the fact that foodstuffs are free of certain preservatives or pesticides. This builds satisfaction and positions competitors negatively if they have not made such claims.

Use salient problems

Gains to be made when a competitor upsets customers and makes certain services deficiencies more salient. For example, Broadband service may be intermittent or slower than expected. If a competitor has irritated customers in this way, it is worth stressing that your service lacks these problems.

Do not draw attention to the unnoticed

Do not overreact to minor deficiencies in your product. People may not notice or bother about small discrepancies between expectation and outcome. Apologies for minor shortfalls may increase dissatisfaction by drawing attention to a problem that customers had ignored.

3 Damage Limitation

Company policy should be designed to reduce dissatisfaction when a product has fallen short of expectation by:

- listening to and responding politely to complaints,
- recognizing the deficiency,
- apologizing and accepting responsibility to assist customers, but not necessarily responsibility for causing the problem,
- explaining what's gone wrong, describing any steps taken by the company to prevent it happening again, and inviting customer comment,
- compensating customers where appropriate.

This last heading, damage limitation, leads us on to a discussion of complaining behaviour.

SECTION 4: COMPLAINING

Factors Affecting Complaining Behaviour

People are often reluctant to complain when they are dissatisfied with goods or services. There is evidence that the degree of dissatisfaction has a modest relationship with the likelihood of complaint (Day, 1984; Malafi et al. 1993; Oliver, 1981, 1987; Singh and Howell, 1985). Andreasen (1988) and Stø and Glefjell (1990) both found that 60 per cent of dissatisfied consumers did nothing. Benterud and Stø (1993) found that 95 per cent of those dissatisfied with their TV shopping did not complain. Oliver (1981) reports a correlation of about 0.4 between dissatisfaction and complaining. However, some of us may complain about policies that do not bring much personal discomfort (see Box 8.4).

Box 8.4	Complaints

Although a grievance is usually required to make a complaint, some of us scarcely need it. Complaining also has its entertaining aspect. Here are two examples of teasing the great and the good.

Sir John Krebs
Chairman, Food Standards Agency

Dear Sir John

For some time I have been concerned about the emphasis placed by the FSA on the absence of micro-organisms in food. There is evidence that those exposed to soil bacteria have improved resistance to disease, probably because bacterial challenge improves the function of the immune system. Whilst in medicine the development of immunity is much supported, it seems that your Agency gives little or no consideration to this potential effect of food. Too little bacterial content in food could lead to increased morbidity when food does become contaminated. This thinking suggests that some controls on the production and sale of food could be counter-effective and that some death and disease from contaminated food is acceptable because of the resistance conferred on the rest of the population. I would be glad if the FSA could endorse a more pro-bacterial policy.

Yours sincerely

Ken Livingston
Mayor of London

Dear Ken

'This train terminates at High Barnet'. It is the *service* that terminates at High Barnet. The train terminates with its first and last carriages. I was so cross when I heard this that I forgot to get out at Tufnell Park and had to come back from Archway. Do you think that you could do something about these announcements?

Yours sincerely

Day (1984) and Singh and Howell (1985) have noted that complaining is affected by how people attribute product failure, their expectation of redress and the likely time-cost and effort involved. We suggest that people may also complain out of a sense of social obligation. Research on complaining needs to take account of all the possible reasons that people might have for this behaviour. We can cover these reasons by using Ajzen's (1985, 1991) theory of planned behaviour, as discussed in Chapter 6. This deals with three types of influence.

1 **Expected outcomes** (gains and losses, including opportunity costs, that follow complaining). Hirschman (1970) suggested that complaining was related to the expected returns and opportunity costs. Positive outcomes may include replacement, apology and better goods or service in the future, while negative outcomes may include lost opportunities, wasted time and embarrassment. The perceived likelihood of success in obtaining redress has been found to be associated with complaining in a number of studies (Day and Landon, 1976; Granbois, Summers and Frazier, 1977; Richins, 1983, 1987; Singh, 1990). Richins (1985) also found evidence that the importance of the product affects the likelihood of complaining.
2 **Normative influences** (what people think reference persons or groups think they should do). Consumers may also be influenced by what they believe others think they should do, even when these other people are not present. Normative influences on complaining have not been studied systematically, although Richins (1981) has noted instances where consumers felt that they *ought* to complain.
3 **Control factors** (that make it more or less easy to register a complaint). These are knowledge, skills, time and other factors that can make complaining easier or harder. Examples are the ease of access to key personnel, an understanding of the workings of the organization causing dissatisfaction and confidence about complaining. Control factors help us to distinguish between those who complain and those who do not. Two studies (Caplovitz, 1967; Warland, Herrman and Willits, 1975) found that non-complainers seemed powerless and had less knowledge of the means of redress. Also, Grønhaug (1977) found that there were more complaints to a Norwegian consumer

protection agency from citizens who lived closer to it. Grønhaug and Zaltman (1981) also recognized the importance of resources such as time, money and confidence and this study is cited by Yi (1990) as important in showing differences between complainers and non-complainers. A matter of concern is that vulnerable consumers (the old, ill and disadvantaged) complain less than others (Andreasen and Manning, 1990) and this is likely to be related to the reduced control that such consumers have.

East (2000) used the theory of planned behaviour to investigate complaining. He found that complaining was based mainly on getting a refund or replacement, standing up for one's rights, doing what friends expected and confidence about complaining. Such evidence helps us to see what may encourage complaining. For example, in order to increase confidence, suppliers should make it clear that they welcome complaints and that they have a clear procedure for handling them.

The Benefits of Receiving Complaints

Fornell and Wernerfelt (1987) argued that, within cost limits, it is profitable to gather and evaluate complaints from dissatisfied customers and some companies – particularly in the USA – put toll-free telephone numbers on goods packaging for this purpose. One reason for the profitability of receiving complaints is that these supply information about product deficiencies, which can then be corrected. A second reason is to gather further sales when the complainer gets in touch. For example, the complainer may be advised that there is a newer version of software or an improved design of outdoor clothing and this information may lead to purchase. A third reason is that an effective response to the aggrieved customer by the company may reduce negative word of mouth to other potential customers, which could damage sales. Finally, if the complaint is well handled, the company may be able to stop defection or recover customers who have already left.

There is evidence that customers who are retained after a service failure may be more satisfied than they are without the failure. This is called the service recovery paradox (SRP). If customers are more appreciative of the company, they may recommend it more and be more inclined to repurchase. An SRP was found by TARP (1979) and Gilly and Gelb (1982) but Solnick and Hemenway (1992) found that those who complained about health provision were over four times more likely to defect than those who did not. More patronage after complaint may occur because the complaint handling resolved the customer's dissatisfaction and exceeded expectation, but it is also possible that those who intend to remain with the supplier complain because they want to benefit from changes induced by their complaining.

Magnini et al. (2007) used role-play studies to investigate the SRP. They found that the effect occurred when the failure was not severe, the firm had not failed the customer before, the cause of the failure was seen as unstable and the customer believed that the company had little control over the failure. In a meta-analysis, De Matos et al. (2007) found a significant SRP effect for satisfaction but not for repurchase intention or word of mouth. The satisfaction effect varied from service to service.

SECTION 5: THE CONSUMER'S RESPONSE TO DELAY

The Frequency of Delay

Delay in the delivery of service is a perennial feature of retailing and other services. Indeed, it is an inherent liability of a product that is produced and consumed in an interval of time (see illustration). Consumers wait for counter service in post offices, for train tickets in booking offices and at the checkout in supermarkets they also wait for public transport and get held up in traffic jams; they may have to wait to talk to someone on the telephone. For the individual, delay is frustrating and for the economy it is wasteful because people waiting in line are neither producing nor consuming. Pruyn and Smidts (1993) found that Dutch consumers waited, on average, over half an hour per day and that supermarket checkout delay was the most irritating hold-up. In Britain, 70 per cent of respondents in a Consumers' Association report on supermarkets (*Which?*, February 1990) mentioned 'a lot of staffed checkouts' as desirable, placing it fourth in importance compared with other store features and another report on post offices (*Which?*, September 1989) put cutting queuing time at the top of service improvements suggested by respondents even though the research recorded an average wait of only 3½ minutes. Bitner, Booms and Tetreault (1990) noted that delay was a major feature of incidents causing dissatisfaction.

Evidence on the Response to Delay

It is important that delays are minimized. A number of studies have shown that the longer the wait, the lower the evaluation of the whole service (Feinberg, Widdows and Steidle, 1996; Katz, Larson and Larson, 1991; Taylor, 1994; Tom and Lucey, 1995). It appears that dissatisfaction with waiting can affect the whole service experience. Organizations may not notice the irritation that delay causes because of perceptual differences. Feinberg and Smith (1989) found that when the customer at the checkout thought the average delay was 5.6 minutes the staff perception was 3.2 and the actual time was 4.7 minutes.

It is likely that people are less bothered by delay when it is expected (Maister, 1985). Supporting this, an experiment on bank queues by Clemmer and Schneider (1989) showed that the more unexpected the delay, the more it was

Queuing for crêpes in Hampstead.

disliked. This suggests that we can identify two types of dissatisfaction with delay: a low involvement discontent when the delay is predicted and a high involvement disconfirmation effect. As delays get more common they also become more predictable and, paradoxically, consumers may put up with them more easily. This may be why Taylor (1994) did not find that common delays were associated with significantly more irritation.

Maister (1985) proposed that people tolerate a wait better if they have a reason for the delay. The provision of delay information is standard for airlines and London Transport provides display boards reporting the wait before the next train or bus arrives. This information seems to be much appreciated despite the fact that it does nothing to reduce the waiting time. Another useful innovation is queue position information when waiting on the telephone.

Maister also notes that people are less irritated by delay if they are occupied in some way. One example here is the way in which Disneyland entertains its queues, another is the provision of mirrors in places where people have to wait, for example at lifts. Taylor (1995) used two groups in an experiment to test the effect of occupying people when they had to wait. Both groups were delayed by ten minutes but only one was allowed activities to offset the delay. In this study, the evaluation of the service was reduced by delay but the reduction was less when people were occupied. In fact, some of those who were delayed did not even realize that they had been held up and most of these people were in the 'occupied' group. Taylor's work also suggested that, if the service provider was thought to have control, customers assessed the service more negatively. This is consistent with Weiner's (1980, 1990) suggestion that people become more irritated when they believe that the service provider has control of the situation.

Studies by Dubé-Rioux, Schmitt and Leclerc (1989, 1991) showed that when delay occurred at the beginning or end of a process, in this case a meal, it was evaluated more negatively than mid-process delays. It was better to take the order, and then impose the delay, than to wait before taking the order. However, it is not always clear when a service starts and finishes. For example, delays to air travel occur when going to the airport, at check-in, baggage check, passport control, the departure lounge, in the plane before take-off, before landing, at baggage reclaim and again at passport control and customs. People may think of this sequence as a number of services or just one and the way they regard it may affect how they tolerate delay at different points.

A study by East, Lomax and Willson (1991b) showed that 31 per cent did not mind waiting at the checkout in supermarkets. In banks and post offices this figure rose to 50 per cent and in building societies to 57 per cent. A cynic might see this as evidence of British stoicism, and Maister (1985) has noted dryly that, if the British see a queue, they join it. Further evidence showed that most people (52 per cent in the UK and 63 per cent in the USA), either did not mind, or minded a little, when delayed at the checkout (East et al., 1992). The data suggest that delay is tolerated in the USA more than in the UK. However, the dislike of delay was related to how long people expected to be delayed; the US respondents expected delays to be briefer and this probably explains their greater tolerance. In the East, Lomax and Willson study it was clear that people expected to be delayed longer in supermarkets than in other outlets and this may explain why they were less tolerant of waiting in supermarkets than in banks, building societies and post offices.

Dislike of queuing is also likely to be related to the reason for waiting and the amount of spare time that people have. Table 8.2 shows the evidence on post offices subdivided by age and whether the customer was paying or receiving money. Older people, who might be expected to have more spare time, were more tolerant of delay. People were also more tolerant when they were receiving a benefit rather than paying for something.

Table 8.2   Percentage who dislike waiting at the post office (East, Lomax and Willson, 1991b)

Age	Those buying stamps, licences or paying bills (%)	Those receiving pensions, allowances or other benefits(%)
Under 65	61	49
65+	50	18

Perceived Responsibility for Delay

Of particular interest is the way people explain who is responsible when they have to wait for service. If customers see the service provider as responsible, they are likely to be more irritated by the delay and complain more (Weiner, 1980).

Folkes, Koletsky and Graham (1987) found that customers became more angry and expressed more resistance to repurchase when they saw that a delay was avoidable by management. Taylor (1994) also found that those who blamed management were more angry about the wait.

In the study by East, Lomax and Willson (1991b), respondents were asked whom they held responsible when they were delayed at the checkout of a supermarket. Table 8.3 shows that more of the people who blamed management disliked waiting. The investigations of delay in post offices, building societies and banks gave very similar results. We see from the bracketed numbers in Table 8.3 that few people are self-blaming; they are much more likely to blame other customers than themselves. This is consistent with the actor–observer bias (Jones and Nisbett, 1972), that an actor tends to see others as choosing and therefore responsible for their behaviour while the actor sees the same behaviour in himself as caused by the situation (e.g. circumstances or other people).

Table 8.3   Those held responsible for delay in the supermarket (East, Lomax and Willson, 1991b)

Response to delay	No one (99) (%)	Self (9) (%)	Other customers (96) (%)	Checkout staff (19) (%)	Management (208) (%)	Total (431) (%)
Don't mind	48	33	46	37	16	31
Dislike it	52	67	54	63	84	69

Delay Management

Research on the response to delay helps us to understand how to manage this service problem better. There are three approaches:

1   **Operations management.** Where feasible, managements should try to avoid delays by increasing service supply in line with demand. For example, supermarket managements can count shoppers entering the store and open checkouts in advance of the calculated demand and they can use their fastest checkout operators at peak times.
2   **Influencing demand.** The second approach uses regulation and incentives to draw demand away from busy periods and towards quiet periods. A reservation system is used for many services and differential pricing may also shift demand, e.g. Monday is often a cheap day at the cinema in Britain. However, East, Lomax, Willson and Harris (1994) judged that the scope for promoting the off-peak periods in supermarkets was limited (Chapter 10).
3   **Perception management.** The third approach is to try to ensure that the customer sees the delay in a way that does least damage. Tom and Lucey (1995) suggest putting literature at the checkout and suggest that this is a good location for free samples. Maister (1985) also recommends diverting the queue but the form of the diversion should be chosen carefully; it is easy to irritate customers with mindless music on the telephone and irrelevant advertising on screens set up for the queue. Such arrangements imply that the delay is normal (stable) and management is interested in alleviating, rather than eliminating, the discomfort of waiting.

When serious delays occur, managements may receive much of the blame. Often the cause is accidental or brought about by other service providers on whom a firm had relied. This suggests that management needs to distinguish between the cause of the delay and responsibility for its consequences. Staff should clearly accept responsibility for remedying a problem, but it will help if they can explain that they did not create the problem, since Taylor (1994) has shown that the service is liked less when blame is attributed to the service provider. For example, the cause of an take-off delay may be that a service company has failed to deliver airline food on time, a mechanical fault has been revealed by standard checks before take off, bad weather has delayed the plane's arrival, or that airport congestion is worse than normal. In all these cases, timely announcements may help to deflect blame.

Queues can be organized as either multiple-line or as single-line. Sometimes it is possible to use a queuing ticket system, which allows people to conduct other business while they wait. The relative attraction of these three systems was tested by East, Lomax, Willson and Harris (1992) in their investigation of bank and building society use (see Table 8.4).

Table 8.4   If there were queues, would you rather have? (East, Lomax, Willson and Harris, 1992)

System	Banks (%)	Building societies (%)	Mean (%)
... separate queues at each counter	15	12	14
... a single queuing system	78	81	79
... queuing tickets	7	7	7

The single-line queuing system is much preferred despite the fact that this introduces a slight delay as customers make their way to a vacant counter. The advantages of single-line systems are twofold: delays are approximately equal and therefore fair and they are more predictable since excessive delays at one counter will not affect waiting time much when there are several counters in use. A single-line system seems particularly useful when the start of a service is impending; for example, in train stations where there is a danger of missing the train. Work by Pruyn and Smidts (1993) indicates that, although people may prefer the single line, the queuing system is of less consequence than the duration of delay and the quality of the waiting environment.

SUMMARY

Consumer satisfaction, dissatisfaction, quality perception and complaining behaviour are important because they relate to profit via word of mouth and repeat purchase. A particular emphasis in this field has been on the quality of services because service work constitutes a large and growing proportion of modern economies.

Consumers are contented when products meet positive expectations and are discontented with goods and services that show expected weaknesses, but this fulfilment of expectations normally produces little arousal and, therefore, little exit or voice. Much research has now focused on those occasions where product performance surprises the consumer (the disconfirmation model). Surprise is arousing and causes more behavioural response and, therefore, more potential impact on profit. There is some variation in the way researchers describe the detail of the disconfirmation model but there is agreement that the discrepancy between expectation and perception creates disconfirmation and that expectations and perceptions may have additional direct effects on dis/satisfaction. In addition, researchers now recognize an interpretative phase in which consumers' explanations of their experience may modify their responses to it.

Work on service quality has focused on an instrument called SERVQUAL which has been developed as a measure of quality in any service field. The instrument has attracted substantial criticism and, although it has been modified, there are continuing concerns about what it measures and how well it applies across different services.

Research has related complaining behaviour to the level of dissatisfaction and to outcomes such as redress and time cost. When all salient factors were measured in a planned behaviour framework, other factors (the views of others, standing up for rights and confidence about complaining) had strong influence on whether or not a complaint was made. This suggests that redress may have been given too much importance as a response to complaining.

Delay is a general liability of service provision. Unexpected delay (causing disconfirmation) is more disliked. When it occurs, the delay is tolerated better if people understand why they are delayed and how long it will last. Also, if consumers can occupy their time they are less bothered. It is better to start a service and then impose a delay rather than to begin or end with the delay. Resentment at delay varies quite widely; it is greater among those who attribute blame to management.

Additional Resources

For reviews of SERVQUAL, see Smith (1995) and Buttle (1996). For evidence of the impact of satisfaction on shareholder value, see Anderson et al. (2004) and Gruca and Rego (2005).

Note

1 A firm's q value is the ratio of its market value to the current replacement cost of its assets (Tobin, 1969). Thus it is higher for those firms that are perceived to be using their assets more effectively.

Part 4
Market Response

9 Consumer Response to Price and Sales Promotions

LEARNING OBJECTIVES

When you have completed this chapter, you should be able to:

1 Describe how consumers process price information.
2 Explain how marketers assess consumers' price sensitivity.
3 Evaluate the different tactics you observe in the marketplace to present prices and price changes.
4 Assess the effectiveness of promotions by distinguishing between possible sources of extra sales.
5 Compare the advantages and disadvantages of price discounting versus couponing.
6 Discuss the long-term effectiveness of promotions.

OVERVIEW

Consumers verify prices of products in order to make sure they buy at the right price and, for expensive items, stay within budget. Buying at the right price means getting good value for money, compared to alternative products and buying at the right moment and place. Benchmark prices may be externally available but oftentimes consumers have to rely on their memory of previously encountered prices to make comparisons. Price memory, unfortunately, appears to be rather unreliable.

Marketers have developed different methodologies to estimate how consumers react to price changes. Price increases, though often necessary and justified, are unpopular and are often considered unfair. Consumer researchers have examined under which conditions perceptions of fairness or unfairness occur.

Price decreases are usually sales promotions. Two decades of access to scanner data has given researchers the opportunity to develop sophisticated quantitative models to evaluate promotion

(Continued)

effectiveness. Combining a price cut with additional promotional activities, such as in-store displays and advertising features, may have a synergistic effect. Promotions usually have large short-term effects on sales, but there is doubt about their long-term effectiveness and contribution to profit.

SECTION 1: CONSUMER RESPONSE TO PRICE

Reference Prices

A price is rarely treated in isolation: prices become informative by relating them to other prices, a phenomenon studied under the heading of reference price. A price in combination with a reference price, whether accurate or not, allows a consumer to determine whether it is better to buy here and now or to wait and buy elsewhere. When a product is cheaper than expected it is more likely to be purchased and vice versa.

The concept of reference price was introduced to marketing by Monroe (1973). It was inspired by Helson's (1964) adaptation-level theory that states that stimuli are judged with respect to internal norms. These internal norms represent the aggregate effect of past and present stimulation. There are two views on the origin of reference prices. According to the first view, consumers call on their memory of past prices they paid or encountered. They hold what is referred to as internal reference prices (IRP). The second view posits that reference prices are formed during the shopping occasion itself, based on prices observed, known in the literature as external reference prices (ERP).

Interestingly, research on reference price does not ask consumers for their reference prices but instead infers them from choice models estimated on panel data (Winer, 1986). These models include as independent variables the elements of the marketing mix, including price, but also a reference price term. This term captures the difference between the current price of the product and its competitors at the moment of choice and some mathematical function of past prices (in the case of IRP) or currently observable other prices (in the case of ERP). The fact that this difference variable helps explain choice is taken as evidence that consumers make comparisons with reference prices. The wide availability of individual-level scanner data has permitted an extremely productive stream of research in this area (see the review in Mazumdar, Raj and Sinha, 2005).

Researchers have provided a broad range of reference price models. Hardie, Johnson and Fader (1993) compared a model with ERP and one with IRP and found that, at least for orange juice, the category they examined, ERP was a better representation of reference price. Briesch et al. (1997), however, showed that IRP gave a better model fit in other categories. It is of course possible that the use of IRP or ERP varies between consumers and situations. Mazumdar and Papatla (2000) pursue this idea and show that there are segments of consumers that differ in the extent to which they use IRP or ERP. They also show that IRP is more frequently used for more expensive product categories while ERP is more often used in categories with a longer interpurchase time and greater frequency of promotions.

Although most research examines ERP and IRP as defined above, a number of alternative definitions of reference price have been proposed. People may compare with the price they *usually* pay but they may also compare with the price they would *like* to pay, the price they *expect* to pay, given the expected evolution of prices, or the price they regard as *fair*. Winer (1988) even proposed eight different possible definitions of price reference.

Although most research treats reference prices as precise points, it may be that consumers actually have price zones in mind. Kalyanaram and Little (1994) estimate a 'latitude of acceptance' around the reference price. This is a zone in which the consumer is indifferent to deviations between the observed price and the reference price. They also show that the width and variability differ for different market segments. As with most reference price models, they find the asymmetric price effect predicted by prospect theory (see Chapter 7), with stronger negative responses to price increases than positive responses to price decreases.

EXERCISE 9.1   YOUR PRICE KNOWLEDGE

Keep the till receipt of one of your next trips to the supermarket. When you get home, unpack your products and, without looking at your receipt, write down the prices you paid. Indicate each time whether you think you remember the price accurately or whether you are just making an estimate. Also indicate how accurate you think you are (very accurate, rather accurate, not accurate). Score your responses according to whether they are exactly right, within 10 per cent or outside this range. Compare your results with others.

1   How easy or difficult was it to determine whether your knowledge is directly pulled from memory (accurate) or constructed (estimated)? In other words, how good is your introspective access to the cognitive processes you use to answer the questions?
2   Is there any evidence that frequently bought items are better remembered?
3   Do you have other hypotheses on why you remembered some prices better than other ones?
4   How can these hypotheses be tested in a study?
5   Are students likely to remember prices better than other consumers? If so, for which reasons?

Price Memory

If consumers use IRP to assess the attractiveness of an offer, it is interesting to verify how accurate their knowledge of prices is. An early study by Gabor and Granger (1961) observed that 82 per cent of Nottingham housewives could state a price for products that they had bought in the previous week and of these at least 70 per cent were correct. It should be noted that this study was conducted when manufacturers could enforce prices and there was little price variability between stores or over time. In the USA, there was no price control and price recall figures were lower. More recently, Dickson and Sawyer (1990) found that less than half of US shoppers could give the correct price for the item that they had just put into their shopping trolley. They mention in their article that marketing executives and academics who attended presentations of this study were surprised by how imperfect shoppers' attention to, and retention of, price information was at the point of purchase. Nevertheless, the finding was corroborated by Le Boutillier, Le Boutillier and Neslin (1994) for coffee, but not for soda, where 71 per cent could recall the exact price they paid. In addition, using the same interviewing procedure, Wakefield and Inman (1993) report percentages of correct responses ranging from 52 to 78 per cent for four product categories.

These in-the-aisle price knowledge surveys have received two types of response. Some researchers consider that these survey results bring reference price findings into question, because price knowledge is much lower than most researchers intuitively expected (Kalyanaram and Winer, 1995). A second type of response concerns the interpretation of the results. The Dickson and Sawyer results are often interpreted as indications that price memory is poor. Vanhuele and Drèze (2002) point out that what is actually measured in these in-the-aisle surveys is short-term memory, not long-term price memory.

Vanhuele and Drèze (2002) examined how price information is stored in long-term memory and, based on theories from numerical cognition, hypothesized that three types of coding are used: verbal (similar to recording your voice), visual (photographic) and magnitude coding (you automatically remember some area on a hypothetical number line; what you remember is that the price was somewhere between 35 and 40). They show that recall questions measure only part of price memory. Recognition memory is clearly better and some knowledge is also only present in an approximate form in memory.

Overall, price knowledge surveys may suggest that the current price is of no consequence to many purchasers but this simplifies the issue too much. Although consumers may take prices on trust on many occasions, they may, at other times, check on how much they are paying and react against suppliers who are seen to overcharge. In addition, the price of a limited number of goods may be used as a key to the overall value for money offered by a store. Even if there is only a small segment of consumers who examine prices carefully most of the time, this segment of so-called price vigilantes (Wakefield and Inman, 1993) may be sufficiently important for retailers to keep prices low.

Although some price learning may be incidental and unconscious – and therefore less available to recall (Monroe and Lee, 1999; Vanhuele and Drèze, 2002) – other price learning may be intentional and conscious, especially for motivated price-sensitive consumers. What if we are motivated to learn prices? How good can we become at price recall? How well is our cognitive system adapted to memorizing prices? Vanhuele, Laurent and Drèze (2006) examined the first step of the process with a series of experiments on how the immediate memory for prices functions. Participants had to keep prices for two or three products in a given category (DVDs, cameras and candy) in memory for five seconds before feeding them back. Analyses of the responses confirmed that the three types of numerical coding discussed by Vanhuele and Drèze (2002) are used: verbal, visual and magnitude coding. Most intriguing is the effect of verbal coding. If people want to hold a price (or whatever other information) in short-term memory, they cycle it through a subsystem of working memory. Because the capacity of this subsystem is restricted to 1.5 to 2 seconds of length of speech, prices that take longer to report are less well remembered. Consumers who speak slower have poorer immediate memory, because of this capacity restriction. And consumers who do not respect the official pronunciation of prices and use shortcuts instead (e.g. twelve ninety instead of one thousand two hundred and ninety) have a memory advantage. An implication of this finding, not examined in the article, is that, across regions, language differences handicap some consumers in their price memory. For the French, for instance, a price of ninety euro is pronounced as 'quatre-vingt dix euro', but Belgians and Swiss know it in a shorter form as 'nonante euro'.

The Price–Quality Relationship

When comparing different goods, consumers may use price as an indicator of quality. In a review of over 40 studies, Rao and Monroe (1989) found robust, but moderate, evidence that consumers use price as a proxy for product quality. If such inferences occur, they may actually be mistaken. An analysis of US studies by Tellis and Wernerfelt (1987) found a mean correlation between price and *objective* product quality of 0.27; this relationship is statistically significant, but we note that the effect is small. At the subjective level, Etgar and Malhotra (1981) showed evidence that price was unimportant to consumers as an indicator of quality for some products and Zeithaml (1988) reviewed nearly 90 studies and found mixed support for a relationship between price and subjectively assessed quality. It seems that the inference of quality from price is therefore rather less ubiquitous than has been supposed. One important reason is probably that quality perceptions obviously depend on a number of factors in addition to price, such as the appearance of the product, the reports of others, the brand and the store that sells the product. Consumers who believe that price and quality are related may persist in this belief because they selectively focus on cases that confirm their belief, i.e. they attend most to high-price/high-quality and low-price/low-quality products. Kardes et al. (2004) show, however, that belief-inconsistent information can be processed for price–quality inferences when consumers are motivated and have the opportunity to do so.

In a variation on the price–quality inference theme, Shiv, Carmon and Ariely (2005) show that consumers who pay a discounted price for an existing energy drink that is thought to enhance mental acuity are, after consumption of the drink, able to solve fewer word-jumble puzzles than consumers who paid the regular price. An additional surprising finding is that the effect, which in the medical world would be called a placebo effect, is apparently unconscious.

Combining this review with that on reference price, we see that price can influence acceptability either because of quality inferences or because of reference prices. This gives us the model shown in Figure 9.1. Notice that, as price rises, the acceptability of the product is raised by the price–quality relationship but reduced by the comparison against reference prices. Normally we expect the reference price effect to be stronger since otherwise sales would rise with increase in price, which is not usually observed.

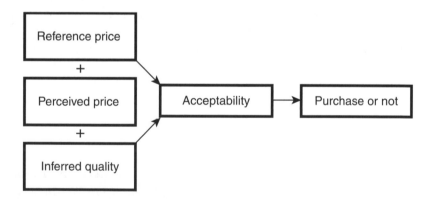

Figure 9.1   Price, acceptability and purchase

SECTION 2: ESTIMATING PRICE SENSITIVITY

The sensitivity of sales to changes in prices is usually quantified as price elasticity. Price elasticity is the ratio of sales change to price change, expressed in relative terms. Thus, if sales go up 20 per cent when the price is cut by 10 per cent (a negative change), the price elasticity would be –2. For some products, for instance prescription drugs, price changes produce very little change in demand. Price elasticity is close to zero and demand is called 'inelastic'. Conversely, the price elasticity for any supplier in a commodity market is highly 'elastic'; the absolute value of price elasticity is very high, indicating that sales will drop steeply if price is increased, but will also increase considerably when price is dropped. It is important to keep in mind that price elasticities are not the same at all price levels. A price elasticity estimation is therefore only valid for the region of prices used for its estimation. Price elasticities can, of course, also change with general economic conditions or changes in specific market factors (for instance, the development of new distribution channels such as the Internet).

In consumer markets three methods are used to estimate price sensitivity. For new products, customer surveys are often used. For new and established products, price experiments can be run. When historical information on the market is available, econometric modelling can be applied. Quantitative research in marketing has made enormous progress over the past 15 years in developing models to evaluate the impact of marketing actions in general and price in particular. In parallel, the wide use of checkout scanners and other forms of information technology have permitted detailed recording of transaction data. The result has been an enormous increase in the ability of researchers to evaluate price effects.

Customer Surveys

There are two approaches to surveying consumers to assess their price sensitivity. In the direct-survey approach, consumers receive a product description, or are exposed to the product itself and then have to react to potential prices. This method, developed in the 1960s, is simple to apply and easily understood by respondents (Gabor and Granger, 1961, 1966; Wedel and Leeflang, 1998). There are a number of biases that typically lead consumers to overstate their willingness to pay, but corrections are possible. An important drawback is, however, that price is treated in isolation in these surveys while, in real-life choices, product characteristics have to be weighed against price.

Conjoint analysis (Green and Krieger, 2002) is a widely used customer survey method that presents consumers with simplified product descriptions and asks them for their preference among these products while considering all information conjointly. Price sensitivity and the sensitivity to changes in other attributes are then inferred using estimation methodology. Conjoint analysis is widely applied for new product designs in general, not just for price analysis. Running conjoint surveys by computer and on the Internet has now become standard practice. The method is rarely used in consumer research but has become a standard tool for commercial market researchers and a large number of applications have been published (see reviews in Green, Krieger and Wind, 2001; Wittink, Vriens, and Burhenne, 1994).

Price Experiments

The objective of an experiment is to control for factors that influence the outcome of interest (usually sales) but that are not the object of the study. Sales are not only influenced by price changes but also by all the marketing actions of the firm, those of its competitors and changes in the context. Running a price experiment in one store and comparing sales at the end of the experiment with sales before is therefore rarely conclusive; an observed change in sales can usually be attributed to different factors.

The art of running a good price experiment is in selecting a good comparison basis, usually called the control group, which cancels out the influence of other factors. Price experiments can be carried out in a simulated shopping environment, but large market research companies, such as TNS, Nielsen or GfK in Europe, have test cities in different countries in which they run experiments with consumer goods on a regular basis. All the variables of the marketing mix can be controlled during these experiments (for an example see Fader, Hardie and Zeithammer, 2003).

Ehrenberg and England (1990) investigated price elasticity using a field experimental method. Staff made fortnightly home visits to housewives and offered a limited selection of cereal, confectionery, soup, tea and biscuit brands for sale at prices that were a little below those in local supermarkets. After two visits, the prices of some brands were raised or lowered. The order of price changes was altered for different sub-groups so that any effects based on price sequence could be detected. The authors found that the response to price changes was immediate and was unaffected by the order of earlier changes, i.e. it was zero order. Price increases had slightly less percentage impact on sales than decreases. The mean elasticity obtained by Ehrenberg and England (weighted by brand size) was –2.6. There was little variation in price elasticity when categories or brands were compared. One possible explanation for this result is that the field experimental design encouraged participants to buy brands that they would normally avoid with the result that all the brands in a field experiment have rather similar buyer groups and hence tend towards a common elasticity.

Box 9.1	**Price experiments on the Internet**

Technically, the Internet allows price experimenting on a constant basis. In practice, consumer reactions may complicate things (but see Exercise 9.2). In early September 2000, Computerworld reported that consumers logging on to Amazon at about the same time could be charged very different prices for the same DVD. For example, at 2.40 pm a search for the *Planet of the Apes* DVD on the Amazon site using a Netscape Web browser turned up a quoted price of $64.99 – 35 per cent off the original price of $99.98 but, several seconds later, a similar search performed with Microsoft Corp.'s Internet Explorer browser resulted in a price of $74.99 for the same product. A company spokesperson acknowledged that Amazon was running price experiments. 'Some customers will pay the same for a certain item as customers paid last week, some will pay more and some will pay less', she said. In a statement several weeks later, Amazon formally denied published rumours that the price differences in the test were based on customer demographic information and said that the price reductions, which were in the 20–40 per cent range, aimed at determining how much sales are affected by lower prices. Amazon also promised that, if they ever were to run such a test again, they would automatically refund customers who purchased at a price higher than the lowest test price for the same item.

Econometric Estimation

Econometric estimation of price elasticities has a long history and research has sought to combine the knowledge accumulated over decades of pricing research. A meta-analysis by Tellis (1988b) brought together 367 elasticities, drawn from 42 prior studies using a variety of estimation methods. Tellis showed that a number of market factors were related to elasticity and that the mean elasticity across all the studies was −1.8. He found more dispersion of price elasticities than Ehrenberg and England (1990), a result that is to be expected from the wide range of market conditions under which the elasticities were estimated.

Bijmolt, van Heerde and Pieters (2005) presented a more recent meta-analysis and across 1,851 price elasticities drawn from 81 studies, they found a substantially larger average of −2.6. They examined the evolution over time between 1961 and 2004 and found that the (absolute) sales elasticity became larger every year, at a rate of one percentage point per 25 years. They also compared different market and category characteristics and found that price elasticities have greater magnitude in the introduction and growth stages of the product life cycle compared with the maturity and decline stages. Consumers are more price elastic for durables than for other products. Inflation also increases the magnitude of price elasticity. They found no effects of country, income, data source (firms, retail panels, household panels) and brand ownership (private labels versus manufacturer brands).

SECTION 3: PSYCHOLOGICAL REACTIONS TO PRICES AND PRICE CHANGES

Perceived (Un)fairness of Prices and Price Changes

Consumers can react to prices and price changes by purchasing now – and even stockpiling – if the current price is attractive, or by cancelling or postponing a planned purchase if the current price is unattractive. They may, however, in addition develop perceptions of fairness or, more commonly, unfairness about the seller. These perceptions can lead to negative attitudes about a company or an entire industry (e.g. 'pharmaceutical prices should be controlled more strongly because of the excess profits of the industry'), boycotts and negative word of mouth.

What is considered as fair or unfair? Fairness is a judgement about the justness, reasonableness or acceptability of an outcome (the price) or the process to reach the outcome (often communicated by the seller as a reason for a change, or inferred by the consumer). It is a judgement that is induced by a comparison to another outcome, such as 'I paid more than another customer did' or 'I paid more than I usually do' (Xia, Monroe and Cox, 2004).

Kahneman, Knetsch and Thaler (1991a, 1991b), in a series of surveys and experiments, identified the price conditions that consumers consider as fair or unfair. They developed the principle of dual entitlement as an explanation, arguing that fairness perceptions are determined by a belief that firms are entitled to a certain profit and customers are entitled to a certain price. Increasing prices to increase profits when there is heavy demand is considered unfair, but it is fair to protect profit from rising costs. The classic example is that a retailer is entitled to raise the price of snow shovels in reaction to an increased wholesale price, but not in response to extra demand brought about by a snowstorm.

Campbell (1999) expands on the dual entitlement principle and identifies two important factors that affect the perceived fairness of a price change: consumers' inferences about the firm's motive for a price change and inferred profit, relative to the past. She also finds that a company's prior reputation moderates the effect of inferred relative profit. The core idea is that consumers make inferences about a marketer's motive or intention for a particular price increase. The idea is based on attribution research, indicating that people search for causal explanations for negative and unexpected events. When consumers infer that the firm has a negative motive (e.g. exploiting a sudden increase in demand), the increase is considered unfair. When the firm has a good reputation, consumers give it the benefit of the doubt. Even when the scenario suggests a negative motive, if the firm does not appear to make extra profit, consumers infer a more positive motive. Like most price fairness researchers, Campbell presents scenarios to the participants of her studies who, in this case, judge whether a described price increase is fair, unfair or neither.

EXERCISE 9.2   PRICE DISCRIMINATION

Yield management is a pricing practice in which prices are adapted over time to optimize profits and capacity usage. It is used in industries where capacity is fixed, such as the hotel and airline business. Marginal revenue at a low price may be worthwhile if the room or seat would otherwise be empty, but not if it forces a reduction of the overall price level. So, while a tourist might get a concessionary rate on the weekend, this should not undermine the full price charged to business travellers. It is now commonly accepted that, on any given flight, passengers pay widely varied prices for their tickets as a result of yield management pricing software. This restricts the availability of cheaper prices to more price-conscious consumers, who are able to book well in advance or be flexible in travel times.

Pick with a friend a couple of flying destinations that are served by a low-cost carrier (like Ryanair or EasyJet). Agree on a departure date and hour and check the prices of your flights a couple of times over the next week. Do prices change? By how much and in which direction? Why do they change? Would you find it acceptable if your friend found a lower price than you for a given flight? Under which conditions? What if you both logged on at the same time, and got a different price quote?

Bolton, Warlop and Alba (2003) examine, in ten different studies, how information about prices, profits and costs influences consumer perceptions of price fairness. They show that consumers underestimate inflationary trends, even when provided with explicit quantitative information, and therefore overestimate the profits that sellers are drawing from price increases. When comparing the price of the same product in different types of store (such as a department store versus a discount store), they tend to attribute price differences to different profit motives instead of to different cost levels. Some marketing strategies are considered unfair, even when they are not under the store's control. When they are given information about the cost structure of a firm, consumers tend to focus on the cost of goods sold and ignore other cost categories. In conclusion, unfavourable comparisons seem to dominate: consumers apparently have a tendency to believe that the selling price of a good (or service) is substantially higher than its fair price.

Framing of Price and Price Reductions

Prices sometimes can be presented in different ways in order to make them look more attractive, a practice that is referred to as 'framing'. Also, temporary price reductions can be presented in different formats, such as 'up to 50% off', '30–50% off', or 'buy two get one free'. Rationally speaking, consumers should be indifferent to different frames that result in the same cost. However, Chapter 7 showed how framing can affect people's judgements. The frequency of use of price framing suggests that it is an effective pricing tool.

To encourage subscriptions, magazines present their per-issue subscription price. Membership fees of clubs can be framed in terms of the amount per day (only \$2.50 per day) instead of the actual total amount to pay (\$912). Mail order suppliers may separate postage and packaging (\$4.95) from the cost of the product (\$24.95). Charitable donations apparently also find framing effective and explain the benefits you can bring to children in poverty 'for less than a dollar per day'. Gourville (1998) posits that consumers evaluate unfamiliar single-alternative transactions by comparing them to known transactions that involve similar expenses. Different frames therefore foster the retrieval of different comparison bases and influence the evaluation of the offer and compliance. The 'pennies-a-day' frame, as Gourville describes it, triggers comparisons to small ongoing expenses like buying a cup of coffee or a train ticket, which makes the transaction more acceptable.

The Effect of Price Endings

Prices often fall just below a round number, a practice referred to as odd pricing. A price of, for instance, \$100 is converted to \$99.95. According to some counts, between 30 and 65 per cent of all prices end in the digit 9 (Schindler and Kirby, 1997; Stiving and Winer, 1997). The clearest demonstration of the effect of 9-endings on sales comes from Anderson and Simester (2003), who varied prices on identical items in different clothing catalogues that were sent to tens of thousands of randomly selected customer samples. In the different experiments demand for the items with 9-ending prices increased between 7 and 35 per cent. The effect was stronger for new items.

There are two dominant explanations of the phenomenon. A first theory posits that consumers ignore the right-most digits or at least do not give them sufficient weight because of left-to-right processing. A price starting with a 2 therefore looks a lot smaller than a price starting with a 3, even if the complete price is 2.99. According to a second theory, the 9-ending signals a good deal or a promotion. However, Schindler (2006) found that prices ending in 99 increased sales but those ending in 95 did not. Since these prices shared the first digit it seems likely that the signalling hypothesis is correct. Interestingly, Schindley found that 99 products were not objectively cheaper than more roundly priced product.

SECTION 4: CONSUMER RESPONSE TO SALES PROMOTIONS

Introduction

Sales promotion is a fairly recent topic in the marketing literature. It appeared primarily from the 1980s onwards when the use of promotions increased considerably with the arrival of scanner data. Before the introduction of checkout scanning, companies had to rely on store audit data, collected by auditors on a sample of stores, which were released on only a bimonthly basis. These data did not have the detail necessary to see the real effect of promotions that are usually run on a week-to-week basis. When weekly data became available and marketers realized the full size of the boost to sales, they started investing much more in promotions (see Figure 9.2). Promotions usually have a clearly identifiable impact on sales. Graphs of sales over time clearly show a sales spike after a promotion launch, a phenomenon that is rarely observed for advertising (unless, of course, the advertisement communicates a promotion). Despite enthusiasm for promotions, the consulting company Accenture found, in 2001, that 80–90 per cent of trade promotions do not generate a positive return on investment.

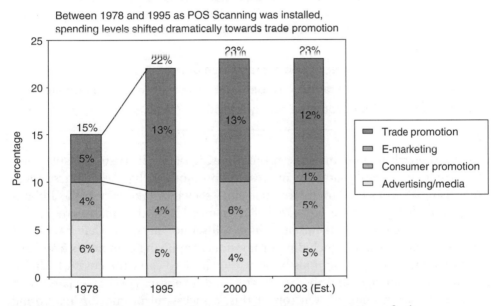

Figure 9.2   Promotion spending in packaged goods as a percentage of sales

Source: Accenture

In reaction to the increased use of promotions, academics oriented their research attention to the analysis of promotional effectiveness, usually by using sophisticated quantitative modelling. In his 1995 review of the promotion literature, Chandon counted 200 academic studies published over the previous ten years, while for the period between 1965 and 1983 he only found 40.

Promotions can take many forms but promotional campaigns are usually short-lived (see Box 9.2). The distinction has to be made between promotions offered by retailers and manufacturers to consumers and trade promotions offered to retailers by manufacturers. Examples of trade promotions are co-op advertising funds and display allowances. The retailer may or may not pass on cost savings to the consumer (called the 'pass-through').

Box 9.2	Types of promotion

- **Direct price reduction** – also known as 'discounts' or, in the USA, as 'deals'.
- **Couponing** – refers to the distribution of certificates that can be redeemed for a discount when purchasing.
- **Rebates or cash back** – price refunds that can only be obtained after the purchase by mailing an application, for instance.
- **Display** – refers to in-store display.
- **Feature advertising** – refers to stand-alone circulars, also known as flyers, that consumers receive in their mailbox. This is a form of cooperative advertising in which manufacturers pay retailers to feature their products.
- **Games and contests**.
- **Multibuy** – for example, three for the price of two.
- **Extra quantity** – for example, 10 per cent extra length on a chocolate bar.
- **Bonus offers** – buy product X and get product Y free.

Most research focuses on price promotions, feature advertising, display and couponing. In recent years the interest of promotions has been questioned. Advertising agencies tend to dislike them since they may take part of the ad budget, although this attitude has somewhat changed now that many advertising agencies have converted themselves into full-service agencies that handle all forms of communication, including promotions. Supplying companies also have mixed feelings about promotions because they have to carry the costs of administration, pack changes and the production and inventory costs associated with peaks and dips in demand. On top of this, a successful promotion may bring retaliation from competitors, which damages later profits. In aggregate, the effects of competing sales promotions may cancel out, leaving a cost that has to be added to the price of goods. Maybe all players (except the sales promotion agencies) would be better off if discounting in mature markets was limited (see Exercise 9.3)?

Much of our evidence on sales promotions comes from the USA, where marketing practices are rather different from those applying in Europe. In the USA, we find:

- more lines are normally offered on deal,
- discounts are usually larger,
- promotion periods are usually a week – shorter than in Europe – and they are often driven by short-life coupons. In other countries coupons are less popular.

EXERCISE 9.3   COUPON WAR

In autumn 2002, Tesco and Sainsbury became involved in a coupon war in the UK. Sainsbury had issued coupons on its home delivery service, offering, for instance, discounts of £2 for every £20 of shopping. Tesco reacted by announcing that it would itself honour these coupons on its own service. In retaliation, Sainsbury's printed thousands of coupons to send to customers in areas where it was not present, hoping that customers would redeem them with Tesco. Its objective was to decrease Tesco's margins. A Tesco spokesperson replied: 'It is usually our job to promote shopping with Tesco, but if our competition want to do that as well, that is fine with us. … The risk is that by encouraging consumers to get discounts with us, it actually makes them more loyal to the Tesco brand.'

Analyse the moves of the two players. Were there alternatives? Under what conditions is there an interest in this type of escalation and for whom? What would you do next if you were Sainsbury?

Sources of Extra Sales

Observing a promotional sales spike or bump does not necessarily mean the promotion was effective. Whether a sales promotion is beneficial, from a managerial perspective, depends on whether the additional sales can be attributed to brand switching (usually good news for the manufacturer, but the retailer's evaluation depends on the relative margins of the competing brands), category expansion effects (even better news, both for manufacturer and retailer) or purchase acceleration and stockpiling (usually mixed news because this can be considered as 'borrowing' sales from the future). Researchers therefore have built sophisticated econometric models to decompose the promotional bump into these three sources of sales.

Initial results were conflicting, with some researchers finding that most promotional sales volume comes from brand switchers (e.g. Gupta, 1988; Totten and Block, 1987) and others observing that category expansion is a more important source of additional sales (e.g. Chintagunta, 1993). One possible explanation of the contrasting findings is product category differences. When comparing category expansion, brand switching and purchase acceleration, Pauwels, Hanssens and Siddarth (2002) found a breakdown of 66/11/23 for a storable product (canned soup) and 58/39/3 for a perishable product (yoghurt). In the most recent analysis to date, van Heerde, Leeflang and Wittink (2004) found that each source contributes to about one-third of the sales bump on average; they used four products, two from an American and two from a Dutch data set.

As already mentioned, stockpiling is considered the least interesting contributor to promotional sales, because it is assumed that consumers would otherwise buy the brand later, at the regular price. However, Ailawadi et al. (2007) demonstrate that stockpiling can also have benefits in two forms: category consumption can increase because consumers have (more of) the product at home and the extra inventory of the promoted brand may pre-empt the purchase of a competing brand. They observe that the first benefit is the most important and that together the two offset the downside of stockpiling.

So far we have taken the manufacturer's perspective on promotions. Yet price promotions are also an important competitive tool for retailers. In a large-scale experiment over 16 weeks in 86 stores across 26 product categories, Hoch, Drèze and Purk (1994) compared an everyday low price (EDLP) strategy (more or less constant low prices) with a Hi-Lo strategy (higher prices but with frequent promotions). For the EDLP condition, they lowered prices by 10 per cent while they increased those for the Hi-Lo condition by 10 per cent. As a result, sales increased by 3 per cent in the EDLP condition while they decreased by 3 per cent in the Hi-Lo condition. There were, however, also large differences in profitability, but now in the opposite direction. EDLP reduced profits by 18 per cent and Hi-Lo increased them by 15 per cent. The authors explain that in general the results depend on how the customer base is divided among price-sensitive store switchers and store-loyal customers. The main interest of the EDLP strategy is that it attracts switchers from other stores. If many consumers are loyal, this will not work well and the profit level will be deteriorated because everyone will pay a lower price. In the Hi-Lo strategy, loyal customers purchase their product basket both when the products are on deal and when the price is at the normal level. On average they therefore generate more profit than in the EDLP strategy. Store switchers, on the other hand, will buy more when prices are lower. Overall, the Hi-Lo strategy is therefore a good price discriminator, while the drawback of EDLP is that it offers low prices to everyone, irrespective of price sensitivity.

The Combined Effect of Discount, Display and Ad Features

Research reports by practitioners and consulting agencies claim that the best promotion campaigns are built on synergies between price deals, feature advertising and display. For instance, IRI (1989) have circulated an analysis of these effects based on their 1988 data on sales in 2,400 grocery stores in 66 markets in the USA. The data are normalized on a price cut of 15 per cent. The main findings are shown in Figure 9.3. The price cut on its own increases sales by 35 per cent (an elasticity of −2.3). When the discount is coupled with an ad feature the effect is 173 per cent, i.e. 138 per cent more than the price cut on its own, and when the price cut is paired with an in-store display the sales gain is 279 per cent, 244 per cent more than the sales gain alone. Of particular interest is what happens when price cut, ad feature and display are combined. The sales effects could simply add together, thus:

35% + 138% + 244% = 417%

Figure 9.3 shows instead that there is a gain of 128 per cent above the 417 per cent, which suggests that the three components of promotion act synergistically.

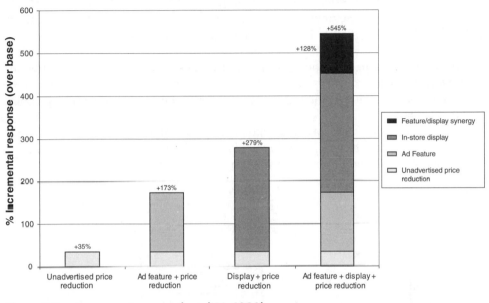

Figure 9.3   Response to promotions (IRI, 1989)

Later academic research, however, reported mixed findings. Gupta (1988) observed negative interactions of display and feature with price cuts, which he attributes to a possible overlap or substitutability among these promotional instruments. Lemon and Nowlis (2002) found, across different brands, a mix of small positive and negative interactions of display and price cut and a negative interaction of feature and price cut. In an experimental setting, East, Eftichiadou and Williamson (2003) found no synergistic effect for a double, as opposed to a single display. Zhang (2006) provided an explanation of these mixed patterns. She observes first that promotion markers can serve as a proxy for a price cut, as shown by Inman, McAlister and Hoyer (1990); a promotion signal is in this case taken as a cue for a price cut that influences choice even in the absence of a real reduction in price. Second, another stream of research has shown that in-store displays and feature ads can influence the formation of consideration sets (e.g. Allenby and Ginter, 1995). Zhang builds a model of brand choice that incorporates both processes: consumers use promotion markers either as price cut proxies or for consideration set formation, or for both. If display and feature have mainly a price cut proxy effect, then negative interactions are observed in choice models. In contrast, if they help get a product into the consideration set, then they create a positive interaction. Differences across past studies can therefore be explained by the mechanism that dominates the choice process.

Carryover Effects

What happens after the sales promotion has finished? This depends partly on the mix of category expansion, brand switching and purchase acceleration or stock-piling, but also on the extent to which these effects persist after the promotion. Consider the possibilities (which are illustrated in Figure 9.4):

- Some consumers may buy and consume a discounted brand more with no effect on later consumption.
- Some buyers may switch brands or maintain a raised consumption after trying a brand on promotion.
- Some regular consumers may accelerate purchase and stockpile a brand on a deal; as a result they may buy less later. Though plausible this requires more planning than is usually found among consumers of frequently purchased goods.

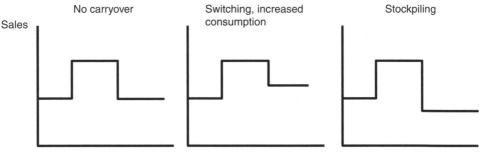

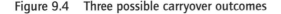

Figure 9.4   Three possible carryover outcomes

The availability of scanner data has made research on carryover effect more feasible and the *overall* picture shows little carryover effect. The most compre-hensive study in this area is by Ehrenberg, Hammond and Goodhardt (1994) using panel data from Britain, Germany, America and Japan on 25 established grocery products. The researchers identified 175 sales peaks of 25 per cent or more for different brands in these product fields and compared sales levels before and after these promotional episodes. The procedure excluded cases where the sales pattern was irregular either before or after the peak.

The overall outcome of this study was a sales increase of 1 per cent which is effectively no effect. A check was made by measuring the repeat buying rates for the 8-week period after the peak; the average was 43 per cent, almost the same as the 44 per cent inferred from NBD theory (see Chapter 4) which showed that buying was stationary in the post-promotion period. Differences between coun-tries were small and there was no evidence that categories showed a consistent movement when data were available on the same category from more than one country.

In sum, these studies show little evidence of carryover effect. A lack of carryover effect is quite difficult to explain. How is it that a spike of extra sales, often several times the normal level, does not disturb the base-level sales? One explanation offered by Ehrenberg et al. is that deals touch only a minority of the brand's customer base; many regular buyers would not see a promotion and their behaviour could not be affected. A second explanation offered by Ehrenberg et al. is that the extra purchasers attracted by the deal were nearly always people who had bought the brand in the past (see Table 9.1); thus a promotion does not introduce *new* buyers to the brand. Those who respond to promotions are past and current buyers who are already familiar with the brand characteristics.

Table 9.1   Percentage of those buying on promotion who had bought the brand before (adapted from Ehrenberg, Hammond and Goodhart, 1994)

Product	Bought promoted brand in previous:			
	6 months (%)	1 year (%)	2 year (%)	$2\frac{1}{2}$ years (%)
Ground coffee (Germany)	78	83	91	95
Detergent (USA)	76	76	88	93
Yogurt (USA)	71	78	90	91
Ketchup (USA)	52	68	88	91
Detergent (Germany)	61	90	98	na
Soup (USA)	75	90	91	na
Carbonated drinks (Germany)	70	79	90	na
Instant coffee (USA)	70	80	90	na
Crackers (USA)	55	65	78	na
Average	68	79	89	93

A thoughtful paper by Neslin and Stone (1996) compared seven different explanations for the lack of post-promotion effect. They suggest that many people are insensitive to the stock of purchases already made so that household inventory has little effect on purchase decisions. But the enlarged inventory will eventually slow purchasing and produces a generally lower sales level rather than a post-promotion dip. So, the effect of discount sales is to reduce base-level sales; without promotions the base rate would rise.

Long-term Effects of Promotions

There has been concern that there may be a long-term negative effect of promotions that is not revealed in the shorter-term studies that test for carryover effect. Broadbent (1989) and Ogilvy (1987) are among those who have suggested that the heavy use of sales promotions will degrade brand equity.

There are four bases for concern about promotional activity. The first comes from reference price research. Promotional prices may become integrated in the reference price and consumers therefore start perceiving the normal, non-promoted, price as high (Kalwani and Yim, 1990). A second basis for concerns comes from attribution theory, suggesting that consumers make causal attributions of promotional events; they wonder why the brand is promoted. Lichtenstein and Bearden (1989), for instance, concluded that consumers' reactions are more positive when they think that a promotion aims to attract customers, as opposed to when they think the promotion's objective is to get rid of unwanted goods. Third, customers may see the lower price as evidence of poorer quality. Finally, frequent promotions may condition consumers to only buy on deal. Bolton (1989) and Raju (1992), for instance, observed that the sales spikes are smaller when promotions are more frequent.

In a review of research up to 1995 on the possible negative effect of promotions, Blattberg, Briesch and Fox (1995) conclude that, given the mixed evidence, the 'jury is still out'. However, more recent studies, based on time-series analysis converge on an absence of positive and a possibility of negative long-term effects. Dekimpe, Hanssens and Silva-Risso (1999) find positive effects for only one brand out of 13 in an analysis of four categories. Nijs et al. (2001) examine the possibility of category expansion but find this type of effect in only 36 of 560 product categories. Pauwels, Hanssens and Siddarth (2002) find no permanent effects of promotions for purchase incidence or purchase quantity. In only one of the 29 cases do they find permanent effects on brand choice.

Couponing

Couponing is vastly popular in the USA. For packaged goods a total volume of almost 300 billion coupons were printed in 2005. For groceries specifically, the total face value of coupons issued that year added up to $190 billion, of which $3 billion were effectively redeemed (Harnett, 2006). Research has mainly focused on whether and, if so, how coupons create incremental sales. Coupons can increase category consumption (Ailawadi and Neslin, 1998), encourage brand switching (Neslin, 1990), trigger trial (Neslin and Clarke, 1987), but also reward brand loyalty. Neslin (2002: 49) reports several studies that show that brand-loyal consumers are more likely than others to redeem coupons.

Coupons can be considered as an instrument for price discrimination. Instead of giving a discount to all buyers, coupons reserve the discount for consumers who make the effort to obtain the saving. Coupons have to be found, stored, organized and redeemed before expiry for the correct product. The 'cost' associated with this effort, including the opportunity cost of time, is higher for some individuals than for others. Narasimhan (1984) develops this argument in more detail and his analyses conclude that users of coupons are more price-sensitive than non-users of coupons.

American consumers are attached to coupons (see Box 9.3). An explanation for consumers' attachment to coupons is that highly coupon-prone consumers are not only drawn to reduced prices but are also seeking psychological benefits. For instance, they get a sense of achievement by purchasing products on deal and view themselves as smart shoppers, an idea Garretson and Burton (2003) confirmed in a store exit survey.

Box 9.3	Life without coupons?

Procter & Gamble launched in January 1996 an 18-month 'no-coupon' test in upstate New York, a region where 90 per cent of shoppers used coupons. Procter & Gamble believed that across-the-board lower prices offered more efficient savings than coupons. In a survey by the trade journal *Supermarket Business*, 80 per cent of manufacturers and 69 per cent of retailers and wholesalers considered that Procter & Gamble was on the right track and some manufacturers followed its lead (Partche, 1996). However, consumers reacted fiercely with public hearings, petition drives and boycotts. Some put up 'Save Our Coupons' signs on their front lawns. A county official claimed that the elimination of coupons by the 'big guys' was intended to hurt the 'average Joe'. The *Wall Street Journal* observed that 'coupons, to many people, are practically an inalienable right' (Narisetti, 1997: 1). Procter & Gamble stopped the test after 14 months.

Heilman, Nakamoto and Rao (2002) examine responses to in-store instant coupons such as electronic shelf coupons and peel-off coupons on product packages. They show that these 'surprise' coupons increase market basket sales for two reasons: unplanned purchases are made as the result of the psychological income effect in reaction to the unexpected financial gain and the coupons raise the consumers' mood.

In conclusion, coupons – and promotions in general – are not just forms of price reduction. As Chandon, Wansink and Laurent (2000) show, promotions give consumers hedonic benefits (opportunities for value expression, entertainment and exploration) in addition to utilitarian benefits (savings, the possibility to upgrade to higher product quality and improved shopping convenience).

EXERCISE 9.4   OPTIMAL DISCOUNTS

Plus is a canned soft drink selling at $1 for a 4-pack. The margin is 50 cents and the elasticity is –4.

1   Assuming no additional fixed costs or competitor retaliation, would a discount of 12.5 per cent make money?

(Continued)

2   What is the optimal discount? The profit is given by the number sold multiplied by the margin, i.e. profit = $(100+4d)(50-d)$ where d is the discount as a percentage. If you multiply this out, differentiate, equate the differential to zero (the slope is zero at highest point), you can calculate the optimum discount.

3   Is the promotion still profitable if sales over the period of the promotion are 1 million and fixed costs for the promotion are $40,000, ignoring competitor response?

4   If competitor retaliation reduces subsequent profits by $20,000, is the promotion still worthwhile?

Answers:

1   For every 100 sales at normal price there will be 100+4×12.5 sales at the 12.5 per cent discount, i.e. 150 sales, and the profit will be 0.375×150= $56.25 instead of 0.5×100=$50. Therefore the discount is more profitable than the usual price, assuming no other costs.

2   Multiplying out, profit=$5000+100d-4d^2$. Differentiating, slope=$100-8d$. Therefore, equating slope to zero, $d = 12.5$ per cent. In words, the optimal discount is 12.5 per cent.

3   On a million sales the profit is 0.375×1,000,000=$375,000 and without the discount the profit on the reduced sales would be $333,333. The profit advantage is $41,667, reduced to $1,667 after taking account of fixed costs.

4   If competitor retaliation costs a further $20,000 the exercise would be loss making.

SUMMARY

Consumers compare observed prices to reference prices in order to determine their interest in buying a particular product at a particular time and a particular place. Reference prices can be externally available or have to be recalled from memory. Price memory is, unfortunately, not reliable for many people. One reason is that prices are not encoded correctly because of their verbal length.

When comparing different products, consumers do not necessarily prefer the product with the lowest price because many associate low prices with low quality. In reality, however, price is not a good predictor of quality.

Market researchers apply different methodologies to assess consumers' price sensitivity. For hypothetical new products they often use conjoint analysis and direct questioning. To examine reactions to large changes in existing prices or to different alternative prices for new products, price experiments are used. When historical data are available, econometric estimation of price elasticity is possible.

Consumers react to price changes by adapting their purchase behaviour, but they may also express their agreement or disagreement in ways that affect a company's image and, possibly, its brand equity. There is a clear bias to interpret price increases as unfair. If companies do not explicitly give explanations for price increases that show that increasing profit is not the motive, consumers often infer that profit is the motive.

Promotions can clearly boost sales temporarily, but long-term positive effects seem to be absent. Even the obvious short-term effects have to be interpreted with caution, because promotions ultimately risk becoming a costly zero-sum game among competitors. Everything depends on the source of the additional sales. If promotions increase switching and bring new customers to the market, they can be profitable. If they just offer the product at a lower price to brand-loyal customers, they may be counter-productive.

Consumer like promotions, not only because they lower the cost of the product, but also because they create excitement, satisfaction about being a smart shopper and because they simplify the purchase decision.

Additional Resources

An excellent overview of pricing research is given in Gijsbrechts, E. (1993). This overview not only shows what the main findings are but also explains how they were obtained. It is not restricted to pricing and also covers some promotion issues. Schindler has published a lot of research on odd pricing and nine endings. Schindler, R.M. (2006) is a nice example of how simple observations of the marketplace can be very insightful. This chapter referred several times to meta-analyses. A good recent example of this type of analysis can be found in Del Vecchio, D., Henard, D.H. and Freling, T.H. (2006).

10 The Retail Context

LEARNING OBJECTIVES

When you have completed this chapter, you should be able to:

1   Understand the main ideas about gravity models.
2   Discuss the reasons why people use different types of store and how they use them at different times.
3   Report on the factors related to compulsive, heavy and loyal shoppers.
4   Discuss the evidence on store atmospheric effects and explain these effects.

OVERVIEW

Over the last decade, retailing has evolved in a number of ways. There are fewer but bigger store groups. The supermarket share of retail spending has grown steadily in many countries. In the UK, the big four, Tesco, Asda, Sainsbury and Morrison, accounted for over 75 per cent of all grocery sales in 2007 according to Taylor Nelson Sofres. Some chains, such as Tesco, Walmart and Boots, have extended their operations to more countries. In the UK, supermarket groups have introduced new small-store formats that compete with convenience stores. As often happens when firms get larger, there has been a groundswell of resistance to some aspects of modern store management. Firms such as Primark, Asda and Tesco are accused of ignoring the working conditions of those who produce their remarkably cheap clothing. There have been complaints about the air freighting of vegetables from Africa to Europe because of carbon emissions. There has been worry about the power of the retailer over suppliers. There have been demands for more local sourcing, though local markets can probably do a better job in supplying local produce than the store groups, which cannot easily handle small quantities.

And yet, the use of stores has probably changed little in the last decade. People are likely to have much the same reasons for using particular stores, which continue to be accessed mostly by car. The largest change in the last decade must be the continuing growth in shopping via the

Internet, introduced in Chapter 1. In addition to the purchase of new products via the Internet, the growth of auction sites, principally eBay, has assisted the trade in second-hand goods.

Stores need to be well located if they are to be profitable. We consider location effects briefly and then examine the criteria that people use to select supermarkets and consider the way in which customer demand varies over time. Then, we focus on three types of customer: heavy buyers, loyal buyers and compulsive shoppers. We also review loyalty schemes briefly. After this, we turn to the store environment and the ways in which this can influence spending. Finally, we describe research on atmospherics; this is the impact on shoppers of music, smell, colour and crowding in the retail outlet.

SECTION 1: SHOPPER CHOICE

Gravity Models

Gravity models explain demand for shopping at a location in terms of the local population and the accessibility of the retail location. The number of people who buy from a particular store depends upon nearby population densities, transport access, the store development at the location and the presence of competing retail locations. These models have directed attention to the way shops, stores, shopping centres and cities draw customers from the surrounding environment.

The early research in this area focused on the attraction exerted on a shopper by two cities at varying distances. Reilly (1929) argued that trade was attracted in direct proportion to the population of each city and inverse proportion to the square of the distance from the city. The similarity with Newton's explanation for the movement of planets, in terms of gravitational attraction, led to theories of this sort being called *gravity models*. Reilly's model implies that there will be a *breaking point* between two cities where customers are equally attracted to each city. The model was tested on 30 pairs of cities and found to be quite accurate. However, it does not allow for the strong appeal of particular stores. In the UK, for example, John Lewis stores have exceptional attraction, since a John Lewis store offers a product range and standard of service that is not easily found in other stores. In addition, distance is only an approximate indicator of travel time and cost which really control customer demand. Reilly's model is less applicable when good transport facilities make distant locations easily accessible. Another consideration is that neighbourhoods vary in their preferences and spending, so that the revenue obtained may vary according to the characteristics so that population size is only a crude indicator of expenditure per head.

Store operators want more precise answers to their location problems, and Huff's (1962, 1981) retail gravitation model was developed to describe the pulling power of a retail centre within a city. In this model the attraction of a centre, A_1, is a function of its selling area (S), divided by a power λ (lambda) of the travel time (T):

$$A_1 = S/T^\lambda$$

The probability of a consumer using a shopping area is a function of A_1 divided by the sum of the attractions of all the available shopping centres, i.e.

$$p = A_1/\Sigma(A_1 \ldots A_n)$$

Wee and Pearce (1985) note that a large number of studies have supported Huff's model and have generally found that the exponent, λ, is approximately two, as Reilly hypothesized. Huff's approach includes all the possible shopping centres, although in practice a consumer might rule many of these out. Wee and Pearce modified Huff's model and used only the shopping centres that the shopper considered. With this adjustment, predictions were better but even the improved model gave an R^2 of only 0.25, showing that three-quarters of shopping location preference remained unexplained. This is hardly surprising since a gravity model cannot take account of the detail of a particular shopping environment. For example, Foxall and Hackett (1992) found that stores that were located at path junctions were better remembered.

Another use of this work is the impact on sales in existing stores when a new store is opened in a particular location. Using Wee and Pearce's (1985) approach, it should be possible to calculate the loss of trade.

Because shoppers are attracted to centres, growth also happens at these centres. *Central place theory* (Christaller, 1933; Losch, 1939) uses the importance of a centre and the economic distance as basic concepts explaining how centres develop and how retail units tend to cluster together, with each taking advantage of the custom generated by the others. Businesses in the same field can benefit from proximity since together they increase the total custom. We can find examples of this effect in most cities; one example is the concentration of restaurants, particularly Chinese restaurants, in London's Soho (see Box 10.1).

Box 10.1	**Retail clusters**

Some quite small locations can become specialists in a particular field. In the ancient Shropshire town of Ludlow there are four restaurants with Michelin stars, more than any other place outside London in the UK. People can take a long weekend in Ludlow and eat excellent cuisine at a different restaurant each day. As a result, Ludlow may draw gourmets from great distances. A similar effect is found in Ireland, at Kinsale, which again has a fine selection of restaurants.

Store Preferences

Gravity models and central place theory provide explanations of retail attractiveness at an aggregate level. However, they describe only some of the reasons for store attractivness and say nothing about the shopper's criteria for choosing stores or the timing and frequency of shopping trips. We now consider these matters.

EXERCISE 10.1   SUPERMARKET USE

Which supermarket do you use most? What is the reason for this? Do you have a regular day and time of day for doing your shopping? Many people do have regular times – why do you think this is so? Would you say that you were loyal to your main supermarket? What does this mean?

    Try and answer these questions now. In the sections below, we provide our answers.

Criteria for Using Supermarkets

Surveys on supermarket use have been conducted at Kingston University in the UK in concert with colleagues in the USA and New Zealand. These surveys sought the reasons why respondents used their main supermarket (the one where they spent most). Table 10.1 shows the principal reasons in different years. The two most important criteria are location and good value; these account for an average of 55 per cent of the main reasons given for patronizing a supermarket. There is more interest in good value in the USA and New Zealand, compared with the UK. When the USA figures are compared for 1992 and 1994, we find that good value dominates over location in 1992, probably because of a recession at that time. Recession hit the UK rather later and we see an increase in the importance of good value there from 1992 to 1994. Then, as the economy became more settled from 1994 to 1998, the importance of good value eased slightly. This evidence shows that supermarket choice criteria can change in response to economic conditions; retailers should be alert to such changes and adjust their offering accordingly. However, the main message from Table 10.1 is that the reasons for shopping at supermarkets do not vary much either over time or between different advanced economies.

    Data from Nielsen (2005) for the UK in 2004 gave less importance to location and more to quality. The Nielsen question was: *Which of the following factors do you consider the most important when choosing where to do your grocery shopping?* East, Lomax and Willson (1991b) asked respondents why they used their main store. We prefer the East et al. question because it requires an explanation for past behaviour that has occurred rather than for potential behaviour. Nielsen's (2005) result for location (11 per cent of responses) also seems at odds with the findings of retail location theory.

Table 10.1   Reasons for patronizing main supermarkets

	1992		1994		1998		
Reason	UK (%)	USA (%)	UK (%)	USA (%)	UK (%)	New Zealand (%)	Mean (%)
Location (easy to get to)	32	25	29	33	31	24	29
Good value/lowest price/ sales promos	14	34	24	29	20	35	26
Good quality	15	15	14	11	14	5	12
Wide choice	18	13	13	12	10	7	12
Other (familiarity with store, parking, etc.)	21	13	20	15	25	29	21

Sources: Consumer Research Unit, Kingston University, UK; Debra Perkins, Florida Memorial University, USA; Phil Gendall, Massey University, New Zealand

In the grocery sector, convenience stores (local food shops) and supermarkets are regarded somewhat differently and customers provide different reasons for their patronage. Table 10.2 shows the attractions of convenience stores and supermarkets in Britain according to a 1991 survey (East, Lomax and Willson, 1991b). Closeness and convenient opening times were the main attractions of the local shop while the supermarket scored better on wide choice, good value and easy parking. The small shop is clearly not immune from attack by the super-markets. In the UK, supermarkets have extended their opening hours and have introduced small format stores to compete with convenience stores.

Table 10.2   'Thinking about the last time you went to the supermarket/convenience store, what was your main reason for shopping there?'

Reason	Supermarket (%)	Convenience store (%)
Near where I live/convenient opening times	34	66
Good value/lowest price/sales promos	14	8
Good quality/wide choice	27	8
Easy parking	14	5
Other (including familiarity with store, parking)	11	13

Sources: East, Lomox and Wilson, 1991b

Perceived Differences between Store Groups

Supermarket customers also give different reasons for patronage of different store groups. Tables 10.3 and 10.4 show examples for Britain and New Zealand. In Britain, Sainsbury was rated high on quality compared to Tesco. Asda was reckoned to provide good value but was low on quality. In New Zealand, Pak'n'Save was less accessible than other stores but was seen as very good value. Woolworth was more accessible and scored on wide choice and quality. Thus, the different store groups have different functional images. Some of the reasons for patronage may reflect the social segments that are attracted to different store groups though there is little social difference in the customers of Tesco,

Table 10.3   Store user's main reasons for patronizing store groups in Britain, 1998

Reason	Tesco (%)	Sainsbury (%)	Asda (%)	Other (%)
Location (easy to get to)	27	30	28	35
Good value/lowest price/sales promos	17	10	38	21
Wide choice	16	10	13	5
Good quality	12	25	6	12
Other (including familiarity with store, parking)	28	25	21	27

Table 10.4   Store user's main reasons for patronizing store groups in New Zealand, 1998

Reason	New Word (%)	Pak'n'Save (%)	Woolworth (%)	Other (%)
Location (easy to get to)	27	13	37	25
Good value/lowest price/sales promos	20	67	9	32
Wide choice	4	3	19	9
Good quality	6	2	11	4
Other (including familiarity with store, parking)	43	15	24	30

Sainsbury and Asda. When the share of social grade is standardized on 100, the figures for the AB grade share are: Tesco, 104; Sainsbury, 117; and Asda, 94 (Nielsen, 2005). There is even less difference between the stores on age profile, size of household and work status.

Customers seem to retain store images over long periods, even when they are hard to justify. In the UK, for example, it took Tesco many years to shake off a low-quality image despite the fact that its product range had been comparable in quality to Sainsbury for a long time. We can see from Table 10.3 that the quality aspect of Tesco's image was well below that of Sainsbury in 1998, even though there was no objective basis for this assessment.

Shopping Trip Patterns

The previous section outlined the reasons shoppers offer for their choice of store or store group. However, it is important to understand not just why and where people shop but also when. The timing of shopping trips has many managerial implications, ranging from staff and stock management to store layout, parking requirements, likely effectiveness of in-store promotions and the best time to conduct product sampling. The store may be little used over much of the day while, at other times, congestion and delay may reduce the quality of service delivered. Off-peak periods are useful for staff relaxation, cleaning, restocking, training and maintenance, as Sasser (1976) notes, but smoothing demand remains a desirable managerial objective.

Frequency of Shopping Trips

Consumers go shopping for a great variety of goods, but researchers have learned most about grocery shopping. Many studies have shown that households have a routine of supermarket shopping that often includes one weekly main trip and one or more secondary 'quick' trips. In the USA, McKay (1973) and Frisbie (1980) found this pattern. Kahn and Schmittlein (1989), also in the USA, report similar findings; they were able to distinguish between those who relied principally on the main trip and those whose shopping included more quick trips than main trips. In Britain, Dunn, Reader and Wrigley (1983) also found evidence of weekly trips and Nielsen (2005) reports shopping trip frequencies of approximately 50 per year for most supermarket groups. Thus many people appear to make a once-a-week main shopping trip which might be supplemented by secondary trips.

Time of Store Use

Store use varies over the year; it rises before holiday periods and can be affected by bad weather. The weekend is a holiday too and shopping tends to be heavier on Thursday, Friday and Saturday, as shown in Figure 10.1. There has not been much change over the years though comparison with data gathered in 1992 by East et al. (1994) shows that Saturday and Sunday have become more popular in the UK.

East et al. (1994) also investigated whether fully employed customers used supermarkets at different times from other shoppers. Figure 10.2 shows the way 1,012 shoppers in 1992 were divided over the week and Figure 10.3 shows the distribution of these shoppers over the day, by employment status.

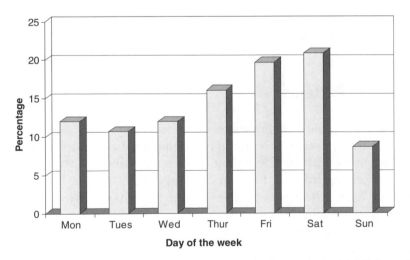

Figure 10.1   Grocery shopping by day of the week in the UK in 2001 (Nielsen, 2003)

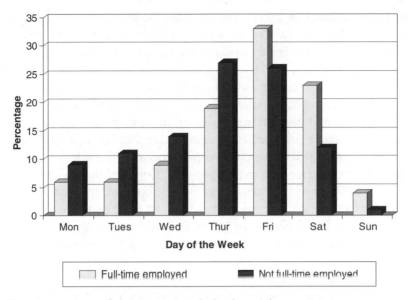

Figure 10.2   Percentage of shoppers on each day by employment status (East et al., 1994)

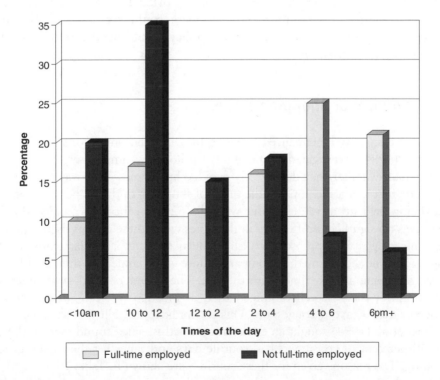

Figure 10.3   Percentage of shoppers at different times of the day by employment status (East et al., 1994)

These figures show that those who are full-time employed tend to shop later in the week and later in the day. We can infer from these two distributions that those shopping late on a Friday or on Saturday are very likely to be employed full-time. This separation of the employment segments could be useful to store owners; if these groups prefer different goods, additional display space and in-store promotions could be switched to take account of these preferences. There may also be opportunities for price discrimination, with mid-week shoppers potentially being more price-sensitive than Friday and Saturday shoppers.

Figure 10.3 shows that there are two main periods of high demand over the day. The first is in the morning, peaking at 10–11am, and the second, in the early evening. It is difficult to provide a clear figure showing the combined effect of day and hour preferences but our analysis shows that, as the week progresses, the morning peak is distributed in much the same way each day. The evening peak only occurs Wednesday to Friday. Saturday shopping is concentrated on the morning.

This evidence indicates that it could be profitable to alter prices and promotions over the day. Some supermarket groups, such as New World in New Zealand, have switched their larger stores to display prices on miniature LCD displays attached to the shelf. This allows computerized price updating that may provide the infrastructure to allow time-of-day pricing in the future. However, supermarket pricing is complex and shoppers could resent short-term price changes, so any major changes in pricing policy would need careful evaluation before being implemented.

The Flexibility of Shopping Times

Store efficiency may be enhanced by smoothing out the timing of shopping trips. East et al. (1994) investigated the flexibility of shoppers' times of use of stores and, in particular, whether they deliberately avoided busy times. This was tested in two ways. The first method compared the times of shopping of the 48 per cent who disliked being held up at the checkout with the 52 per cent who minded this less. There was no significant difference in the times when these groups used supermarkets, which suggests that those who disliked delay took no particular action to avoid congestion. The second method compared those who claimed to often avoid supermarket shopping at busy times with the rest. The 'avoiders' used quiet times only slightly more; the researchers judged that, at most, 6 per cent of all shoppers changed times to avoid congestion. This shows little flexibility in shopping times and East et al. (1994) sought an explanation for this. They found that, in the UK, over 60 per cent of consumers had routine days and times for their main grocery shopping. The reasons given for these routines are shown in Table 10.5.

These data support the view that many shopping trips are related to situational factors over which shoppers have little or no control. They cannot choose when they are paid or when they have to collect their children from school.

Table 10.5 What was your main reason for shopping ... (East et al., 1994)

On a specific day	%	At a specific time of day	%
Near weekend	28	Fitted in with other shopping	25
Day not working	16	Store less busy	25
Store less busy	13	Left work then	15
Ran out of food, needed item	13	Car/lift/help available	13
Wages/pension day	12	Ran out of food, needed item	6
Car/lift/help available	12	On route to/from work	5
Food fresher/better stocked	5	On route to/from school	4
Open late	2	Easier parking	4
		Happened to pass store	3
		To meet people	1

Because of this, their shopping times are fairly rigid; shoppers *could* shop at other times, and they reported this in the survey, but they have good reasons for their present practices and stores would have to offer substantial inducements at off-peak times to change their customers' shopping trip behaviour. It is also clear that the reasons shoppers have for their habits are relatively unchanging so that any inducements that a store might offer would have to be sustained.

Two other factors may deter the use of off-peak times. East et al. (1994) found that customers were put off from shopping on an off-peak day, such as Monday, because more products were thought to be out of stock at such times and because there were still queues at the checkouts. A second factor was lack of knowledge of when the off-peak times were. East et al. found that customers knew the *days* when demand was low in supermarkets but had more limited knowledge about the quiet times *during the day*. Customers might use off-peak hours somewhat more if these were advertised. Overall, these findings suggested limited scope for redistributing demand in supermarkets.

EXERCISE 10.2   ANALYSIS OF STORE DATA

On the website associated with this book (ww.sagepub.co.uk/east) you will find uk98, which is the data from a survey conducted in the UK. Findings from this survey were used in the production of Tables 10.1 and 10.4. The questionnaire for the survey is supplied as su6. Use SPSS to compare stores (question 3) in respect of comparative checkout delay, how much the store is recommended and the relative share of requirements (questions 13, 16 and 21). Use **Compare means, means,** to get the means per store. How would you establish the significance of differences between means?

For all stores, what factors are associated with the rating of the store? To do this, select potential predictors and run an ordinal regression to predict the answers to question 17. Is rating related to recommendation and share of requirement? Use a Spearman correlation to test for this.

How strong are these findings? What alternative explanations are there for the associations you find?

SECTION 2: CUSTOMER TYPOLOGIES

Textbooks sometimes contain classifications of customer types. These may be hypothetical or derived empirically from data. For example, one might hypothesize that shoppers divide into 'prospecting' and 'reluctant' shoppers. The 'prospectors' are generally positive about shopping and see the retail environment as a hunting ground for new ideas, fashions and bargains; these people play a game with retailers in which they win when they get good value for their money. The 'reluctants' have little interest in shopping, seeing it as a necessary means for achieving other goals. Using this classification, we might be able to predict other behaviour. For example, we might expect more window shopping by prospectors. Another approach is Nielsen's (2005) classification of shoppers into branded EDLP (everyday low price) seekers, low price fixture ferrets, promotion junkies, stockpilers, budget bound, promotion opportunists and promotionally oblivious. This classification uses evidence of past purchase to classify shoppers. Many of these typologies include a position for the cost saving, economizing customer who searches for cheapness or good value for money (Jarratt, 1996).

Perhaps the most sophisticated classification is made by Dunn-Humby in their analysis of Tesco's loyalty data. Dunn-Humby uses a selection of frequently bought products to classify customers on 30 criteria. For example, a large size of oven-ready chips will indicate positively for budget consciousness and negatively for health consciousness and gourmet propensity. Those who purchase organic produce indicate another type of concern and those who buy Tesco's own label disproportionately may be classified as a Tesco loyalist. These behaviour-based classifications are used to ensure that coupons go to those who will appreciate them and new products are promoted to customers who are likely to buy them.

Heavy Shoppers

Some shoppers are obviously more important than others; in particular, heavy buyers and loyal buyers should be the focus of management attention. According to the 'heavy half' principle (Chapter 3), the heaviest 50 per cent of buyers will make about 80 per cent of all purchases. Retailers should be alert to heavy buyers and should try to target promotions to these shoppers in order to recruit and retain them.

It might be thought that those who spend more would use more shops and therefore have lower loyalty but Dunn and Wrigley (1984) and Mason (1991) found that first-store loyalty did not change with increasing total expenditure in supermarkets. Tate (1961), Enis and Paul (1970) and East, Harris, Willson and Lomax (1995) found a positive relationship between loyalty and primary grocery store expenditure. Knox and Denison (2000) also found a small positive association ($r = 0.24$) between store loyalty and total spending for supermarkets and a negative relationship for other types of retail outlet. If bigger spenders are more loyal, it follows that they will spend a lot more in their primary store than others because they spend more in total and a higher proportion of this spending goes to their favourite store. High spending customers may therefore seem very attractive to supermarket managers and may be courted through loyalty programmes. However, the fact that heavy buyers are more loyal does not imply that all loyal customers are heavy buyers. There may be many light buyers who show high purchase loyalty simply because they have fewer opportunities to visit different stores.

Some data were gathered at Kingston University on heavy supermarket shoppers. This work suggested that, more than others, these people tend to have larger incomes and households, be under age 45, prefer large out-of-town stores, shop later in the day and less often and have a regular day for shopping. This type of work may help us to understand the heavy buyer but stores may be able to bypass this sort of analysis because their databases should reveal directly how much different customers buy.

Store-loyal Customers

Like brand loyalty (Chapter 2), store loyalty can be defined in a number of ways. The attitude to the store provides one measure of loyalty. This is much the same as satisfaction with the store. As behaviour, loyalty can be measured by *share-of-category requirement* (SCR); high SCR loyalty to a store occurs when customers devote a large proportion of their spending to that store. Another behavioural measure is *retention* of the store; high retention loyalty occurs when customers patronize the store for a long time. Despite the assumption that they have some common basis, these different measures may show little association. East et al. (2005a) found that the SCR for the primary store and attitude to the store showed only weak correlations of 0.13 and 0.15 in the UK and New Zealand respectively.

Store loyalty can be investigated using the market regularities described in Chapter 4. We may use models like the Dirichlet to show the relationship at an aggregate level between SCR requirement and factors such as penetration, purchase frequency and market share (Kau and Ehrenberg, 1984; Uncles and Ehrenberg, 1990; Uncles and Hammond, 1995; Wright, Sharp and Sharp, 1998). We demonstrated this method of analysis for brands in Chapter 3. We may also search for economic, demographic, behavioural or attitudinal factors that predict SCR or retention at an individual level. In particular, we are interested in whether a shopper's store loyalty relates to age, the frequency of store use, the accessibility of the store, brand loyalty, shopping on a particular day, the amount spent in the retail category, income, attitude to the store and free time. Retailers will also be interested in whether the customers of different store groups show differences in average loyalty (Box 10.2).

East et al. (2000) used regression analysis on survey data to examine the effect of various factors on SCR and retention for UK supermarkets. They found that age was negatively related to SCR, but positively related to retention. More generally, although SCR and retention had three predictors in common (brand loyalty, attitude to the store chain and age), five other factors applied to one measure but not the other. The R^2 for the model predicting SCR, was 0.14. However, for the model predicting retention, it was only 0.04, suggesting that attempts to influence store retention using these variables would have little value for management.

Box 10.2	Average supermarket loyalty

Average levels of loyalty to different stores depend on the retail category, market concentration, average store size and the period of time taken for measurement. For supermarkets in the UK, AGB (1992) reported that over an 8-week period approximately 75 per cent of expenditure took place in the primary supermarket. Also in the UK, Mason (1991) reported the SCR for the primary store was 72 per cent over one month, 65 per cent over 12 weeks and 60 per cent over 24 weeks. Loyalties to the store group are slightly higher than the loyalty to the individual store. It is difficult to compare these figures with earlier ones that included convenience store purchases, e.g. 42 per cent was found in Cardiff by Dunn and Wrigley (1984), but it seems likely that loyalties to the store group rose when grocery trade concentration, store size and the number of outlets per store group increased. The recent growth of small store formats may have reduced average loyalty.

Theories of Store Loyalty

There may be no overarching explanations for SCR and retention. These effects may be the result of a large number of weak influences that have little in common. However, it is reasonable to look for one or two mobilizing influences that are responsible for much of the effect and here there have been two competing theories about the nature of store loyalty. We report these theories and suggest a third possibility.

Resource constraint

The first theory was specified by Charlton (1973), who drew on earlier work by Enis and Paul (1970). In this theory, store loyalty is the outcome of limited resources: those who lack money, time and transport, or whose environment lacks choice (Tate, 1961), are forced to use one store much of the time and are therefore obliged to be loyal. Carman (1970) offered a variation of this model, suggesting that some people had little interest in shopping and therefore did not use the choice that they had. Such people had a lifestyle with commitments outside the home, full-time work, little home entertaining and a lack of interest in deals, advertising and shopping. As a result, they were loyal to both brands and stores because they did not seek alternatives. However, East, Harris, Willson and Lomax (1995) found that shoppers with different loyalty levels gave similar ratings for the pleasantness of supermarket shopping which does not support Carman's lifestyle theory.

Carman (1970) and Enis and Paul (1970) found that those with low incomes were more loyal so this theory probably did apply at one time. But it is unlikely that it applies now. Shoppers are more able to make choices, have wider access to stores (car ownership) and better storage capacity (home freezers).

Discretionary loyalty

Dunn and Wrigley (1984) argued that Charlton's negative concept of store loyalty needed review. They suggested that some store loyalty arose from a pattern of one-stop shopping, often in large supermarkets. We call this *discretionary store loyalty*. It implies that resources are used by shoppers to make positive choices that raise SCR. For example, the car may be used to do most of the shopping in one hypermarket, thus avoiding shopping in many outlets. Discretionary loyalty differs from Carman's account by implying a more positive approach to brands and shopping and it may be seen as an adaptation to being time poor and money rich. People can spend less if they use several stores and cherry pick the bargains (leading to low loyalty) but this takes time and effort. Those with less time and more money may choose to buy most of what they need from one outlet because this is easier; as a result, they will show high loyalty. This can be seen as a rational choice. Mason (1991) found that store loyalty was higher when the housewife worked and was under 45 years of age (when family commitments are likely to take a lot of time). Flavián, Martínez and Polo (2001) found general support for discretionary loyalty in Spain. However, East et al. (2000) found that neither free time nor income was significantly related to SCR in a regression analysis covering many factors.

Loyalty as habit

An alternative way of thinking about loyalty is that it is a habit. The habit may be set by the conditions under which a person lives; for example, those with routine work patterns are free at specific times and may fit shopping into one of these times because this is convenient and after a while this arrangement will become routine. Another basis for habit is personal disposition; some people may find routines more attractive than other people. Either way, we would expect to find that those with high store loyalty tend to have other similar habits, such as brand loyalty and a regular day for shopping. Evidence from East et al. (2000) gave support to this explanation.

| **Box 10.3** | **Purchase and loyalty on the Internet** |

In Chapter 1, we drew attention to the rapid growth of Internet purchase. In the early days of Internet use, it was argued that this channel was particularly suited to 'bit-based' products such as music, booking travel, share purchase, banking, gambling and pornography. These fields have certainly prospered but it is also the case that the Internet has been used to purchase a range of physical products. Some of these are familiar, such as groceries, books, CDs and clothing, while others are more unusual and benefit from the ability to search the Web for unusual products. For example, a person wanting a spray against clothes moths can find this on the Internet but might be hard put to find it in ordinary stores.

From the standpoint of the supplier, the Internet may save costs, particularly for bit-based products that can be directly distributed 'down the wire'. Some use of the Internet is driven by cost saving but, in other cases, it is the convenience of this method of purchase that appeals, e.g. grocery purchase and also the superior quality of information, e.g. for share purchase. Often the convenience is enhanced by the very accurate delivery of advertising that is possible when people search for products on the Web.

Grocery buying has been studied to see whether brand loyalty is stronger when purchase is made on the Internet. Degeratu, Rangaswamy and Wu (2001) found that brand names played a stronger role in choice and that fewer brand switches were made in the online environment. But Degeratu et al. compared those who shopped online with those who shopped offline and any differences may be due to the different abilities and interests of the two groups rather than to the channel used. Arce and Cebollada (2006) improved the analysis by comparing the online and offline grocery purchasing of the same people. They confirmed that there was less brand switching online. One explanation for this is that, on the Web, buyers may work from a list of past purchases and take less advantage of the discount opportunities available. As a result, they stick to the same brands and have high loyalty.

The Effects of Loyalty Schemes

Loyalty schemes take a variety of forms. All schemes have some form of customer incentive. Some schemes raise service levels for a more valuable part of the customer base, for example the provision of executive lounges for frequent air travellers. Many schemes, such as supermarket loyalty programmes, give cash incentives. A loyalty scheme has two potential effects. First, the incentives, it may raise customer acquisition, share of wallet and retention by directly influencing customers. Second, when data on the purchases of different card holders are collected, the store owner may use that data to target shopper segments more accurately and produce further gains in acquisition, share and retention.

Incentives are very expensive. If they take 1 per cent of turnover and the store group makes 5 per cent on turnover, the incentives take 20 per cent of profit if turnover is unchanged. To pay for the loyalty scheme, the turnover would have to increase by 25 per cent. Furthermore, competitors can run loyalty schemes which may make it very difficult to achieve a 25 per cent increase. In an effort to reduce the effect of competitor response, some schemes, such as Air Miles and Fly Buys, only allow one operator in each sector. If Shell gives Air Miles, BP, Esso and so on are excluded. However, competitors can still run other schemes.

A loyalty scheme provides a database covering most customers together with information about their purchases. Retailers can use this information to ensure that promotions (often by vouchers) are well targeted. Tesco, with its analysis agency Dunn-Humby, is recognized as a world leader in this respect.[1] Tesco is interested in the types of purchase made – and not made – by a card holder. If the customer buys no meat, vouchers for meat are never sent to avoid offending vegetarians, but if the customer does not buy toothpaste at Tesco, vouchers might be used in an effort to switch their purchasing of toiletries to Tesco. A similar inducement might be given to those who appear to buy most of their wine elsewhere; alternatively, the wine buff may be invited to wine tasting events. In other cases, vouchers may be for what the customer already buys; this is a reward for loyalty and makes the vouchers more interesting to the customer. The database also reveals customers who have switched to competitors (they can differentiate this from going on holiday by the nature of the purchases before the customer leaves). Defecting customers can be sent vouchers in order to recover them. Customer purchase information also helps to sell items that never go through the stores, such as gardening equipment and baby buggies (certain items purchased, together with customer age, can indicate when a customer may be pregnant). The customer database allows Tesco to launch financial products, such as credit cards and insurance, with little risk. The pattern of demand in stores allows the management to fine tune the inventories for different stores. Tesco can also sell data to manufacturers because the system shows the relative performance of brands over time.

This sophisticated operation has helped to expand Tesco's total business and, in the view of the company, it is the information rather than the direct incentive effect that justifies the scheme. However, researchers remain interested in the incentive effect of loyalty cards; this is difficult to measure because other factors may be involved. For example, Tesco took share from Sainsbury when the loyalty scheme was introduced in 1995 but much of this change might have happened in any case because Tesco built more stores, many of which were in Sainsbury territory (East and Hogg, 1997). Although Tesco gained market share, the firm's customers did not show a disproportionate increase in the share-of-category requirement (SCR). This is despite the fact that Tesco was targeting those with intermediate loyalty to the store in an effort to expand their SCR. The data in Table 10.6 from Taylor Nelson Sofres shows that in 1996, a year after the introduction of the loyalty scheme, Tesco had the same SCR for a slightly greater market share as Sainsbury had in 1994 when this group had no loyalty scheme. Table 10.6 shows that SCR is tied to market share for all the store groups

Table 10.6   Market share and share-of-category requirement for five UK store groups, 1994–7

Store Group	1994		1996		1997	
	MS	SCR	MS	SCR	MS	SCR
Tesco	18	44	21	46	22	48
Sainsbury	20	46	19	45	20	48
Asda	11	42	12	42	13	44
Safeway	9	34	10	35	10	36
Somerfield	7	31	6	29	5	28

Source: Data from Taylor Nelson Sofres

The evidence in Table 10.6 does not show that the loyalty scheme had no effect but indicates that it could have increased customer acquisition as well as retention and SCR. If the new customers were often light buyers, some of the longer-term customers could have increased SCR to produce the average pattern observed in Table 10.6. Some evidence of customer acquisition by Tesco at this time comes from a study of 541 shoppers who answered questionnaires before and after the introduction of the Tesco loyalty scheme (East and Hogg, 1997). This showed that Tesco gained share by customer retention *and* customer acquisition whereas Sainsbury lost ground because this group failed to acquire new customers. We discussed the importance of growth through customer acquisition in Chapter 2. It seems to get insufficient attention in marketing.

Meyer-Waarden (2007) reviews studies of incentive effect. In general, there is little or no effect of SCR from loyalty schemes; for example, Sharp and Sharp (1997) found that the firms in the Fly Buys scheme in Australia did not show a significant increase in SCR compared with Dirichlet norms. Meyer-Waarden used panel data in his own research and found that customers who were holders of one card showed single-figure increases in lifetime duration (retention) and more share of wallet but customers with several cards did not show these effects. However, multiple card holding has become the norm so that single card holders may be a minority, which means there is little effect on profits. Also, membership may involve a self-selection effect, whereby those who join a loyalty scheme are already highly loyal customers.

Leenheer et al. (2007) took account of self-selection effects in a study of loyalty schemes in Dutch supermarkets. They found a naïve model estimated that loyalty schemes increased share of wallet by 29.8 percentage points if self-selection was ignored but when self-selection effects were taken into account, the increase in share of wallet attributable to loyalty programme membership averaged 4.1 per cent. The size of the effect varied slightly between schemes and reduced as the customers joined additional loyalty programmes. A 4.1 per cent gain is not going to cover the cost of the scheme but it is a mistake to focus only on share of wallet when customer acquisition and retention may be involved and these would raise the return. From this work it appears that loyalty schemes cannot be justified on the basis of incentive effect but may bring benefit.

Compulsive Shoppers

In advanced economies a phenomenon of compulsive shopping has emerged. This is not simply a pastime of the rich. In the USA, 15 million people are estimated to exhibit the deviant pattern of compulsive purchase; they buy clothes, shoes and other goods which they do not need and sometimes never use (Arthur, 1992). Scherhorn, Reisch and Raab (1990) have reported on compulsive shopping in Germany and Elliott (1993, 1994) has researched this phenomenon in the UK. Faber and O'Guinn (1988) saw this type of shopping as part of a wider range of compulsive behaviour, which they describe as: 'A response to an uncontrollable drive or desire to obtain, use, or experience a feeling, substance, or activity that leads an individual to repetitively engage in behaviour that will ultimately cause harm to the individual and/or others.'

Compulsive shopping is clearly a serious problem, which often causes financial and psychological distress to the shoppers themselves and to their families. One reason for compulsive shopping is the more attractive shopping environment of the present day but, to explain why some people suffer from this compulsion more than other people, we need to focus on the behaviour and background of the compulsive shopper. D'Astous (1990) argues that this type of behaviour is the extreme end of a continuum and that many people have strong urges to buy that they can barely hold in check. If we accept this view, we can learn about compulsive behaviour by examining those who are less extreme (Magee, 1994).

Compulsive shoppers tend to be owners of credit cards (D'Astous, 1990), are usually women (92 per cent in Faber and O'Guinn's study, 1992) and some research has revealed them to be younger and to have lower self-esteem. Research in this area is by survey and it is difficult to assign cause and effect; compulsive shoppers may have low self-esteem because of their behaviour but it seems likely that it is a cause, rather than an effect, of their behaviour.

Compulsive shoppers appear to get some emotional release, or temporary 'mood repair', out of the process of buying. Elliott, Eccles and Gournay (1996) interviewed 50 compulsive shoppers and probed their thinking and motivation. The respondents accepted that their behaviour was abnormal and potentially very damaging but they could not easily control it. In this respect it functioned rather like a drug and Elliott et al. emphasize this by describing the behaviour as addictive. Elliott et al. also found that this type of shopping was often related to unsatisfactory relationships with partners. Women whose partners worked excessively, ignored them, or were controlling, were more likely to be compulsive shoppers. In many cases, their behaviour was a form of revenge or was deliberately designed to rile their partner. In other cases, their treatment by their partner may have lowered their self-esteem and made compulsive shopping more attractive.

Dittmar, Beattie and Friese (1995) suggested that the way in which products are bought reflects the way in which people see themselves. These researchers suggested that the sexes might differ in this respect. They found that men tend to buy instrumental and leisure items impulsively, reflecting their independence and activity, while women tend to buy symbolic and self-expressive goods concerned with appearance and the emotional aspects of self. The researchers suggested that this difference might be found in compulsive shoppers. Dittmar (2005) stresses that materialistic values are one key to compulsive shopping. Those with low self-esteem can only get mood repair from shopping if possessions have importance to them (see Figure 10.4).

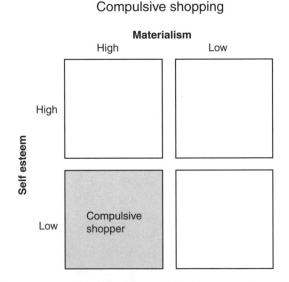

Figure 10.4   Compulsive shopping as a product of high materialism and low self-esteem

SECTION 3: THE STORE ENVIRONMENT

Store Layout, Location and Space

Actions occur when the environment presents opportunities, stimuli and rewards. The store layout should therefore be decided by reference to increasing spending opportunities, presenting purchase cues and making the store an easy and pleasant place to use. These different considerations do not always coincide. IKEA uses a layout that requires the customer to move through the whole store in order to reach the exit; this may raise spending opportunities but it can be a near-claustrophobic experience for some customers who find it difficult to get out.

In supermarkets, specific locations in the store are associated with different rates of purchase. For example, the end-aisle position induces more purchase and eye-level shelves sell nearly twice as much as the lowest shelf. One of the applications of scanner technology, called direct product profitability (DPP), is to measure the profit from a given stock keeping unit (SKU)[2] in a specific location. This technology identifies 'hot-spots' in the store and can be used to vary the location and space given to an SKU so that profit is optimized. Space use studies are complicated by the fact that sales gains for categories given more space or better locations are off-set by losses from categories that lose space or go to a worse location. Drèze, Hoch and Purk (1994) showed a potential profit gain of about 15 per cent, comparing the worst to best configurations of location and space but, in practice, the authors estimated that the feasible changes would produce a much smaller gain. Drèze et al. found that more effect came from location than from the amount of space given to an SKU. Experimental studies on varying shelf space in grocery categories show that a doubling of space leads to sales increases in the region of 20 per cent (Cox, 1970; Curhan, 1972; Kotzan and Evanson, 1969; Krueckeberg, 1969). Display is also important in supermarkets as a large proportion of grocery purchase decisions are made at the point of purchase (Dagnoli, 1987).

Atmospherics

Store Features

The store environment includes the amount of space, the layout, fittings, colours, aromas, sound and the density of customers in the outlet. There are some standard display features used by stores that affect the impression given by the store. For example, discount stores sell out of cases to emphasize low prices, shopping centres create central areas with entertaining features, fashion shops use music that suits the age and taste of their clientele. In Britain, Oddbins wine shops use handwritten prices, enhancing an image of a knowledgeable management. Such features are an extension of product display and are chosen to enhance the store image. These signs help to define the store offering and to differentiate it from that of other stores. In this sense, store design and the display of goods have parallels with advertising and packaging.

EXERCISE 10.3   ASSESSING ATMOSPHERIC FEATURES

Describe a shop which you find to be attractive and also stimulating. What is the basis for this? Is space, colour, sound or odour used? Do these environmental features affect your spending in the store?

Kotler (1973) suggested that these store features create an *atmosphere*, modifying the buyer's knowledge and mood and thus affecting behaviour. Kotler also noted that atmospherics could be used to de-market; for example, State liquor stores in some countries are deliberately off-putting environments. There is no doubt that environmental features can have a strong effect on in-store behaviour. Bellizzi, Crowley and Hasty (1983) found that people were more aroused by red than blue or green and suggested that red will speed up behaviour and might be appropriate where quicker action is more profitable, e.g. in fast-food restaurants. Babin, Hardesty and Suter (2003) found that blue was associated with greater purchase intention, compared to orange, but this effect was largely nullified under subdued lighting. Milliman (1982) found that fast-tempo music speeded up supermarket customers and reduced their purchasing. Slower music slowed them down and produced expenditures that were 38 per cent above those in the fast music condition. Customers were not aware of these influences. Areni and Kim (1993) found that, compared with popular music, classical background music in a wine store led to the choice of more expensive wines. North, Hargreaves and McKendrick (1999) followed up Areni and Kim's study by using either French accordion music or German beer cellar music in a wine store. More French wine was sold when the French music played and more German wine was sold when the German music played and customers were unaware of this influence on their behaviour.

Another study by Yalch and Spangenberg (1993) showed that music could affect sales in a departmental store. The music had to be appropriate for each department; for example, music in departments with younger customers needed to be played at high volume. Other work has looked at the way different stimuli work together. For example, Mattila and Wirtz (2001) showed that, when music and scent were similar in terms of arousing properties, they worked together to increase the evaluation of the environment. Similarly, a 'Christmas' scent raised the evaluation of the store environment only when accompanied by Christmas music (Spangenberg, Grohmann and Sprott, 2005). Bosmans (2007) found that scents had a powerful influence on evaluations in the store as long as they were congruent with the product. Meyers-Levy and Zhu (2007) found that ceiling height could affect the way consumers processed information; they suggested that people felt freer when the height was greater.

What is the explanation for these effects? One proposal is that the impact on purchase is mediated by mood. In a preliminary study, Donovan and Rossiter (1982) used a classification of mood states described by Mehrabian and Russell (1974). They found that a store's atmosphere produced mood effects in consumers which could affect the time and money spent in the store. Figure 10.5 shows this stimulus → organism → response (SOR) model with the intervening moods of pleasure and arousal. Donovan and Rossiter expected that high arousal would act with pleasure to raise spending and with displeasure to reduce spending and more rapid departure from the store. The first was supported but there were too few unpleasant environments to test the second effect.

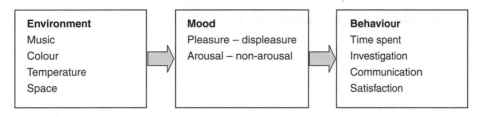

Figure 10.5   The role of moods in mediating atmospheric effects on shopping behaviour

There is a variety of evidence available on mood effects. A paper by Smith and Sherman (1992) showed that store image was associated with mood, which then predicted the amount of time and money spent in the store. Mehrabian and Russell (1974) thought that more novel and complex environments would raise interest and Gröppel (1993) observed that supermarkets with high novelty and complexity levels did give more pleasure, that customers spent more time and bought more in such stores. Swinyard (1993) argued that only the more elaborate processing of the highly involved consumer would be affected by mood and that this mood change would affect shopping intentions. This was supported in a scenario-based experiment, i.e. only the highly involved shoppers modified their shopping intentions. Sharma and Stafford (2000) found that store design affected the persuasiveness of sales personnel, an effect that may be mediated by mood. Eroglu, Machleit and Davis (2003) even found support for mood effects in an online environment.

Donovan et al. (1994) reviewed research in this area. They noted weaknesses in their earlier paper and those of others. In particular, they suggested that it was necessary to distinguish moods induced by the environment from emotions associated with purchase. Donovan et al. conducted a further study which avoided these problems. They found that pleasure did contribute to time in the store and extra spending and that arousal did reduce spending in environments rated as unpleasant, but arousal did not increase spending when the environment was pleasant. One problem that has not been addressed is that window shoppers may be drawn into stores with pleasant atmospheres but may not buy because that is not their purpose. In some retail sectors, window shoppers are as common as active shoppers (Nielsen, 2005) and these people may react differently to store atmospherics than other shoppers.

While mood may act as an intervening variable to modify levels of spending, there are cases where this explanation is inadequate. In particular, the North et al. (1999) study indicates that behaviour can be modified directly by the French and German music cues (there are no French and German moods). Also, the effect of the tempo of music, observed by Milliman (1982), may be automatic and not mediated by mood. This fits a stimulus–response (SR) model rather than a SOR model. Many stimuli affect behaviour without much awareness; this is part of our low involvement response to the environment which helps us to cope with the wide variety of stimuli that impinge on our senses. By acting in this way, we leave ourselves free to concentrate on other features of the environment.

Morin, Dubé and Chebat (2007) suggest a dual model whereby stimuli can affect shoppers' perceptions by two paths. Ambient environmental cues operate at an unconscious level – as pre-attentional signals – and induce limited processing, but focal cues with more value may be selected for attention. The authors suggest that some stimuli, such as pleasant music, may influence behaviour through both channels.

What other explanations might be relevant to the effect of atmospherics? As Kotler (1973) suggested, some environmental features may be informative and these cognitive effects may influence behaviour. Also, some retail interiors are so dramatic that people talk about them. For example, the vastness of the Mall of America and the video screens of Niketown may cause so much interest that these places are easily mentioned in conversations. However, we believe that the explanation of atmospheric effects remains rather limited; if store atmospherics are a kind of advertising, some of the explanations from the advertising field may be applicable.

Crowding

A common problem in stores, banks, post offices, restaurants and so on is the level of congestion or crowding. People have a complex response to crowding and, in different contexts, may find it attractive or aversive. Hui and Bateson (1991) found that an important factor in determining whether crowding was liked or disliked is the control that customers feel that they have in the situation. People seek to preserve their control (Brehm, 1989; Brehm and Brehm, 1981). In Hui and Bateson's study, high densities of people were associated with *increased* control in a bar and *reduced* control in a bank. People go to banks for instrumental reasons and bars for recreation and it seems likely that this different usage is associated with the way crowding affects perceived control since crowding is more likely to obstruct activity in banks than in bars. In shops, therefore, people are likely to dislike densities that impede action and store designs should aim to reduce such congestion. However, there may be some recreational shoppers who have little to buy but who enjoy store congestion. It is also likely that people are put off when a store appears empty. Wicker (1984) has suggested that every setting has an optimal number of occupants. For example, some people feel reluctant to go into a near-empty restaurant.

Milgram (1970) saw crowding as stressful, making people quicker, less exploratory and more inclined to omit purchases. The impact of stress is to narrow concentration so that central tasks may be performed better but more complex operations, which require more peripheral perceptions and memories for their completion, may be performed less efficiently. This means that the key functions of shopping may be done more efficiently under crowded conditions but shoppers may forget items that are peripheral to their needs. Anglin, Stuenkel and Lepisto (1994) found that shoppers who scored high on measures of stress engaged in more comparison shopping and were more price-sensitive, these behaviours might be seen as central to shopping. This is another reason why stress-reducing atmospheric factors may raise spending.

Michon, Chebat and Turley (2005) found that scents made people more positive about their environment when the shopping density was at a medium level. this may be because scents tend to reduce stress. In psychology, it has been found that there is a preferred level of stimulation: people seek minimum arousal; they are more aroused when there are no stimuli (and they are bored); and they are more aroused when there are many stimuli so that they cannot process them all. This model is shown in Figure 10.6. This suggests that store interiors, including crowding, can be too stimulating or not stimulating enough and that the optimum will vary across consumers and types of outlet.

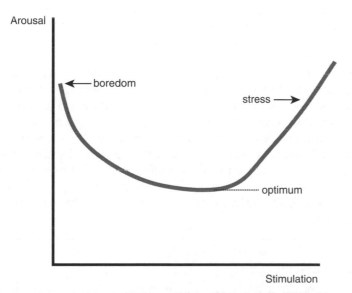

Figure 10.6   There is an optimum level of stimulation

SUMMARY

Retail use is explained at the aggregate level by gravity models and at the individual level by identifying the preferences of customers. Shoppers are strongly affected by convenience and price and, to a lesser extent, by wide choice and quality. Retail use varies by day and time of day and stores are under-used much of the time. Investigations of the

(Continued)

reasons for use at different times shows that many of these reasons stem from the shopper's situation and this limits change. There are two distinct time–use segments which are based on work: fully employed people shop later in the day and later in the week compared with those not in full-time employment.

A number of typologies have been suggested for shoppers. One important group for retailers are high spenders. Among grocery shoppers these heavy buyers are found to be wealthier, have larger households and to use a car. A second group is high-loyalty customers. Store loyalty, like brand loyalty, has two basic behavioural forms: the proportion of patronage given to a store in the retail category and the duration of patronage, or store retention. Early studies suggested that people were more loyal (measured as a proportion) when they lacked the time, money, transport resources or interest to spread their custom. A second theory, called discretionary loyalty, was that certain people, who had resources, used them to choose a shopping pattern that gave high loyalty. Such people were time poor and money rich and could afford to spend a little more and save time by shopping at one store. Recent evidence in the UK did not support the first and gave limited support to the second of these theories. The results fitted a different theory, that store loyalty was a habit that was conditioned by circumstances or personality.

Compulsive shoppers buy things that they do not need and may not use. This pattern of behaviour has raised concern because of the financial devastation that uncontrolled spending can produce. These people tend to have low self-esteem, which is temporarily alleviated by shopping.

In all types of store, spending may be affected by *atmospherics* – the impact of environmental features such as space, colour, sound, odour and crowding. Here, we have evidence of the effects but the explanations are limited.

Additional Resources

There is a large literature in this area, as well as a specialist journal (the *Journal of Retailing*). For particular topics, see Donovan et al. (1994) for store atmosphere, Morin, Dubé and Chebat (2007) for the effect of music, Meyer-Waarden (2007) on loyalty programmes, and Arce and Cebollada (2006) for recent work on online versus offline shopping behaviour. There are also popular texts, notably Underhill (1999). The interested reader may wish to start with some retailing textbooks, such as McGoldrick (2002) or Weitz and Levy (2004).

Notes

1　Dunn-Humby advises other companies, such as Kroger (USA) and Coles (Australia).
2　Brands come in different sizes, flavours etc.; the SKU used by retailers will have a unique combination of these attributes.

11 Word-Of-Mouth Influence

LEARNING OBJECTIVES

When you have completed this chapter, you should be able to:

1 Discuss the difficulty of conducting research on word of mouth (WOM).
2 Describe how product decisions in different categories are affected by WOM.
3 Report on the relative occurrence and impact of positive and negative WOM in familiar categories.
4 Describe variations in WOM that affect its impact: solicited or volunteered, strongly or mildly expressed, from people who are close or distant from the receiver.
5 Report how WOM relates to the current and past usage of brands and to market share.
6 Suggest how marketers might apply knowledge about WOM.

OVERVIEW

As we saw in Chapter 5, word of mouth (WOM) has been treated mainly as a latent influence in the diffusion of innovation. Some 'who spoke to whom?' research has been conducted in this field so we also have an understanding of network processes in the adoption of new practices. But WOM has effects beyond innovation; in particular, it affects how consumers replace one brand with another in categories that they understand well. In this chapter, we focus on brand choice in familiar markets, rather than new markets.

We assess the relative importance of WOM and other information channels in the selection of brands in different categories. We describe research on the relative frequency of positive and negative WOM (PWOM, NWOM). We report evidence on the relative impact of PWOM

(Continued)

and NWOM and we explain how different factors contribute to that impact. We identify whether brands that are cited in PWOM and NWOM have been owned – or are currently owned – and we describe how WOM production is related to market share. These reports draw on research conducted by the authors.

Why has such evidence not been available before? The main explanation is that it is very difficult to study word of mouth. It occurs infrequently and consumer surveys must be used to find out about it. Such survey evidence is prone to bias and is rightly treated with caution.

SECTION 1: THE NATURE OF WORD OF MOUTH

In Chapter 5, we described the way in which innovations became accepted. At the centre of the adoption process is the communication of information. A person who adopts a new idea or product must find out about it, either through the mass media (advertising, editorial), or through personal discovery (e.g. seeing it in a shop), or from other people (salespersons, other consumers). A substantial part of the success of innovations depends upon the influence of one consumer on another. Sometimes, consumers just see what others do and copy them, but much social influence starts with word of mouth (WOM). WOM may be positive (recommendation, advocacy, PWOM) or negative (advising against, NWOM). Unlike rumour, WOM is, or is believed to be, founded on verified evidence (see Box 11.1).

Box 11.1	Rumour

Rumours are unverified topical beliefs that circulate between people. Early thinking about rumour was presented by Knapp (1944) and by Allport and Postman (1947). Rumours may be based on hope, fear or hatred and may make claims about conspiracies or dangers. The Internet now provides a means for the rapid circulation of rumours and many companies have suffered from this hazard. The financial marketplace is particularly susceptible to rumour (Kimmel, 2004a). Rosnow (2001) argues that uncertainty, credibility and importance (personal relevance) are the primary drivers of rumours, which will spread faster in contexts of high anxiety. Kimmel and Audrain-Pontevia (2007) found that roughly three-fifths of rumours were negative, one-fifth positive and one-fifth neutral. They confirmed that credibility, importance and uncertainty were the most important factors in rumour transmission. This subject is reviewed by Kimmel (2004b).

Advice occurs in direct exchanges when people are face to face, when they are connected via telephones and email and, more remotely, via blogs and message boards on the Internet where the person posting the advice is unlikely to be known by others. Some advice occurs in a commercial context, e.g. from sales personnel and on sponsored websites; here the influence process may be more persuasive than informative.[1] We focus on the advice that is offered by one consumer to another. In this situation, in which commercial interests are usually absent, people can drop their guard and treat WOM as impartial. We describe all such advice as WOM, even though some of it is written and not oral (see Box 11.2).

Box 11.2	Definitions

'Word of mouth is product-related, oral, person-to-person communication.' (Arndt, 1967).

'Word of mouth is the most important marketing element that exists.' Gordon Weaver, of Paramount Pictures, quoted in the *Wall Street Journal* (1984)

'The ultimate test of the customer relationship.' (Bendapudi and Berry, 1997: 30).

'Word of mouth is typically considered a face-to-face spoken communication, although phone conversations, text messages sent via *SMS* and web dialogue, such as online profile pages, blog posts, message board threads, instant messages and emails are often now included in the definition of word of mouth.' (Wikipedia)

In this chapter, we move from the innovations studied in Chapter 5 to mature categories. Innovations are usually new concepts or products, or new features of existing products. Many of the classic studies on WOM were concerned with innovations; for example, Whyte (1954) on air conditioners, Coleman, Katz and Menzel (1957) on the prescribing of new drugs by physicians and Katz's (1961) work on farming innovations. In mature categories, WOM tends to induce switching between familiar brands rather than first-time adoption. Sometimes a brand will have new features not offered by others and here switching may occur because consumers want to adopt these new features. For example, a 3G mobile phone network operator may offer services not available from other operators. By contrast, mature brands, such as China Mobile, Orange, Optus and Vodafone, are familiar to people and usually offer much the same services. Here, the reason for switching to a new supplier may not be an innovation but some advantage that can be drawn to a consumer's attention. On phone networks, one person might advise another about relative cost, or the coverage of a network in a particular location. This is useful information to a prospective buyer but it is *not* an innovative feature of the service. We should study such WOM because brand switching is so common: about 15 per cent of customers per year switch brands according to Reichheld (1996b).

Research on WOM has been difficult to conduct, so we begin by reviewing how WOM may be studied. Then, using the methods that are available, we answer the questions below.

- How does the effect of WOM on brand choice vary by category?
- Under what circumstances does WOM occur?
- How frequently do PWOM and NWOM occur?
- How much do people talk about their current main brand?
- How does the occurrence of WOM relate to the market share of the brand?
- How can we explain word-of-mouth production?
- Which has most impact on purchase probability, PWOM or NWOM?
- What aspects of word of mouth are associated with more impact?
- What are the applications of these findings in marketing?
- What problems need further research?

How Can We Study Word of Mouth?

Research on WOM is limited by the methods available. Ideally, we would observe WOM as it occurs and monitor the consequences. In practice, WOM occurs too rarely and any effect may be delayed, so that direct observation of the outcomes of WOM may be impossible. As a result, other methods have to be used, which are reviewed below.

Text Mining on the Internet

Although we cannot observe WOM as it happens, we may be able to measure it as comments posted on the Internet. WOM is not hard to find in consumer-generated media but there are two problems. First, those who set up websites may encourage either more positive or more negative WOM than is typical in everyday life and, second, those who post comments on the Internet may be different from those who give offline advice. One study that sought to predict the success of TV programmes from Internet comment had mixed success. The volume of comment was not predictive but another measure was indicative of programme success (Godes and Mayzlin, 2004b). However, another study using Internet comment (Liu, 2006) found that the volume of comment about movies predicted box office returns. It seems likely that, as the Internet becomes more widely used, Web recommendation will become more predictive.

Experiments

A number of laboratory experiments have examined the impact of positive and negative information (e.g. Ahluwalia, 2002; Herr, Kardes and Kim, 1991). The main problem here is that the artificiality of the laboratory situation restricts generalization to naturally occurring behaviour. This artificiality has several aspects:

1 **The stimulus is not like real WOM.** In experiments, the 'WOM' is often written information which has less impact than spoken (Herr, Kardes and Kim, 1991), and is not requested, which is often an aspect of real advice WOM (East et al., 2005b). In experiments, it is customary to use symmetrically expressed PWOM and NWOM but, in everyday life, WOM varies from neutral to strong expression, and PWOM and NWOM could differ in this emphasis.
2 **The response measures may be inappropriate.** Although it is not a necessary feature of experiments, most experimental studies of WOM have used attitude and belief items to measure impact (e.g. Ahluwalia, 2002); marketers should be more interested in the impact on purchase or purchase probability.
3 **Experiments make no allowances for the fact that some people give more WOM than others.** Each participant in an experiment makes an equal contribution to the outcome; in everyday life, some people say nothing while others give a lot of WOM.
4 **Experiments rush the process.** Experimental studies usually take measures of effect shortly after exposure to the stimulus. After a longer period, the effects may have changed. In natural settings, people who receive WOM may not act on it for months, so delayed measurement is better.

Some escape from these problems is provided by role-play experiments. In a role-play experiment, the subject may be asked what he or she would do in a specified situation, e.g.: 'If someone asked you about mobile phones, would you recommend/advise against ...?' Participants can be more dispassionate under these circumstances but there is no guarantee that they would do as they claim. Another possibility is to use field experiments. Arndt (1967) introduced a new brand into a community and measured sales and the reported PWOM and NWOM. Godes and Mayzlin (2004a) used a field experiment to compare the extra effect on sales of WOM from loyal and non-loyal customers. Unfortunately, this method is very expensive and, to measure WOM, the experimenter may still have to ask participants to recall what they have given or received.

Retrospective Surveys

The major problem associated with retrospective surveys is that respondents have to recall the WOM that they have given or received and the circumstances relating to such WOM. As a result, their reports may be systematically distorted by recall bias. If PWOM is more easily recalled than NWOM, a measure of relative frequency will be biased in favour of PWOM; if NWOM is believed to generally have more impact than PWOM, this could affect respondent reports on impact.

EXERCISE 11.1   QUESTIONNAIRE

Fill out this questionnaire:

1   Do you own a mobile phone?

No	[1]
Yes	[2]

2   Which make of mobile phone do you have?

Have no mobile phone	[1]
Nokia	[2]
Sony Ericsson	[3]
Motorola	[4]
Samsung	[5]
Siemens	[6]
Panasonic	[7]
NEC	[8]
Airtime supplier phone (O_2, 3 etc.)	[9]
Other brand of mobile phone	[10]

3   In the last six months, how many times have you *received positive* advice about any mobile phone handset?
Write in number (0, 1, 2 etc. ......)
If you answered 0, then please go to Q.9

4   The last time you received positive advice, did you ask for advice or was it just given?

Just given	[1]
Asked for it	[2]

5   What was your relationship to the person who last gave you positive advice?

Casual acquaintance [1]
More distant family, friend or colleague [2]
Close family, close friend or colleague [3]

6 About which brand was the last positive advice received? *Please write in the make of mobile phone (Nokia, Sony Ericsson etc.)* ....

7 Did the last positive advice that you received affect your handset choice or intended handset choice?

No [1]
Yes [2]

8 How strongly expressed was the last negative advice?

Hardly at all strongly [1]
Moderately strongly [2]
Fairly strongly [3]
Very strongly [4]

9 In the last six months, how many times have you *received negative* advice about any mobile phone handset?
Write in number (0, 1, 2 etc. ......)
If you answered 0, then please go to Q.15

10 The last time you received negative advice, did you ask for advice or was it just given?

Just given [1]
Asked for it [2]

11 What was your relationship to the person who last gave you negative advice?

Casual acquaintance [1]
More distant family, friend or colleague [2]
Close family, close friend or colleague [3]

12 About which brand was the last negative advice received? *Please write in the make of mobile phone (Nokia, Sony Ericsson etc.)* ....

13 Did the last negative advice received affect your handset choice or intended handset choice?

No [1]
Yes [2]

14 How strongly expressed was the last negative advice?

Hardly at all strongly [1]
Moderately strongly [2]
Fairly strongly [3]
Very strongly [4]

(Continued)

15 In the last six months, how many times have you *given negative* advice about any mobile phone handset?
    Write in number (0, 1, 2 etc. ......)
    If you answered 0, then please go to Q.17

16 About which brand did you last *give positive* advice? *Please write in the make of mobile phone (Nokia, Sony Ericsson etc.)* ....

17 In the last six months, how many times have you *given positive* advice about any mobile phone handset?
    Write in number (0, 1, 2 etc. ......)

18 About which brand did you last *give negative* advice? *Please write in the make of mobile phone (Nokia, Sony Ericsson etc.)* ....

The purpose of this exercise is to show you how aspects of WOM are measured. Consider how answers to these questions provide explanation, e.g. what affects the impact of PWOM and NWOM?

A second complaint about surveys relates to the recruitment of the sample, which is often based on convenience. In this sort of research, we are interested in the comparison between one variable and another; for example, whether PWOM is more common than NWOM. It is argued that such relationships between variables are less affected by sampling effects than the raw frequencies, but this may not be true. However, problems about convenience sampling recede as we gather more data. If we have 20 studies using diverse population samples which are focused on different categories and these all show the same pattern, we can be more confident about the findings.[2] Representative sampling is not just about populations. Campbell (1957) pointed out that variables and settings need to be sampled as well as people. In consumer research, this means that a variety of brands and categories should be studied.

Scientific Procedure

When no method is satisfactory, researchers may give up and investigate something else. This has probably led to a lack of research on WOM. But this is something that we can ill afford. In many categories, WOM is the most powerful influence on consumption and, outside the commercial arena, WOM assists many social changes. In these circumstances, even weak findings should be put into the public domain.

To some extent, the problems that affect measurement in this area may be offset by using multiple methods and measures and a wide range of categories. We report on such work in this chapter but, because of the problems of research method, many of the findings are provisional and some revision may be needed when better methods of investigation are devised.

How Does Word of Mouth Affect Brand Choice in Different Categories?

Despite the difficulties in studying WOM, enough work has been done to cast some light on the subject. We focus on the role on WOM in brand purchase. It is generally believed that WOM can have a powerful effect and it is worth considering why this may be so. First, WOM is quick and saves time and effort. In most situations, WOM occurs in a social exchange: people may ask for advice and, when they receive it, they may follow up with secondary questions so that they end up with the information that they need. It is also worth noting that, in some cases, there is little alternative to word of mouth. For example, a person who has to find a new dentist has few sources of relevant information on a dentist's competence. Because of this, advice from other people is probably the best way of finding a good dentist. When there is advertising or when sales staff can provide useful information, WOM will be less important. This means that the need for WOM will vary between categories. It is often said that WOM reduces risk – and this is true – but risk exists when there is a lack of information on a product and little opportunity to find out about it by direct experience with the product.

In early work, WOM was credited with very large effects. Dichter (1966) claimed that advice figured in as many as 80 per cent of brand decisions. Katz and Lazarsfeld (1955) claimed to show that WOM was seven times as effective as newspapers and magazines, four times as effective as personal selling and twice as effective as radio advertising in influencing consumers to use brands. As we noted, some of these early studies applied more to the adoption of new categories than to brand switching, so these claims may not tell us much about brand choice in familiar categories. However, Keaveney (1995) found that about 50 per cent of service provider replacements occurred primarily through WOM.

East et al. (2005b) asked about the *main* source of information in a study focusing on services. Table 11.1 shows the results. The main source was divided into recommendation, personal search, advertising and 'other'. The 'other' category included non-commercial editorial advice in the mass media and situations where people had no choice because of contracts, gifts or other circumstances that were compelling. At the base of the table, we see that recommendation was the main factor in about one-third of the choices. In this work, the same people were asked about two or three categories and the data

Two out of three customers come to us by word of mouth.

are blocked accordingly in Table 11.1. We can see that, in the first block, coffee shops and mobile airtime providers are more often chosen on recommendation than credit cards. Also, dentists are chosen on recommendation much more often than cars (third block). This is hardly surprising since cars can be tried out and are the objects of substantial advertising.

Services are probably more responsive to WOM than most goods but this is not clear from the limited evidence that we have on goods. In other studies (not shown), we have noted: cars 12 per cent, mobile phones 18 per cent, Patagonia outdoor clothing (USA) 52 per cent and hair colourant (Japan) 11 per cent.

Stages in Influence

We also lack evidence on the way in which information from different sources is combined by consumers who make switching decisions; advice may be the main factor behind a decision or it may contribute in a minor way. In the diffusion of innovation literature, opinion leaders are seen as gatekeepers to ad messages. For example, a person may see ads for satellite navigation products and then check with more knowledgeable friends about how well these products work, their costs, the alternative models and their general usefulness.

Table 11.1 Choice of brand provider (from East, Gendall, Hammond and Lomax 2005)

| Category (Country) | Main source when choosing new brand/provider (%) | | | |
	Recommendation	Personal search	Advertising/Promotion	Other
Coffee shop (UK)	65	20	1	14
Mobile phone airtime provider (UK)	50	24	6	20
Credit card (UK)	20	16	20	44
Car insurance (Mauritius)	60	16	6	18
Car servicing (Mauritius)	56	17	3	14
Dentist (UK)	59	3	9	30
Current car (UK)	13	42	13	33
Education institution (UK)	48	19	2	31
Mobile phone airtime provider (UK)	25	22	9	44
Optician (UK)	21	16	8	56
Bank (UK)	43	20	13	24
Mobile phone brand (UK)	21	26	16	37
House contents insurance (UK)	33	12	34	21
Car insurance (UK)	27	19	34	20
Car servicing (UK)	32	9	1	58
Dry cleaning (UK)	14	26	4	56
Hairdresser (Mexico)	32	29	5	34
Fashion store (Mexico)	13	27	43	17
Supermarket (Mexico)	10	36	33	21
Mobile phone airtime provider (UK)	29	13	21	37
Internet service provider (UK)	24	26	26	24
Fashion store (France)	15	47	9	29
Supermarket (France)	9	29	8	54
Means	31	22	14	**32**

Alternatively, an earlier conversation with a friend may sensitize a consumer so that ad messages are received more readily when they are encountered. This *two-step flow* can sometimes have several person-to-person links before it affects behaviour (when it may be called *multi-step flow*). Research by Watts and Dodds (2007) suggests that this description of mass influence fits some cases but, often, wide acceptance of new products is a critical-mass effect that occurs only when receivers have reached a ready-to-change state. Think of a sand hill where adding a few more grains of sand causes a slip. Clearly, a number of factors can contribute to this ready-to-change state, including ads, editorial and discussion among friends.

It seems likely that some switching in familiar categories has such a two-step flow. For example, a critical mass consensus might form about the value of cameras in phones so that large numbers of people are then ready to switch to models with these features. However, we should not forget that consumers often have little interest in brands and may be more concerned to solve a problem quickly. When the category is familiar and not very important, we may find that recommendation plays a small role and that decisions are based more directly on advertising or on seeing the product in a shop. This *one-step* flow is sometimes called the *hypodermic needle effect*.

SECTION 2: THE OCCURRENCE OF WORD OF MOUTH

Under What Circumstances Does WOM Occur?

The previous section examined the nature of WOM and its use in brand choice. But we would also like to know the circumstances under which WOM occurs. This question often leads to comments about satisfied and dissatisfied people producing different levels of advice to others (see Box 11.3). But think back to the last advice that you gave. Was it driven by satisfaction or dissatisfaction, or were you trying to provide information that would help someone with a decision? Our satisfaction or dissatisfaction with a product may sometimes be the main basis for advice but often we are influenced more by the other person's needs and here our personal satisfaction may be of limited importance.

Box 11.3	Comparing dissatisfied and satisfied consumers

Marketing textbooks such as Heskett, Sasser and Schlesinger (1997) and Hanna and Wosniak (2001) report NWOM to PWOM ratios of two or three to one *when comparing dissatisfied and satisfied customers*. The origin of these reports is work by a US agency, the Technical Assistance Research Program (TARP), which finds that NWOM from dissatisfied customers occurs about twice as frequently as PWOM from satisfied customers, though the ratio varies with the category (Goodman and Newman, 2003). Anderson's (1998) comprehensive study also showed greater WOM among those who were very dissatisfied compared with those who were very satisfied, but he commented: 'The widespread belief in a high degree of word of mouth by dissatisfied customers may be unwarranted. In fact, in a sizable proportion of cases, the difference between the two is probably not significant' (Andersen, 1998: 15).

People may confuse the WOM from dis/satisfied customers with WOM in general. This may be why Silverman (2001: 134) claims that studies have shown that most word of mouth is negative. The truth is the reverse; since most products are satisfactory, people may not know of unsatisfactory products that they could advise against. Peterson and Wilson (1992) conducted a comprehensive review of satisfaction studies in the USA. In one table they show that, on average, 83 per cent of customers were satisfied, with the remaining 17 per cent distributed between neutrality and dissatisfaction.

We see from Anderson (1998) and from Mangold, Miller and Brockway (1999) that only a small part of WOM is driven primarily by satisfaction and dis-satisfaction. To establish the ratio of PWOM to NWOM, we need studies on the occurrence of PWOM and NWOM that are *not* based on dis/satisfaction.

The fact that advice is often independent of satisfaction is indicated by a study conducted by Anderson (1998), who used the Swedish Customer Satisfaction Barometer and the American Customer Satisfaction Index, which each cover many industries. The results were very similar for the two countries and Figure 11.1 illustrates the data for Sweden. We see that there is a little more WOM when people are very satisfied or very dissatisfied, but that, when they are neutral about an issue, WOM is still produced at about 80 per cent of the maximum level. This indicates that satisfaction and dissatisfaction are relevant to the production of WOM but that other circumstances are important.

These other circumstances are illustrated by Mangold, Miller and Brockway (1999), who asked respondents to describe the last time they

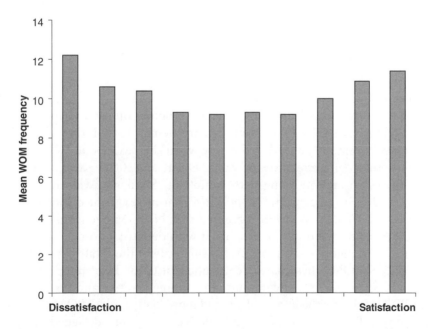

Figure 11.1   Frequency of word of mouth in relation to satisfaction and dissatisfaction in Sweden (adapted from Anderson, 1998)

received positive and negative advice about a service. Mangold et al. identified ten catalysts that set off WOM, which are shown in Table 11.2. The most common catalyst was the receiver's felt need, which was either implicit in the situation or made explicit by a request for advice. Coincidental conversation occurred when a conversation led to advice, e.g. when a discussion of weekend plans led to a destination recommendation. The communicator's dis/satisfaction with the service (as judged by the receiver) was the third catalyst. The fourth catalyst occurred when the recipient made a comment that related to the service, e.g. about the communicator's hair, which led the communicator to recommend her hairdresser. The fifth catalyst was the effort to make a joint decision, such as which restaurant to go to together.

Table 11.2   Catalysts that stimulate word of mouth (adapted from Mangold, Miller and Brockway, 1999)

Stimulus	Positive communication (%)	Negative communication (%)	Total (%)
Receiver's felt need	54	47	50
Coincidental communication	16	21	18
Communicator's dis/satisfaction	5	13	9
Receiver's comment about effect of service	9	4	7
Joint decision on service	6	6	6
Marketing organization's promotion	2	5	3
Receiver's dis/satisfaction	3	3	3
Another's comment about the effect of service	4	1	2
Media exposure (not marketing organization)	1	1	1
Unsolicited comment	1	0	1

When the dis/satisfaction of both communicator and receiver are combined, it constitutes only 12 per cent of the total WOM catalysts. This evidence means that those researchers who have gathered evidence on WOM in relation to dis/satisfaction have focused on only a part of the WOM that is produced. Richins (1983) treated NWOM in this way when she described NWOM as communication that *denigrated* the product. Halstead (2002) saw NWOM as a product of dissatisfaction along with complaint. Similarly, Wetzer, Zeelenberg and Pieters (2007) concentrate on NWOM that arises from dissatisfaction. In contrast to this, Asugman (1998) observed that NWOM occurred as an everyday occurrence and need not be associated with dissatisfaction.

A feature of Mangold et al.'s study is the similarity of the catalyst frequencies for PWOM and NWOM; these have a correlation of 0.96. This shows that there is not much difference in the circumstances governing positive and negative advice. Clearly, PWOM makes the choice of a brand more likely and NWOM makes it less likely, but usually they are both constructive comments designed to aid the receiver. In this respect, PWOM and NWOM differ from compliment and complaint to a supplier where the emotional involvement is likely to be quite different.

Is There More PWOM than NWOM?

Godes and Mayzlin (2004b) studied TV comment on websites and found that positive appraisals occurred nearly twice as often as negative appraisals. Chevalier and Mayzlin (2003) found that the majority of book reviews on two websites were positive. Naylor and Kleiser (2000) studied users of a health and fitness resort and also found more positive comment than negative. East, Hammond and Wright (2007) examined the ratio of PWOM to NWOM in 15 different studies, covering all the brands in a range of widely used categories (mostly services). In every case, the PWOM incidence exceeded the NWOM incidence and the average ratio was 3.1 to 1. This work was conducted by asking respondents about the PWOM and NWOM that they had *given* in the last six months. In follow-up studies, respondents were asked about the WOM they had *received*, and the WOM they *would give, if asked.* These gave ratios of 2.4 to 1 and 3.4 to 1 respectively.

How Much Do People Talk about Their Current Main Brand?

In some cases, East, Hammond and Wright (2007) asked about the ownership of the brand that was referred to in PWOM and NWOM. Roughly, four-fifths of PWOM and one-fifth of NWOM were about the current main brand. In the case of repertoire categories, such as restaurants, where people spread their usage across several brands, about 60 per cent of PWOM was about the main brand. In five cases, a more detailed investigation was made and these findings are shown in Table 11.3. The last two columns of this table show that people rarely recommend a previously owned brand, or one that they never owned, but that people often advise against previously owned brands and ones that they have not owned. Wangenheim (2005) also found that NWOM was often about previously owned brands and Winchester and Romaniuk (2008) found that, when people expressed negative beliefs about brands,

Table 11.3   Ownership of the brand cited in positive word-of-mouth (P) and negative word of mouth (N) (from Hammound, 2007)

Ownership	Mobile phone handsets		Mobile phone airtime		Computers		Leather goods		Cameras		Means	
	P	N	P	N	P	N	P	N	P	N	**P**	**N**
	%	%	%	%	%	%	%	%	%	%	**%**	**%**
Current brand	81	20	79	19	70	24	63	7	88	33	**76**	**21**
Previous brand	5	45	4	32	15	14	10	24	8	17	**8**	**26**
Owned earlier	10	26	5	24	4	5	19	45	4	17	**8**	**23**
Never owned	5	9	12	26	12	58	8	24	0	33	**7**	**30**

these were often about previously owned brands. The large amount of NWOM for brands that have never been owned suggests that, sometimes, brands become widely discussed because of their deficiencies. Although, *in the category*, there is more PWOM than NWOM, some *brands* could attract more NWOM than PWOM if they got into difficulties. This would be a serious worry for managers.

How Does the Occurrence of WOM Relate to the Market Share of the Brand?

Bigger brands, with more users, will get more recommendations because 80 per cent of recommendations are for the current main brand. As a result, the rate of recommendation will tend to relate to market share. Recommendations for previously owned brands will reflect the market share that applied earlier and, if the market has not changed much, this will approximate to current market share. Similarly, when NWOM is about previously owned brands and market shares have not changed much, there should also be a market share effect, but comments about brands that have never been owned may not relate to market share. This implies that NWOM production will not follow market share as closely as PWOM. Table 11.4 shows that the production of PWOM is closely correlated with market share in five categories. This is true for three categories in the case of NWOM, but not for mobile phone airtime and cameras. More detailed examination of the data on airtime showed that two small suppliers were strongly criticized for service and coverage, and some of this NWOM could have been spread by non-users of these brands. Mobile phone airtime and cameras are fairly rapidly changing markets and this may also help to explain the lack of correlation between NWOM and market share (since NWOM relates more to a previous market share).

Table 11.4   Correlations between market share and the production of WOM (from East, Hammond and Wright, 2007)

Category	PWOM	NWOM
	r	r
Mobile phones	0.97*	0.85*
Mobile phone airtime	0.90*	0.13
Cameras	0.91*	0.02
Coffee shops	0.99*	0.97*
Computers	0.94*	0.87*

*$p<0.05$

This evidence shows that if one brand gets more PWOM than another, it is not necessarily performing better. To do well, a brand must get more PWOM and less NWOM than would be expected on the basis of market share.

Explaining Word-of-Mouth Production?

In a famous paper, Dichter (1966) explored the motivations of those who gave PWOM. On the basis of in-depth interviews, Dichter suggested that people gave PWOM because they were involved with the product, with expressing themselves, with relating to others and with the processes of information transfer. However, this is only half the story. Motivations tell us *why* people do things but people also do things because they *can* do them – they have the opportunity to do them. Mangold et al. (1999) described some of the circumstances that create this opportunity, for example, when people were asked about a product, or when a conversation was related to the product. In work at Kingston, it was found that recommendation was often related to:

- **Relative attitude to the brand**. Relative attitude is the rating of the brand compared with other available brands and, for practical purposes, this is the same as relative satisfaction.
- **The referral status of the communicator.** This is whether that person was recruited to the brand by recommendation or not. Mostly, those who were recruited by recommendation also tended to give more recommendations. This was also found by Wangenheim and Bayón (2004) when they investigated German utility customers. This effect is likely to depend on the size of a person's circle of friends. Those who interact more with others have more opportunity both to be recruited by recommendation and to give advice. Godes and Mayzlin (2004a) stimulated PWOM and found that the extra sales that resulted were related to the size of a person's social circle.
- **Whether the communicator recommended other categories**. The size of a person's circle of friends will affect his or her recommendation of any category, so a person who advises on Category A is more likely to advise on Category B. There is also a disposition, called *mavenism*, which characterizes those who give advice across a wide range of products. We found that, often, the recommendation of one category was associated with more recommendation of another, but not always. There seemed to be areas of interest and, sometimes, one area of interest had no link to another.
- **Customer tenure (duration of time as a customer of the brand).** The relationship between tenure and recommendation was described in Chapter 2. In brief, East et al. (2005a) found that tenure was negatively related to recommendation in some categories (credit cards, bank accounts, motor insurance and supermarkets) and positively related in others (car servicing and fashion shops in Mexico city). Other categories were neutrally related. This pattern can be explained by considering the character of the service. Services that are unchanging, simple or frequently used can be recommended once to friends but then most users are likely to lose interest and not think or talk about such services. Consistent with this, Wangenheim and Bayón (2004) found that those who had recently switched to a new energy supplier recommended the new supplier more than those who stayed with an existing supplier. By contrast, when a service is complex and infrequently used (so that it takes time to get to know about it and to appreciate the supplier),

recommendation may be initially subdued and then increase with tenure. This helps to explain why car service agents were recommended more with longer tenure. We found that long-term customers of servicing agents knew more about car service and liked the agent more and these factors were responsible for the tenure effect.

The same study also found that the rate of recommendation was sometimes related to whether the respondent had heard others recommending the brand, category spending, category knowledge and age. We did not find that recommendation was related to share of category requirement. This may be because those who buy a variety of brands are better able to compare them.

Finally, we believe that there are cultural and fashion effects. When the same questionnaire on holiday destinations and credit cards was given to population samples in New York and Chichester (in the UK), the New Yorkers gave about twice as many recommendations as the residents of Chichester. When similar surveys on mobile phones and airtime were conducted in 2005 and 2007 to similar samples in the UK, recommendation levels were lower in 2007. This may have been because a range of new phones with extra features was available in 2005.

We can make sense of these findings in a conceptual framework that assumes that behaviour depends upon motivation and opportunity. Often, opportunity is subdivided into ability and environmental opportunity (as in Figure 11.2). This explanative framework is the 'plain vanilla' of explanation. Any behaviour that is subject to personal control will occur more frequently when people *want*

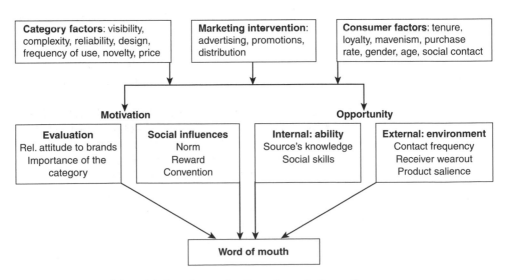

Figure 11.2   Model explaining the production of word of mouth

(motivation) to engage in the behaviour and when they *can* do so (opportunity and ability). In Figure 11.2, opportunity has two aspects: internal, which is about ability – and external – which is about the scope offered by the physical and social environment for doing an action. Motivation is divided into personally-based and socially-based aspects.

This framework explains why some factors are more associated with recommendation. Working from the right on the second level, a wide circle of friends and associates gives more contact frequency. 'Receiver wearout' is when it would be difficult to repeat recommendations without boring the receiver. This reduces the opportunity to give advice when the service is dull and unchanging. Salience is exemplified by products which are frequently used or seen, such as mobile phones and, because of this, generate comment and advice. These effects will be amplified if a person is more knowledgeable and skilled in dealing with others, since these abilities make it easier to give advice. Social influences encourage recommendation in three ways: other people indicate what they think you *should* do (social norm), what they would *like* you to do (reward) and what is *usually done* (convention), which establishes everyday practice when this is uncertain. Finally, people are more likely to recommend brands when the brands are better than alternative brands and when the category is important. These opportunity and motivation factors are themselves controlled by category, marketing and consumer factors, as illustrated on the top level of Figure 11.2.

SECTION 3: THE IMPACT OF WORD OF MOUTH

What is the Impact of Positive and Negative Word of Mouth on Brand Choice?

PWOM may be more common than NWOM, but perhaps it has less impact when it occurs? There seems to be a belief that an instance of NWOM has more impact than an instance of PWOM and there is evidence that suggests that this *might* be true. One field study of WOM effect by Arndt (1967) showed twice as much impact on purchase from NWOM than from PWOM, but he studied only one brand in one category. Also, a series of studies has shown a 'negativity effect' – that negative information has more impact on judgements than positive information (Anderson, 1965; Chevalier and Mayzlin, 2003; Fiske, 1980; Herr, Kardes and Kim, 1991; Mittal, Ross and Baldasare, 1998; Mizerski, 1982). In these studies, negative information is less common than positive information and a widely accepted explanation for the negativity effect relates to this. Fiske (1980) argued that the rarity of negative information made it more useful than positive information because the latter can often be presumed. For example, evidence that a brand is unreliable is more useful than evidence that the brand is reliable because reliability may be assumed as normal for modern products.[3] Under these circumstances, we would expect negative information to have more effect on judgement.[4]

Fiske's explanation for the negativity effect may be expressed as an effect of the gap between the position supported by the message and the position held by the receiver. The excess of positive information ensures that the position taken by most receivers is positive so there will be a larger gap and more impact when negative information is received. Exceptionally, when the receiver's expectation is negative and the information received is positive, there could be a 'positivity effect'.

Some work has not supported the negativity effect. One study by Charlett, Garland and Marr (1995) found more effect from positive information. Ahluwalia, Burnkrant and Unnava (2000) suggested that prior commitment to a brand may prevent consumers from fully accepting negative information about that brand. This was confirmed in two experiments. The high-commitment participants treated written negative information as less useful and they mobilized a larger number of counter-arguments to this information compared with low-commitment participants.

Wilson and Peterson (1989) and Sundaram and Webster (1999) showed that the impact of WOM was much reduced when the product was familiar. Supporting this, Ahluwalia (2002) compared responses to written positive and negative information on a brand when participants were familiar or unfamiliar with the brand. When the brand was familiar, there were no significant differenccs in the impact of positive and negative information. One way of thinking about these results is that commitment and familiarity both indicate cognitive network complexity (Chapter 3) and this complexity could anchor beliefs and prevent change.

PWOM tends to increase purchase probability and NWOM to reduce it. East, Hammond and Lomax (2008) used the shift in purchase probability to measure the impact of WOM and applied Fiske's gap explanation. They pointed out that positive advice will have more effect if the receiver has a low likelihood of purchase before the PWOM is received because this leaves a large gap and therefore more 'room for change'. Similarly, NWOM will have more effect when the initial probability of purchase is high. This thinking suggests that NWOM could have *less* impact on the probability of purchase if the likelihood of purchase before the WOM is received is below 0.5.

In their empirical work, East and Hammond examined the reported impact of PWOM and NWOM in three ways. First, they conducted 15 role-play

Table 11.5   The impact on brand choice of PWOM and NWOM (from East et al. 2008)

Category	Percent claiming effect on decision of...		Probability of purchase (%)		Shift in probability of purchase	
	PWOM	PWOM	Prior to PWOM	prior to NWOM	PWOM	NWOM
Supermarket	33	54	0.44	0.39	0.16	−0.16
Computer	60	68	0.53	0.49	0.20	−0.20
Mobile phone airtime	61	53	0.32	0.41	0.19	−0.10
Luxury brands	64	44	0.38	020	0.12	−0.06
Leather goods, Lebanon	65	34	0.48	0.46	0.23	−0.14
Camera	65	44	0.53	0.34	0.17	−0.12
Coffee shop	66	43	0.54	0.42	0.19	−0.11
Holiday destination	66	62	0.48	0.42	0.18	−0.19
Mobile phone handset	70	35	0.39	0.36	0.20	−0.07
Restaurant, favourite	72	87	0.35	0.58	0.39	−0.47
Restaurant, ethnic types	83	48	0.36	0.41	0.34	−0.23
Restaurant, Iranian in London	86	43	0.44	0.22	0.31	−0.03
Mean	**66**	**51**	**0.44**	**0.39**	**0.22**	**−0.16**

experiments in which they asked respondents how much effect symmetrically expressed positive and negative advice would have on their decisions. In all cases, the respondents were users of the category. This showed that, on average, PWOM had a little more impact than NWOM. Second, they conducted studies in which respondents were asked if they had received PWOM and NWOM in the last six months. Twelve of these studies are shown in Table 11.5. Those that had received PWOM or NWOM were asked whether the last instance had affected their decision (see Table 11.5, columns 2 and 3). Across the 12 studies, 66 per cent stated that PWOM and 51 per cent that NWOM had affected their decision so, again, PWOM had a little more effect. Third, in these 12 studies, East and Hammond also used the Juster (1966) scale (Chapter 6) to measure purchase probability before and after receiving WOM. Table 11.5 shows that the purchase probability averaged 0.44 before receiving PWOM and 0.39 before receiving NWOM (bottom, columns 4 and 5). This means that there is more room for PWOM to increase purchase likelihood than for NWOM to reduce it and this was supported by the measured shifts in purchase probability of 0.22 and −0.16 (bottom, columns 6 and 7).

This work suggests that PWOM has a little more impact on brand choice than NWOM, contrary to a widespread assumption in marketing. However, as we stated at the beginning of this chapter, it is difficult to study WOM effects and estimates of past probabilities of purchase could easily be biased by selective recall. For this reason we should be cautious about the findings from this research.

What Other Factors Affect Brand Choice

East et al. (2008) also measured the impact of four other factors. These were: how strongly expressed the WOM was; the closeness of the communicator to the receiver (that is, whether a close friend or relative, or not); whether the WOM was solicited or not; and how much advice the respondent reported *giving* on the category that was studied.

It seems likely that the *strength of expression* of WOM affects its impact. However, sometimes people react against advice (even when they agree with it). This reactance effect was first documented by Brehm (1966) as a motivation that helped people to preserve their autonomy. In an experiment, Fitzsimons and Lehmann (2004) found support for reactance effects. This raises some doubt about the effect of strong recommendations; perhaps, mildly expressed advice has more impact.

The *closeness* of the relationship between the communicator and receiver has quite complicated effects. Granovetter (1973) has argued that weak ties are important in the transmission of information between social groups because the people who form weak ties do so with a large number of groups. As a result, weak ties are better at diffusing information through a social network. Brown and Reingen (1987) conducted a 'who told whom?' study which supported Granovetter's thesis by showing a greater network effect, but they also showed that receivers thought that strong ties had more direct effect on their behaviour.[5]

The relative impact of solicited and unsolicited WOM has been studied by East et al. (2005b). They found that the impact ratio for both PWOM and NWOM was in the region of 1.5 to 1 but these results were obtained without taking account of the effect of other variables. It is possible that another variable, say the closeness of the communicator, is correlated with whether or not the advice is solicited. This could occur if people ask for advice more often from those to whom they are close. Finally, East et al. (2008) tested whether those who gave more advice were more influenced by the advice that they received.

Table 11.6 shows the output from the multiple regression analysis conducted by East et al. (2008). We see that the prior probability of choice is the most significant factor. For PWOM, the sign is negative, indicating that the greater the prior probability, the less the change (and the reverse for NWOM). The strength of expression and the closeness of the communicator have the most impact according to the estimates and whether the advice was sought or not is only significant for PWOM. The amount of WOM given by the respondent was only significant for PWOM. An interesting feature of Table 11.6 is the similarity in the effect of the different determinants as shown by the beta coefficients. Remember that we have argued that PWOM and NWOM are similar in kind, save for the fact that they have opposite effects. Table 11.6 supports this claim.

Table 11.6   Regression analysis: variables related to impact (NWOM impact treated as positive)

Variable	PWOM		NWOM	
	Beta	Sig.	Beta	Sig.
Probability of purchase pre-WOM	−0.38	<.001	0.35	<.001
Strength of expression of WOM	0.29	<.001	0.23	<.001
Closeness of communicator	0.16	<.001	0.13	<.001
Whether advice was sought	0.08	0.006	0.04	0.148
Amount of WOM given	0.07	0.015	0.03	0.402
R^2	0.27		0.23	

EXERCISE 11.2   ANALYSING DATA ON WOM

On the website supporting this book you will find the SPSS data file WOMcomposite. This is the data used for Table 11.6. See if you can reproduce Table 11.6. What other analyses can you conduct?

The Effect of Brand Commitment

East, Hammond and Lomax (2008) aggregated all the data and plotted the shift in purchase probability against the probability of purchase prior to receiving WOM. The result for 12 categories is shown in Figure 11.3. What we see here is a close relationship between impact, measured as shift and prior probability of purchase for most of the range. The plots then turn towards the x-axis in a way that suggests that brand commitment affects their response to PWOM and NWOM. People who are very likely to buy a brand give less weight to NWOM on that brand and people who are very unlikely to buy a brand (perhaps because they intend to buy another brand) give less weight to PWOM. Figure 11.3 is useful because it helps us to see how consumers differ in their response to WOM (and other information) depending on their prior position. When we are able to judge the prior probability of purchase, the graphs show the potential responsiveness of different consumer segments to a positive or negative message.

SECTION 4: APPLICATIONS OF WORD-OF-MOUTH RESEARCH

Consumer-generated media (CGM) on the Internet, such as blogs, discussion groups and emailing, has produced a form of influence very similar to WOM. Often called 'buzz', Internet advice has renewed interest in word of mouth among ad agencies, market research organizations and business organizations in general. The term 'viral marketing' has been coined to describe campaigns where

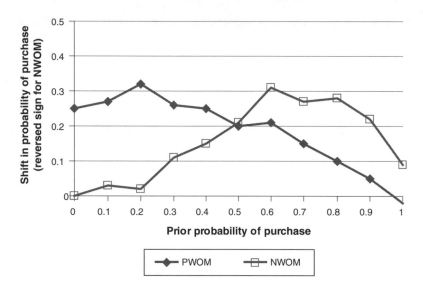

Figure 11.3   Impact (shift in the probability of purchase after WOM) as a function of prior probability of purchase

copy is spontaneously propagated by Internet users and we have even seen the emergence of a new medium, 'direct WOM', where agencies such as Tremor and BzzAgent recruit consumers, supply them with products, and ask them to advise their friends about this merchandise.[6]

In the flurry of enthusiasm for WOM, pundits have come forward to suggest how it works. Gladwell (2000), in an engaging book called *The Tipping Point*, gives examples of mass changes via WOM. Gladwell draws attention to the fact that WOM is often spontaneous and uncontrollable. Silverman (2001) suggests that the speed of WOM can help to put a product ahead of competitors. Rosen (2000) focuses particularly on the Internet and argues that there is a need to identify and use the more influential consumers, or hubs. Interest in WOM has had an impact on advertising but we leave this until the next chapter. Here we look at the way it has affected market research and marketing practice.

Text Mining

One area of interest has been to use comment on the Internet as a predictor of future trends in brand and category sales. When future demand can be estimated, manufacturers can adjust production to meet demand and investors can buy the potential risers and sell the potential fallers. Despite this, the initial enthusiasm for analysing Web comment seems to have waned and it is worth examining whether brand popularity can be predicted from word on the Web. The method for doing this often uses Internet robots. These 'bots' crawl through the Web and assemble a balance sheet of positive and negative comment on brands. However, distinguishing positive from negative comment is not easily done by an automatic process and human intelligence may be required to check the bots. The managing director of one company told one of the authors that their accuracy was 72 per cent but much the same level of accuracy would be obtained if all comments were assumed to be positive since the majority of Web comments are positive (Chevalier and Mayzlin, 2003; Godes and Mayzlin, 2004b). To work out the effect of Web advice, weights must be assigned to positive and negative comment and these may vary from category to category and brand to brand. Also, websites may be designed to be supportive or critical of brands so that Web comment may not bear much relationship to advice in the everyday world where most word of mouth takes place. Carl (2006a) estimated Web comment at 10 per cent of total WOM and, in a more detailed analysis, Keller and Fay (2006) found the following:

70%	Face to face
19%	Phone
4%	Email
3%	Text message
1%	Online chat or blog
3%	Other

Despite these problems, text mining may yet provide a reliable form of market research, particularly in those areas where Web advice is often used, for example in the selection of postgraduate courses by international applicants where some limited work by one of the authors suggested that 60 per cent of decisions rested primarily on Internet information and 30 per cent on WOM.

Net Promoter Score

One measure of the effect of advice was designed by Reichheld (2003). From correlational research, he found that the Net Promoter Score (NPS) provided a prediction of company revenue (see Figure 11.4).

The NPS is intended to measure the number of people who are positive about the brand (promoters) minus the number who are negative (detractors). The question is framed as in Figure 11.4. Many firms now use this measure to judge their performance. The measure taps likelihood of future recommendation, which may not be as reliable as recall of past recommendation. The NPS scoring does not vary for different brands and categories, which is difficult to justify. A more serious weakness is that the amount of NWOM is derived from low PWOM. East, Hammond and Wright (2007) found that those who give little PWOM on their brand are likely to give little NWOM on it too and that NWOM was mainly produced on brands *other than* the respondent's main brand. Also, the NPS is based on the amount of WOM *given* and the WOM that is received is more relevant,

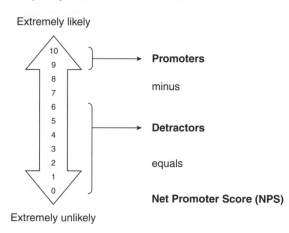

Figure 11.4   Measuring the Net Promoter Score

since this is what influences us. Morgan and Rego (2004) criticized the NPS in a letter to the *Harvard Business Review* and later published a more detailed critique (2006). They constructed a measure that was similar to the NPS and found that this was not as effective at predicting company revenue as other measures of performance. In particular, they found that satisfaction measures were better. Further work by Keiningham et al. (2007a), using the industries studied by Reichheld, again gave a poor prediction of performance. In a further study Keiningham et al. (2007b) showed that a multiple-item measure, rather than the single-item NPS, gave a better prediction of retention and recommendation. The poor prediction of NPS may relate to the design of the measure, or it may be that WOM simply does not predict brand/company performance.

This focuses attention on alternative measures of WOM. A measure could be based on the measurement of both the amount and impact of PWOM and NWOM for each brand, using the measures in the East, Hammond and Lomax (2008) research. The East et al. (2008) measures may be compared with the measures used in the American Consumer Satisfaction Index to see which predicts profit best. More elaborate predictive designs might take account of other factors such as the quality of advertising. We are a long way off the accurate prediction of future brand performance but this is a potential development.

Identifying the Influentials

A third concern of market researchers is to identify those who give more advice (opinion leaders, influentials, hubs) so that communications can be targeted at this group for onward dissemination. This manner of thinking follows the tradition of identifying early adopters and opinion leaders in the field of new product diffusion, and is widely accepted by practitioners (e.g. Rosen, 2000). More influential people have wider social networks and higher standing among their friends but, even when these people are identified, they may not account for much of the total WOM. Feick and Price (1987) suggested that market mavens could be found, i.e. those who advise across a range of categories but these seem to be rare individuals. Feick and Price found that less than half of the US population could identify one or more people among their associates who fitted the description of the market maven. Research by Goodey and East (2008, forthcoming) showed that those who scored high on the maven index did not give much more word of mouth than those who scored low. Obviously, some people recommend more than others but, typically, about half the user base will recommend a brand in a category once or more in six months (from East, Hammond and Wright, 2007). This spread in recommendation makes it quite difficult to identify a group of influentials who are responsible for the majority of advice. Reflecting this problem, Balter and Butman (2005) argue that WOM is more effective when it is delivered by ordinary people (we would say by the users of products). Balter is the founder of BzzAgent.

As reported earlier, research at Kingston University showed that about 80 per cent of PWOM came from existing users. This means that any supplier who has a customer database can direct communications to most of the people who might recommend their products. The decision on whether to focus on influentials or all users depends partly on costs. If consumers are given products, there may be a substantial cost per person and then it pays to focus on the influentials, but if consumers are merely given information to keep them well informed about the merits of the products that they use, the costs are low (very low when the Internet is used) and it makes more sense to focus on the whole user base. However, there is a need for research to find out what information people are inclined to pass on and what information, if passed on, has most impact on receivers.

Incentivized Word of Mouth

Companies often encourage referrals. There is evidence that this can be a very effective strategy (Buttle, 1998; Danaher and Rust, 1996). One problem is that it is not clear quite how much a receiver is put off when the communicator is incentivized, even when the incentive is shared by the communicator and the receiver. A recent study by Carl (2006b) relates to this issue. Carl studied the contacts of agents who had been enlisted by a WOM agency. He found that three-quarters of those receiving advice were unworried by the agent's affilation; what mattered was whether they trusted the agent to be honest and to consider their interests. This indicates that consumers are relatively unworried by the possibility that an agent could be motivated by self-interest.

Stopping Negative and Promoting Positive Comments

Companies can facilitate comment on the Internet by providing websites where users can express their views. When the product performs well, comment is likely to be predominantly positive and any negative comments can be quickly addressed. Well-managed websites may add to customer satisfaction and make positive comment still more likely. Some companies which actively engage and listen to their customers in the context of private, online branded communities seem to generate higher levels of customer recommendation (commercial research by Communispace).

Suppliers may be able to use their customer databases to direct information to groups who could be critical. In Table 11.3, we showed that about one-fifth of negative advice relates to the communicator's main brand. Some of this negative advice is not because the brand is disliked but because it is deemed unsuitable for another person and it is probably unrealistic to try to reduce this sort of NWOM. The rest of the NWOM about a currently used brand may reflect dissatisfaction with the brand and, where possible, this sort of WOM should be counteracted. Even if it is impossible to detect the minority who criticize their main brand, it may still be possible to deal with common complaints by communicating with all customers. If this can be done, both NWOM and defection may be reduced.

Most cases of NWOM come from past customers. Normally, past customers are contacted with a view to recovering them but, even if this is unlikely, there may be value in contact if it can be used to counteract NWOM. When products have improved, those who no longer buy them are unlikely to know about the improvement and may continue to criticize their previous brand on the assumption that it is unchanged. By sending past customers information about brand improvements, suppliers may be able to stop this NWOM. The research at Kingston University showed that those who gave NWOM were much more likely to give PWOM on some other brand; suppliers who successfully counteract NWOM may generate PWOM instead.

Customer databases make it easy to send information to customers though they will often ignore it. We need a better understanding of what customers will attend to and what they are likely to pass on in advice to others. It is possible that the standard method of presenting information to customers makes it less likely that it will be passed on – who wants to repeat ads? Customers who find out information for themselves, for example on websites, may be more inclined to pass it on.

Information, Not Hearsay

Sometimes, a better understanding of social and commercial processes allows business people to make more informed and more realistic assessments of business prospects. When there are widespread misunderstandings, there is a danger that strategies will be misjudged. Many beliefs about WOM appear to have been mistaken. It is not true that NWOM is more common or more powerful than PWOM according to the evidence that has now accumulated. It is not true that most WOM is driven primarily by satisfaction or dissatisfaction, though this is often involved. Nor is it true that long-term customers usually recommend more than short-term customers. Information from research is needed to displace such false hearsay and to provide a basis for well thought-out marketing strategies.

SUMMARY

PWOM and NWOM are powerful influences on consumption but they are difficult to study. Experimental research lacks relevance to natural settings and survey research is prone to bias. In the absence of much evidence, some misunderstanding has occurred. It appears that much of WOM is given to help others and is not strongly driven by dis/satisfaction. Therefore, comparisons between satisfied and dissatisfied customers are inappropriate for determining the occurrence and impact of PWOM and NWOM.

Recent research suggests that PWOM is more common than NWOM. In familiar categories, PWOM usually has somewhat more impact on the probability of purchase than NWOM. This is related to the strength of expression of advice, the relationship with the communicator and the probability of purchase before the WOM is received.

PWOM tends to be about the communicator's current main brand and NWOM about previously owned brands and brands that have never been owned. These patterns produce a strong association between the production of PWOM and market share. The relationship between NWOM and market share is more erratic. However, when brands are performing well both PWOM and NWOM are related to market share, which provides a norm for assessing the amount of comment brands receive. The associations between WOM and past/present ownership can be used to combat NWOM and promote PWOM.

In an effort to increase WOM, information can be targeted to more influential persons or more generally to the user base. The best strategy depends on costs; when these are low it is better to target the whole user base.

Predicting brand performance from WOM measures has had little success so far. In Particular, the Net Promoter Score (Reichheld, 2003) has not been found to be a strong predictor of brand/company performance.

Additional Resources

To see how word of mouth varies between categories and for a further review of the literature, see East, Hammond and Wright (2007). Gladwell

(2000) is an entertaining read about word of mouth, and is also worth considering for a popular account of some of the dynamics discussed in Chapter 5. It is worth checking the websites for the WOM agencies mentioned earlier, www.bzzagent.com, business.tremor.com and also www.womma.org.

Notes

1 There is a substantial literature on persuasion techniques, which are usually well covered in social psychology textbooks. These techniques can assist managers and salespersons but are rarely used by consumers who are trying to help others by supplying useful information. We do not deal with persuasion techniques here.
2 This problem of convenience sampling also affects experiments where participants may even be restricted to a single population segment, such as students. Despite this fact, experiments are rarely criticized for inadequate sampling.
3 One problem about applying this to WOM is that people usually try to give useful advice and might therefore avoid facts that can be assumed.
4 There are other explanations for the impact of rare negative information, e.g. surprise (Berlyne, 1954) and attribution (Laczniak, DeCarlo and Ramaswamy 2001; Mizerski, 1982). Research on the negativity effect is reviewed in detail by Skowronski and Carlston (1989).
5 In some fields, expertise is particularly important and may be more common among weak ties. For example, physicians are usually not close but their advice is likely to have more impact than that of a family member. In such fields, we would expect weak ties to have more impact.
6 An interesting paper on buzz marketing is available from Knowledge@Wharton.

12 The Response To Advertising

LEARNING OBJECTIVES

When you have completed this chapter, you should be able to:

1 Describe what is meant by effective advertising, giving examples.
2 Discuss the issues relating to effective frequency and concentration.
3 Explain how advertising could have primary and secondary effects on sales and the possible bases for these effects.
4 Report evidence on the decay in the effect of advertising.
5 Discuss which product fields and which segments are more responsive to advertising.
6 Consider how the Internet is changing advertising.

EXERCISE 12.1   WHAT DO YOU EXPECT?

Go through the objectives above and decide what you think the answers are. This helps you to take in the evidence presented in this chapter.

OVERVIEW

Advertising can sometimes have a powerful impact on consumption but its effect is quite variable and often there is no discernable outcome. We review research on the effects of the frequency and concentration of exposures. High concentrations may break through the resistance established by competitor brands.

Sales effects appear to have two components: a short-term effect that is largely dissipated within a month and a long-term effect that only occurs if there is a short-term effect, which can last for more than a year. We discuss the bases for these effects.

(Continued)

Ads have more effect in certain product fields and have more impact on certain consumer segments. We illustrate these effects and consider which segments provide most extra sales volume. The Internet may affect the way consumers respond to advertising. Ad agencies are concerned about this and there are signs that it is changing their practice.

SECTION 1: EFFECTIVE ADVERTISING

Ads may affect our beliefs and attitudes but, ultimately, they must affect behaviour if they are to be useful. In social applications, ads must reduce accidents, increase voting rates, promote healthy eating and get people to report suspicious behaviour that might indicate terrorist activity. In commercial applications, advertising must increase purchase and subscription, or hold purchase rates when the price goes up. Sometimes the profit-making behaviour occurs at the end of a chain of prior actions and the links in this chain may be strengthened by advertising, e.g. by getting consumers to go to a showroom, or to check a product on the Internet. Advertising campaigns vary in effectiveness (how much change they achieve) and also in efficiency (how much change they achieve for a given cost). Ambler and Broadbent (2000) discuss this.

In the commercial arena, three particular outcomes may be derived from advertising, which we discuss in more detail in following sections. These are:

- **Price support**. Buyers pay more per unit and thus increase the profit on a sale.
- **Sales support**. Buyers buy more than they would have done without the advertising. This is usually used as a criterion of ad effectiveness.
- **Cost saving**. Costs are reduced.

These outcomes can occur via a number of mechanisms. For example, advertising may:

- be based on a new analysis of the product range and consumer segments (a re-launch). For example, Virgin focused more on text messaging and its younger customers when it re-launched the Australian service in 2004 (*Effective Advertising 8*, 2006[1]).
- induce WOM and media comment that eventually results in purchase. Murray-Burton, Dyke and Harrison (2007) report on a live Monopoly game, which could be played over the Internet and which generated measurable WOM.
- increase retailer stocking, raising the opportunity to purchase. For example, the Felix cat food campaign (Broadbent, 2000) boosted distribution so that a third of the extra sales effect came from this source. In many cases, an enlarged distribution will produce a sales gain without the help of advertising.
- raise demand for scarce items such as property and shares. In the case of the One2One (now T-Mobile) telephone company, ads lifted share values so that capital could be raised at lower cost (Kendall, 1998).

Price Support

Some ads make consumers aware of discounts and the possibility of saving money. This price-related advertising tends to be associated with increased price sensitivity on the part of the consumer (Bolton, 1989; Kaul and Wittink, 1995). When this occurs, margins are squeezed and any benefits must come via increased sales. By contrast, most brand advertising is designed to raise perceptions of quality and thus increase the appreciation of the brand. This sort of advertising tends to reduce price sensitivity, which allows the brand owner to raise margins. For example, Broadbent (2000) showed that price sensitivity about Lurpak butter dropped in regions that received more advertising for this brand. In a more systematic analysis, Hamilton, East and Kalafatis (1997) found that well-advertised brands usually had either slightly lower price elasticity or were more highly priced than others. The research showed that brand leaders advertised twice as heavily as follower brands and the main difference in price sensitivity occurred between leader and follower brands. This combination of high adspend and high price is a common pattern for leading brands (Farris and Reibstein, 1991). Sometimes, it is suggested that the high level of advertising could be a consequence of the brand's success but the case histories provide quite good evidence that the reduction in price sensitivity *follows* the advertising. For example, in the Stella Artois case, the ads seemed to lead the sales (see Box 12.1).

Box 12.1	Stella Artois

Price support has been demonstrated by the success of Stella Artois advertising in Britain (Baker, 1993). Stella was advertised as 'reassuringly expensive', to imply high quality. It attracted a large proportion of lager drinkers despite a trade price premium of 7.5 per cent. Publicans more than recovered this premium when they sold Stella at its higher retail price. In 1999, Stella was priced 14 per cent above the premium lager average and the profit increment was estimated at six times the ad cost (Broadbent, 2000).

Mela, Gupta and Lehmann (1997) studied the impact of brand advertising and sales promotion on price sensitivity over an 8-year period. They focused on a mature product where life-cycle effects were minimal and found that *reductions* in brand advertising were associated with increased price sensitivity. Most of this effect occurred among the less brand loyal customers, showing that price support from advertising occurs mainly because it affects low-loyalty buyers.

Squeezing the Retailer

So far we have not distinguished between the margins of the retailer and those of the manufacturer. Steiner (1973, 1993) found that advertising in the toy industry could both reduce the price to the customer and raise manufacturer margin. He found that the ads created a consumer demand for products which compelled retailers to stock them so they had to pay the manufacturer's price. At the same time, competition between retailers forced them to reduce the selling price. As a result, consumers and manufacturers did well at the expense of retailers. This effect is likely to be particularly strong when the product is a 'must have', such as the last Harry Potter book (see Box 12.2). Farris and Albion (1980) reviewed this subject and concluded that advertising generally exerted pressure on retailers' margins and that the net effect of such advertising often lowered the price to the consumer. When retailers have great power, as in the case of the supermarket groups, this effect may be less apparent but even in groceries there is evidence that manufacturers have adjusted production to emphasize the stronger brands where they have more leverage. In the 1990s, Procter & Gamble and Unilever dropped a large number of small brands and focused on the *power brands* which supermarkets had to stock.

Box 12.2	**The trouble with Harry** **(from The *Guardian*, 4 May 2007)**

Waterstone's owner HMV yesterday defended its decision to sacrifice profits and offer the forthcoming Harry Potter book at half price, suggesting a price war had left it with little choice.

HMV chief executive Simon Fox said the whole market for the final instalment of the boy wizard's tale would be at half price and cited Ottakar's, now owned by HMV, as an example of the price to be paid for not joining in a Harry Potter price battle. 'Not being price competitive on the book seemed to set a perception that the store was high price. There are very few books that have that level of publicity,' said Mr Fox. 'If we try to be anything other than half price we are setting the Waterstone's brand off as high price and that's something we are trying to change.'

When Supply is Limited

When supply is relatively fixed – as in auctions, the services of top professionals and houses for sale – increased demand will result in an increase in price. In equity markets, where the available stock is fixed in the short term, corporate

advertising may have a direct effect on the share price. Evidence for this effect is sketchy but Moraleda and Ferrer-Vidal (1991) showed that advertising raised the intention to apply for shares in the Spanish oil company, Repsol, in the run-up to privatization.

In monopoly situations, customers may feel that a product that they have to buy is poor value. Here, advertising can be used to raise the perceived value. Kendall (1998) showed how ads were used to raise the evaluation of North West Water in the United Kingdom (where water companies have monopolies). Before the advertising, customers were hostile to the company and objected to increases in their water costs. The advertising drew attention to the benefits offered by the company and raised the perceived value of the service.

Sales Support

The cases in the *Advertising Works* (UK) and *Effective Advertising* (Australia) series demonstrate that advertising can increase sales. On rare occasions the effect is large, as in the case of Levi 501 jeans in the UK. Here, campaigns from 1984 to 1987 raised sales 20 times (Feldwick, 1990). But the Levi 501 case was quite exceptional. Even when the best campaigns are reviewed, a sales gain of 100 per cent or more is uncommon and tends to go to small brands, which can increase share substantially without much effect on the size of the market. In *Advertising Works 15* (Green, 2007), a small volume brand, Actimel, secured a year-on-year sales gain of 426 per cent while O_2 gained about 35 per cent of contract customers and 100 per cent of pre-pay customers as a result of a very successful campaign in a rising market. The payback of a campaign can be very substantial when the brand is big. The O_2 payback was as much as 80 times the ad cost when all possible benefits were included. The Actimel payback was much lower at about 1.7 times because of the small size of the brand. Other examples are found in *Effective Advertising 8* (2006). Here, the Sunbeam electric blanket brand gained 83 per cent but the return payback was only 1.8 because the market was relatively small. Compare this with a campaign for Australian lamb that raised sales by about 25 per cent over five years; the payback in this big market was 53 times the ad cost. So ad campaigns can give very good returns on big brands, but it is hard to show large returns from small brands, even when market share is much increased.

Taking account of this, small brands may sometimes be able to band together and fund generic advertising for the whole industry. This works when suppliers are trying to overcome consumer inertia rather than displace each other. An example might be beds, where weak brand awareness makes individual brand advertising risky. Collectively, bed manufacturers might show a good return on advertising designed to get consumers to replace sagging beds and lumpy mattresses.

The Australian lamb advertising corrected a long-term decline in lamb sales, so the 25 per cent gain on sales at the start of the campaign was probably an underestimate of the advertising achievement. Sometimes, even static sales are an achievement if, without the advertising, there would have been a decline. Hahn Premium light beer expected to lose its leading position because of a build-up of intense competition but its campaign successfully countered the attack and the brand even gained a little share (*Effective Advertising 8*, 2006).

One very successful campaign in the UK was conducted by the ad agency TBWA for Wonderbra. These ads featured a self-assured model (Eva Herzigova) and enigmatic captions. The cost of the initial four-month campaign was only £330,000 because the medium was largely restricted to billboards (Baker, 1995). Over a two-year period, a gain in sales of 120 per cent was achieved although Wonderbra was selling above the price of many other brands. The key to this success was almost certainly the substantial editorial comment and WOM that the advertising provoked, including discussion of how advertising could distract drivers and cause accidents (see Box 12.3).

Box 12.3	**Successful ads**

The wide variation in the effectiveness of ads has led to speculation among practitioners about which elements of the ad make it effective. It might be thought that copy tests would isolate the key factors but, although these tests show that one copy is superior to another, any useful recipes for success are hard to find. Mostly, the key elements that are proposed refer to rather obvious features of an ad. For example, Moldovan (1984) focused on ad credibility and Brown (1986) on the power of the ad to arrest attention. These claims are sensible but they are of limited value to those trying to create good copy. By its nature, creativity cannot be anticipated. But, after its creation, we can see features of an ad that help to make it successful. For example, the Wonderbra campaign was noticed because it created curiosity at a number of levels. Among these are the enigmatic and challenging character of the model, the oddity of putting such ads on billboards and, in the ad shown, uncertainty about the origin of captions such as 'or are you just pleased to see me'. This comes from a line by Mae West to Cary Grant in the film *She Done Him Wrong*. The full line is 'Is that a pistol in your pocket, or are you just glad to see me?'

The *Advertising Works* and *Effective Advertising* cases are selected because they are successful. Most advertising for established brands produces far less sales response. This is illustrated by a report by Riskey (1997) on 23 Frito-Lay ad campaigns. This study compared brand sales when ads were running with a

no-ad control condition. The study was conducted using the BehaviorScan method of Information Resources Inc. (IRI), which is described in more detail in Box 12.4. Twelve campaigns showed effects and these cases produced an average sales increase of 15 per cent.

Box 12.4	BehaviorScan

Information Resources Inc. (IRI) uses cable TV in specific towns to test ads. Households are recruited to a panel and agree to receive television that may be modified by IRI. The BehaviorScan technology swaps commercials so that some households receive trial ads or extra exposures of normal ads when compared with other households. The former allows *copy* tests to be conducted, the latter *weight* tests. Members of the panel show an identification number when they buy groceries in town. IRI finances the scanners in the town's stores and downloads sales information each night from these scanners. This system allows sales to be tied to households receiving different frequencies of advertising. Malec (1982) describes the system in more detail. GfK has used the same technology in Germany (Litzenroth, 1991).

This system permits experimental tests but suffers from some weaknesses:

- Members of the household may not be watching a TV set when it is on.
- Out-of-town purchases (out-shopping) are missed.
- The tests exclude trade response. National advertising may generate more retailer stocking and competitor advertising than in the test communities.
- The brands that are tested are chosen for commercial reasons and this may bias the sampling.
- There may be a 'hothouse' effect if panellists guess that commercials are on test and, as a consequence, take more interest in them.

As a method of testing copy, the BehaviorScan procedure takes a long time and is expensive. A cheaper and quicker method uses the shift in intention to purchase after exposure to test ads. This ARS Persuasion Measure is discussed by Blair and Rabuck (1998).

Cost Saving

In some cases, advertising can produce efficiencies that reduce cost. For example, Volkswagen saved on storage costs when extra demand meant that they had fewer cars unsold (Kendall, 1998). Costs may also be saved when advertising is accurately targeted and irrelevant inquiries are avoided. This problem is particularly relevant to industrial and personnel advertising where unproductive responses need to be avoided. Internet job advertising can get replies from anywhere in the world and should be designed to cut out applicants who cannot be appointed by virtue of their location or nationality. Kendall (1998) showed the value of well-targeted advertising in the campaign to recruit personnel to the British Army. In 1994, one person from every 6.7 inquirers was enlisted. Following the advertising campaign, the conversion ratio improved to 1 in 3.4. In the analysis, it was estimated that this change in ratio saved the Army £16 million after deducting the cost of the advertising. In addition, it appeared that better recruits were enlisted since they were less likely to drop out during the period of initial training.

The Effects of Social Advertising

Large paybacks are quite often found in social applications of advertising. For example, a £1 million campaign to raise rear seat belt usage in the UK gave a directly quantifiable return of £18 million, and, when further assumptions were made about the costs of injury and death, the return was £73 million (Broadbent, 2000). Another campaign in Australia achieved a drop in smoking of over 7 per cent, equivalent to 190,000 fewer smokers. The healthcare saving was $24 million (*Effective Advertising* 6, 2001). Often, social advertising has no opposing advertising but has to work against consumer inertia (e.g. energy saving) or self-indulgence (e.g. eating less).

SECTION 2: ADVERTISING FREQUENCY AND CONCENTRATION

Schedules

Advertising is presented according to a schedule. Ad exposures may be *continuous* (delivered at a steady frequency per month) or in *bursts* (e.g. one month on and two months off). When the bursts are short-interval (e.g. a week) this pattern may be called *pulsing*. Sometimes, a low level of advertising or *drip* is maintained in the gaps between bursts. The choice of schedule should be determined primarily by its sales impact on consumers. Continuous schedules spread the advertising across a larger number of people so that each person tends to see fewer exposures compared with bursting. As the time for the burst is reduced, there is more *concentration* (the exposures occur over a shorter period).

In order to choose the most effective schedule, we need to know how individuals respond to each additional ad exposure and how they react to the same number of exposures when these are concentrated into different time intervals. Work in this field has been hampered in the past by the poor quality of the data available. Now, with actual sales data on individual respondents, the effect of each extra exposure can be measured. If each additional exposure produces a smaller sales effect than the last, the response is *concave to the x-axis* and is an example of *diminishing marginal returns* (see Figure 12.1). When this occurs, the most cost-effective number of exposures (known as the *effective frequency*) is *one per person* and it is best to use a continuous schedule that spreads the advertising across the target population as widely as possible. In this way, more people are reached at lower frequencies. But if additional exposures produce increasing and then decreasing increments in sales, which is an *S-shaped* response curve, then the best strategy is to use a schedule that takes the audience quickly to the point where their sales response is steepest. This strategy sacrifices penetration for frequency. It is achieved best by irregular schedules (bursting and pulsing).

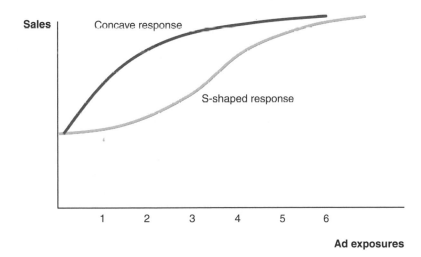

Figure 12.1   Concave and S-shaped responses to exposures

S-Shaped or Concave Response?

A better understanding of ad effects comes from using single-source data, i.e. data on the exposures and purchases of single households. Simon (1979) analysed data from a study by Zielske (1959) and found that the second and later exposures gave diminishing returns. In further evidence, Simon and Arndt (1980) reviewed 37 advertising studies and found that the great majority showed a concave response function. Roberts (1996) found that the response curve was concave in 15 out of 17 cases of mature brands. McDonald (1995) also argued that the true pattern of sales response to advertising exposures is concave for mature brands; his earlier work supported this when it was re-analysed (McDonald, 1970).[2] McDonald was influenced in part by work done by Jones on single-source data (Jones, 1995a, 1995b, 1995c), which showed little gain after the first exposure.

Studies by Adams (1916) and by Burnkrant and Unnava (1987) are relevant to this issue. In these studies, three showings of different ads for a brand were compared with three showings of the same ad. There was more effect on purchase propensity when the ads were different. This indicates that the second and third exposures of the same ad had less effect.

Despite this evidence, there is support for the S-shaped response. This is partly because the difficulties of research in this field make results uncertain. In particular, there is a problem posed by the decay of any ad effect as the period of time between exposure and measurement increases. Also, a given number of exposures can occur over different periods of time, thus varying the concentration. Broadbent (1998) pointed out that there is very little agreement among researchers and practitioners on the period over which exposures should occur when frequency effects are studied; three exposures could occur in a day, a week, or a month.

In addition, there are good reasons why the response to exposures *should be* S-shaped. An important argument is based on the idea of *breakthrough*, getting over a threshold of attention so that the audience cannot miss the message (Broadbent, 1998). This is discussed in more detail in the section below (Explaining Breakthrough). The attention to an ad is affected by other advertising in the category, which means that the effective frequency is affected by the exposure rates of competitive brands. An S-shaped response is also implicit in Krugman's (1972) three-hit theory. Krugman argued that on first exposure viewers are curious, on the second the meaning of the ad may become clear and they endorse or reject the message, and on the third and subsequent exposures they are reminded of the message again and may take action. In this account, the second and third exposures are more effective than the first. An influential book by Naples (1979) endorsed the three-hit theory.

Some aggregate evidence also supports an S-shaped response function. Lodish and Lubetkin (1992) analysed IRI data and found that both new and established products did better when the advertising was initially concentrated rather than spread over time. This suggests that exposures need to exceed some threshold level if they are to have optimum effect.

This evidence has left considerable uncertainty, but this may be resolved by work on concentration, below.

Concentration

Roberts (1999) has provided fresh evidence on the way concentration affects the outcome of repeated exposures to ads. He used a UK data set on 750 households from Taylor Nelson Sofres' Superpanel, which was gathered by TVSpan. Each household was equipped with a TV 'setmeter' so that viewing could be recorded.

Ad exposures were related to household purchases recorded through Superpanel. One hundred and thirteen brands from ten categories were studied. These were advertised over a two-year period from March 1996 to March 1998. This method does not produce data that controls for covariates and care must be taken to reduce the effects of such biases. Roberts controlled for major biases: concurrent sales promotions and weight of television viewing. He compared respondents who had received exposures on a brand with *these same respondents* when, over another period, they had not received any ad exposures on the brand for 28 days.

Roberts (1999) conducted a number of analyses. Here, we focus on the effects of three exposures in three different intervals: one day, three days and 28 days. Figure 12.2 shows the sales recorded after the end of the exposure interval. When the exposures occur over 28 days the additional effect of the second and third exposures is small and follows the familiar concave pattern. When all three exposures occur in the same day (and in practice this is often over a few hours) the effect of the second and third exposures is large and produces a convex sales response, which could be the lower part of an S-curve. Over three days, the pattern is more linear. This seems like a real advance in our knowledge of how multiple exposures work. There appears to be an interaction between exposures when these occur over a short period. It seems that, when close together, multiple exposures assist each other and achieve breakthrough. In further work, Roberts confirmed that the extra sales achieved by a high concentration decayed at the same rate as sales achieved by low concentration.

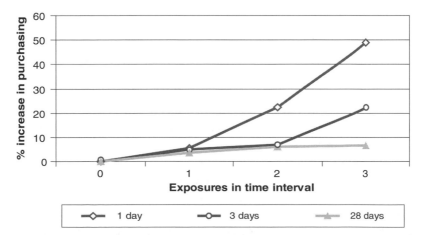

Figure 12.2   Percentage increase in sales for different frequencies and concentrations (from Roberts, 1999)

In an unpublished analysis, Roberts calculated how concentration might affect sales under continuous, monthly burst and weekly pulse schedules. One-week pulsing was best and continuous was worst. The degree of superiority of pulsing over the continuous schedule is estimated to be from 4 to 13 per cent depending on the total weight of advertising employed.

Roberts' evidence, though persuasive, is the first of its kind to be published and should be closely scrutinized. First, we note that the data are gathered in Britain where ad clutter is relatively low. This raises the possibility that stronger effects from concentration might be observed in high-clutter environments. Second, the study is restricted to groceries. Third, doubts may be felt about the effectiveness of the control comparison used in this work (the purchases made by the same respondents when they have not been exposed to the advertising for 28 days). However, in this study control subjects had shown themselves to be in the market by making purchases in other categories and this limits the discrepancy possible between control and test groups.

Explaining Breakthrough

Breakthrough relates to the psychological concept of interference, which occurs when a change in the strength of one idea affects the strength of another idea. In the competition between brands in a category, more recent ads for Brand A tend to displace the propensity to buy Brand B by retroactive interference, i.e. the new learning about Brand A displaces the previously learned responses to buy Brand B. Prior ads for Brand B prevent this by proactive interference, i.e. previous learning makes it harder to acquire new learning that is similar to the previous learning. Breakthrough occurs when more concentrated exposure to ads for Brand A overcomes the proactive interference set up by other brands.

A study by Burke and Srull (1988) showed proactive and retroactive interference effects in the recall of advertising. In their study, the target brand ad frequency was manipulated from 1 to 3 exposures while competitive advertising was manipulated from 0 to 3 exposures. The study showed that, as competitive brand advertising was increased, the recall of target brand details decreased. The study showed that recall accelerated with exposures of the target brand when there was no competition but became concave when competition was high. These findings correspond with the concentration effect observed by Roberts (1999) and suggest that Roberts' results could have been found because the greater concentration overcame any interference from competitive brand ads. A weakness of this study is that it was based on recall and lacked any observation of sales effect. Now the effect has been found in market data. Danaher, Bonfrer and Dhar (2008) examined the impact on sales of a focal brand when competitors advertised within a week and found a substantial reduction compared with the sales that would have occurred without the competitor advertising.

Practitioners have always been concerned by share of voice, the proportion of advertising exposure that a brand gets compared to all others. The work on concentration suggests that this simplifies the issue too much and that the competition for mind space occurs over short intervals. Consider a situation in which two brands, A and B, have equal strength so that the ad for one always displaces the other brand from the minds of consumers. If the ads for Brand A immediately follow those for Brand B and then there is a delay before Brand B advertises again, Brand A will have more impact although the two Brands have equal strength, advertise equally and their share of voice is the same.

Share of voice relates to the associative network discussed in Chapter 3. Interference should vary with the closeness and the linkage strength of competitive brands – some competitors are more of a threat than others. There is also a background level of interference set up by all the advertising in a medium (called clutter). This inhibits response to any ad and concentrated exposures may also help to overcome this clutter, thus increasing attention to the focal brand. These interference effects are more apparent when the material that is remembered is trivial, which fits most advertising.

SECTION 3: A MODEL OF ADVERTISING EFFECT

Despite evidence that ads lose effect with each exposure, it is apparent that some ads are aired a great number of times. This suggests that there is some residual effect of an ad after the initial effect of early exposures. It may be that brand name repetition helps to keep the brand salient relative to competitors. One mechanism for this is the effect of mere exposure which was discussed in Chapter 7 (Zajonc, 1968; Zajonc and Rajecki, 1969). Therefore, we need a model of advertising effect that describes the effect of early exposures as well as the continuing effect from what is often a large number of subsequent exposures. Figure 12.3 illustrates such a model in which advertising has two types of *primary* effect on an audience.

We suggest that the first few presentations of the ads may secure attention and may modify thinking about a brand. It is likely that this thoughtful initial response has a substantial sales effect when it occurs but that this is not usually repeated on later exposures when only the second primary effect occurs. This second primary effect takes the form of passive, low-involvement automatic mechanisms that help to maintain brand awareness. Mechanisms of this sort produce weak effects but may continue to work over many repetitions. This dual-process account has some parallel in work on persuasion by Fazio (1990) and Petty and Cacioppo (1985).

Figure 12.3 also shows secondary processes that may occur later. These secondary effects on sales are generally weak but, because they are sustained over long periods, may contribute substantially to the total sales benefit from advertising. Studies of the connection between primary and secondary effects

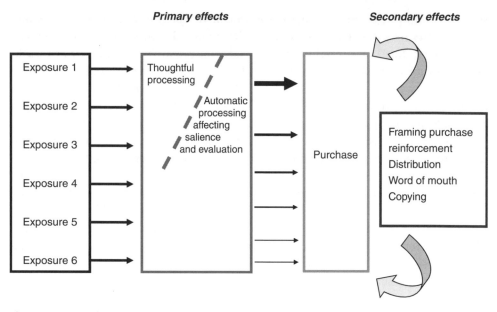

Figure 12.3   Primary and secondary responses to advertising

consistently show that a secondary effect occurs only when there has been a primary effect on sales. Abraham and Lodish (1990) reported that, if advertising tests do not show an effect after six months, they are unlikely to show any effect later. Jones (1995a) found that no one-year ad effect was observed if a short-term effect was not detected in the first seven days after exposure. Riskey (1997) observed that longer-term effects in 12 ad campaigns occurred only when there were shorter-term effects. Lodish et al. (1995b) found no delayed effects from ads that were ineffective in their test year. This evidence shows that any secondary effect is an outcome of the primary effect, but a primary effect does not guarantee a secondary effect.

The secondary effect could arise in a number of ways. There may be framing when ads modify thinking and produce a persisting change in the way that a product or brand is perceived. For example, ads may persuade customers to think of their phone as a replacement for their camera. Usually, the changes produced by advertising involve a more modest change in thinking that adjusts the positioning of the brand rather than its categorization. For example, ads may establish that a car model is more economical than previously thought. These shifts in thinking, whether dealing with the category or the attribute, are likely to be first produced by the thoughtful primary processes rather than by automatic mechanisms.

Another process that could produce a secondary effect is *purchase reinforcement*. When a short-term ad effect induces extra purchase, this additional purchase experience may strengthen the propensity to buy the brand in the future. Purchase reinforcement could occur because, after buying a brand, it comes to mind more easily because behaviour-based information is more easily recalled (Fazio, 1986; Fazio, Powell and Herr, 1983; Fazio and Zanna, 1981). Purchase reinforcement could also be based on better knowledge of where to buy the brand (which store and the location in the store) because these skills are learned from previous purchase. Two objections may be made to the purchase reinforcement explanation for the secondary effect of advertising. The first is that there can be no such effect in the case of consumer durables; people who have just bought a new cooker are not in the market for another one. Because of this, Givon and Horsky (1990) suggest that advertising induces a different effect for durables. They suggest that those who receive the advertising may become *potential* adopters and then may find out more about the product from others, particularly those who have already acquired it. The second objection asks why an ad-induced increase in purchasing produces purchase reinforcement but the extra sales from sales promotions generally show no appreciable carryover effect (Ehrenberg, Hammond and Goodhardt, 1994). This suggests that it is not purchase, as such, that creates a continuing effect but some change in thinking about the brand that is associated with purchase – this indicates framing.

A third secondary effect occurs when advertising raises *distribution* and reduces *stockouts* so that the product is more easily purchased. Better stocking may occur either because retailers anticipate demand and order more when they are advised about ad campaigns, or because the extra demand from an ad campaign forces retailers to increase stock. Retailers may maintain the higher stock level after the advertising has finished.

A fourth process is social influence, either as positive *word of mouth* when consumers recommend the product to others or as copying when publicly used products catch the fancy of others, as with fashion goods. The idea that new usage and brand switching is often started by recommendation is undeniable. The role of social influence is implicit in the diffusion of new ideas and products (Chapter 5) and is often explicitly cited when people replace one brand with another (Chapter 11). We can see that ads may instigate recommendation by simulating social influence or by providing facts that can be used when people recommend. For example, a British ad for Lavazza coffee stated that it was the most popular coffee in Italy. This can impress those who respect Italians for their discrimination with regard to food and drink and the message is easily repeated. This suggests that an important function of media is to impart information that people are likely to pass on and websites can be good at this.

How Long Do Advertising Effects Last?

Decay of advertising effect occurs when the extra propensity to buy declines over time. This decay process will affect both the primary and the secondary effects of advertising. Decay usually shows an exponential pattern, like that of radioactivity; the rate of decay is constant but, since it applies to a diminishing quantity, the change in the whole becomes less and less as it approaches some base level. Such patterns are usually described by their half-life, the period of time required for activity to decay to half its original level. Some of the decay may be due to forgetting and some to interference effects from competitive brands.

Short-term Decay

To a large degree, the short-term decay relates to primary effects and the long-term decay to the secondary effects of advertising, represented in Figure 12.3. Earlier studies estimated advertising half-lives on the assumption that there was a single process of ad decay. On this basis, Broadbent (1984) claimed that, for most brands, half-lives were in the region of 4–6 weeks and a meta-study of 70 brands by Clarke (1976) indicated half-lives in the range of 4–12 weeks. Then, Broadbent and Fry (1995) suggested that ad decay had both short-term and long-term components and Roberts (1999) measured an average short-term ad decay for frequently purchased brands. He found that this fitted an exponential curve with a half-life of 16 days. This means that, on average, an exposure loses 4.4 per cent of its sales effect each day and 72 per cent after 28 days. This rapid loss of effect has practical implications (see Exercise 12.2).

EXERCISE 12.2   WHICH DAY SHOULD YOU ADVERTISE?

Groceries have an uneven pattern of purchase over the week. Spending is heavier on Thursday, Friday and Saturday when compared with Sunday, Monday, Tuesday and Wednesday. The Nielsen (2003) figures are shown below:

Weekly supermarket expenditure by day of the week (percentage of total, Nielsen 2005):

Monday	Tuesday	Wednesday	Thursday	Friday	Saturday	Sunday
11.7	12.1	12.8	15.8	19.5	20.2	7.9

Which day should you advertise if the impact of your ads decays each day? What factors beside decay might affect your decision?

Long-term Decay

Lodish and Lubetkin (1992) used IRI data on upweight tests to measure the persistence of ad-induced sales gains. In this study, 44 brands received 50–100 per cent extra advertising during a test year only and sales of these brands were then followed for the ensuing two years and compared with a control condition. Approximately half of the brands showed a sales increase in the test year. Lodish and Lubetkin analysed the extra sales for these brands and compared results with consumers who had not received extra advertising. Table 12.1 shows the extra sales in the upweight group over three years and demonstrates that the extra sales that occurred in years 2 and 3, after the upweight had finished, were roughly equal to the extra sales during the test year. This work was criticized for excluding unsuccessful weight tests that might have shown a response in later years but Lodish et al. (1995b) found that there was no such later response.

Table 12.1 Percentage sales gain in upweight group (adapted from Lodish and Lubetkin, 1992)

	Test year	Year 2	Year 3
	(%)	(%)	(%)
Sales gain	22	14	7

Roberts (2000) has also studied the effect of advertising over a longer period. He divided customers into those who had – and those who had not – been exposed to advertising for grocery brands in the previous 28 days. The analysis took account of weight of viewing, concurrent promotions and brand size. Repeat purchase of the brand in the subsequent 12 months was higher if the ad had been seen. Roberts assessed the extra sales in the year as 5.6 times the short-term increase in sales over a month. When these extra sales are taken into account, advertising will often pay off over a year. Hanssens, Parsons and Schultz (2001) also find evidence of a substantial long-term ad effect. Figure 12.4 is designed to incorporate these different effects. In Figure 12.4, a burst of advertising produces a short-term primary effect. The long-term secondary effect is derived from the extra sales generated by the short-term effect; it has a much smaller amplitude but lasts much longer. The combined effect aggregates the base sales, long-term and short-term effects.

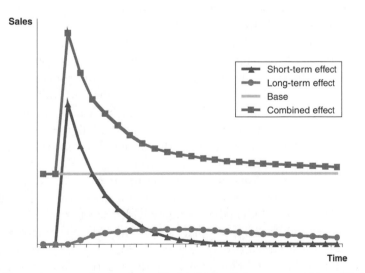

Figure 12.4 How primary and secondary effects of advertising may combine with base sales

SECTION 4: SPECIFIC EFFECTS

Segments

Advertising will have more effect on some segments than others. Identifying these segments helps us to understand how advertising works and, more practically, how it may be used.

Loyalty

Raj (1982) found the maximum sales response to advertising among those with a share-of-category requirement (SCR) loyalty of 50–70 per cent. One explanation for the lesser response of the very loyal (above 70 per cent) is that these buyers have fewer other-brand purchases to switch to the focal brand. However, Raj found that the purchases of other brands were not much affected when the focal brand gained. In his study, the extra sales in the 50–70 per cent loyalty group came mainly from an increase in category volume. Tellis (1988a) studied one mature product category and also found that ads had more sales effect on loyal buyers with an SCR greater than 50 per cent. Those who had not bought the brand before showed only a small volume sales response to the advertising compared with loyal buyers.

Roberts (1999) looked at percentage increase rather than volume. He found that the low-loyalty segment (SCR less than 10 per cent) showed the greatest and the high-loyalty group (SCR more than 50 per cent) the least, proportionate increase in sales per buyer. Making reasonable assumptions about the volume previously bought, we still find that loyal buyers buy more as a result of advertising. However, the large number of consumers in the low-loyalty segment complicates this issue. Baldinger and Rubinson (1996) found that there were three times as many buyers with an SCR of less than 10 per cent compared with buyers with an SCR greater than 10 per cent. Although the extra volume per individual low-loyalty buyer may be small, the aggregate gain in volume from the whole segment of low-loyalty buyers can be very substantial when compared with the gain from the smaller number of buyers in the high-loyalty segment. We computed that the low-loyalty segment gave a larger increment in volume than all the rest of the buyers.

This evidence helps us to understand the rather different roles performed by one-to-one direct marketing and media advertising. Where an approach to a buyer is expensive, as in some direct marketing, it pays to focus on those with high initial loyalty. If costs are low, this constraint does not apply and all buyers should be approached. Media advertising provides access to the large number of low-loyalty buyers and non-buyers that can provide a large volume of extra sales. Also, some low-loyalty buyers may evolve into high-loyalty buyers and advertising can start this process. This analysis indicates that advertising and direct marketing have different functions and that a sound marketing strategy may need both of them.

Heavy and Light Buyers

We should be careful not to relate loyalty and weight of purchase too closely because some light buyers are 100 per cent loyal. Even so, some of the foregoing argument about low and high loyalty segments applies to light and heavy buyers. In Chapter 3, we saw that the distribution of purchase frequencies of a sample of buyers follows a Gamma distribution. This means that there are many more light than heavy buyers so that the small volume changes made by many light buyers (and non-buyers) can aggregate to a much bigger increase in sales than the large volume changes made by few heavy buyers. This is what we see: sales growth comes principally from the light buyer segment. Advertising can reach light buyers and non buyers and is usually involved when a brand gains share.

Heavy and Light Television Viewers

Heavy viewers are less sensitive to television ads. Roberts (1999) divided households into the 40 per cent with the lightest viewing pattern and the rest. When he compared these light and heavy viewers, the light viewers had over twice the sales response of the heavy viewers. Roberts suggests that the greater responsiveness of light viewers is a 'share-of-mind' effect, i.e. the light viewer experiences less clutter so that each ad has more effect. Light viewers tend to watch during the peak evening period – it is their extra viewing that makes it a peak period. Roberts compared off-peak only and peak only viewers and showed that peak only viewers had three times the sales response of the off-peak only viewers.

Do Some Brands Get More from Their Advertising?

Big Brands

Brands are big mainly because they have more buyers rather than because each buyer buys them more frequently (Ehrenberg, 1988). If the sales response from advertising depends mainly on the number of buyers, big brands will get more total volume uplift from an ad campaign, other things being equal. But the evidence often shows stronger gains for smaller brands. Riskey (1997) found that ads for small brands delivered greater volume increases than ads for big brands. Riskey suggested that this may be because the small brand ads tended to report some advance in the brand and these 'newsy' ads were more effective. Sometimes, the buyer base of the small brand is actually quite large; long-established small brands can have a large number of past buyers who may be activated by advertising. Another factor against big brands is that they may have reached a ceiling where there are few potential recruits; when this applies, advertising serves to retain buyers rather than to increase sales. In addition, the advertising of small brands is often infrequent and this may make it more effective when it does occur. An example of a small brand that benefited that from advertising is the Co-operative Society (Broadbent, 2000). Here, an old and relatively small store brand, which was very well known and had not advertised for some time, did very well when it returned to advertising.

In summary, although big brands usually have more buyers, a small brand may get a good response from advertising if it has not advertised for a while, has something new to say and has a long history.

New Brands

New brands are often introduced by advertising. Unless the new brand can be directly marketed, it must use media advertising to let potential customers know that it exists. The responsiveness to ads, measured as advertising elasticity, is high for new brands. Advertising elasticity is the ratio of the proportional increase in sales to proportional increase in advertising. Lodish et al. (1995a) found an elasticity of 0.05 for established brands and 0.26 for new brands. The novelty of a product may help it to gain attention but, even though a new brand shows a high elasticity, the gain in volume can still be modest because there are few base sales. Furthermore, buyers of new brands may not stay. If they are willing to try new brands, they may move later to yet newer brands.

Elastic Categories

In some fields the boundaries between categories have little meaning to buyers. Consumers may replace Coca-Cola with beer and the cinema may replace the theatre. Thus, an increase in consumption of one brand may occur at the expense of other brands in the category *or* brands outside the category. As a result, the whole category can grow and individual brand sales may be more responsive to advertising. Because of gains from other categories, food and drink brands are particularly responsive to advertising in comparison to toiletries and cleaners, where brands can only gain at the expense of other brands in the category. Supporting this effect, unpublished Unilever research showed a greater ad response among food and drink categories than among cleaning and toiletry products. However, the greater ad response of food and drink brands has its reverse side since, in these fields, gains in sales can be whittled away by same-category competitors *and* by brands in other categories.

SECTION 5: ADVERTISING AND THE INTERNET

The growth of the Internet is changing the face of advertising. Blogs, message boards, emails and personal websites allow large numbers of people to put ideas into the public domain with great ease. As a result, an increasing proportion of consumer choice is directed by consumer-generated media (CGM), over which suppliers have limited control. Because the Internet is used so widely, more and more of the ad budget goes to this medium. Much of this spending on ads is related to search engines because of the exceptional precision of search-related advertising.

The character of ads on the new media may have altered audience expectations. The Internet can present material that would not be aired on commercial television. For example, the Trojan Games website shows risqué videos of sham sexual athleticism with voice-overs that are reminiscent of a darts match commentary. Visitors to the website who are amused can easily pass on details of the site to others. As a result, people may become aware of the Trojan brand of condoms at a very low cost. A further case is a video of a suicide bomber detonating a bomb in a Volkswagen Polo. The bomb explodes but the Polo contains the explosion. This ad is not claimed by Volkswagen but it is likely to enhance the Polo's reputation for toughness.

Blogs and discussion sites have much of the character of personal communication, even though the communicators and receivers are usually not personally acquainted. Generally, comment on the Internet is treated as another form of word of mouth (WOM) and it may be passed on from consumer to consumer. This emphasis on WOM seems to have refocused ad agencies on producing copy that people talk about. In an effort to induce such comment, *live* ads have been created. For a period, those going by train to Heathrow airport could have found themselves listening to a conversation between two actors about the advantage of checking in online. At the end of the performance, the actors explained to the travellers what they had been doing. In the USA, some Burger King ads have been deliberately bizarre so that people discuss them. One poster ad in the UK presented a new remedy for gastric problems with the invocation to 'pass it on'. It is easy to imagine those who see this ad saying to their friends that the last thing that they would do is to talk about such medication – only to realize that that is just what they had done! In some ways this is not so new. Public relations has always been concerned with creating comment, either between consumers or in editorial content. One example of this was the launch of the telephone directory inquiry number 118 118 in the UK. To emphasize the number, twins were used in the advertising. The twins were portrayed as runners and one technique was for them to run through public areas so that people who saw them talked about them to their friends. This case is reported by Hoad (2005).

EXERCISE 12.3   WHERE IS THE INTERNET
GOING TO TAKE US?

Ads on the Web are exceptionally precise when they are associated with search machines but other aspects of the Web are less controllable since consumers can broadcast to other consumers. How is advertising on the Web going to develop? How is this going to affect other forms of advertising?

SUMMARY

Commercial advertising targets behaviours that affect profit, such as purchase and rental. Social advertising may target behaviours such as smoking and dangerous driving. The benefit from commercial advertising may be via more sales, greater margins or lower costs. Ad campaigns usually have quite small effects on sales but, in large markets, the payback on advertising can be many times.

We now understand better how individuals react to different frequencies and concentrations of advertising. Extra exposures tend to give increasing sales effects when these exposures are concentrated into a short interval; otherwise, extra ads have a diminishing effect. This is probably because concentrated exposures give better breakthrough. This evidence suggests that a schedule of short concentrated periods of advertising (pulsing) is the most effective.

A model is presented in which ads may have two sorts of primary effect: one is thoughtful, and the effect is quite strong if it occurs; the other is automatic and weak. Thoughtful processes occur early in the sequence of ad exposures if they occur at all; automatic mechanisms can occur at each exposure so ads can continue to have some effect for a long period.

When primary effects occur there may be consequential secondary effects that include framing (persisting change in thinking about the brand), purchase reinforcement (later purchase is facilitated by the occurrence of the earlier purchase), better distribution, word of mouth and copying.

Corresponding to these primary and secondary effects, sales appear to have short-term and long-term decay rates. In one study, the short-term component had an average half-life of 16 days. The long-term component can persist for a year or more after the advertising has finished.

Although low-loyalty and light buyers show less individual volume response to advertising, the large numbers of these buyers ensure that these segments provide more sales gain. Advertising is effective at

> reaching such consumers and contrasts with direct marketing, which is better when there is a need to focus on the smaller number of high-loyal or heavy buyers. In the response to television advertising, more sales response comes from light viewers than heavy viewers.
>
> Although they have more buyers, studies have sometimes shown that big brands do not gain as much as smaller brands from advertising.

Additional Resources

You should read at least one of the cases in the *Advertising Works* series (or the equivalent in another country). This indicates the concerns of ad agencies and the difficulties of measuring effects. For reasons of space, this chapter omits some of the psychological explanations for ad effect which are covered in East (2003). If you are more interested in the decisions that have to be made in ad agencies, one textbook that is based on research is Rossiter and Bellman (2005).

Notes

1 The Advertising Federation of Australia (AFA) supports the publication *Effective Advertising* and, in the UK, the Institute of Practitioners in Advertising (IPA) supports *Advertising Works*. These publications, usually issued at two-year intervals, are dedicated to showing how competent and creative advertising can bring returns to the advertiser.
2 There is more agreement between researchers and practitioners on ad frequency when the advertising or product is new or complex. It is widely held that a linear or S-shaped response may be expected under these conditions. Roberts (1996) found that the response was effectively linear in five out of seven cases where the brand was new or re-launched.

References

Aaker, D.A. (1991) *Managing Brand Equity: Capitalizing on the Value of a Brand Name*, New York: The Free Press.

Aaker, D.A. and Keller, K.L. (1990) Consumer evaluations of brand extensions, *Journal of Marketing*, 54(1), 27–41.

Abraham, M.M. and Lodish, L.M. (1990) Getting the most out of advertising and promotion, *Harvard Business Review*, 68(3), 50–60.

Adams, H.F. (1916) *Advertising and its Mental Laws*, New York: Macmillan.

AGB (1992) Revealed: The nation's shopping habits, *SuperMarketing*, Aug 14th.

Ahluwalia, R. (2002) How prevalent is the negativity effect in consumer environments?, *Journal of Consumer Research*, 29 (September), 270–279.

Ahluwalia, R., Burnkrant, R.E. and Unnava, H.R. (2000) Consumer response to negative publicity, *Journal of Marketing Research*, 37(2), 203–214.

Ailawadi, K.L., Gedenk, K., Lutzky, C. and Neslin, S.A. (2007) Decomposition of the sales impact of promotion-induced stockpiling, *Journal of Marketing Research*, 44(3), 450–467.

Ailawadi, K.L. and Neslin, S.A. (1998) The effect of promotion on consumption: buying more and consuming it faster, *Journal of Marketing Research*, 35(3), 390–398.

Ajzen, I. (1971) Attitude vs. normative messages: an investigation of the differential effects of persuasive communications on behavior, *Sociometry*, 34(2), 263–280.

Ajzen, I. (1985) From intentions to actions: a theory of planned behavior. In J. Kuhl and J. Beckmann (eds), *Action-Control: From Cognition to Behavior*, Heidelberg: Springer, 22–39.

Ajzen, I. (1991) The theory of planned behavior. In E.A. Locke (ed.), *Organizational Behavior and Human Decision Processes*, 50, 179–211.

Ajzen, I. (2002) Perceived behavioral control, self-efficacy, locus of control and the theory of planned behavior, *Journal of Applied Social Psychology*, 32(4), 665–683.

Ajzen, I. and Driver, B.L. (1992) Application of the theory of planned behavior to leisure choice, *Journal of Leisure Research*, 24(3), 207–224.

Ajzen, I. and Fishbein, M. (1969) The prediction of behavioral intentions in a choice situation, *Journal of Experimental Social Psychology*, 5(4), 400–416.

Ajzen, I. and Fishbein, M. (1972) Attitudinal and normative beliefs as factors influencing behavioral intentions, *Journal of Personality and Social Psychology*, 21(1), 1–9.

Ajzen, I. and Fishbein, M. (1977) Attitude–behavior relations: a theoretical analysis and review of empirical research, *Psychological Bulletin*, 84, 888–918.

Ajzen, I. and Fishbein, M. (1980) *Understanding Attitudes and Predicting Social Behavior*, Englewood Cliffs, NJ: Prentice-Hall.

Ajzen, I., Nichols, A.J. and Driver, B.L. (1995) Identifying salient beliefs about leisure activities: frequency of elicitation versus response latency, *Journal of Applied Social Psychology*, 25(16), 1391–1410.

Ali, M. (1977) Probability and utility estimates for racetrack bettors, *Journal of Political Economy*, 85, 803–815.

Allais, M. (1953) Le comportement de l'homme rationel devant le risque: critique des postulats et axiomes de l'ecole americaine, *Econometrica*, 21(4), 503–546.

Allenby, G.M. and Ginter, J.L. (1995) The effects of in-store displays and feature advertising on consideration sets, *International Journal of Research in Marketing*, 12(1), 67–80.

Allport, G.W. (1935) Attitudes. In C. Murchison, (ed.), *A Handbook of Social Psychology*, Worcester, MA: Clark University Press, 798–844.

Allport, G.W. and Postman, L. (1947) *The Psychology of Rumor*, New York: Holt, Rinehart and Winston.

Ambler, T. and Broadbent, S. (2000) A dialogue on advertising effectiveness and efficiency, *Admap*, July/August, 29–31.

Anand, P., Holbrook, M.B. and Stephens, D. (1988) The formation of affective judgments: the cognitive–affective model versus the independence hypothesis, *Journal of Consumer Research*, 15, 386–391.

Anand, P. and Sternthal, B. (1991) Perceptual fluency and affect without recognition, *Memory and Cognition*, 19(3), 293–300.

Anderson, E.I. and Simester, D. (2003) Effects of $9 price endings on retail sales: evidence from field experiments, *Qualitative Marketing and Economics*, 1(1), 93–110.

Anderson, E.W. (1998) Customer satisfaction and word of mouth, *Journal of Service Research*, 1(1), 5–17.

Anderson, E.W., Fornell, C. and Lehmann, D.R. (1994) Customer satisfaction, market share and profitability, *Journal of Marketing*, 58(3), 53–66.

Anderson, E.W. and Mittal, V. (2000) Strengthening the satisfaction–profit chain, *Journal of Service Research*, 3(2), 107–120.

Anderson, E.W., Fornell, C. and Mazvancheryl, S.K. (2004) Customer satisfaction and shareholder value, *Journal of Marketing*, 68(4), 172–185.

Anderson, N.H. (1965) Averaging versus adding as a stimulus-combination rule in impression formation, *Journal of Experimental Psychology*, 70, 394–400.

Andreasen, A.R. (1985) Consumer responses to dissatisfaction in loose monopolies, *Journal of Consumer Research*, 12(2), 135–141.

Andreasen, A.R. (1988) Consumer complaints and redress: what we know and what we don't know. In E.S. Maynes (ed.), *The Frontier of Research in Consumer Interest*, Columbia: University of Columbia and American Council of Consumer Interest, 675–721.

Andreasen, A.R. and Manning, J. (1990) The dissatisfaction and complaining behavior of vulnerable consumers, *Journal of Consumer Satisfaction, Dissatisfaction and Complaining Behavior*, 3, 12–20.

Anglin, L.K., Stuenkel, J.K. and Lepisto, L.R. (1994) The effect of stress on price sensitivity and comparison shopping. In C.T. Allen and D.R. John (eds), *Advances in Consumer Research*, 21, 126–131.

Arce, M. and Cebollada, J. (2006) The role of loyalty in online and offline shopping behaviour: an empirical application to the grocery industry, *Conference Proceedings of the European Marketing Academy*, Athens.

Areni, C.S. and Kim, D. (1993) The influence of background music on shopping behavior: classical versus top-forty music in a wine store. In L. McAlister and M.L. Rothschild (eds), *Advances in Consumer Research*, 20, 336–340.

Armitage, C.J. and Conner, M. (2001) Efficacy of the theory of planned behaviour: a meta-analytic review, *British Journal of Social Psychology*, 40(4), 471–499.

Armstrong, J.S. (1985) *Long-range Forecasting: From Crystal Ball to Computer*, 2nd edition. London: Wiley.

Arndt, J. (1967) The role of product-related conversations in the diffusion of a new product, *Journal of Marketing Research*, 4 (August), 291–295.

Arthur, C. (1992) Fifteen million Americans are shopping addicts, *American Demographics*, March, 14–15.

Assael, H. (2004) *Consumer Behavior: A Strategic Approach*, Boston: Houghton Mifflin Company.

Asugman, G. (1998) An evaluation of negative word-of-mouth research for extensions, *European Advances in Consumer Research, 3*, 70–75.

Babacus, E. and Boller, G.W. (1992) An empirical assessment of the SERVQUAL scale, *Journal of Business Research*, 24(3), 253–268.

Babin, B.J., Hardesty, D.M. and Suter, T.A. (2003) Color and shopping intentions: the intervening effect of price fairness and perceived affect, *Journal of Business Research*, 56(7), 541–551.

Bagozzi, R.P. (1981) Attitudes, intentions and behavior: a test of some key hypotheses, *Journal of Personality and Social Psychology*, 41(4), 607–627.

Bagozzi, R.P. (1984) Expectancy-value attitude models: an analysis of critical measurement issues, *International Journal of Research in Marketing*, 1(4), 295–310.

Bagozzi, R.P. (1992) The self-regulation of attitudes, intentions and behaviors, *Social Psychology Quarterly*, 55, 178–204.

Bagozzi, R.P. and Kimmel, S.K. (1995) A comparison of leading theories for the prediction of goal directed behaviours, *British Journal of Social Psychology*, 34(4), 437–461.

Baker, C. (1993) *Advertising Works 7*, Henley-on-Thames: Institute of Practitioners in Advertising, NTC Publications.

Baker, C. (1995) *Advertising Works 8*, Henley-on-Thames: Institute of Practitioners in Advertising, NTC Publications.

Baldinger, A.L. and Rubinson, J. (1996) Brand loyalty: the link between attitude and behavior, *Journal of Advertising Research*, 36(6), 22–34.

Baldwin, M.W. and Holmes, J.G. (1987) Salient private audiences and awareness of the self, *Journal of Personality and Social Psychology*, 52(6), 1087–1098.

Balter, D. and Butman, J. (2005) *Grapevine: The New Art of Word-of-Mouth Marketing*, New York: Penguin Portfolio.

Bargh, J.A., Chaiken, S., Govender, R. and Pratto, F. (1992) The generality of the automatic activation effect, *Journal of Personality and Social Psychology*, 62(6), 893–912.

Bartlett, F.C. (1932) *Remembering*, Cambridge: Cambridge University Press.

Barwise, P. (1993) Brand equity: Snark or Boojum?, *International Journal of Research in Marketing*, 10(1), 93–104.

Bass, F.M. (1969) A new product growth model for consumer durables, *Management Science*, 15(5), 215–227.

Bass, F.M. (1995) Empirical generalizations and marketing science: a personal view, *Marketing Science*, 14(3), Part 2 of 2, G6–G18.

Bass, F.M., Givon, M.M., Kalwani, M.U., Reibstein, D. and Wright, G.P. (1984) An investigation into the order of the brand choice process, *Marketing Science*, 3(4), 267–287.

Bass, F.M., Jeuland, A.P. and Wright, G.P. (1976) Equilibrium stochastic choice and market penetration theories: derivation and comparisons, *Management Science*, 22(10), 1051–1063.

Bass, F.M., Krishnan, T.V. and Jain, D.C. (1994) Why the Bass model fits without decision variables, *Marketing Science*, 13(3), 203–223.

Bayus, B.L. (1985) Word of mouth: the indirect effects of marketing efforts, *Journal of Advertising Research*, 25(3), 31–39.

Bayus, B.L. (1991) The consumer durable replacement buyer, *Journal of Marketing*, 55 (January), 42–51.

Beales, H.J., Mazis, M.B., Salop, S.C. and Staelin, R. (1981) Consumer search and public policy, *Journal of Consumer Research*, 8(1), 11–22.

Beatty, S.E. and Smith, S.M. (1987) External search effort: an investigation across several product categories, *Journal of Consumer Research*, 14(1), 83–95.

Bellizzi, J.A., Crowley, A.E. and Hasty, R.E. (1983) The effects of color in store design, *Journal of Retailing*, 59(1), 21–44.

Bemmaor, A.L. (1995) Predicting behavior from intention-to-buy measures: the parametric case, *Journal of Marketing Research*, 32(2), 176–191.

Bendapudi, N. and Berry, L.L. (1997) Customers' motivations for maintaining relationships with service providers, *Journal of Retailing*, 73(1), 15–37.

Benoulli, D. (1738) Specimen Theoriae Novae de Mensura Sortis. *Comentarii Academiae Scientiarum Imperiales Petropolitanae*, 5, 175–92. Translated by L. Sommer in *Econometrica*, 1954, 22(1), 23–36.

Benterud, T. and Stø, E. (1993) TV shopping in Scandinavia: Consumer satisfaction, dissatisfaction and complaining behavior, *Journal of Consumer Satisfaction, Dissatisfaction and Complaining Behavior*, 6, 196–203.

Bentler, P.M. and Speckart, G. (1981) Attitudes 'cause' behaviors: A structural equation analysis, *Journal of Personality and Social Psychology*, 40, 226–38.

Bentler, P.M. and Speckart, G. (1979) Models of attitude–behavior relations, *Psychological Review*, 86(5), 452–464.

Berlyne, D.E. (1954) A theory of human curiosity, *British Journal of Psychology*, 45, 80–191.

Berlyne, D.E. (1965) *Structure and Direction in Thinking*, London: Wiley.

Berlyne, D.E. and McDonnell, P. (1965) Effects of stimulus complexity and incongruity on duration of EEG desynchronisation, *Electroencephalography and Clinical Neurophysiology*, 18(2), 156–161.

Benartzi, S. and Thaler, R.H. (1995) Myopic loss aversion and the equity premium puzzle, *Quarterly Journal of Economics*, 110(1), 73–92. Reprinted in Kahneman, D. and Tversky, A. (2000) *Choices, Values, and Frames*, New York: Russell Sage Foundation, Cambridge University Press, 301–316.

Berry, L.L. (1983) Relationship marketing. In L.L. Berry, G.L. Shostack, and G.D. Upah (eds), *Emerging Perspectives on Service Marketing*, Chicago: American Marketing Association, 25–28.

Bettman, J.R. (1979) *An Information Processing Theory of Consumer Choice*, Reading, MA: Addison-Wesley.

Biel, A.L. (1991) The brandscape: Converting brand image into equity, *Admap*, Oct, 41–6.

Bijmolt, T.H.A., van Heerde, H.J. and Pieters, R.G.M. (2005) New empirical generalizations on the determinants of price elasticity, *Journal of Marketing Research*, 42(2), 141–156.

Bird, M. and Ehrenburg, A.S.C. (1966) Intentions-to-buy and claimed brand usage, *Operational Research Quarterly*, 17, 27–46.

Bitner, M.J., Booms, B.H. and Tetreault, M.S. (1990) The service encounter: diagnosing favourable and unfavourable incidents, *Journal of Marketing*, 54(1), 71–84.

Blair, M.H. and Rabuck, M.J. (1998) Advertising wearin and wearout: ten years later – more empirical evidence and successful practice, *Journal of Advertising Research*, 38(5), 7–18.

Blattberg, R.C., Briesch, R. and Fox, E.J. (1995) How promotions work, *Marketing Science*, 14(3), G122–G132.

Blodgett, J.G., Granbois, D.H. and Walters, R.G. (1993) The effects of perceived justice on complainants' negative word-of-mouth behavior and repatronage intentions, *Journal of Retailing*, 69(4), 399–428.

Bolton, L.E., Warlop, L. and Alba, J.W. (2003) Consumer perceptions of price (un)fairness, *Journal of Consumer Research*, 29(4), 474–491.

Bolton, R.N. (1989) The relationship between market characteristics and promotional price elasticities, *Marketing Science*, 8(2), 153–169.

Bolton, R.N. (1998) A dynamic model of the duration of the customer's relationship with a continuous service provider: the role of satisfaction, *Marketing Science*, 17(1), 45–65.

Bosmans, A. (2007) Scents and sensibility: when do (in)congruent ambient scents influence product evaluations?, *Journal of Marketing*, 71(3), 32–43.

Bottomley, P.A. and Holden, S.J.S. (2001) Do we really know how consumers evaluate brand extensions? Empirical generalizations based on secondary analysis of eight studies, *Journal of Marketing Research*, 38(4), 494–500.

Brehm, J.W. (1966) *A Theory of Psychological Reactance*, New York: Academic Press.

Brehm, J.W. (1989) Psychological reactance: theory and applications. In T.K. Srull (ed.), *Advances in Consumer Research*, 16, 72–5.

Brehm, S.S. and Brehm, J.W. (1981) *Psychological Reactance*, New York: Academic Press.

Briesch, R.A., Krishnamurthi., Loo Muzumdar, T. and Raj, S.P. (1997) A comparative analysis of reference price models, *Journal of Consumer Research*, 24 (September), 202–214.

Broadbent, S. (1984) Modelling with adstock, *Journal of the Market Research Society*, 26(4), 295–312.

Broadbent, S. (1989) *The Advertising Budget: The Advertiser's Guide to Budget Determination*, Henley: NTC Publications.

Broadbent, S. (1998) Effective frequency: there and back, *Admap*, May, 34–38.

Broadbent, S. and Fry, T. (1995) Adstock modelling for the long term, *Journal of the Market Research Society*, 37(4), 385–403.

Broadbent, T. (2000) *Advertising Works 11*, Henley-on-Thames: Institute of Practitioners in Advertising, World Adverstising Research Centre (WARC)

Brown, G. (1986) Monitoring advertising performance, *Admap*, 22(3), 151–153.

Brown, G.H. (1953) Brand loyalty, *Advertising Age*, 24, 28–35. Reproduced in A.S.C. Ehrenberg and F.G. Pyatt (eds), *Consumer Behaviour*, Harmondsworth: Penguin Books, 28–35.

Brown, J.J. and Reingen, P.H. (1987) Social ties and word-of-mouth referral behavior, *Journal of Consumer Research*, 14(3), 350–362.

Buday, T. (1989) Capitalizing on brand extensions: lessons of success and failure, *Journal of Consumer Marketing*, 6(4), 27–30.

Budd, R. (1986) Predicting cigarette use: the need to incorporate measures of salience in the theory of reasoned action, *Journal of Applied Social Psychology*, 16, 663–685.

Burke, R.R. and Srull, T.K. (1988) Competitive interference and consumer memory for advertising, *Journal of Consumer Research*, 15(1), 55–68.

Burnkrant, R.E. and Unnava, H.R. (1987) Effects of variation in message execution on the learning of repeated brand information. In M. Wallendorf and P. Anderson (eds), *Advances in Consumer Research*, 14, 173–176.

Burns, D.J. and Perkins, D. (1996) Accounts in post-purchase behavior: excuses, justifications and meta-accounts, *Journal of Satisfaction, Dissatisfaction and Complaining Behavior*, 9, 144–157.

Buttle, F. (1996) SERVQUAL: review, critique, research agenda, *European Journal of Marketing*, 30(1), 8–32.

Buttle, F.A. (1998) Word of mouth: understanding and managing referral marketing, *Journal of Strategic Marketing*, 6, 241–254.

Buzzell, R.D. and Gale, B.T. (1987) *The PIMS Principles: Linking Strategy to Performance*, New York: The Free Press.

Buzzell, R.D., Quelch, J.A. and Salmon, W.J. (1991) The costly bargain of trade promotion, *Harvard Business Review*, 68(2), 141–149.

Camerer, C.F. (2000) Prospect theory in the wild. In D. Kahneman and A. Tversky (eds), *Choices, Values and Frames*, New York: Russell Sage Foundation, 288–300.

Campbell, D.T. (1957) Factors relevant to the validity of experiments in social settings, *Psychological Bulletin*, 54(4), 297–312.

Campbell, M.C. (1999) Perceptions of price unfairness: antecedents and consequences, *Journal of Marketing Research*, 36(2), 187–199.

Caplovitz, D. (1967) *The Poor Pay More*, 2nd edition, N.Y. The Free Press.

Cardozo, R.N. (1965) An experimental study of consumer effort, expectation and satisfaction, *Journal of Marketing Research*, 2(3), 244–249.

Carl, W.J. (2006a) What's all the buzz about? Everyday communication and the relational basis of word-of-mouth and buzz marketing practices, *Management Communication Quarterly*, 19(4), 601–634.

Carl, W.J. (2006b) To tell or not to tell? Assessing the practical effects of disclosure for word-of-mouth marketing agents and their conversational partners. Working Paper, Northeastern University, Department of Communication Studies, Boston, MA.

Carman, J.M. (1970) Correlates of brand loyalty: some positive results, *Journal of Marketing Research*, 7(1), 67–76.

Carman, J.M. (1990) Consumer perceptions of service quality: an assessment of the SERVQUAL dimensions, *Journal of Retailing*, 66(1), 33–55.

Chandon, P. (1995) Consumer research on sales promotions: a state-of-the-art literature review, *Journal of Marketing Management*, 11(5), 419–441.

Chandon, P., Morvitz, V.G. and Reinartz, W.J. (2005) Do intentions really predict behavior? Self-generated validity effects in survey research, *Journal of Marketing*, 69(2), 1–14.

Chandon, P., Wansink, B. and Laurent, G. (2000) A benefit congruency framework of sales promotion effectiveness, *Journal of Marketing*, 64(4), 65–81.

Channon, C. (1985) *Advertising Works 3*, London: Holt, Rinehart and Winston.

Charlett, D., Garland, R. and Marr, N. (1995) How damaging is negative word of mouth?, *Marketing Bulletin*, 6, 42–50.

Charlton, P. (1973) A review of shop loyalty, *Journal of the Market Research Society*, 15(1), 35–51.

Chatfield, C. and Goodhardt, G. (1975) Results concerning brand choice, *Journal of Marketing Research*, 12(1), 110–113.

Chevalier, J.A. and Mayzlin, D. (2003) The effect of word of mouth on sales: online book reviews, *Journal of Marketing Research*, 44(3), 345–354.

Chintagunta, P.K. (1993) Investigating purchase incidence, brand choice and purchase quantity decisions of households, *Marketing Science*, 12(2), 184–208.

Christaller, W. (1933) *Central Places in Southern Germany*, translated by C.W. Baskin (1966), Englewood Cliffs, NJ: Prentice-Hall.

Churcher, P.B. and Lawton, J.H. (1987) Predation by domestic cats in an English village, *Journal of Zoology*, 212, 439–55.

Churchill, G.A. Jr. and Surprenant, C. (1982) An investigation into the determinants of customer satisfaction, *Journal of Marketing Research*, 19(4), 491–504.

Churchill, H. (1942) How to measure brand loyalty, *Advertising and Selling*, 35(24).

Clare, J.E. and Kiser, C.V. (1951) Preference for children of a given sex in relation to fertility. In P.K. Whelpton and C.V. Kiser (eds) *Social and Psychological Factors Affecting Fertility*. New York: Milbank Memorial Fund, 621–673.

Clarke, D.G. (1976) Econometric measurement of the duration of advertising effect on sales, *Journal of Marketing Research*, 13(4), 345–357.

Clemmer, E.C. and Schneider, B. (1989) Towards understanding and controlling dissatisfaction with waiting during peak demand times. In M.J. Bitner and L.A. Crosby (eds), *Designing a Winning Service Strategy*, Chicago: American Marketing Association, 87–91.

Coleman, J., Katz, E. and Menzel, H. (1957) The diffusion of an innovation among physicians, *Sociometry*, 20(4), 253–270.

Collins, M. (1971) Market segmentation – the realities of buyer behaviour, *Journal of the Market Research Society*, 13(3), 146–157.

Conner, M., Lawton, R., Parker, D., Chorlton, K., Manstead, A.S.R. and Stradling, S. (2007) Application of the theory of planned behaviour to the prediction of objectively assessed breaking of posted speed limits, *British Journal of Psychology*, 98(3), 429–453.

Copeland, M.T. (1923) Relation of consumer's buying habits to marketing methods, *Harvard Business Review*, 1, 282–289.

Cowley, E. and Mitchell, A.A. (2003) The moderating effect of product knowledge on the learning and organization of product information, *Journal of Consumer Research*, 30(3), 443–454.

Cox, D. and Cox, A.D. (2002) Beyond first impressions: the effects of repeated exposure on consumer liking of visually complex and simple product designs, *Journal of the Academy of Marketing Science*, 30(2), 119–130.

Cox, K.K. (1970) The effect of shelf space upon sales of branded products, *Journal of Marketing Research*, 7(1), 55–58.

Crawford, C. and Di Benedetto, A. (2006) *New Products Management*, 8th edition, New York: McGraw-Hill/Irwin.

Crocker, J., Fiske, S.T. and Taylor, S.E. (1984) Schematic bases of belief change. In J.R. Eiser (ed.), *Attitudinal Judgement*, New York: Springer-Verlag.

Cronin, J.J. Jr. and Taylor, S.A. (1992) Measuring service quality: a re-examination and extension, *Journal of Marketing*, 56(3), 55–68.

Crosby, L.A. and Stephens, N. (1987) Effects of relationship marketing on satisfaction, retention, and prices in the life insurance industry, *Journal of Marketing Research*, 24(4), 404–411.

Cunningham, R.M. (1956) Brand loyalty – what, where, how much?, *Harvard Business Review*, 34 (Jan./Feb.), 116–128.

Curhan, R.C. (1972) The relationship between shelf space and unit sales in supermarkets, *Journal of Marketing Research*, 9(4), 406–412.

Dabholkar, P.A., Thorpe, D.I. and Rentz, J.O. (1996) A measure of service quality for retail stores, *Journal of the Academy of Marketing Science*, 24(1), 3–16.

Dacin, P.A. and Smith, D.C. (1993) The effect of adding products to a brand on consumers' evaluations of new brand extensions. In L. McAlister and M.L. Rothschild (eds), *Advances in Consumer Research*, 20, 594–598.

Dagnoli, J. (1987) Impulse governs shoppers, *Advertising Age*, 5th October, 93.

Dall'Olmo Riley, F.D., Ehrenberg, A.S.C., Castleberry, S.B., Barwise, T.P. and Barnard, N.R. (1997) The variability of attitudinal repeat-rates, *International Journal of Research in Marketing*, 14(5), 437–450.

Danaher, P. and Rust, R. (1996) Indirect financial benefits from service quality, *Quality Management*, 3(2), 63–75.

Danaher, P.J., Bonfrer, A. and Dhar, S. (2008) The effect of competitive advertising interference on sales for packaged goods, *Journal of Marketing Research* 44 (April).

D'Astous, A. (1990) An inquiry into the compulsive side of normal consumers, *Journal of Consumer Policy*, 13(1), 15–32.

Davidson, A.R. and Jaccard, J.J. (1975) Population psychology: a new look at an old problem, *Journal of Personality and Social Psychology*, 31, 1073–1082.

Davis, F.D. (1989) Perceived usefulness, perceived ease of use, and user acceptance of information technology, *MIS Quarterly*, 13(3), 319–339.

Dawar, N. and Anderson, P.F. (1993) *Determining the Order and Direction of Multiple Brand Extensions*, INSEAD Working Paper 93/17/MKT.

Day, D., Gan, B., Gendall, P. and Esslemont, D. (1991) Predicting purchase behaviour, *Marketing Bulletin*, 2(May), 18–30.

Day, G.S. (1969) A two-dimensional concept of brand loyalty, *Journal of Advertising Research*, 9, 29–35.

Day, R.L. and Landon, E.L. (1976) Collecting comprehensive complaint data by survey research. In B.B. Anderson (ed.) *Advances in Consumer Research*, 3, 263–268.

Day, R.L. (1984) Modeling choices among alternative responses to dissatisfaction. In Kinnear, T.C. (ed.) *Advances in Consumer Research*, 11, 496–499.

De Matos, C.A., Henrique, J.L., Vargas, R. and Carlos, A. (2007) Service recovery paradox: a meta-analysis, *Journal of Service Research*, 10(1), 60–77.

Degeratu, A.M., Rangaswamy, A. and Wu, J. (2001) Consumer choice behavior in online and traditional supermarkets: the effects of brand name, price, and other search attributes, *International Journal of Research in Marketing*, 17(1), 55–78.

Dekimpe, M.G., Hanssens, D.M. and Silva-Risso, J.M. (1999) Long-run effects of price promotions in scanner markets, *Journal of Econometrics*, 89(1/2), 269–291.

DelVecchio, D., Henard, D.H. and Freling, T.H. (2006) The effect of sales promotion on post-promotion brand preference: a meta-analysis, *Journal of Retailing*, 82(3), 203–214.

DeSarbo, W.S., Huff, L., Rolandelli, M.M. and Choi, J. (1994) On the measurement of perceived service quality. In R.T. Rust and R.L. Oliver (eds), *Service Quality: New Directions in Theory and Practice*, London: Sage, 201–222.

Deutch, M. and Gerard, H.B. (1955) A study of the normative and informational influences upon individual judgment, *Journal of Abnormal and Social Psychology*, 51(3), 629–636.

Dichter, E. (1966) How word-of-mouth advertising works, *Harvard Business Review*, 44(6), 147–166.

Dick, A.S. and Basu, K. (1994) Customer loyalty: towards an integrated framework, *Journal of the Academy of Marketing Science*, 22(2), 99–113.

Dickson, P.R. and Sawyer, A.G. (1990) The price knowledge and search of supermarket shoppers, *Journal of Marketing*, 54(3), 42–54.

Dimson, E., Marsh, P. and Staunton, M. (2004) Low-cap and low-rated companies, *The Journal of Portfolio Management*, Summer, 1–12.

Dittmar, H. (2005) Compulsive buying – a growing concern? An examination of gender, age, and endorsement of materialistic values as predictors, *British Journal of Psychology*, 96(4), 467–491.

Dittmar, H., Beattie, J. and Friese, S. (1995) Gender identity and material symbols: objects and decision considerations in impulse purchases, *Journal of Economic Psychology*, 16(3), 491–512.

Donovan, R.J. and Rossiter, J.R. (1982) Store atmosphere: an environmental psychology approach, *Journal of Retailing*, 58(1), 34–56.

Donovan, R.J., Rossiter, J.R., Marcoolyn, G. and Nesdale, A. (1994) Store atmosphere and purchasing behaviour, *Journal of Retailing*, 70(3), 283–294.

Dowling, G.R. and Uncles, M.D. (1997) Do customer loyalty programs really work?, *Sloan Management Review*, 38(Summer), 71–82.

Doyle, P. (1989) Building successful brands: the strategic options, *Journal of Marketing Management*, 5(1), 77–95.

Drèze, X., Hoch, S.J. and Purk, M.E. (1994) Shelf management and space elasticity, *Journal of Retailing*, 70(4), 301–326.

Driesener, C. and Romaniuk, J. (2006) Comparing methods of brand image measurement, *International Journal of Market Research*, 48(6), 681–698.

Dubé-Rioux, L., Schmitt, B.H. and Leclerc, F. (1989) Consumers' reactions to waiting: when delays affect the perception of service quality. In T.K. Srull (ed.), *Advances in Consumer Research*, 16, 59–63.

Dunn, R.S., Reader, S. and Wrigley, N. (1983) An investigation of the assumptions of the NBD model as applied to purchasing at individual stores, *Applied Statistics*, 32(3), 249–259.

Dunn, R.S. and Wrigley, N. (1984) Store loyalty for grocery products: An empirical study, *Area*, 16(4), 307–314,

Eagly, A.H. and Chaiken, S. (1993) *The Psychology of Attitudes*, Orlando, FL: Harcourt, Brace, Jovanovitch.

East, R. (1973) The duration of attention to alternatives and re-evaluation in choices with two and three alternatives, *European Journal of Social Psychology*, 3(2), 125–144.

East, R. (1992) The effects of experience on the decision making of expert and novice buyers, *Journal of Marketing Management*, 8(2), 167–176.

East, R. (1993) Investment decisions and the theory of planned behaviour, *Journal of Economic Psychology*, 14(2), 337–375.

East, R. (2000) Complaining as planned behavior, *Psychology and Marketing*, 17(12), 1077–1095.

East, R. (2003). *The Response to Advertising and Display: Assessing the Research on Effectiveness*, Boston: Kluwer Academic Publishers.

East, R., Eftichiadou, V. and Williamson, M. (2003) Point-of-purchase display and brand sales, *The International Review of Retail, Distribution and Consumer Research*, 13(1), 127–134.

East, R., Harris, P., Willson, G. and Lomax, W. (1995) Loyalty to supermarkets, *International Review of Retail, Distribution and Consumer Research*, 5(1), 99–109.

East, R., Gendall, P., Hammond, K. and Lomax, W. (2005a) Consumer loyalty: singular, additive or interactive?, *Australasian Marketing Journal*, 13(2), 10–26.

East, R., Hammond, K., Lomax, W. and Robinson, H. (2005b) What is the effect of a recommendation?, *The Marketing Review*, 5(2), 145–157.

East, R. Grandcolas, U. and Dall'Olmo Riley, F. (2007a) New evidence on the reasons for switching services. Paper presented at ANZMAC, Otago, New Zealand.

East, R. and Hammond, K. (1996) The erosion of repeat-purchase loyalty, *Marketing Letters*, 7(2), 163–172.

East, R., Hammond, K. and Lomax, W. (2008) Measuring the impact on brand purchase probability of positive and negative word of mouth, Forthcoming in *International Journal of Research in Marketing*.

East, R., Hammond, K. and Gendall, P. (2006) Fact and fallacy in retention marketing, *Journal of Marketing Management*, 22(1–2), 5–23.

East, R., Hammond, K., Harris, P. and Lomax, W. (2000) First-store loyalty and retention, *Journal of Marketing Management*, 16(4), 307–325.

East, R., Hammond, K.A. and Wright, M. (2007b) The relative incidence of positive and negative word of mouth: a multi-category study, *International Journal of Research in Marketing*, 24(2), 175–184.

East, R., Harris, P., Willson, G. and Hammond, K. (1995) Correlates of first-brand loyalty, *Journal of Marketing Management*, 11(5), 487–497.

East, R. and Hogg, A. (1997) The anatomy of conquest: Tesco versus Sainsbury, *Journal of Brand Management*, 5(1), 53–60.

East, R., Lomax, W. and Narain, R. (2001) Customer tenure, recommendation and switching, *Journal of Consumer Satisfaction, Dissatisfaction and Complaining Behavior*, 14, 46–54.

East, R., Lomax, W. and Willson, G. (1991a) *Demand Over Time: Attitudes, Knowledge and Habits that Affect When Customers Use Supermarkets*, Working Paper, Kingston Business School.

East, R., Lomax, W. and Willson, G. (1991b) Factors associated with service delay in supermarkets and post offices, *Journal of Consumer Satisfaction, Dissatisfaction and Complaining Behaviour*, 4, 123–128.

East, R., Lomax, W., Willson, G. and Harris, P. (1992) *Demand Over Time: Attitudes, Knowledge and Habits that Affect When Customers Use Banks and Building Societies*, Working Paper, Kingston Business School.

East, R., Lomax, W., Willson, G. and Harris, P. (1994) Decision making and habit in shopping times, *European Journal of Marketing*, 28(4), 56–71.

East, R., Whittaker, D. and Swift, A. (1984) *Measuring the Factors that Affect Product Take-up: Key Beliefs about Breakfast TV in Britain*, Working Paper, Kingston Business School.

Edwards, W. (1954) The theory of decision making, *Psychological Bulletin*, 51(4), 380–417.

Effective Advertising 6 (2001) Advertising Federation of Australia, South Yarra, Victoria, Hardie Grant Books.

Effective Advertising 8 (2006) Sydney: Advertising Federation of Australia Advertising Effectiveness Awards.

Ehrenberg, A.S.C. (1959) The pattern of consumer purchases, *Applied Statistics*, 8, 26–41.

Ehrenberg, A.S.C. (1969) The discovery and use of laws of marketing, *Journal of Advertising Research*, 9(2), 11–17.

Ehrenberg, A.S.C. (1986) Pricing and brand differentiation, *Singapore Marketing Review*, 1, 5–15.

Ehrenberg, A.S.C. (1988) *Repeat Buying: Theory and Applications* (2nd edn), London: Charles Griffin & Co. (first published in 1972 by North Holland)

Ehrenberg, A.S.C. and England, L.R. (1990) Generalising a pricing effect. *The Journal of Industrial Economics*, 39(1), 47–68.

Ehrenberg, A.S.C. and Goodhardt, G.J. (1968) Repeat-buying of a new brand – a 10-point case history, *British Journal of Marketing*, 2(3), 200–205.

Ehrenberg, A.S.C and Goodhardt, G.J. (1979) *Essays on Understanding Buyer Behavior*, New York: J. Walter Thompson Co. and Market Research Corporation of America.

Ehrenberg, A.S.C., Goodhardt, G.J. and Barwise, T.P. (1990) Double jeopardy revisited, *Journal of Marketing*, 54(3), 82–90.

Ehrenberg, A.S.C., Hammond, K.A. and Goodhardt, G.J. (1994) The after-effects of price-related consumer promotions, *Journal of Advertising Research*, 34(4), 11–21.

Ehrenberg, A.S.C., Uncles, M.D. and Carrie, D. (1994) Armed to the teeth: an exercise in brand management. Cranfield, UK: European Case Clearing House (reference M94-005:594-039-1/594-039-4/594-040-1/594-040-4).

Ehrenberg, A.S.C., Uncles, M.D. and Goodhardt, G.J. (2004) Understanding brand performance measures: using Dirichlet benchmarks, *Journal of Business Research*, 57(12), 1307–1325.

Ehrenburg, A.S.C. and Goodhardt, G.J. (2001) New brands: Near-instant loyalty, *Journal of Targeting, Measurement and Analysis in Marketing*, 10(1), 9–16.

Elliott, R. (1993) Shopping addiction and mood repair. In M. Davies et al. (eds), *Emerging Issues in Marketing: Proceedings of the Marketing Education Group*, Loughborough, Loughborough University Press, 287–296.

Elliott, R. (1994) Addictive consumption: function and fragmentation in postmodernity, *Journal of Consumer Policy*, 17, 159–179.

Elliott, R., Eccles, S. and Gournay, K. (1996) Man management? Women and the use of debt to control personal relationships, *Proceedings of the XXnd Marketing Education Group Conference*, Strathclyde, available on compact disk, Buyer Behavior track.

Elliott, R., Jobber, D., and Sharp, J. (1995) Using the theory of reasoned action to understand organizational behaviour: The role of belief salience, *British Journal of Social Psychology*, 34(2), 161–172.

Elliott, R. and Jobber, D. (1990) Understanding organizational buying behaviour: the role of cognitions, norms and attitudes, *Proceedings of the 23rd Marketing Education Group Conference*, Oxford Polytechnic, 402–423.

Ennew, C.T. and Binks, M.R. (1996) The impact of service quality and service characteristics on customer retention: small businesses and their banks in the UK, *British Journal of Management*, 7, 219–230.

Enis, B.M. and Paul, G.W. (1970) Store loyalty as a basis for marketing segmentation, *Journal of Retailing*, 46(3), 42–56.

Eroglu, S.A., Machleit, K.A. and Davis, L.M. (2003) Empirically testing a model of online store atmospherics and shopper responses, *Psychology and Marketing*, 20(2), 139–150.

Eskin, G. (1973) Dynamic forecasts of new product demands using a depth of repeat model, *Journal of Marketing Research*, 10(2), 115–129.

Etgar, M.E. and Malhotra, N.K. (1981) Determinants of price dependency: personal and perceptual factors, *Journal of Consumer Research*, 8(2), 217–223.

Faber, R.J. and O'Guinn, T.C. (1992) A clinical screener for compulsive buying, *Journal of Consumer Research* 19(3), 459–469.

Faber, R.J. and O'Guinn, T.C. (1988) Compulsive consumption and credit abuse, *Journal of Consumer Policy*, 11, 97–109.

Fader, P.S., Hardie, B.G.S. and Huang, C.Y. (2004) A dynamic changepoint model for new product sales forecasting, *Marketing Science*, 23(1), 50–65.

Fader, P.S., Hardie, B.G.S. and Zeithammer, R. (2003) Forecasting new product trial in a controlled test market environment, *Journal of Forecasting*, 22(5), 391–410.

Farris, P.W. and Albion, M.S. (1980) The impact of advertising on the price of consumer goods, *Journal of Marketing*, 44(3), 17–35.

Farris, P.W. and Reibstein, D.J. (1991) How prices, ad expenditures, and profits are linked, *Harvard Business Review*, 57(6), 173–184.

Fazio, R.H. (1986) How do attitudes guide behavior? In R.M. Sorrentino and E.T. Higgins (eds), *The Handbook of Motivation and Cognition: Foundations of Social Behavior*, New York: Guilford Press, 204–243.

Fazio, R.H. (1990) Multiple processes by which attitudes guide behavior: the mode model as an integrative framework. In M.P. Zanna (ed.), *Advances in Experimental Social Psychology*, 23, 75–109.

Fazio, R.H., Powell, M.C. and Herr, P.M. (1983) Toward a process model of the attitude–behavior relation: accessing one's attitude upon mere observation of the attitude object, *Journal of Personality and Social Psychology*, 44, 723–735.

Fazio, R.H. and Zanna, M. (1981) Direct experience and attitude–behavior consistency. In L. Berkowitz (ed.), *Advances in Experimental Social Psychology*, 14, New York: Academic Press, 161–202.

Feick, L.F. and Price, L.L. (1987) The market maven: a diffuser of marketplace information, *Journal of Marketing*, 51(1), 83–97.

Feinberg, R.A. and Smith, P. (1989) Misperceptions of time in the sales transaction. In T. Srull (ed.), *Advances in Consumer Research*, 16, 56–58.

Feinberg, R.A., Widdows, R., Hirsch-Wyncott, M. and Trappey, C. (1990) Myth and reality in customer service: good and bad service sometimes lead to repurchase, *Journal of Consumer Satisfaction, Dissatisfaction and Complaining Behavior*, 3, 112–113.

Feinberg, R.A., Widdows, R. and Steidle, R. (1996) Customer (dis)satisfaction and delays, *Journal of Consumer Satisfaction, Dissatisfaction and Complaining Behavior*, 9, 81–85.

Feldwick, P. (1990) *Advertising Works 5*, Henley-on-Thames: Institute of Practitioners in Advertising, NTC Publications.

Ferber, R. (1954) The role of planning in consumer purchase of durable goods, *American Economics Review*, 44(5), 854–874.

Finn, D.W. and Lamb, C.W. Jr. (1991) An evaluation of the SERVQUAL scale in a retail setting. In R.H. Holman and M.R. Solomon (eds), *Advances in Consumer Research*, 18, 483–490.

Fishbein, M. (1963) An investigation of the relationships between beliefs about an object and attitudes to that object, *Human Relations*, 16, 233–240.

Fishbein, M. (1977) *Consumer Beliefs and Behavior with Respect to Cigarette Smoking: A Critical Analysis of the Public Literature. A Report to the U.S. Federal Trades Commission*.

Fishbein, M. and Ajzen, I. (1975) *Belief, Attitude, Intention and Behavior*, Reading, MA: Addison-Wesley.

Fishbein, M.F. and Ajzen, I. (1981) On construct validity: a critique of Miniard and Cohen's paper, *Journal of Experimental Social Psychology*, 17, 340–350.

Fisher, J.C. and Pry, R.H. (1971) A simple substitution model of technological change, *Technological Forecasting and Social Change*, 3, 75–88.

Fiske, S.T. (1980) Attention and weight in person perception: the impact of negative and extreme behavior, *Journal of Personality and Social Psychology*, 38(6), 889–906.

Fitzsimons, G.J. and Lehmann, D.R. (2004) When unsolicited advice yields contrary responses, *Marketing Science*, 23(1), 82–95.

Flavián, C., Martínez, E. and Polo, Y. (2001) Loyalty to grocery stores in the Spanish market of the 1900s, *Journal of Retailing and Consumer Services*, 8(2), 85–93.

Folkes, V.S. (1984) Consumer reactions to product failure: an attributional approach, *Journal of Consumer Research*, 10(4), 398–409.

Folkes, V.S. (1988) The availability heuristic and perceived risk, *Journal of Consumer Research*, 15(1), 13–23.

Folkes, V.S., Koletsky, S. and Graham, J.L. (1987) A field study of causal inferences and consumer reaction: the view from the airport, *Journal of Consumer Research*, 13(4), 534–539.

Fornell, C. (1992) A national customer satisfaction barometer: the Swedish experience, *Journal of Marketing*, 56(1), 6–21.

Fornell, C and Wernerfelt, B. (1988) A model for customer complaining management, *Marketing Science*, 7(3), Summer, 187–98.

Fornell, C., Mithas, S., Morgeson, F. and Krishnan, M.S. (2006) Customer satisfaction and stock prices: high returns, low risks, *Journal of Marketing*, 70(1), 3–14.

Fournier, S., Dobscha, S. and Mick, D.G. (1998) Preventing the premature death of relationship marketing, *Harvard Business Review*, January/February, 42–51.

Fourt, L.A. and Woodlock, J.W. (1960) Early prediction of market success for new grocery products, *Journal of Marketing*, 25(2), 31–38.

Foxall, G. and Hackett, P.M.W. (1992) Consumers' perception of micro-retail location: wayfinding and cognitive mapping in planned and organic shopping environments, *International Review of Retail, Distribution and Consumer Research*, 2(3), 309–327.

Fredricks, A.J. and Dossett, K.L. (1983) Attitude–behavior relations: a comparison of the Fishbein–Ajzen and the Bentler–Speckart models, *Journal of Personality and Social Psychology*, 45, 501–512.

Frisbie, G.A. Jr. (1980) Ehrenberg's negative binomial model applied to grocery store trips, *Journal of Marketing Research*, 17, 385–390.

Fulgoni, G.M. (1987) The role of advertising – is there one? *Admap*, 262, 54–57.

Gabor, A. and Granger, C.W.J. (1961) On the price consciousness of consumers, *Applied Statistics*, 10, 170–188.

Gabor, A. and Granger, C.W.J. (1966) Price as an indicator of quality: report on an inquiry, *Economica*, 32, 43–70.

Gabor, A. and Granger, C.W.J. (1972) Ownership and acquisition of consumer durables: report on the Nottingham consumer durables project, *European Journal of Marketing*, 6(4), 234–248.

Gardner, A.G. and Levy, S.J. (1955) The product and the brand, *Harvard Business Review*, 33 (March–April), 33–39.

Garretson, J.A. and Burton, S. (2003) Highly coupon and sale prone consumers: benefits beyond price savings, *Journal of Advertising Research*, 43(2), 162–172.

Gerard, H.B. (1967) Choice difficulty, dissonance and the decision sequence, *Journal of Personality and Social Psychology*, 35(1), 91–108.

Gigerenzer, G. (1991) How to make cognitive illusions disappear: beyond 'heuristics and biases'. In W. Stroebe, and M. Hewstone (eds), *European Review of Social Psychology*, 2, 83–115.

Gijsbrechts, E. (1993) Prices and pricing research in consumer marketing: some recent developments, *International Journal of Research in Marketing*, 10(2), 115–151.

Gilly, M. and Gelb, B. (1982) Post-purchase consumer processes and the complaining consumer, *Journal of Consumer Research*, 9(3), 323–328.

Givon, M. and Horsky, D. (1990) Untangling the effects of purchase reinforcement and advertising carryover, *Marketing Science*, 9(2), 171–187.

Gladwell, M. (2000) *The Tipping Point*, Boston: Little Brown and Co.

Godes, D. and Mayzlin, D. (2004a) *Firm-created Word-of-mouth Communication: a Field-based Quasi-experiment*, Harvard Business School Marketing Research Papers No. 04–03.

Godes, D. and Mayzlin, D. (2004b) Using online conversations to study word-of-mouth communication, *Marketing Science*, 23(4), 545–560.

Goodey, C. and East, R. (2008, forthcoming). Testing the market maven concept, *Journal of Marketing Management*.

Goodhardt, G.J. and Ehrenberg, A.S.C. (1967) Conditional trend analysis: a breakdown by initial purchasing level, *Journal of Marketing Research*, 4(2), 155–161.

Goodhardt, G.J., Ehrenberg, A.S.C. and Chatfield, C. (1984) The Dirichlet: a comprehensive model of buying behaviour, *Journal of the Royal Statistical Society*, A, 147, 621–655.

Goodhardt, G.J., Ehrenberg, A.S.C. and Collins, M.A. (1975) *The Television Audience: Patterns of Viewing*, Lexington, MA: Lexington Books.

Goodhardt, G.J., Ehrenberg, A.S.C. and Collins, M.A. (1987) *The Television Audience: Patterns of Viewing, An Update*, Aldershot: Gower.

Goodman, J. and Newman, S. (2003) Understanding customer behavior and complaints. TARP (Technical Assistance Research Programs), available via www.asq.org.

Gourville, J.T. (1998) Pennies-a-day: the effect of temporal reframing on transaction evaluation, *Journal of Consumer Research*, 24(4), 395–409.

Granbois, D., Summers, J.O. and Frazier, G.L. (1977) Correlates of consumer expectation and complaining behavior. In Day, R.L. (ed) *Consumer Satisfaction, Dissatisfaction and Complaining Behavior*. Bloomington, Indiana University, 18–25.

Granovetter, M.S. (1973) The strength of weak ties, *American Journal of Sociology*, 78(6), 1360–1380.

Green, L. (2007) *Advertising Works 15*, IPA Effectiveness Awards 2006, Henley-on-Thames: World Advertising Research Center (WARC).

Green, P.E. and Krieger, A.M. (2002) What's right with conjoint analysis?, *Marketing Research*, 14(1), 24–27.

Green, P.E., Krieger, A.M. and Wind, Y. (2001) Thirty years of conjoint analysis: reflections and prospects, *Interfaces*, 31(3), S56–S73.

Greenfield, S. (1997) *The Human Brain: A Guided Tour*, London: Phoenix.

Grewal, D., Kavanoor, S., Fern, E.F., Costley, C. and Barnes, J. (1997) Comparative versus non-comparative advertising: a meta-analysis, *Journal of Marketing*, 61(4), 1–15.

Grønhaug, K. (1977) Exploring complaining behavior: a model and some empirical results. In Perreault, W.D.Jr. (ed.) *Advances in Consumer Research*, 4, 159–163.

Grønhaug, K. and Zaltman, G. (1981) Complainers and noncomplainers revisited: Another look at the data. In Monroe, K.B. (ed.) *Advances in Consumer Research*, 8, 83–87.

Grönroos, C. (1978) A service-oriented approach to marketing service, *European Journal of Marketing*, 12(8), 588–601.

Grönroos, C. (1994) From marketing mix to relationship marketing: towards a paradigm shift in marketing, *Management Decision*, 32(2), 4–20.

Gröppel, A. (1993) Store design and experience-orientated consumers in retailing: comparison between United States and Germany. In W.F. van Raaij and G.J. Bamossy (eds), *European Advances in Consumer Research*, 1, 99–109.

Gruca, T.S. and Rego, L.L. (2005) Customer satisfaction, cash flow and shareholder value, *Journal of Marketing*, 69(3), 115–130.

Gupta, S. (1988) Impact of sales promotions on when, what, and how much to buy, *Journal of Marketing Research*, 25(4), 342–355.

Gupta, S., Lehmann, D.R. and Stuart, J.A. (2004) Valuing customers, *Journal of Marketing Research*, 41(1), 7–18.

Gupta, S., Van Heerde, H.J. and Wittink, D.R. (2003) Is 75% of the sales promotion bump due to brand switching? No, only 33% is, *Journal of Marketing Research*, 40(4), 481–491.

Habel, C. and Rungie, C. (2005) Drawing a double jeopardy line, *Marketing Bulletin*, 16, Technical Note 1, 1–10.

Halstead, D. (1993) Five common myths about consumer satisfaction programs, *Journal of Service Marketing*, 7(3), 4–12.

Halstead, D. (2002) Negative word of mouth: substitute for or supplement to consumer complaints, *Journal of Consumer Satisfaction, Dissatisfaction and Complaining Behavior*, 15, 1–12.

Hamilton, W., East, R. and Kalafatis, S. (1997) The measurement and utility of brand price elasticities, *Journal of Marketing Management*, 13(4), 285–298.

Hammond, K.A. and Ehrenberg, A.S.C. (1995) Heavy buyers: how many do you have? How important are they? In M. Bergardaá (ed.), *Marketing Today and for the 21st Century. 24th EMAC Conference Proceedings*, Essec, Paris, 1651–1656.

Hammond, K.A., Ehrenberg, A.S.C. and Goodhardt, G.J. (1996) Market segmentation for competitive brands, *European Journal of Marketing*, 30(12), 39–49.

Hanna, N. and Wosniak, R. (2001) *Consumer Behavior: An Applied Approach*. Englewood Cliffs, NJ: Prentice-Hall.

Hanssens, D.M., Parsons, L.J. and Schultz, R.L. (2001) *Market Response Models: Econometric and Time Series Analysis*, 2nd edition Dordrecht, Netherlands: Kluwer Academic Publishers.

Hardie, B.G.S., Fader, P.S. and Wisniewski, M. (1998) An empirical comparison of new product trial forecasting models, *Journal of Forecasting*, 17(3/4), 209–229.

Hardie, B.G.S., Johnson, E.J. and Fader, P.S. (1993) Modeling loss aversion and reference dependence effects on brand choice, *Marketing Science*, 12(4), 378–395.

Harrison, A.A. (1968) Response competition, frequency, exploratory behavior and liking, *Journal of Personality and Social Psychology*, 9(4), 363–368.

Hartman, C.L., Price, L.L. and Duncan, C.P. (1990) Consumer evaluation of franchise extension products. In M.E. Goldberg, G. Gorn and R. Pollay (eds) *Advances in Consumer Research*, 17, 110–127.

Hartnett, M. (2006) Coupons still king, *Frozen Food Age*, 55(3) October.

Heilman, C.M., Nakamoto, K. and Rao, A.G. (2002) Pleasant surprises: consumer response to unexpected in-store coupons, *Journal of Marketing Research*, 39(2), 242–252.

Helson, H. (1964) *Adaptation Level Theory*, New York: Harper & Row.

Hennig-Thurau, T. and Klee, A. (1997) The impact of customer satisfaction and relationship quality on customer retention: a critical reassessment and model development, *Psychology and Marketing*, 14(8), 737–764.

Hensher, D.A., Rose, J.M. and Greene, W.H. (2005) *Applied Choice Analysis: A Primer*, Cambridge: Cambridge University Press.

Herr, P.M., Kardes, F.R. and Kim, J. (1991) Effects of word-of-mouth and product-attribute information on persuasion: an accessibility-diagnosticity perspective, *Journal of Consumer Research*, 17(March), 454–462.

Heskett, J.L., Sasser, W.E. Jr. and Schlesinger, L.A. (1997) *The Service Profit Chain*. New York: The Free Press.

Hirschman, A.O. (1970) *Exit, Voice and Loyalty: Responses to Decline in Firms, Organizations and States*, Cambridge, MA: Harvard University Press.

Hoad, A. (2005) *Advertising Works 13*, Henley-on-Thames: Institute of Practitioners in Advertising, World Advertising Research Center, 123–144.

Hoch, S.J., Drèze, X. and Purk, M.E. (1994) EDLP, Hi-Lo, and margin arithmetic, *Journal of Marketing*, 58(4), 16–28.

Howard, J.A. and Sheth, J.N. (1969) *The Theory of Buyer Behavior*, New York: Wiley.

Huefner, J.C. and Hunt, H.K. (1994) Extending the Hirschman model: when voice and exit don't tell the whole story, *Journal of Satisfaction, Dissatisfaction and Complaining Behavior*, 7, 267–270.

Huff, D.L. (1962) *Determination of Intra-Urban Retail Trade Areas*, Los Angeles: University of California, Real Estate Research Program.

Huff, D.L. (1981) Retail location theory. In R.W. Stampfl and E.C. Hirschman (eds), *Theory in Retailing: Traditional and Non-Traditional Sources*, Chigago: American Marketing Association, 108–121.

Hui, M.K. and Bateson, J.E.G. (1991) Perceived control and the effects of crowding and consumer choice on the service experience, *Journal of Consumer Research*, 18(2), 174–184.

Hunt, H.K., Hunt, D. and Hunt, T. (1988) Consumer grudge holding, *Journal of Consumer Satisfaction, Dissatisfaction and Complaining Behavior*, 1, 116–118.

Inman, J.J., McAlister, L. and Hoyer, W.D. (1990) Promotion signal: proxy for a price cut?, *Journal of Consumer Research*, 17(1), 74–82.

IRI (1989) Larger sample, stronger proof of P-O-P effectiveness. Reprinted from IRI which enlarges on a report that first appeared in *P-O-P Times*, March/ April, 28–32, 1989.

Jaccard, J.J. and Davidson, A.R. (1972) Toward an understanding of family planning behaviors: an initial investigation, *Journal of Applied Social Psychology*, 2(3), 228–235.

Jacoby, J. and Olson, J.C. (1970) *An Attitudinal Model of Brand Loyalty: Conceptual Underpinnings and Instrumentation Research*. Purdue Paper in Consumer Psychology, No. 159, Purdue University, West Lafayette, IN.

Jarratt, D.E. (1996) A shopper typology for retail strategy development, *The International Journal of Retail, Distribution and Consumer Research*, 6 (2), 196–215.

Jones, E.E. and Nisbett, R.E. (1972) The actor and observer: divergent perceptions of the causes of behavior. In E.E. Jones, D.E. Kanouse, H.H. Kelley, R.E. Nisbett, S. Valins and B. Weiner (eds), *Attribution: Perceiving the Causes of Behavior*, Morristown, NJ: General Learning Press, 79–94.

Jones, J.P. (1995a) *When Ads Work: New Proof that Advertising Triggers Sales*, New York: Lexington Books.

Jones, J.P. (1995b) Single source research begins to fulfill its promise, *Journal of Advertising Research*, 35(3), 9–16.

Jones, J.P. (1995c) Advertising exposure effects under a microscope, *Admap*, February, 28–31.

Jones, T.O. and Sasser, W.E. (1995) Why satisfied customers defect, *Harvard Business Review*, Nov.–Dec., 88–99.

Juster, F.T. (1966) Consumer buying intentions and purchase probability: an experiment in survey design, *Journal of the American Statistical Association*, 61(September), 658–696.

Kahn, B.E. and McAlister, L. (1997) *Grocery Revolution: The New Focus on the Consumer*, Reading, MA: Addison-Wesley.

Kahn, B.E., Morrison, D.G. and Wright, G.P. (1986) Aggregating individual purchases to the household level, *Marketing Science*, 5(3), 260–268.

Kahn, B.E. and Schmittlein, D.C. (1989) Shopping trip behavior: an empirical investigation, *Marketing Letters*, 1(1), 55–69.

Kahneman, D. (2002) Presentation following the award of the Nobel Prize for Economics. http://nobelprize.org/nobel_prizes/economics/laureates/2002/kahneman-lecture.html.

Kahneman, D., Knetsch, J. and Thaler, R. (1991a) Anomalies: the endowment effect, loss aversion, and status quo bias, *Journal of Economic Perspectives*, 5(1), 193–206. Reprinted in D. Kahneman and A. Tversky (2000) *Choices, Values, and Frames*, New York: Russell Sage Foundation, Cambridge University Press, 159–170.

Kahneman, D., Knetsch, J.L. and Thaler, R.H. (1991b) Fairness as a constraint on profit seeking: entitlements in the market. In R.H. Thaler (ed.), *Quasi Rational Economics*, New York: Russell Sage Foundation, 199–219.

Kahneman, D., Knetsch, J.L. and Thaler, R.H. (1991c) Fairness and the assumption of economics. In R.H. Thaler (ed.) *Qusai Rational Economics*. New York: Russell Sage Foundation, 220–235.

Kahneman, D. and Tversky, A. (1979) Prospect theory: an analysis of decision under risk, *Econometrica*, 47, 263–291. Reprinted in D. Kahneman and A. Tversky (2000) *Choices, Values, and Frames*, New York: Russell Sage Foundation, Cambridge University Press, 17–43.

Kahneman, D. and Tversky, A. (1996) On the reality of cognitive illusions, *Psychological Review*, 103(3), 582–591. Also available at: http://psy.ucsd.edu/~mckenzie/KahnemanTversky1996 PsychRev.pdf

Kahneman, D. and Tversky, A. (2000) *Choices, Values and Frames*, New York: Russell Sage Foundation, Cambridge University Press.

Kahneman, D., Slovic, P. and Tversky, A. (1982) *Judgment under Uncertainty: Heuristics and Biases*, Cambridge: Cambridge University Press. pp. 117–28.

Kalwani, M.U. and Yim, C.K. (1990) A price expectations model of customer brand choice, *Journal of Marketing Research*, 27(3), 251–262.

Kalyanaram, G. and Little, J.D.C. (1994) An empirical analysis of latitude of price acceptance in consumer package goods, *Journal of Consumer Research*, 21(3), 408–419.

Kalyanaram, G. and Winer, R.S. (1995) Empirical generalizations from reference price research, *Marketing Science*, 14(3), G161–G170.

Kamakura, W.A. and Russell, G.J. (1991) *Measuring Consumer Perceptions of Brand Quality with Scanner Data: Implications for Brand Equity*, Report 91–122, Cambridge, MA: Marketing Science Institute.

Kardes, F.R., Cronley, M.L., Kellaris, J.J. and Posanac S.S. (2004) The role of selective information processing in price-quality inference, *Journal of Consumer Research*, 31(2), 368–374.

Katona, G. (1947) Contribution of psychological data to economic analysis, *Journal of the American Statistical Association*, 42, 449–459.

Katz, E. (1961) The social itinerary of technical change: two studies on the diffusion of innovation, *Human Organization*, 20(Summer), 70–82.

Katz, K., Larson, B. and Larson, R. (1991) Prescription for waiting-in-line blues: entertain, enlighten, and engage, *Sloan Management Review*, 32, 44–53.

Katz, E. and Lazarsfeld, P.F. (1955) *Personal Influence*, Glencoe, IL: The Free Press.

Kau, A.K. and Ehrenberg, A.S.C. (1984) Patterns of store choice, *Journal of Marketing Research*, 21(4), 399–409.

Kaul, A. and Wittink, D.R. (1995) Empirical generalizations about the impact of advertising on price sensitivity and price, *Marketing Science*, 14(3, Part 2 of 2), G151–G160.

Keaveney, S.M. (1995) Customer switching behavior in service industries: an exploratory study, *Journal of Marketing*, 59(2), 71–82.

Keiningham, T.L., Cooil, B., Andreasson, T.W. and Aksoy, L. (2007a) A longitudinal examination of 'net promoter' and firm revenue growth, *Journal of Marketing*, 71(3), 39–51.

Keiningham, T.L., Cooil, B., Aksoy, L., Andreassen, T.W. and Weiner, J. (2007b) The value of different customer satisfaction and loyalty metrics in predicting customer retention, recommendation, and share-of-wallet, *Managing Service Quality* 17(4), 361–384.

Keller, E. and Fay, B. (2006) Single-source WOM measurement: bringing together senders' and receivers' inputs and outputs. In W.J. Carl (ed.), *Measuring Word of Mouth,* (Vol. 2), Chicago: Word of Mouth Marketing Association, 31–41.

Keller, K.L. (2002) Branding and brand equity. In Weitz, B. and Wensley, R. (2002), (Eds) *Handbook of Marketing*, London: Sage Publications Ltd, 155–178.

Keller, K.L. (1993) Conceptualizing, measuring, and managing customer-based brand equity, *Journal of Marketing*, 57(1), 1–22.

Keller, K.L. and Aaker, D.A. (1992) The effects of sequential introduction of brand extensions, *Journal of Marketing Research*, 29(1), 35–52.

Kendall, N. (1998) *Advertising Works 10*, Henley-on-Thames: NTC Publications.

Kimmel, A. and Audrain-Pontevia, A.-F. (2007) *Consumer Response to Marketplace Rumors: An Exploratory Cross-Cultural Analysis*. Proceedings of the 36th EMAC conference, Reykjavik University, Iceland.

Kimmel, A.J. (2004a) Rumors and the financial marketplace, *The Journal of Behavioral Finance*, 5, 232–239.

Kimmel, A.J. (2004b) *Rumors and Rumor Control: A Manager's Guide to Understanding and Combating Rumors*, Mahwah, NJ: Lawrence Erlbaum Associates Inc.

Klein, G.A. (1989) Recognition-primed decisions. In W.B. Rouse (ed.), *Advances in Man–Machine System Research*, 5, Greenwich, CT: JAI Press, 47–92.

Knapp, A. (1944) A psychology of rumor, *Public Opinion Quarterly*, 8, 22–27.

Knox, S.D. and de Chernatony, L. (1994) Attitude, personal norms and intentions. In M. Jenkins and S. Knox (eds), *Advances in Consumer Marketing*, London: Kogan Page, 85–98.

Knox, S.D. and Denison, T.J. (2000) Store loyalty: its impact on retail revenue. An empirical study of purchasing behaviour in the UK, *Journal of Retailing and Consumer Services*, 7(1), 33–45.

Koelemeijer, K. (1992) Measuring perceived service quality in retailing: a comparison of methods. In K. Grunert (ed.), *Marketing for Europe – Marketing for the Future*, Proceedings of the 21st Annual Conference of the European Marketing Academy, Aarhus, Denmark, 729–744.

Koepp, S. (1987) Pul-eeze! Will someone help me? *Time*, 2 February, 28–34.

Kordupleski, R.E., Rust, R.T. and Zahoric, A.J. (1993) Why improving quality does not improve retention (or whatever happened to marketing?), *California Management Review*, Spring, 82–95.

Kotler, P. (1973) Atmosphere as a marketing tool, *Journal of Retailing*, 49(4), 48–63.

Kotzan, J.A. and Evanson, R.V. (1969) Responsiveness of drug stores sales to shelf space allocations, *Journal of Marketing Research* 6(4), 465–469.

Krishnan, H.S. (1996) Characteristics of memory associations: a consumer-based brand equity perspective, *International Journal of Research in Marketing*, 13(4), 389–405.

Kristiansen, C.M. (1987) Salient beliefs regarding smoking: consistency across samples and smoking status, *Journal of the Institute of Health Education*, 25, 73–6.

Krueckeberg, H.F. (1969) The significance of consumer response to display space reallocation, *Proceedings of the American Marketing Association Fall Conference*, 30, 336–339.

Krugman, H.E. (1972) Why three exposures may be enough, *Journal of Advertising Research*, 12(6), 11–14.

Kuehn, A.A. (1962) Consumer brand choice as a learning process, *Journal of Advertising Research*, 2(December), 10–17.

Kumar, N., Scheer, L.K. and Steenkamp, J.-B.E.M. (1995) The effects of supplier fairness on vulnerable resellers, *Journal of Marketing Research*, 32(1), 54–65.

Kunst-Wilson, W.R. and Zajonc, R.B. (1980) Affective discrimination of stimuli that cannot be recognised, *Science*, 207, 557–558.

Laczniak, R.N., DeCarlo, T.E., and Ramaswamy, S.N. (2001) Consumers' responses to negative word-of-mouth communication: An attribution theory perspective, *Journal of Consumer Psychology*, 11(1), 57–74.

Lapersonne, E., Laurent, G. and Le Goff, J-J. (1995) Consideration sets of size one: an empirical investigation of automobile purchases, *International Journal of Research in Marketing*, 12(1), 55–66.

LaTour, S.A. and Peat, N.C. (1979) Conceptual and methodological issues in consumer satisfaction research. In W.L. Wilkie (ed.), *Advances in Consumer Research*, 6, 431–437.

Le Boutillier, J., Le Boutillier, S.S. and Neslin, S.A. (1994) A replication and extension of the Dickson and Sawyer price-awareness study, *Marketing Letters*, 5(1), 31–42.

Leclerc, F., Schmitt, B.H. and Dubé, L. (1995) Waiting time and decision making: is time like money?, *Journal of Consumer Research*, 22(1), 110–119.

Lee, A.Y. (1994) The mere exposure effect: is it a mere case of misattribution? In C.T. Allen and D.R. John (eds), *Advances in Consumer Research*, 21, 270–275.

Leenheer, J., van Heerde, H.J., Bijmolt, T.H.A. and Smidts, A. (2007) Do loyalty programs really enhance behavioural loyalty? An empirical analysis accounting for self-selecting members, *International Journal of Research in Marketing*, 24(1), 31–47.

Lees, G.J., Garland, B.R. and Wright, M.J. (2007) Switching banks: old bank gone but not forgotten, *Journal of Financial Services Marketing*, 12(2), 146–156.

Lemon, K.N. and Nowlis, S.M. (2002) Developing synergies between promotions and brands in different price-quality tiers, *Journal of Marketing Research*, 39(2), 171–185.

Lichtenstein, D.R. and Bearden, W.O. (1989) Contextual influences on perceptions of merchant-supplied reference prices, *Journal of Consumer Research*, 16(1), 55–67.

Lichtenstein, S., Slovic, P., Fischoff, B., Lyman, M. and Combs, B. (1978) Judged frequency of lethal events, *Journal of Experimental Psychology: Human Learning and Memory*, 4, 551–578.

Lilien, G.L. and Rangaswamy, A. (2002) *Marketing Engineering: Computer-assisted Marketing Analysis and Planning* (2nd edn), Upper Saddle River, NJ: Prentice-Hall.

Litzenroth, H. (1991) A small town in Germany: single source data from a controlled micro-market, *Admap*, 26(5), 23–27.

Liu, Y. (2006) Word of mouth for movies: its dynamics and influence on box office revenue, *Journal of Marketing*, 70(3), 74–89.

Lodish, L.M., Abraham, M., Kalmansen, S., Livelsberger, J., Lubetkin, B., Richardson, B. and Stevens, M.E. (1995a) How TV advertising works: a meta-analysis of 389 real-world split cable TV advertising experiments, *Journal of Marketing Research*, 32(2), 125–139.

Lodish, L.M., Abraham, M., Livelsberger, J., Lubetkin, B., Richardson, B. and Stevens, M.E. (1995b) A summary of fifty-five in-market experiments on the long-term effect of TV advertising, *Marketing Science*, 14(Part 2 of 2), G133–G140.

Lodish, L.M. and Lubetkin, B. (1992) How advertising works. General truths? Nine key findings from IRI test data, *Admap*, February, 9–15.

Loken, B. (1983) The theory of reasoned action: examination of the sufficiency assumption for a television viewing behavior. In R.P. Bagozzi and A.M. Tybout (eds), *Advances in Consumer Research*, 10, Ann Arbor, MI: Association for Consumer Research, 100–105.

Lomax, W., Hammond, K., Clemente, M. and East, R. (1996) New entrants in a mature market: an empirical study of the detergent market, *Journal of Marketing Management*, 12(4), 281–95.

Losch, A. (1939) *The Economics of Location*, translated by W.H. Woglom and F. Stolper (1954), New Haven, CT: Yale University Press.

Macintosh, G. and Lockshin, L.S. (1997) Retail relationships and store loyalty: a multi-level perspective, *International Journal of Research in Marketing*, 14(5), 487–497.

Madden, T.J., Ellen, P.S. and Ajzen, I. (1992) A comparison of the theory of planned behavior and the theory of reasoned action, *Personality and Social Psychology Bulletin*, 18(1), 3–9.

Magee, A. (1994) Compulsive buying tendency as a predictor of attitudes and perceptions. In C.T. Allen and D.R. John (eds), *Advances in Consumer Research*, 21, 590–4.

Magnini, V.P., Ford, J.B., Markowski, E.P. and Honeycut, E.D. Jr (2007) The service recovery paradox: justifiable theory or smouldering myth, *Journal of Services Marketing*, 21(3), 213–224.

Mahajan, V., Muller, E. and Bass, F.M. (1990) New product diffusion models in marketing: a review and directions for research, *Journal of Marketing*, 54(1), 1–26.

Maister, D.H. (1985) The psychology of waiting lines. In J.A. Czepiel, M.R. Solomon and C.F. Surprenant (eds), *The Service Encounter*, Lexington, MA: D.C. Heath, 113–124.

Malafi, T.N., Cini, M.A., Taub, S.L. and Bertolami, J. (1993) Social influence and the decision to complain: investigations on the role of advice, *Journal of Consumer Satisfaction, Dissatisfaction and Complaining Behavior*, 6, 81–89.

Malec, J. (1982) Ad testing through the marriage of UPC scanning and targetable TV, *Admap*, May, 273–279.

Mangold, W.G., Miller, F. and Brockway, G.R. (1999) Word-of-mouth communication in the service marketplace, *Journal of Services Marketing*, 13(1), 73–89.

Marcel, J. (1976) Unconscious reading: experiments on people who do not know they are reading. Paper presented at the British Association for the Advancement of Science, Lancaster, UK.

Markus, H. and Zajonc, R.B. (1985) The cognitive perspective in social psychology. In G. Lindzey and E. Aronson (eds), *Handbook of Social Psychology*, 3rd edition, (Vol. 1), New York: Random House, 137–230.

Marsh, P., Barwise, P., Thomas, K. and Wensley, R. (1988) *Managing Strategic Investment Decisions in Large Diversified Companies*, Working Paper, London Business School reviewed in *The Economist*, 9 July, 1988.

Marsh, A. and Matheson, J. (1983) *Smoking Attitudes and Behaviour: An Enquiry Carried Out on Behalf of the Department of Health and Social Security*, London: HMSO.

Marx, K. (1930) *Capital*, vol. 1, 2 and 3. London: J.M. Dent & Sons Ltd.

Mason, N. (1991) *An Investigation into Grocery Shopping Behaviour in Britain*, Headington, Oxford: Nielsen Consumer Research.

Mattila, A.S. and Wirtz, J. (2001) Congruency of scent and music as a driver of in-store evaluations and behavior, *Journal of Retailing*, 77(2), 273–289.

Mazumdar, T. and Papatla, P. (2000) An investigation of reference price segments, *Journal of Marketing Research*, 37(2), 246–258.

Mazumdar, T., Raj, S.P. and Sinha, I. (2005) Reference price research: review and propositions, *Journal of Marketing*, 69(4), 84–102.

McDonald, C. (1970) What is the short-term effect of advertising? *Proceedings of the ESOMAR Congress*, Barcelona, 463–485.

McDonald, C. (1995) *Advertising Reach and Frequency*, Chicago: NTC Business Books.

McGoldrick, P. (2002) *Retail Marketing*, 2nd edition, London: McGraw Hill.

McGoldrick, P.J. and Andre, E. (1997) Consumer misbehaviour: promiscuity or loyalty in grocery shopping, *Journal of Retailing and Consumer Services*, 4.

McKay, D.B. (1973) A spectral analysis of the frequency of supermarket visits, *Journal of Marketing Research*, 10(February), 84–90.

McPhee, W.N. (1963) *Formal Theories of Mass Behavior*, Glencoe, IL: The Free Press.

McQuarrie, E.F. (1988) An alternative to purchase intentions: the role of prior behaviour in consumer expenditure on computers, *Journal of the Market Research Society*, 30(4), 407–437.

McWilliam, G. (1993) The effect of brand typology on the evaluation of brand extension fit: commercial and academic research findings. In W.F. Van Raaij and G.J. Bamossy (eds), *European Advances in Consumer Research*, 1, 485–91.

Mehrabian, A. and Russell, J.A. (1974) *An Approach to Environmental Psychology*, Cambridge, MA: Massachusetts Institute of Technology Press.

Mela, C.F., Gupta, S. and Lehmann, D.R. (1997) The long-term impact of promotion and advertising on consumer choice, *Journal of Marketing Research*, 34(2), 248–261.

Meyer-Waarden, L. (2007) The effects of loyalty programs on customer lifetime duration and share of wallet, *Journal of Retailing*, 83(2), 223–236.

Meyers-Levy, J. and Tybout, A.M. (1989) Schema congruity as a basis for product evaluation, *Journal of Consumer Research*, 16 (1), 39–54.

Meyers-Levy, J. and Zhu, R. (2007) The influence of ceiling height: the effect of priming on the type of processing that people use, *Journal of Consumer Research*, 34(2), 174–186.

Michon, R., Chebat, J.-C. and Turley, L.W. (2005) Mall atmospherics: the interaction effects of the mall environment on shopping behaviour, *Journal of Business Research*, 58(5), 576–583.

Milgram, S. (1970) The experience of living in cities, *Science*, 167, 1464–1468.

Milliman, R.E. (1982) Using background music to affect the behavior of supermarket shoppers, *Journal of Marketing*, 46(3), 86–91.

Mittal, V., Ross, W.T. and Baldasare, P.M. (1998) The asymmetric impact of negative and positive attribute-level performance on overall satisfaction and repurchase intentions, *Journal of Marketing*, 62(1), 33–47.

Mizerski, R.W. (1982) An attributional explanation of the disproportionate influence of unfavorable information, *Journal of Consumer Research*, 9(1), 301–310.

Moldovan, S.E. (1984) Copy factors related to persuasion scores, *Journal of Advertising Research*, 24(6), 16–22.

Monroe, K.B. (1973) Buyers' subjective perceptions of price, *Journal of Marketing Research*, 10(1), 70–80.

Monroe, K.B. and Lee, A.V. (1999) Remembering versus knowing: issues in buyers' processing of price information, *Journal of the Academy of Marketing Science*, 27(2), 207–225.

Moore, W.L. and Pessemier, E.A. (1993) *Product Planning and Management: Designing and Delivering Value*, Singapore: McGraw-Hill.

Moraleda, P. and Ferrer-Vidal, J. (eds) (1991) *Proceedings of the 1990 ESOMAR Conference*, Monte Carlo.

Morgan, N.A. and Rego, L.L. (2004) The one number you need to grow, *Harvard Business Review*, 82(4), 134–136.

Morgan, N.A. and Rego, L.L. (2006) The value of different customer satisfaction and loyalty metrics in predicting business performance, *Marketing Science*, 25(5), 426–439.

Morin, S., Dubé, L. and Chebat, J.-C. (2007) The role of pleasant music in servicescapes: a test of the dual model of environmental perception, *Journal of Retailing*, 83(1), 115–130.

Morrison, D. and Schmittlein, D.C. (1981) Predicting future random events based on past performances, *Management Science*, 27(9), 1006–1023.

Morrison, D. and Schmittlein, D.C. (1988) Generalizing the NBD model for customer purchases: what are the implications and is it worth the effort?, *Journal of Business and Economic Statistics*, 6(2), 145–166.

Murray-Burton, G., Dyke, M. and Harrison, T. (2007) Monopoly here and now. In L. Green (ed.), *Advertising Works 15*, IPA Effectiveness Awards 2006, Henley-on-Thames: World Advertising Research Centre (WARC)

Naples, M.J. (1979) *Effective Frequency: The Relationship Between Frequency and Advertising Effectiveness*, New York: Association of National Advertisers.

Narasimhan, C. (1984) A price discrimination theory of coupons, *Marketing Science*, 3(2), 128–148.

Narisetti, R. (1997) Move to drop coupons puts Procter & Gamble in sticky PR situation, *Wall Street Journal*, 17 April, 1, A10.

Naylor, G. and Kleiser, S.B. (2000) Negative versus positive word-of-mouth: an exception to the rule, *Journal of Satisfaction, Dissatisfaction and Complaining Behavior*, 13, 26–36.

Neslin, S.A. (1990) A market response model for coupon promotions, *Marketing Science*, 9(2), 125–146.

Neslin, S.A. (2002) *Sales Promotion*. Cambridge, MA: Marketing Science Institute.

Neslin, S.A. and Clarke, D.G. (1987) Relating the brand use profile of coupon redeemers to brand and coupon characteristics, *Journal of Advertising Research*, 27(1), 23–32.

Neslin, S.A. and Stone, L.G.S. (1996) Consumer inventory sensitivity and the postpromotion dip, *Marketing Letters*, 7(1), 77–94.

Netemeyer, R.C. and Maxham, J.G. (2007) Employee versus supervisor ratings of performance in the retail customer service sector: differences in the predictive validity for customer outcomes, *Journal of Retailing*, 83(1), 131–145.

Nielsen (2005) *Retail Pocket Book, 2006*. Oxford: WARC and AC Nielsen.

Nielsen (2003) *Retail Pocket Book, 2003*. Oxford: WARC and AC Nielsen.

Nijs, V.R., Dekimpe, M.G., Steenkamp, J-B.E.M. and Hanssens, D.M. (2001) The category–demand effects of price promotions, *Marketing Science*, 20(1), 1–22.

North, A.C., Hargreaves, D.J. and McKendrick, J. (1999) The influence of in-store music on wine selections, *Journal of Applied Social Psychology*, 84(2), 271–276.

Odean, T. (1998) Are investors reluctant to realize their losses?, *Journal of Finance*, 53(5), 1775–1798. Reprinted in D. Kahneman and A.Tversky (2000) *Choices, Values, and Frames*, Cambridge: Russell Sage Foundation, Cambridge University Press, 371–392.

Ogilvy, D. (1987) Sound an alarm!, *International Journal of Advertising*, 6, 81–4.

Oliver, R.L. (1980) Cognitive model of the antecedents and consequences of satisfaction decisions, *Journal of Marketing Research*, 17(4), 460–469.

Oliver, R.L. (1981) Measurement and evaluation of satisfaction processes in retail settings, *Journal of Retailing*, 57(3), 25–48.

Oliver, R.L. (1987) An investigation of the interrelationship between consumer (dis)satisfaction and complaint reports. In Wallendorf, M. and Anderson, P. (eds) *Advances in Consumer Research*, 14, 218–222.

Oliver, R.L. (1989) Processing of the satisfaction response in consumption: a suggested framework and research propositions, *Journal of Consumer Satisfaction, Dissatisfaction and Complaining Behavior*, 2, 1–16.

Oliver, R.L. (1999) Whence customer loyalty?, *Journal of Marketing*, 63(Special Issue), 33–44.

Oliver, R.L. and Swan, J.E. (1989) Consumer perceptions of interpersonal equity and satisfaction in transactions: a field survey approach, *Journal of Marketing*, 53(2), 21–35.

Olshavsky, R.W. and Granbois, D.H. (1979) Consumer decision making – fact or fiction?, *Journal of Consumer Research*, 6(2), 93–100.

Osgood, J.F., Suci, G.J. and Tannenbaum, P.H. (1957) *The Measurement of Meaning*, Urbana: University of Illinois Press.

Parasuraman, A., Berry, L.L. and Zeithaml, V.A. (1991) Refinement and reassessment of the SERVQUAL scale, *Journal of Retailing*, 67(4), 420–450.

Parasuraman, A., Zeithaml, V.A. and Berry, L.L. (1985) A conceptual model of service quality and its implications for future research, *Journal of Marketing*, 49(4), 41–50.

Parasuraman, A., Zeithaml, V.A. and Berry, L.L. (1988) SERVQUAL: a multiple-item scale for measuring consumer perceptions of service quality, *Journal of Retailing*, 64(1), 12–40.

Parasuraman, A., Zeithaml, V.A. and Berry, L.L. (1994) Reassessment of expectations as a comparison standard in measuring service quality, *Journal of Marketing*, 58(1), 111–124.

Partch, K. (1996) Still inching toward efficient promotion, *Supermarket Business*, 51, 16.

Pauwels, K., Hanssens, D.M. and Siddarth, S. (2002) The long-term effects of price promotions on category incidence, brand choice, and purchase quantity, *Journal of Marketing Research*, 39(4), 421–439.

Pavlov, I.P. (1927) *Conditioned Reflexes*, translated by G.V. Anrep, London: Oxford University Press.

Peterson, R.A. and Wilson, W.R. (1992) Measuring customer satisfaction: fact or artifact, *Journal of the Academy of Marketing Science*, 20(1), 61–71.

Petkova, K.G., Ajzen, I. and Driver, B.L. (1995) Salience of anti-abortion beliefs and commitment to an attitudinal position: on the strength, structure and predictive validity of anti-abortion attitudes, *Journal of Applied Social Psychology*, 25(6), 463–483.

Petty, R.E. and Cacioppo, J.T. (1985) The elaboration likelihood model of persuasion. In L. Berkowitz (ed.), *Advances in Experimental Social Psychology*, 19, New York: Academic Press.

Pickering, J.F. (1984) Purchase expectations and the demand for consumer durables, *Journal of Economic Psychology*, 5(4), 342–352.

Pickering, J.F. (1975) Verbal explanations of consumer durable purchase decisions, *Journal of the Market Research Society*, 17(2), 107–113.

Pickering, J.F. and Isherwood, B.C. (1974) Purchase probabilities and consumer durable buying behaviour, *Journal of the Market Research Society*, 16(3), 203–226.

Pieters, R. and Warlop, L. (1999) Visual attention during brand choice: the impact of time pressure and task motivation, *International Journal of Research in Marketing* 16(1), 1–16.

Pritchard, M.P., Havitz, M.E. and Howard, D.R. (1999) Analyzing the commitment–loyalty link in service contexts, *Journal of the Academy of Marketing Science*, 27(3), 333–348.

Pruyn, A.Th.H. and Smidts, A. (1993) Customers' evaluations of queues: three exploratory studies. In W.F. Van Raaij and G.J. Bamossy (eds), *European Advances in Consumer Research*, 1, 371–382.

Putsis, W.M. and Srinivasan, V. (2000) Estimation techniques for macro diffusion models. In V. Mahajan, E. Muller and Y. Wind (eds), *New Product Diffusion Models*, Norwell, MA: Kluwer Academic Publishers, pp. 263–291.

Raj, S.P. (1982) The effects of advertising on high and low loyalty segments, *Journal of Advertising Research*, 9(1), 77–89.

Raju, J.S. (1992) The effect of price promotions on variability in product category sales, *Marketing Science*, 11(3), 207–220.

Randall, D.M. and Wolff, J.A. (1994) The time interval in the intention–behaviour relationship, *British Journal of Social Psychology*, 33(4), 405–418.

Rao, A.R. and Monroe, K.R. (1989) The effect of price, brand name, and store name on buyers' perceptions of product quality: an integrative review, *Journal of Marketing Research*, 26(3), 351–358.

Rao, T.R. (1969) Consumer's purchase decision process: stochastic models, *Journal of Marketing Research*, 6(3), 321–329.

Reichheld, F.F. (1993) Loyalty-based management, *Harvard Business Review*, 71(2), 64–73.

Reichheld, F.F. (1996a) Learning from customer defections, *Harvard Business Review*, 74(2), March/April, 56–69.

Reichheld, F.F. (with Teal, T.) (1996b) *The Loyalty Effect*. Boston: Harvard Business School Publications.

Reichheld, F.F. (2003) The one number you need to grow, *Harvard Business Review*, 81(12), 46–54.

Reichheld, F.F. and Kenny, D.W. (1990) The hidden advantages of customer retention, *Journal of Retail Banking*, 12(4), 19–23.

Reichheld, F.F. and Sasser, W.E. (1990) Zero defections: quality comes to services, *Harvard Business Review*, 68(5), Sept.–Oct., 105–111.

Reilly, W.J. (1929) *Methods for the Study of Retail Relationships*, Austin, TX: Bureau of Business Research Studies in Marketing, No. 4.

Reinartz, W. and Kumar, V. (2000) On the profitability of long-life customers in a non-contractual setting: an empirical investigation and implications for marketing, *Journal of Marketing*, 64(4), 17–36.

Reinartz, W. and Kumar, V. (2002) The mismanagement of customer loyalty, *Harvard Business Review*, 80(7), July, 86–94.

Reinartz, W., Thomas, J.S. and Kumar, V. (2005) Balancing acquisition and retention resources to maximize customer profitability, *Journal of Marketing*, 69(1), 63–79.

Richins, M.L. (1981) An investigation of the consumer's attitudes towards complaining. In Mitchell, A. (ed.) *Advances in Consumer Research*, 9, 502–506.

Richins, M.L. (1983) Negative word of mouth by dissatisfied consumers, *Journal of Marketing*, 47(1), 68–78.

Richins, M.L. (1985) The role of product importance in complaint initiation, *Proceedings of the Eighth and Ninth Conferences on Consumer Satisfaction and Complaining Behavior*, Baton Rouge, Louisiana and Phoenix, Arizona, 50–53.

Richins, M.L. (1987) A multivariate analysis of responses to dissatisfaction, *Journal of the Academy of Marketing Science*, 15(3), 24–31.

Riebe, E., Sharp, B. and Stern, P. (2002) An empirical investigation of customer defection and acquisition rates for declining and growing pharmaceutical brands. Australian and New Zealand Marketing Academy (ANZMAC) 2002 Conference Proceedings, available at: http://members.byronsharp.com/7716.pdf.

Riskey, D.R. (1997) How TV advertising works: an industry response, *Journal of Market Research*, 34(2), 292–293.

Rivis, A. and Sheeran, P. (2003) Descriptor norms as an additional predictor in the theory of planned behaviour: a meta-analysis. *Current Psychology: Developmental, Learning, Personality, Social*, 22(3), 218–233.

Roberts, A. (1996) What do we know about advertising's short-term effects?, *Admap*, February, 42–45.

Roberts, A. (1999) Recency, frequency and the sales effects of TV advertising, *Admap*, February, 40–44.

Roberts, A. (2000) tvSpan: the medium-term effects of TV advertising, *Admap*, November, 12–14.

Rogers, E.M. (1962) *Diffusion of Innovations* 1st edition, New York: The Free Press.

Rogers, E.M. (2003) *Diffusion of Innovations* 5th edition, New York: The Free Press.

Romaniuk, J. (2003) Brand attributes – 'distribution outlets' in the mind, *Journal of Marketing Communications*, 9(2), 73–92.

Romaniuk, J. and Dawes, J. (2005) Loyalty to price tiers in purchases of bottled wine, *Journal of Product and Brand Management*, 14(1), 57–64.

Romaniuk, J. and Gaillard, E. (2007) The relationship between unique brand associations, brand usage and brand performance: analysis across eight categories, *Journal of Marketing Management*, 23(3–4), 267–284.

Romaniuk, J. and Sharp, B. (2003) Brand salience and customer defection in subscription markets, *Journal of Marketing Management*, 19(1–2), 25–44.

Rosen, E. (2000) *The Anatomy of Buzz*, New York: Doubleday.

Rosenberg, L.J. and Czepiel, J.A. (1984) A marketing approach to customer retention, *Journal of Consumer Marketing*, 1(2), 45–51.

Rosenberg, M.J. (1956) Cognitive structure and attitudinal affect, *Journal of Abnormal and Social Psychology*, 53, 367–372.

Rosnow, R.L. (2001) Rumor and gossip in interpersonal interaction and beyond: a social exchange perspective. In R.M. Kowalski (ed.), *Behaving Badly: Aversive Behaviors in Interpersonal Relationships*, Washington, DC: American Psychological Association, 203–232.

Rossiter, J. and Bellman, S. (2005) *Marketing Communications*, Sydney: Pearson Education.

Russo, J.E. and Leclerc, F. (1994) A eye-fixation analysis of choice processes for consumer non-durables, *Journal of Consumer Research*, 21(2), 274–290.

Ryan, B. and Gross, N.C. (1943) The diffusion of hybrid seed corn in two Iowa communities, *Rural Sociology*, 8, 15–24, as cited in E.M. Rogers (2003) *Diffusion of Innovations*, 5th edition, New York: The Free Press.

Saegert, S.C. and Jellison, J.M. (1970) Effects of initial level of response competition and frequency of exposure on liking and exploratory behavior, *Journal of Personality and Social Psychology*, 16(3), 553–558.

Sandell, R. (1981) The dynamic relationship between attitudes and choice behaviour in the light of cross-lagged panel correlations, Dept. of Psychology, University of Stockholm, Report no. 581.

Sasser, W.E. (1976) Match supply and demand in the service industry, *Harvard Business Review*, 54(6), 133–138.

Scherhorn, G., Reisch, L.A. and Raab, G. (1990) Addictive buying in West Germany: An empirical study, *Journal of Consumer Policy*, 13, 355–387.

Schindler, R.M. (2006) The 99 price ending as a signal of a low-price appeal, *Journal of Retailing*, 82(1), 71–77.

Schindler, R.M. and Kirby, P.N. (1997) Patterns of rightmost digits used in advertised prices: implications for nine-ending effects, *Journal of Consumer Research*, 24(2), 192–201.

Schindler, R.M. (2006) The 99 price ending as a signal of a low-price appeal, *Journal of Retailing*, 82(1), 71–77.

Schmittlein, D.C., Bemmaor, A.C., and Morrison, D. G. (1985) Why does the NBD model work? Robustness in representing product purchases, brand purchases and imperfectly recorded purchases, *Marketing Science*, 4(3), 255–266.

Schmittlein, D.C., Cooper, L.G. and Morrison, D.G. (1993) Truth in concentration in the land of (80/20) laws, *Marketing Science*, 12(2), 167–183.

Schuman, H. and Johnson, M.P. (1976) Attitudes and behavior, *Annual Review of Sociology*, 2, 161–207.

Seidler, M. (2006) Near instant loyalty for new brands; further evidence, unpublished honour's dissertation, Wellington, New Zealand: Victoria University of Wellington.

Sharma, A. and Stafford, T.F. (2000) The effect of retail atmospherics on customers' perceptions of salespeople and customer persuasion: an empirical investigation, *Journal of Business Research*, 49(2), 183–191.

Sharp, B. and Sharp, A. (1997) Loyalty programmes and their impact on repeat purchase loyalty patterns, *International Journal of Research in Marketing*, 14(5), 473–486.

Sharp, B.M., Wright, M.J. and Goodhardt, G.J. (2002) Purchase loyalty is polarised into either repertoire or subscription patterns, *Australasian Marketing Journal*, 10(3), 7–20.

Sheppard, B.H., Hartwick, J. and Warshaw, P.R. (1988) The theory of reasoned action: a meta-analysis of past research with recommendations for modifications and future research, *Journal of Consumer Research*, 15(3), 325–343.

Shiv, B., Carmon, Z. and Ariely, D. (2005) Placebo effects of marketing actions: consumers may get what they pay for, *Journal of Marketing Research*, 42(4), 383–393.

Shogren, J.F., Shin, S.Y., Hayes, D.J. and Kliebenstein, J.B. (1994) Resolving differences in willingness to pay and willingness to accept, *The American Economic Review*, 84(1), 255–270.

Shugan, S.M. (1994) Explanations for the growth of services. In R.T. Rust and R.L. Oliver (eds), *Service Quality: New Directions in Theory and Practice*, London: Sage, 223–240.

Silverman, G. (2001) *The Secrets of Word-of-Mouth Marketing*, New York: AMACOM.

Simmel, G. (1908) *The Sociology of Georg Simmel*, translated by Kurt H. Wolf, New York: The Free Press 1964, as cited in E.M. Rogers (2003) *Diffusion of Innovations*, 5th edition, New York: The Free Press.

Simon, H.A. (1957) *Administrative Behavior*, New York: Macmillan.

Simon, J.L. (1979) What do Zielske's real data show about pulsing?, *Journal of Marketing Research*, 16(3), 415–420.

Simon, J.L. and Arndt, J. (1980) The shape of the advertising response function, *Journal of Advertising Research*, 20(4), 11–28.

Simon, C.J. and Sullivan, M.W. (1993) The measurement and determinants of brand equity: A financial approach, *Marketing Science*, 12(1), 28–52.

Singh, J., Ehrenberg, A. and Goodhardt, G. (2004) Loyalty to product variants – a pilot, *Journal of Customer Behaviour*, 3(2), 123–132.

Singh, J. (1990) Voice, exit, and negative word-of-mouth behaviors: An investigation across three categories, *Journal of the Academy of Marketing Science*, 18, 1–15.

Singh, J. and Howell, R. (1985) Consumer complaining behaviour: a review and prospectus. In H.K Hunt and R.L Day (eds) *Consumer Satisfaction, Dissatisfaction and Complaining Behavior.* Bloomington: Indiana University Press, pp. 41–9.

Skinner, B.F. (1938) *The Behaviour of Organisms*. New York: Appleton Century Crofts.

Skinner, B.F. (1953) *Scientific and Human Behavior*, New York: Macmillan.

Skowronski, J.J. and Carlston, D.E. (1989) Negativity and extremity biases in impression formation: a review of explanations, *Psychological Bulletin*, 105(1), 131–142.

Smith, A.M. (1995) Measuring service quality: is SERVQUAL now redundant?, *Journal of Marketing Management*, 11, 257–276.

Smith, D.C. and Park, C.W. (1992) The effects of brand extensions on market share and advertising efficiency, *Journal of Marketing Research*, 29(3), 296–313.

Smith, E.R. and Queller, S. (2001) Mental representations. In A.Tesser and N. Schwarz (eds), *Intra-individual Processes*, Oxford: Blackwell Publishing.

Smith, R.B. and Sherman, E. (1992) Effects of store image and mood on consumer behavior: a theoretical and empirical analysis. In L. McAlister and M.L. Rothschild (eds), *Advances in Consumer Research*, 20, 631.

Smith, W. and Higgins, M. (2000) Reconsidering the relationship analogy, *Journal of Marketing Management*, 16(1–3), 81–94.

Solnick, S.J. and Hemenway, D. (1992) Complaints and disenrollment at a health maintenance organization, *Journal of Consumer Affairs*, 26(1), 90–103.

Soloman, M., Bamossy, G., Askegaard, S. and Hogg, M.K. (2006) *Consumer Behaviour: A European Perspective*, Harlow: Pearson Education.

Spangenberg, E.R., Grohmann, B. and Sprott, D.E. (2005) It's beginning to smell (and sound) a lot like Christmas: the interactive effects of ambient scent and music in a retail setting, *Journal of Business Research*, 58(11), 1583–1589.

Steiner, R.L. (1973) Does advertising lower consumer prices?, *Journal of Marketing*, 37(4), 19–27.

Steiner, R.L. (1993) The inverse association between the margins of manufacturers and retailers, *Review of Industrial Organisation*, 8, 717–740.

Stern, P. and Hammond, K. (2004) The relationship between customer loyalty and purchase incidence, *Marketing Letters*, 15(1), 5–19.

Stern, P. and Wright, M. (2007) Predicting the innovator, *European Marketing Academy Conference* (EMAC).

Stiving, M. and Winer, R.S. (1997) An empirical analysis of price endings with scanner data, *Journal of Consumer Research*, 24(1), 57–67.

Stø, E. and Glefjell, S. (1990) The complaining process in Norway: five steps to justice, *Journal of Consumer Satisfaction, Dissatisfaction and Complaining Behavior*, 3, 92–99.

Sultan, F., Farley, J.U. and Lehmann, D.R. (1990) A meta-analysis of applications of diffusion models, *Journal of Marketing Research*, 27(1), 70–77.

Sundaram, D.S. and Webster, C. (1999) The role of brand familiarity on the impact of word-of-mouth communication on brand evaluations, *Advances in Consumer Research*, 26, 664–670.

Sunde, L. and Brodie, R.J. (1993) Consumer evaluation of brand extensions: Further empirical results, *International Journal of Research in Marketing*, 10(1), 47–53.

Sutton, S., Marsh, A. and Matheson, J. (1990) Microanalysis of smokers' beliefs about the consequences of quitting: results from a large population sample, *Journal of Applied Social Psychology*, 20(22), 1847–1862.

Swan, J.E. and Trawick, I.F. (1980) Satisfaction related to predicted versus desired expectations. In H.K. Hunt and R.L. Day (eds), *Refining Concepts and Measures of Consumer Satisfaction and Complaining Behavior*, Bloomington: School of Business, Indiana University, 7–12.

Swan, J.E. and Trawick, I.F. (1981) Disconfirmation of expectations and satisfaction with a retail service, *Journal of Retailing*, 57(3), 49–67.

Swinyard, W.R. (1993) The effects of mood, involvement and quality of store experience on shopping intention, *Journal of Consumer Research*, 20(2), 271–280.

Tarde, G. (1903) *The Laws of Imitation*, translated by Elsie Clews Parson, New York: Holt (reprinted University of Chicago Press, 1969), as cited in E.M. Rogers (2003) *Diffusion of Innovations* 5th edition, New York: The Free Press.

TARP (Technical Assistance Research Programs) (1979) *Consumer Complaint Handling in America: A Summary of Findings and Recommendation*, Washington, DC: US Office of Consumer Affairs.

Tate, R.S. (1961) The supermarket battle for store loyalty, *Journal of Marketing*, 25(6), 8–13.

Tauber, E.M. (1972) Why do people shop?, *Journal of Marketing*, 36(4), 46–49.

Tauber, E.M. (1981) Brand franchise extension: New product benefits from existing brand names, *Business Horizons*, 24, 36–41.

Tauber, E.M. (1988) Brand leverage: strategy for growth in a cost-conscious world, *Journal of Advertising Research*, 28(4), 26–30.

Taylor, J.W. (1977) A striking characteristic of innovators, *Journal of Marketing Research*, 14(1), 104–107.

Taylor, S. (1994) Waiting for service: the relationship between delays and evaluations of service, *Journal of Marketing*, 58(2), 56–69.

Taylor, S. (1995) The effects of filled waiting time and service provider control over the delay on evaluations of service, *Journal of the Academy of Marketing Science*, 23(1), 38–48.

Taylor, S.E. (1982) The availability bias in social perception and interaction. In D. Kahneman, P. Slovic and A. Tversky (eds), *Judgment under Uncertainty: Heuristics and Biases*, Cambridge: Cambridge University Press, 190–200.

Tellis, G.J. (1988a) Advertising exposure, loyalty and brand purchase: a two-stage model of choice, *Journal of Marketing Research*, 25(2), 134–144.

Tellis, G.J. (1988b) The price elasticity of selective demand: a meta-analysis of economic models of sales, *Journal of Marketing Research*, 25(4), 331–341.

Tellis, G.J. and Wernerfelt, B. (1987) Competitive price and quality under asymmetric information, *Marketing Science*, 6(3), 240–254.

Thaler, R. (1980) Toward a positive theory of consumer choice, *Journal of Economic Behavior*, 1, 39–60. Reprinted in D. Kahneman and A. Tversky (2000) *Choices, Values, and Frames*, New York: Russell Sage Foundation, Cambridge University Press, 269–287.

Thaler, R. (1985) Mental accounting and consumer choice, *Marketing Science*, 4(3), 199–214.

Thaler, R. (1999) Mental accounting matters, *Journal of Behavioral Decision Making*, 12, 183–206. Reprinted in D. Kahneman and A. Tversky (2000) *Choices, Values, and Frames*, New York: Russell Sage Foundation, Cambridge University Press, 241–268.

Theil, H. and Kosobud, R.F. (1968) How informative are consumer buying intentions surveys?, *Review of Economics and Statistics*, 50, 50–9.

Thorndike, E.L. (1911) *Animal Intelligence*, New York: Macmillan.

Tobin, J. (1969) A general equilibrium approach to monetary theory, *Journal of Money, Credit, and Banking*, 1(1), 15–29.

Tom, G. and Lucey, S. (1995) Waiting time delays and customer satisfaction in supermarkets, *Journal of Services Marketing*, 9(5), 20–29.

Totten, J.C. and Block, M.P. (1987) *Analyzing Sales Promotion: Text and Cases*, Chicago: Commerce Communications Inc.

Treasure, J. (1975) How advertising works. In M. Barnes (ed.), *The Three Faces of Advertising*, London: The Advertising Association, 48, 52.

Triandis, H.C. (1977) *Interpersonal Behavior*, Monterey, CA: Brooks Cole.

Trout, J. and Ries, A. (1972) Positioning cuts through chaos in the marketplace, *Advertising Age*, 1 May. Also in B.M. Enis and K.K. Cox (eds), *Marketing Classics* (7th edn), Boston: Allyn and Bacon, 216–233.

Tse, D.K. and Wilton, P.C. (1988) Models of consumer satisfaction formation: an extension, *Journal of Marketing Research*, 25(2), 204–212.

Tversky, A. and Kahneman, D. (1980) Causals schemas in judgements under uncertainty. In Tversky, A. and Kahneman, D. (1981) The framing of decisions and the psychology of choice, *Science*, 211, 453–458.

Tversky, A. and Kahneman, D. (1992) Advances in prospect theory: cumulative representation of uncertainty, *Journal of Risk and Uncertainty*, 5, 297–323. Reprinted in D. Kahneman and A. Tversky (2000) *Choices, Values, and Frames*, New York: Russell Sage Foundation, Cambridge University Press, 44–65.

Uncles, M.D. and Ehrenberg, A.S.C. (1990) The buying of packaged goods at US retail chains, *Journal of Retailing*, 66(3), 278–296.

Uncles, M.D. and Hammond, K.A. (1995) Grocery store patronage, *International Journal of Retail, Distribution and Consumer Research*, 5(3), 287–302.

Underhill, P. (1999) *Why We Buy: The Science of Shopping*, New York: Simon & Schuster.

Van der Plight, J. and van Schie, E.C.M. (1990) Frames of reference, judgement and preference. In W. Stroebe, and M. Hewstone (eds), *European Review of Social Psychology*, 1, Chichester: Wiley and Sons, 61–80.

van Heerde, H.J., Leeflang, P.S.H. and Wittink, D.R. (2004) Decomposing the sales promotion bump with store data, *Marketing Science*, 23(3), 317–334.

Vanhuele, M. (1994) Mere exposure and the cognitive-affective debate revisited. In C.T. Allen and D.R. John (eds), *Advances in Consumer Research*, 21, 264–269.

Vanhuele, M. and Drèze, X. (2002) Measuring the price knowledge shoppers bring to the store, *Journal of Marketing*, 66(4), 72–85.

Vanhuele, M., Laurent, G. and Drèze, X. (2006) Consumers' immediate memory for prices, *Journal of Consumer Research*, 33(2), 163–172.

Vargo, S.L. and Lusch, R.F. (2004) Evolving to a new dominant logic for marketing, *Journal of Marketing*, 68(1), 1–17.

Venkatesh, V. and Davis, F.D. (2000) A theoretical extension of the technology acceptance model: four longitudinal field studies, *Management Science*, 46(2), 186–204.

Verhoef, P.C., Franses, P.H. and Hoekstra, J.C. (2002) The effect of relational constructs on customer referrals and number of services purchased from a multiservice provider: does age of relationship matter?, *Journal of the Academy of Marketing Science*, 30(3), 202–216.

Viscusi, W.K. (1984) The lulling effect: the impact of child resistant packaging on aspirin and analgesic ingestions, *American Economic Review*, 74(2), 324–327.

Wakefield, K.L. and Inman, J.J. (1993) Who are the price vigilantes? An investigation of differentiating characteristics influencing price information processing, *Journal of Retailing*, 69(2), 216–234.

Wangenheim, F. v. (2005) Postswitching negative word of mouth, *Journal of Service Research*, 8(1), 67–78.

Wangenheim, F. v. and Bayón, T. (2004) Satisfaction, loyalty and word of mouth within the customer base of a utility provider: differences between stayers, switchers and referral switchers, *Journal of Consumer Behaviour*, 3(1), 211–220.

Warland, R.H., Herrmann, R.O. and Willits, J. (1975) Dissatisfied customers: Who gets upset and what they do about it, *Journal of Consumer Affairs*, 9, Winter, 152–162.

Watts, D.J. and Dodds, P.S. (2007) Influentials, networks, and public opinion formation, *Journal of Consumer Research*, 34(December), 441–458.

Weber, M. and Camerer, C.F. (1998) The disposition effect in securities trading: an experimental analysis, *Journal of Economic Behavior and Organization*, 33, 167–184.

Wedel, M. and Leeflang, P.S.H. (1998) A model for the effects of psychological pricing in Gabor–Granger price studies, *Journal of Economic Psychology*, 19(2), 237–261.

Wee, C.H. and Pearce, M.R. (1985) Patronage behavior toward shopping areas: a proposed model based on Huff's model of retail gravitation. In E.C. Hirschman and M.B. Holbrook (eds), *Advances in Consumer Research*, 12, 592–597.

Weigel, R.H. and Newman, L.S. (1976) Increasing attitude–behavior correspondence by broadening the scope of the behavioral measure, *Journal of Personality and Social Psychology*, 33, 793–802.

Weiner, B. (1980) *Human Motivation*, New York: Holt, Rinehart and Winston.

Weiner, B. (1990) Searching for the roots of applied attribution theory. In S. Graham and V.S. Folkes (eds), *Attribution Theory: Application to Achievement, Mental Health and Interpersonal Conflict*, Hillsdale, NJ: Lawrence Erlbaum Associates, 1–16.

Weitz, B.A. and Levy, M. (2004) *Retailing Management*, New York: McGraw-Hill/Irwin.

Wellan, D.M. and Ehrenberg, A.S.C. (1988) A successful new brand: Shield, *Journal of the Market Research Society*, 30(1), 35–44.

Wellan, D.M. and Ehrenberg, A.S.C. (1990) A case of seasonal segmentation, *Marketing Research*, 1, 11–13.

Westbrook, R.A. (1980) Intrapersonal affective influences upon consumer satisfaction, *Journal of Consumer Research*, 7(1), 49–54.

Westbrook, R.A. and Oliver, R.L. (1991) The dimensionality of consumption emotion patterns and consumer satisfaction, *Journal of Consumer Research*, 18(1), 84–91.

Wetzer, I., Zeelenberg, M. and Pieters, R. (2007) 'Never eat in that restaurant, I did': exploring why people engage in negative word-of-mouth communication, *Psychology and Marketing*, 24(8), 661–680.

Whyte, W.H. (1954) The web of word of mouth, *Fortune*, 50(November), 140.

Wicker, A.W. (1969) Attitude vs actions: the relationship of verbal and overt behavioral responses to attitude objects, *Journal of Social Issues*, 25, 41–78.

Wicker, A.W. (1984) *An Introduction to Ecological Psychology*, Monterey, CA: Brooks/Cole.

Wilkie, W.L. and Dickson, P.R. (1985) *Shopping for Appliances: Consumers Strategies and Patterns of Information Search*, Cambridge, MA: Marketing Science Institute Research Report No. 85–108.

Williams, L.G. (1966) The effect of target specification on objects fixed during visual search, *Perception and Psychophysics*, 1, 315–318.

Wilson, W.R. and Peterson, R.A. (1989) Some limits on the potency of word-of-mouth information, *Advances in Consumer Research*, 16, 23–29.

Winchester, M. and Romaniuk, J. (2008) Negative brand beliefs and brand usage, *International Journal of Market Research*, 50(3), 1–20.

Winchester, M., Romaniuk, J. and Bogomolova, S. (2008, forthcoming) Positive and negative brand beliefs and brand defection/uptake, *European Journal of Marketing*.

Winer, R.S. (1986) A reference price model of brand choice for frequently purchased products, *Journal of Consumer Research*, 13(2), 250–256.

Winer, R.S. (1988) Behavioral perspectives on pricing: buyers' subjective perceptions of price revisited. In T.M. Divinney (ed.), *Issues in Pricing*, Lexington, MA: Lexington Books, 35–57.

Wittink, D.R., Vriens, M. and Burhenne, W. (1994) Commercial use of conjoint analysis in Europe: results and critical reflections, *International Journal of Research in Marketing*, 11(1), 41–52.

Wright, M., Sharp, A. and Sharp, B. (1998) Are Australasian brands different?, *Journal of Product and Brand Management*, 7(6), 465–480.

Wright, M.J. and Charlett, D. (1995) New product diffusion models in marketing: an assessment of two approaches, *Marketing Bulletin*, 6, 32–41.

Wright, M.J. and MacRae, M. (2007) Bias and variability in purchase intention scales, *Journal of the Academy of Marketing Science*, 35(4), 617–624.

Wright, M.J. and Riebe, E. (2007) Benchmarking brand defection with a stochastic model, Working Paper, Adelaide: Ehrenberg-Bass Institute for Marketing Science.

Wright, M. and Sharp, A. (2001) The effects of a new brand entrant on a market, *Journal of Empirical Generalisations in Marketing Science*, 6, 15-29.

Wright, M.J. and Stern, P. (2006) Extending consumer trial models to national panel data, Working Paper, Victoria University of Wellington, New Zealand.

Wright, M.J., Upritchard, C. and Lewis, A. (1997) A validation of the Bass new product diffusion model in New Zealand, *Marketing Bulletin*, 8, 15–29.

Xia, L., Monroe, K.B. and Cox, J.L. (2004) The price is unfair! A conceptual framework of price fairness perceptions, *Journal of Marketing*, 68(4), 1–15.

Yalch, R. and Spangenberg, E. (2000) Using store music for retail zoning: a field experiment. In L. McAlister and M.L. Rothschild (eds), *Advances in Consumer Research*, 20, 632–636.

Yi, Y. (1990) A critical review of consumer satisfaction. In V.A. Zeithaml (ed.), *Review of Marketing*, Chicago: American Marketing Association, 68–113.

Zajonc, R.B. (1968) Attitudinal effects of mere exposure, *Journal of Personality and Social Psychology Monograph Supplement*, 9(2, Part 2), 1–27.

Zajonc, R.B. (1980) Feeling and thinking: preferences need no inferences, *American Psychologist*, 35, 151–175.

Zajonc, R.B. and Rajecki, D.W. (1969) Exposure and affect: a field experiment, *Psychonomic Science*, 17, 216–217.

Zeithaml, V.A. (1988) Consumer perceptions of price, quality, and value: a means–end model and synthesis of evidence, *Journal of Marketing*, 52(3), 2–21.

Zeithaml, V.A. (2000) Service quality, profitability, and the economic worth of customers: what we know and what we need to learn, *Journal of the Academy of Marketing Science*, 28(1), 67–85.

Zettelmeyer, F., Morton, F.S. and Silva-Risso, J. (2006) How the Internet lowers prices: evidence from matched survey and auto transaction data, *Journal of Marketing Research*, 43(2), 168–181.

Zhang, J. (2006) An integrated choice model incorporating alternative mechanisms for consumers' reactions to in-store display and feature advertising, *Marketing Science*, 25(3), 278–290.

Zielske, H. (1959) The remembering and forgetting of advertising, *Journal of Marketing*, 23(3), 239–243.

Zufryden, F.S. (1996) Multibrand transition probabilities as a function of explanatory variables: estimation by a least squares approach, *Journal of Marketing Research*, 23(2), 177–183.

Author Index

Subject Index